Sunset

COMPLETE
DECK BOOK

By the Editors of Sunset Books

Sunset Books
Vice-President, General Manager: Richard A. Smeby
Production Director: Lory Day
VP, Editorial Director: Bob Doyle
Art Director: Vasken Guiragossian

Sunset Publishing Corporation
Chairman: Jim Nelson
President/Chief Executive Officer: Stephen J. Seabolt
Chief Financial Officer: James E. Mitchell
Publisher: Anthony P. Glaves
Circulation Director: Robert I. Gursha
Director of Finance: Larry Diamond
Vice President, Manufacturing: Lorinda B. Reichert
Editor, Sunset Magazine: William R. Marken

The *Complete Deck Book* was produced in conjunction with
St. Remy Press
President/Chief Executive Officer: Fernand Lecoq
President/Chief Operating Officer: Pierre Léveillé
Vice President, Finance: Natalie Watanabe
Managing Editor: Carolyn Jackson
Managing Art Director: Diane Denoncourt
Production Manager: Michelle Turbide

Staff for this Book:
Senior Editor: Heather Mills
Assistant Editors: Jennifer Ormston, Rebecca Smollett
Senior Art Director: Francine Lemieux
Art Director: Michel Giguère

Special Contributors:
Eric Beaulieu, Michel Blais, Normand Boudreault, François
Daxhelet, Jean-Guy Doiron, Lorraine Doré, Dominique
Gagné, Christine M. Jacobs, Solange Laberge, Joan Page
McKenna, Geneviève Monette, Mark Pechenik, Jacques
Perrault, Judy Yelon

Book Consultants
Richard Day
Don Vandervort

Cover:
Design: Susan Bryant
Photography: Philip Harvey
Photo Direction and Styling: JoAnn Masaoka Van Atta
Landscape Architect: John Montgomery/Garden
   Architecture, Alamo, California
Contractor: Landgraphics Inc.

Note to Readers

*Sunset Publishing Corporation provides no warranties of any
kind, express or implied, regarding the construction and use of
any of the ideas, plans, or designs discussed or illustrated in this
book and shall not be responsible or liable for any injuries or
damages incurred during the construction and/or use of those
ideas, plans, or designs. Before building any projects from this
book, check with your local building department regarding soil
conditions, local codes, and required permits.*

Because outdoor living is enjoyed by people everywhere, a deck has become a basic accoutrement of today's home. It serves as a stage for summer parties, a place to relax or sunbathe, an alfresco dining room, or a garden floor.

This book begins with a gallery of color photos showing how a deck can enhance your outdoor environment. It then takes you through the planning and design process, a crucial stage whether you'll be building your deck yourself or hiring a professional to undertake the project.

Next, you'll find details of the building materials and construction techniques you'll need to build your own deck. You'll also learn how to add benches, overheads, and other amenities to outfit a deck for comfort and convenience. And should you already have a deck that is in need of repair, you'll discover how to bring it back to life.

The last chapter presents 19 deck plans as well as four plans for overheads. These plans solve common site problems and use space in imaginative and aesthetically satisfying ways.

Built above a foggy valley, this deck provides
a beautiful spot to contemplate the view.
(Landscape architects: Royston, Hanamoto, Alley & Abey)

CONTENTS

DECK POSSIBILITIES

The decks shown on the following pages include a wide variety of outdoor structures: modest ground-hugging platforms, spectacular high-level creations, split-level decks, floating islands, and raised poolside platforms. All these decks are designed to enhance the appearance of the home, blend into the natural setting, and expand outdoor living space.

The photos will spark your imagination, helping you create a deck that's just right for your family. Although your site and conditions won't correspond exactly to those shown, you may be faced with similar situations such as a steep slope or a small lot. In this chapter you'll discover how others—in most cases professional designers or builders—have tackled these problems. You can also borrow some of the specific design ideas for your own deck, noticing how the decks shown blend materials, divide space, and make use of pleasing curves and angles. For a closer look at rails, stairs, and other design details, turn to the chapter beginning on page 26.

Even a small corner of your yard can accommodate a deck. This small, compact deck creates a quiet area for reading or conversation.

A deck doesn't have to be a plain rectangle off the back door. This redwood deck makes use of interesting angles, both in the stairway and the seating area; cutouts in the deck house mature oak trees. Carefully placed lighting imparts a beautiful warm glow. (Design: Landgraphics, Inc.)

A low entry deck establishes a transition between house and yard, with leisurely curves leading the eye toward the archway beyond. Redwood decking sits over low-profile footings and beams.
(Architect: Churchill & Hambelton Architects)

A series of small decks links a gazebo and the patio in this yard. The decks surround a fish pond, making it the focus of a tranquil garden. For plans, turn to page 219. (Landscape designer: Jolee Horne)

This wrap-around deck follows the shape of the house. A deck such as this can be designed to provide access from more than one room along its length.

HILLSIDE DECKS

This three-tiered deck leads down to the water in stages, following the slope of the hillside. Stepping down the deck's level partway out from the house permits an unobstructed view from inside.

Trees and rocks are no obstacle to deck design; you can build around them, as in this hillside deck. For plans, turn to page 232. (Landscape contractor: Gary McCook)

These two stunning cedar decks give the effect of theater balconies, each giving more than one vantage point to contemplate a dramatic view. Decks cantilevered over a steep slope the way these are should be designed by a professional. (Architect for the deck shown below: Philip Tattersfield)

MULTILEVEL DECKS

Separate use areas—such as for sunning or entertaining—are kept apart on this cascading deck. While the space is broken up by the different levels, planters visually link the levels and guide foot traffic. The pressure-treated decking was treated with a clear wood finish with a cedar tone.

Although low to the ground, this deck still incorporates subtle level changes. Alternating the direction of the deck boards calls attention to the step up or down, reducing the chance of tripping.

The dramatic starburst decking pattern on this round deck continues onto the lower level, uniting the two areas. An elegant curved bench frames the lower level.

SMALL-SPACE SOLUTIONS

A small deck dresses up this entryway. The railing lends privacy to the entrance while at the same time providing a backrest for the built-in bench.

A deck can provide a low-maintenance surface that enhances a small yard. This practical example is accessible from both floors of the house.

This compact deck is constructed of pressure-treated southern pine, for a long-lasting surface. A screen has been incorporated into the design to block the view from the street.

Tucked into a corner, this deck recovers previously wasted space in a small side yard. (Landscape architect: Fry & Stone Associates)

STAND-ALONE DECKS

A freestanding deck can be built over an existing patio if the patio is in good shape. Here a cedar deck sits atop a stone patio, providing a more comfortable surface for sunning as well as a beautiful contrast in materials. Glass railings allow an unobstructed view. (Landscape architect: Bill Reed)

There will never be a shortage of seating in this backyard, with the integral benches that embellish the deck. Simple enough to be built in a weekend, this deck will give decades of service, thanks to the durable pressure-treated southern pine used in its construction.

This low-level deck is set on sleepers on a gravel base. Staggered ends make the deck look like it's a natural part of the landscape. (Landscape architect: Ransohoff, Blanchfield, Jones, Inc.)

A straightforward single-level deck makes the water's edge more accessible. Easy-to-climb steps that run the entire length of the deck hide the substructure.

POOLSIDE DECKS

*This deck combines the warm colors of redwood decking and brick.
A cutout in the deck boards permitted the tree to remain, providing shade
near the pool. The decking is kept separate from the pool by a brick border.
(Landscape architect: Scott Smith)*

A level change separates the bathing area of this deck from the sitting area. To help unify the deck and the house, the decking is finished to match the house siding. (Designers: Jain Moon and Scott Foell)

This spacious deck provides plenty of room for sunning and relaxing. The decking is mitered to fit around the pool for a sleek, eye-catching look.

This spa deck features an overhead for shade and a screen for privacy. Herringbone decking draws the eye toward the raised spa. In general, spas should be supported underneath by a structure separate from the deck. If a spa is going to be set directly on the deck, the deck will have to be reinforced to take the weight.
(Design: Timothy R. Bitts and Associates, Inc.)

A spa can be flush-mounted in the deck, as shown in this case. In addition to the benches, the steps leading down to the spa provide extra seating.

Small steps spiral around a classic barrel-shaped hot tub. A taper jig and table saw make short work of tapering deck boards. (Design: Roger D. Fiske)

ROOFTOP DECKS

Rooftop decks let you take advantage of a view from on high. They should be designed by a professional—the surface needs to be waterproofed, and the roof framing may have to be reinforced to bear the extra weight.

This rooftop deck gives you a choice between pleasant shade under the arbor or direct sun on the rest of the deck. (Landscape architect: Robert W. Chittock)

A second-floor deck can be built on top of a porch roof. The deck should be waterproofed to keep the area underneath dry. (Design: Richard Schwartz, Builder)

OUTDOOR ROOMS

This Japanese garden room replaced an old concrete patio, providing the owners with year-round indoor-outdoor living. On cool days the room can be closed off with sliding glass partitions. (Architect: Alan Oshima)

A small gazebo is cantilevered over a rock-edged swimming pool. The open-sided redwood structure is styled to resemble a traditional Japanese teahouse. (Design: William Churchill. Landscape design: Edwin Simon)

NONWOOD MATERIALS

Made of a fiberglass composite, these deck boards snap into tracks, leaving no visible fasteners. They are highly durable and can be cleaned with soap and water.

Although these boards resemble wood, they are actually made of a combination of waste wood and reclaimed plastic. They are installed with nails or screws in the same way as wood boards and offer the advantages of long life and easy maintenance.

DECK DETAILS

Though most decks are essentially flat wooden surfaces, their overall appearance can easily be altered to suit your needs and personal taste with the addition of railings, stairs, benches, overheads, and other amenities.

Of course, these details aren't strictly cosmetic—they're usually functional, too. Steps carry you from one level to another, railings provide safety as well as a place to rest your arms as you're admiring a view, benches offer welcome seating, and screens and overheads lend shelter and privacy. Storage compartments help minimize clutter, and planters allow you to bring seasonal color to your deck and to integrate the deck with the surrounding yard.

The photos on the following pages show a variety of functional and aesthetically satisfying deck details. Let them influence the design of your new deck, or adapt them for use with your existing deck.

A railing does not have to be entirely composed of simple, vertical balusters or horizontal rails—this prefabricated starburst panel enlivens an otherwise traditional railing. In this chapter you'll find some classic ideas —and some inspired new ones—for railings, benches, overheads, and other deck amenities.

A spectacular central bench is the focus of this hillside deck. The decking of the upper level forms the seat of the bench, and the surrounding planters hide the structural supports of the bench back. Another interesting feature of this deck is its railings, which have balusters of copper pipe. Plans for this deck begin on page 241. (Design: Robert Engman, AIA, Architect)

STEPS AND STAIRS

Long steps ascending the gentle slope conveniently allow access to the deck from different levels.

The extra width of the lower flight of stairs and the intermediate platform ease the transition from this deck to the yard below. The deck's substructure is hidden with a lattice finished the same color as the railings.

These stairs join two levels of a multilevel deck. Since the landing is off to one side, the stairs take away very little space from the lower deck.

A deck and its amenities should harmonize with its setting. The less formal look of these stairs complements the rough stone wall.

The staircase on this pressure-treated southern pine deck needs a railing only on one side—the other side is enclosed by the deck itself and the privacy screen above it. The lattice beneath both the deck and the stairs hides the substructure from view.

RAILINGS

Different types of railings can be incorporated in a deck's design: Pipe is used for the balusters in the end railing of this lookout deck, while on the other sides, the bench backs double as railings. The hand-crafted lights add style. (Architect: Curtis Gelotte Architects)

The simple, clean lines of the railing shown at left may be just the thing for your deck. By fastening the balusters to a fascia or rim joist, as shown, you will eliminate the need for a bottom rail. Using pressure-treated lumber, such as the southern pine employed here, will result in a very durable deck.

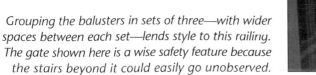

Grouping the balusters in sets of three—with wider spaces between each set—lends style to this railing. The gate shown here is a wise safety feature because the stairs beyond it could easily go unobserved.

This elegant railing is constructed from pre-fabricated panels; other patterns are also available. They can be used for an entire railing, as shown here, or as one or two panels in a standard railing.

A rustic railing of poles and uneven rails is perfect for this beachside deck. On a deck more than 30 inches off the ground, make sure your railing design complies with local building code regulations.

These slim wire rails are perfectly sturdy, can be easily spaced according to building code requirements, and don't obscure the view as much as wood or metal railing members do.

You can have an excellent view as well as a safe barrier with these panels of heavy safety glass installed in an elegant wrought-iron frame. (Landscape architect: James Bradanini, Bradanini & Associates)

SCREENS

Varying widths of lumber add interest to this privacy screen. The deck, with its attractive herringbone decking pattern, is made even more comfortable by the shade-casting overhead. (Landscape architect: Donald G. Boos)

This tall screen of clear acrylic panels blocks the wind but doesn't interfere with the view. (Landscape architect: Ransohoff, Blanchfield & Jones, Inc.)

The combination of a lattice screen and a plant-covered trellis provides a sense of privacy and enclosure on this rooftop deck. The lattice screen's large picture window lets the owners enjoy the view. (Design: Roy Rydell)

An overhead with a solid roof creates an airy outdoor room. You can build a roof over the whole deck, if it's fairly small, or over a portion of a larger deck, as shown here. For an integrated look, you can shingle the overhead to match the roof of your house. A solid-roof overhead should be professionally engineered.
(Design/builder: Imperial Decks & Enclosures)

The ladderlike covering of this open overhead diffuses harsh sun and creates interesting patterns of shade on this cozy raised deck.

Tucked into a grove of cedar trees, this open overhead with its built-in benches and planters offers a peaceful retreat. Plans for this structure begin on page 251. (Architect: Robert C. Slenes and Morton Safford James III for Bennett, Johnson, Slenes & Smith)

The overhead shown here provides shade for the dining area, and helps divide it from the rest of the deck. The integral benches and change in the direction of the decking enhance this effect. (Landscape design: Peter Koenig)

BENCHES

Built between the posts of an overhead, this bench offers a comfortable seat in the shade. The bench has no front legs—it's cantilevered off the railing, with diagonal braces for extra support. The lattice panels in the armrests match those of the overhead. (Design/builder: Bryan Hays)

The mitered 2x2 roofing of this combination bench and overhead diffuses direct sun, providing shade both on the bench and for some distance in front of it. The outdoor cushions make the bench more comfortable, and the light fixtures attached to the joists brighten the space in the evening. You'll find more details on this design on page 160. (Architect: Mark Hajjar)

Most of this bench is built beyond the edge of the deck, so it offers permanent seating without taking any space away from the deck area. The clean lines of the built-in overhead offer shade with style.

A bench such as this one can easily be integrated as part of a complete railing on a high deck.

The narrow seating of the bench surrounding this deck matches the spindles of the built-in hexagonal tables and is further echoed in the tapered backs of the deck chairs. The opening in the central table is sized for a patio umbrella base.

Following the angled edges of the deck, this built-in bench offers ample seating and draws the eye toward the view beyond.

This built-in bench outlines the edge of the deck and provides a convenient seat from which to admire the garden. The light fixtures hidden under the bench provide subtle illumination. (Landscape architect: Lankford Associates)

Built-in benches like this one can divide a large deck into smaller, more intimate spaces. The narrow uprights of the bench back match the balusters of the railing and integrate the deck with the railing system.

STORAGE

The space below a raised deck offers a full-height closet for outdoor gear and pool equipment. For truly sheltered storage, the surface above must be watertight. (Landscape architect: John Herbst, Jr.)

A trapdoor in this deck's surface opens to reveal the hot tub's water-treatment chemicals and equipment. The recessed finger-pull ring lies flat when the lid is closed. (Design: Judith L. Donaghey)

Double doors will open wide to provide easy access to the storage compartment below the upper deck.

Generous storage space, concealed by a lattice screen, is available under the stairway linking this raised deck to the patio below. (Design: Swanson's Nursery & Landscaping)

The decking is cut to fit around these planters made
from corrugated steel culvert pipes. The bottomless
planters drain directly into the soil below the deck.
(Landscape architect: Richard William Wogisch)

With ample space for growing plants,
built-in planters help soften the
angles of this multilevel deck. Plans
for this deck begin on page 238.
(Design: Robert Mowat Associates)

Built-in planters and benches provide a sense of enclosure here, and the tiered planters create a multilevel garden. (Landscape architect: Ken Morrison)

Easy-to-build open boxes on top of closed benches serve a dual purpose in this seating and planter arrangement.

PLANNING YOUR DECK

When you embark upon a project meant to improve your home, it's natural to want to jump right in. Resist the temptation! Planning is your key to success: without it, you're likely to fumble your way through a series of mistakes that are costly and frustrating at best, disastrous at worst. This chapter takes you through the planning sequence, from evaluating your needs to drawing up construction details. You'll find information on site selection, building codes, and plan-drawing techniques.

The chapter beginning on page 61 will show you all the components of a deck and how they fit together. With this information in mind, you'll be ready to start drafting your final plans.

You may decide that you want to leave some part of the design and building process to a professional. Turn to page 58 for tips on making this decision and information on working with professionals. Even if you decide to use one of the plans shown in this book or to have a plan drawn for you, the information in this chapter will help you decide on the kind of plan that will meet your needs.

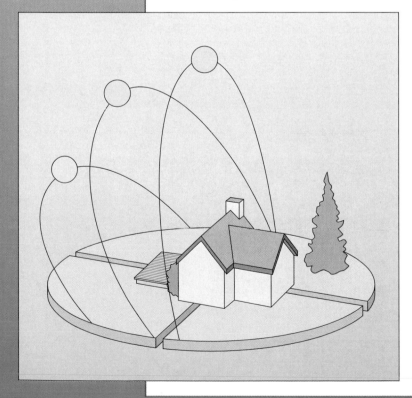

One of the main considerations in locating your deck is the amount of sun the deck will get in different seasons and at different times of day. Starting on page 50, we'll show you how to determine this, as well as how to shelter your deck from wind and rain.

DESIGN CONSIDERATIONS

As you begin to plan your deck, you'll need to consider how your family will use it. Then you can work out an overall shape that will accommodate both those needs and the space available. You'll also want to include design details that will add visual interest and match the style of your house.

MATCHING YOUR NEEDS

How do you and your family spend time outdoors? Do you like to entertain? Do your children need a dry outdoor play area? Do you want to create a poolside place for relaxing? Your answers will help you plan a deck that meets your family's specific needs. These plans may include amenities such as benches, planters, lighting, and storage; see page 153 for information on these additions.

Following are some of the uses you might want to consider in planning your deck.

Entertaining: Sooner or later almost everyone uses a deck for a party. If you entertain often, you'll want to make sure your deck is large enough to handle groups comfortably. How much seating will you need?

Visualize where you might place outdoor furniture. Built-in benches are easy to include if you think of them before you begin construction. Decide where to position them to allow for easy conversation; this is best done with people arranged face to face. For nighttime entertaining, think about installing outdoor lighting; it makes a deck safer and more inviting in the evening.

Dining: If you like to eat outdoors, make sure your deck is large enough to accommodate tables and chairs (a 12-foot square is usually adequate for a table and chairs to seat four). You might want to incorporate a built-in table with benches in the deck's construction. Consider how easy it will be to get from the kitchen to the deck. If a wall separates the two, adding a door *(page 49)* or a service window could make it easier to move food outdoors.

Plan a place for a barbecue. This should be an out-of-the-way spot where no one will bump into the grill and where smoke won't be a nuisance. Barbecuing on a deck can be hazardous—for safety precautions, see the information at right.

Swimming and sunning: When the focus of outdoor living is a swimming pool, the setting can be formal and rectangular or more naturalistic, with the pool's form integrated with an informal landscape. A dining area, a shade-creating roof, or a spa are all delightful extras. Also consider including sunbathing platforms; on a low deck, these can double as railings *(page 159)*.

Gardening: Wooden planters can be handsomely worked into a deck design. Just be sure to allow for proper drainage. Deck construction often covers up outdoor faucets for hoses; move these before you

begin building, or consider installing an automatic irrigation system.

Storage: No matter how you will use your deck, you'll always value storage space. Where will you put the hose and other garden tools or children's play equipment? Where does the garden furniture go in bad weather?

On a sloping property or if the deck is well above the ground, the most obvious place for storage is underneath the deck, where waterproof closets or shelves can be easily built, using the deck's foundation for support. Conceal such storage by skirting around the deck's support posts with lattice panels. You can also build lift-top benches and incorporate closets into the design of stairways.

Privacy: Building an elevated deck can expose as many unpleasant views as attractive ones. Try moving a ladder around and standing on it at the approximate height of your future deck. What can you see? And who can see you? If you value privacy, or if your new view is unsightly, plan to add screens, overheads, or landscaping to remedy the problem.

 PLAY IT SAFE

LOCATING A BARBECUE
Placing a barbecue on a deck can be a fire hazard; not only is the wood combustible, but the finish may be also. To be on the safe side, keep the barbecue off the deck.

If you do decide to put a barbecue on your deck, make sure there is 2 feet of clearance on all sides. In addition, it's wise to place the barbecue on a fireproof surface such as metal, brick, or tile. When designing your deck, consider integrating such a surface.

Do not barbecue under overhanging trees or an overhead; always keep the barbecue attended when in use.

DECK SHAPES

Decks are often built as a simple rectangle off the back door; however, with a little imagination, you can design your deck to take advantage of the shape of your house and lot. Why not consider a detached deck to make use of an attractive corner of your property? Perhaps you can reclaim a forsaken side yard by creating a protected refuge off a bedroom or bath. Some possible deck shapes are shown below and opposite.

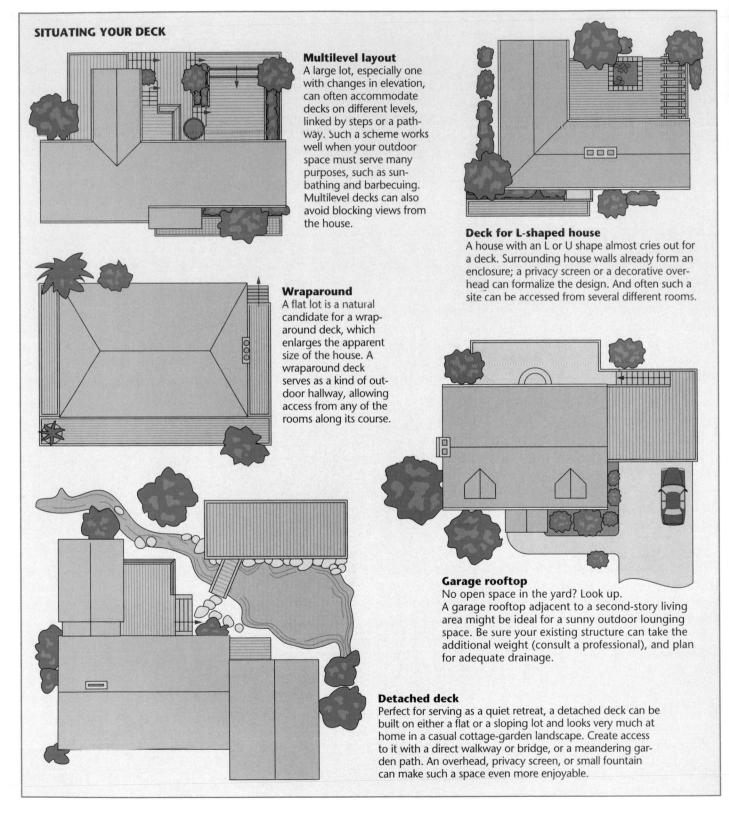

SITUATING YOUR DECK

Multilevel layout
A large lot, especially one with changes in elevation, can often accommodate decks on different levels, linked by steps or a pathway. Such a scheme works well when your outdoor space must serve many purposes, such as sunbathing and barbecuing. Multilevel decks can also avoid blocking views from the house.

Deck for L-shaped house
A house with an L or U shape almost cries out for a deck. Surrounding house walls already form an enclosure; a privacy screen or a decorative overhead can formalize the design. And often such a site can be accessed from several different rooms.

Wraparound
A flat lot is a natural candidate for a wraparound deck, which enlarges the apparent size of the house. A wraparound deck serves as a kind of outdoor hallway, allowing access from any of the rooms along its course.

Garage rooftop
No open space in the yard? Look up.
A garage rooftop adjacent to a second-story living area might be ideal for a sunny outdoor lounging space. Be sure your existing structure can take the additional weight (consult a professional), and plan for adequate drainage.

Detached deck
Perfect for serving as a quiet retreat, a detached deck can be built on either a flat or a sloping lot and looks very much at home in a casual cottage-garden landscape. Create access to it with a direct walkway or bridge, or a meandering garden path. An overhead, privacy screen, or small fountain can make such a space even more enjoyable.

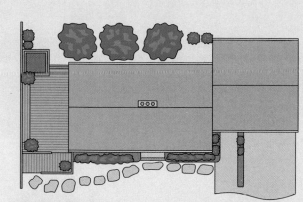

Side-yard space

A neglected side yard may be just the spot for a sheltered out-door sitting area to brighten and expand a small bedroom or bathroom. A sunny breakfast deck off a cramped kitchen can be accessed by way of French or Dutch doors. If you're subject to fence height restrictions, add an overhead to protect privacy.

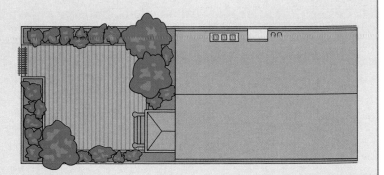

Entry deck

A front deck surrounded by plantings can transform a boring front lawn into a private oasis. Level changes can provide access to a house on a sloping lot. Try using a hedge, lattice screen, or overhead to let in light and air while screening off the street.

BRIDGING THE GAP

A short bridge can be constructed in much the same way as a deck.

Although the bridge illustrated below crosses a terraced ravine between deck and garden, the same sort of bridge could be built to connect two separate elevated decks, to span a garden pond or stream, or simply to allow easy passage over rough or irregular terrain.

Your bridge will need these four components: firm anchorage at each end; sturdy beams to traverse the span; decking; and railings. Be very sure to develop bridge plans in accordance with local building codes.

DESIGN DETAILS

A deck should be more than just functional. When well designed, it adds beauty and character to your home, not to mention value. The deck shown below makes use of level changes to accommodate a sloping lot. One or more flights of stairs could be added to provide access to the ground from different sides of the deck. Planters, benches, angles, and changes in the pattern of the deck boards add visual interest.

The following are some tips to help you make your deck more attractive.

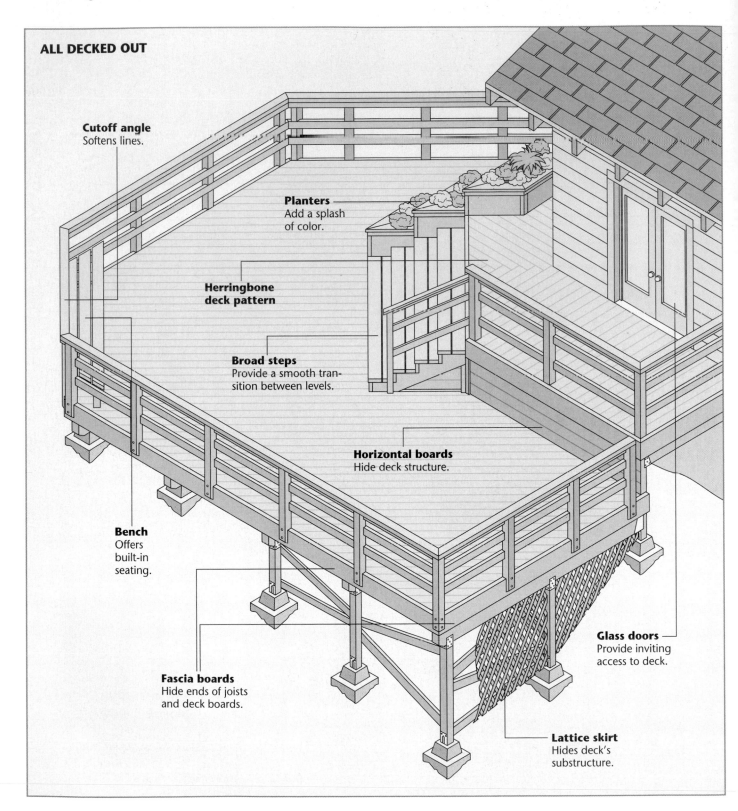

ALL DECKED OUT

Cutoff angle
Softens lines.

Planters
Add a splash of color.

Herringbone deck pattern

Broad steps
Provide a smooth transition between levels.

Horizontal boards
Hide deck structure.

Bench
Offers built-in seating.

Glass doors
Provide inviting access to deck.

Fascia boards
Hide ends of joists and deck boards.

Lattice skirt
Hides deck's substructure.

Match your house: Keep your deck in scale. A large flat deck outside a small house seems out of place—more like a landing platform than an inviting outdoor living area; instead, consider several smaller, multilevel or satellite decks. Likewise, a small deck off a large house feels insecure and uninviting.

To make a new deck seem as though it has always been part of your home, repeat some of your house's features in the deck's design. For example, stain or paint the deck to match or complement the house color. Another trick is to match the railing style to the style of the house trim.

Harmonize with your garden: Highlighting natural features in your garden as part of a deck design can result in a stunningly beautiful outdoor environment. Don't think of large rocks, trees, streams, or rough terrain as obstacles, but as possible focal points. Weave the deck amid the rocks. Let a tree grow up through the deck's surface, and build a bench around it so you can enjoy the shade. Use level changes to accentuate the handsomeness of rugged terrain.

Create smooth transitions: Try to create attractive transitions between different areas of the deck and between the deck and the rest of the garden. Steps should not be too steep, narrow, or intimidating. Railings should be sturdy, and look it. To create a transition between the house and deck, create a flat landing at the doorway, rather than a series of steps. You may also want to create a border of bark chips or gravel between the deck or lawn, or to surround the deck with shrubs.

Use interesting angles: If your initial designs look too blocky, try cutting off some of the sharp corners, creating octagons from squares. Doing so can make the deck itself seem more interesting and can soften the severe look of a rectangular house on a rectangular lot.

Sometimes angling a deck off the back of a house can have a dramatic effect. Besides leading people to a certain part of the yard, it can open up the area alongside the deck for other purposes, such as play space or permanent landscaping.

Vary decking direction: The lines created by decking tend to direct the eye. Consequently, the direction in which you lay the deck boards can have a surprising impact on how people view the deck and the rest of your property. For instance, setting decking parallel to the back of the house makes the deck seem narrower. By angling deck boards you can direct attention to a spectacular view or beautiful part of your garden. You can also change the direction of the decking to create patterns, making the deck more visually interesting and adding an illusion of depth. If overdone, though, this device can make a deck's surface pattern seem too busy or contrived.

Add amenities: Benches and planters can break the open expanse of the deck. Planters can highlight level changes, and a bench can be tucked into a corner as a secluded resting spot.

Incorporating an overhead into your deck design can do much more than provide shade: An overhead connects the vertical mass of the house to the horizontal expanse of the deck. It also yields a look of partial enclosure, which adds to your sense of privacy when you are outdoors.

Amenities such as benches and overheads can be added to a deck after it's built; you can even decide to add them years later. However, you'll save work if you design amenities at the same time as the deck. This will allow you to integrate them into the look of the deck and to anchor them firmly to the deck structure. Furthermore, some must be thought out in the initial planning process. For instance, you may need to use longer posts if an overhead requires them for support.

Choose detailing carefully: A little extra attention paid to the details of a deck can add greatly to its style. Improve the workmanship of the railing and benches, and the whole deck looks more crafted. Add fascia boards around the edges of the decking, and the entire structure becomes more cleanly defined. Build a skirt around the outside of the deck to cover the substructure, and you add a sense of mass and permanence.

Use contrast: Contrasting colors can be achieved by staining different parts of the deck different colors, or by adding plantings. Contrasting materials can also be used, such as by linking sections of a wood deck with stone or brick walkways or patios.

MOVING AND ENLARGING DOORS

A deck should entice people outdoors. Wide French or glass doors that open out onto a deck make the outdoors look inviting. Putting in a wider door will involve enlarging the door opening, and in some cases you may need to cut a brand new door opening to provide access to a deck on a side of the house with no door. When locating a new door, try to route foot traffic around the edges of a room instead of through the middle.

Whether you're enlarging an existing opening or creating a new one, the same basic steps apply. First, the interior and exterior wall coverings must be removed, and the studs and sole plate cut away where the door will be located. Next, the opening must be framed. Finally, the door is hung and door casings are installed. You must avoid cutting into electrical wires or plumbing pipes inside the wall. If you cannot relocate the opening away from wires or pipes, take great care when cutting into the wall covering, and then have the lines rerouted.

SITE CONSIDERATIONS

Deciding where you'll build your new deck is the first step in its design. This choice may seem obvious. For instance, you may know you want your new deck outside your living room. But the implications of your decision may not be as obvious as you think.

First, ask yourself whether the spot you've picked is accessible from both the house and yard, considering established traffic patterns and the location of doors and windows. If a deck isn't in a convenient spot, it may go unused. Also, consider how the deck will affect views from the house, as well as what will be visible from the deck itself. Keep in mind that as well as blocking views, a high-level deck will cool and shade the area it overhangs, and it may also block light to rooms underneath.

Finally, ask yourself what the weather is like in the spot you've chosen. The general climate of your area will determine how and when you use your deck and should influence its design. Do you need an overhead to provide shade during the hottest part of the day? Do you need a barrier to block strong winds? (If you're new to the area, it's a good idea to ask long-time residents about local conditions.) On a smaller scale, the microclimates within your lot may also affect where and how you build your deck. The exposure of your deck to sun, wind, and precipitation will be affected by its orientation and its proximity to buildings and trees.

SUN AND SHADE

In general, a deck that faces north is cool because the sun rarely shines on it, while a south-facing deck is usually warm because, from sunrise to sunset, the sun never leaves it. Yards with an eastern exposure stay cool, receiving only morning sunlight; west-facing areas can be uncomfortably hot, since they absorb the full force of the sun's mid-afternoon rays.

These general rules aren't without exceptions, though. In hot regions of the country, there may be north-facing decks that could hardly be considered cool in summer. And a west-facing deck in San Francisco is rarely hot, since stiff ocean breezes and chilly fogs are common even during the warmer months.

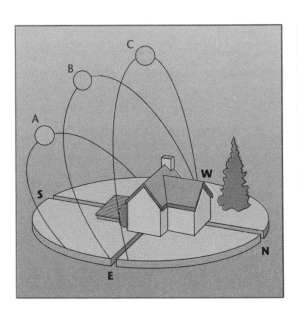

SEASONAL SUN ANGLES	SUN'S POSITION/HOURS OF DAYLIGHT (see map below)		
Season	Area 1	Area 2	Area 3
A) Noon, 12/21	21°/8 hrs.	29°/9 hrs.	37°/10 hrs.
B) Noon, 3/21 and 9/21	45°/12 hrs.	53°/12 hrs.	60°/12 hrs.
C) Noon, 6/21	69°/16 hrs.	76°/15 hrs.	83°/14 hrs.

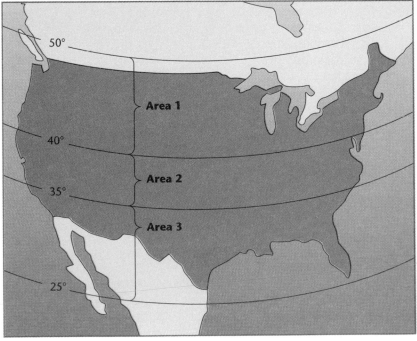

As shown in the illustration on the opposite page, the sun crosses the sky in an arc that changes slightly every day, becoming lower in winter and higher in summer. In the dead of winter, it briefly tracks across the sky at a low angle, throwing long shadows; on long summer days, it moves overhead at a very high angle. As you move farther north from the equator, the difference becomes more dramatic; in Alaska, for example, days are very long in summer, very short in winter. Using both the drawings and the chart, you can determine where the sun will fall on potential deck locations at various times of year. First find your location on the map; then refer to the chart for sun angles.

If you live in an area with hot summers and mild winters, shade may be welcome in summer, but not in winter. A deciduous tree can usually provide shade for a deck when the sun is high in the summer sky but allow sunlight through in winter when the sun is lower and the leaves have fallen. An overhead, particularly one covered with vines, will function the same way.

Keep in mind that certain materials reflect sun and/or heat better than others. Light-colored masonry walls are great for spreading sun and heat but can be uncomfortably bright. Dark masonry materials retain heat longer, making evenings on the deck a little warmer.

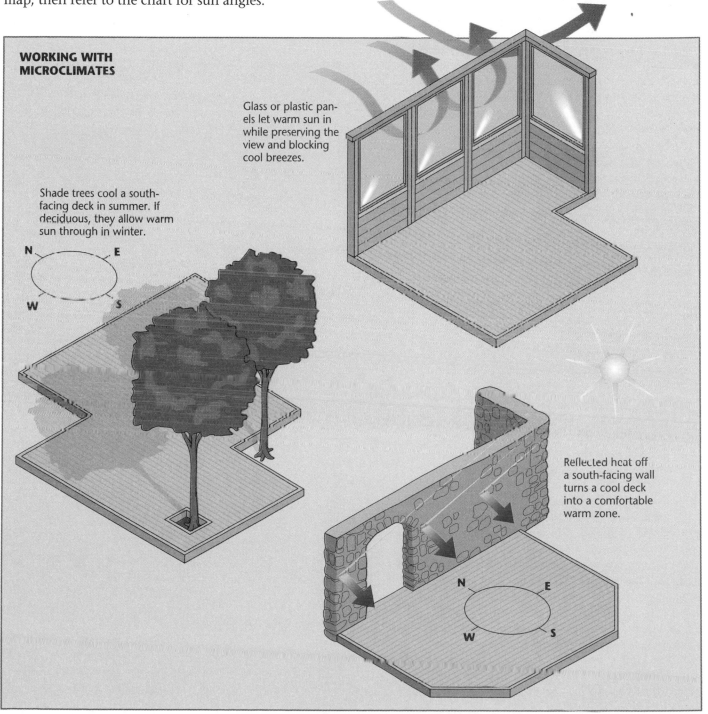

WORKING WITH MICROCLIMATES

Glass or plastic panels let warm sun in while preserving the view and blocking cool breezes.

Shade trees cool a south-facing deck in summer. If deciduous, they allow warm sun through in winter.

Reflected heat off a south-facing wall turns a cool deck into a comfortable warm zone.

WIND PATTERNS

Too much wind can create enough chill on cool days to make a deck unusable. Likewise, if there's no breeze at all, decks in sunny locations can be very uncomfortable in summer weather.

Your deck's location or design may be influenced by three different kinds of winds: annual prevailing winds, very localized seasonal breezes, and occasional high-velocity winds generated by stormy weather.

Even if your proposed deck will face strong winds only occasionally, you may have to strengthen its foundations and substructure. If it will receive mild prevailing breezes, you may wish to modify their effects with vertical screens or fences, as illustrated in the drawings at right. Note that a solid vertical barrier may not be the best choice; angled baffles, lattice-type fencing, or deciduous plantings will disperse wind better. To determine which areas need to be sheltered from the wind, post small flags or ribbons at various places on your proposed site, and take note of their movements during windy periods.

Your house itself can serve as a formidable windbreak. Where regular breezes are a problem, you can shelter your deck by locating it on the side of the house opposite the direction of prevailing winds.

RAIN AND SNOW

Though you're unlikely to use your deck during poor weather, it will take a beating —and age more rapidly—if it's pounded by frequent rains. You may want to locate your deck where the house will shelter it from the weather.

As you evaluate deck locations, note which way your house's roof is pitched; that's where runoff might occur. If necessary, runoff can be redirected with gutters. For information on weatherproofing your deck, turn to page 166.

In areas that experience heavy snowfall, even if only sporadically, any deck must be capable of handling the snow's added weight. Snow is surprisingly heavy; piled 5 to 6 feet deep, it can weigh as much as 80 to 100 pounds per square foot. This standing weight alone can be enough to collapse an improperly designed structure. Make sure you follow all code requirements for your region when constructing your deck. Though code requirements may not cover the strength of railings, they too must be strong enough to support the snow load.

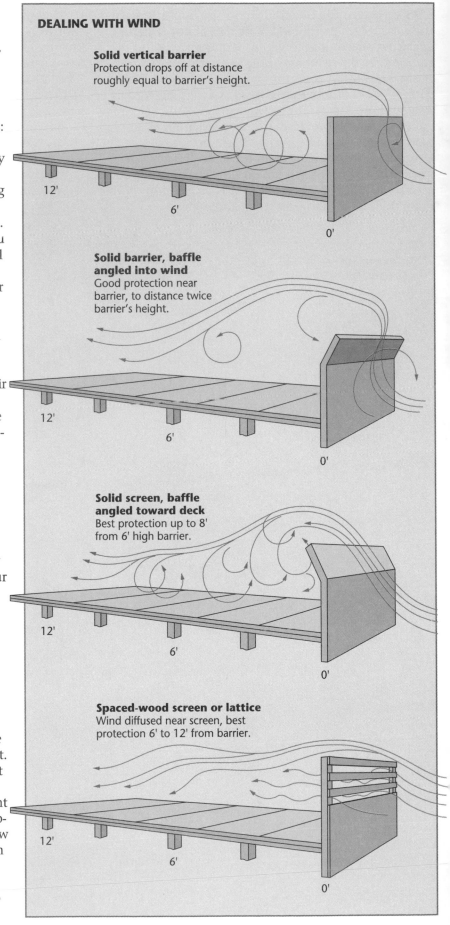

DEALING WITH WIND

Solid vertical barrier
Protection drops off at distance roughly equal to barrier's height.

Solid barrier, baffle angled into wind
Good protection near barrier, to distance twice barrier's height.

Solid screen, baffle angled toward deck
Best protection up to 8' from 6' high barrier.

Spaced-wood screen or lattice
Wind diffused near screen, best protection 6' to 12' from barrier.

LEGAL RESTRICTIONS

Before you've gone too far in planning your deck, consult your local building department for any legal restrictions. In most areas, you'll need to file for a building permit and comply with building code requirements. Also be aware of local zoning ordinances, which normally govern whether or not a deck can be built on your land and where it can be located.

Building permits: Before you pound a single nail, get the needed permits. It's important that the building department check plans before construction begins, to ensure that you don't get off to a substandard start. Negligence may come back to haunt you: Officials can fine you and require you to bring an illegally built structure up to standard or even to dismantle it entirely.

The need for a permit generally hinges on a deck's size and intended use, and on whether or not it's attached to the house. In most areas, any deck more than 30 inches off the ground requires a permit and must be built according to building codes. If the project includes any electrical wiring or plumbing, you may need a separate permit for each of these.

Fees are usually charged for permits. These fees are generally determined by the projected value of the improvement—so when you apply for a permit, be as accurate as possible about the estimated cost. If you overestimate, you might push the fee higher. Many building offices figure a project's value based on standardized construction costs per square foot.

Building codes: Code requirements vary from region to region. They set minimum safety standards for materials and construction techniques: depth of footings, size of beams, and proper fastening methods, for example. Code requirements help ensure that any structures you build will be well made and safe for your family and any future owners of your property.

Zoning ordinances: These municipal regulations restrict the height of residential buildings, limit lot coverage (the proportion of the lot a building and other structures may cover), specify setbacks (how close to the property lines you can build), and—in some areas—stipulate architectural design standards.

Decks rarely exceed height limitations, but they're often affected by setback requirements. They also increase your overall lot coverage—an important consideration, since a deck might limit future additions to your home.

Variances: If the zoning department rejects your plans, you can apply for a variance at your city or county planning department. It's your task to prove to a hearing officer or zoning board of appeal that following the zoning requirements precisely would create "undue hardship," and that the structure you want to build will not negatively affect your neighbors or the community. If you plead your case convincingly, you may be allowed to build.

Architectural review boards: Neighborhoods with tight controls may require that your improvement meet certain architectural standards—and that means submitting your plans to an architectural review board. Going through this process can dramatically increase the time required to get your project moving.

Deeds: Your property deed can also restrict your project's design, construction, or location. Review the deed carefully, checking for easements, architectural-standard restrictions, and other limitations.

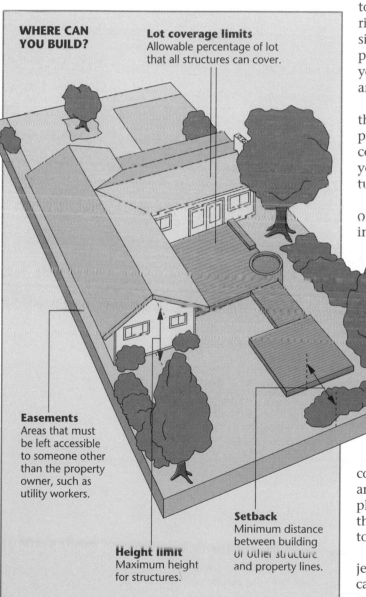

WHERE CAN YOU BUILD?

Lot coverage limits
Allowable percentage of lot that all structures can cover.

Easements
Areas that must be left accessible to someone other than the property owner, such as utility workers.

Height limit
Maximum height for structures.

Setback
Minimum distance between building or other structure and property lines.

DRAWING AND READING PLANS

Once you've determined the best site for your deck, it's time to put your ideas on paper and transform them into a workable design. Before you begin, gather as much information about deck design as you can: Study the deck plans pictured in this book, flip through home improvement magazines to see more examples, and study as many decks as you can at the homes of friends and neighbors.

It doesn't take an artist to design a simple deck. All you need is a few basic drawing tools. If you're not equipped with all the tools shown below, you can make do with a tablet of graph paper and a ruler. (Turn to page 56 for information on drawing to scale.)

First you'll need to obtain or draw a site plan—a plan of your house and property, as shown opposite—and to sketch the overall configuration of the deck; then you'll be ready to draw the working plans. You may decide to hire a professional to draw the final working plans; however, it's still a good idea to develop your own preliminary sketches. For advice on working with professionals, turn to page 58.

If you choose to work from one of the deck plans shown at the end of this book, you may need to adapt it to your situation as discussed on page 183.

ASK A PRO

IS THERE SOFTWARE AVAILABLE TO HELP ME DESIGN MY DECK?

A computer drawing program is easier and more accurate than drawing by hand, and allows you to make changes easily. Software is available specifically intended for deck design. Starting from a basic deck design, the software will allow you to adapt the shape of the deck and to add features such as railings and steps. The program then allows you to view the deck from various angles. Such programs usually generate a materials list based on your design, and provide some how-to information.

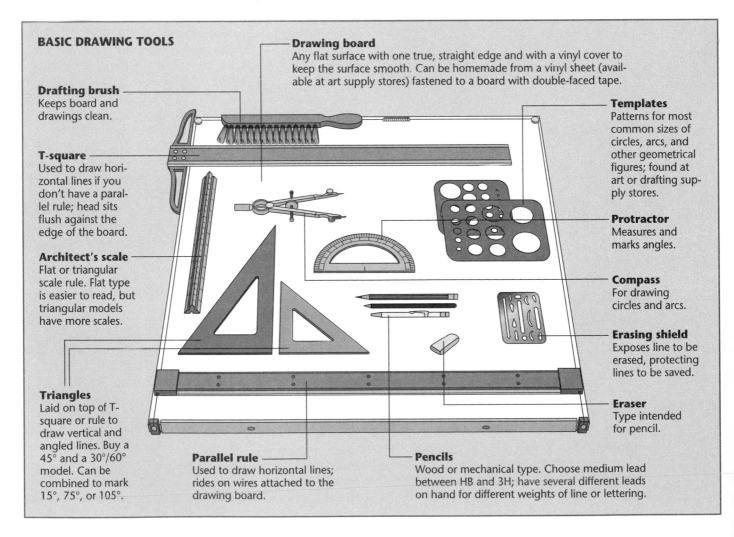

BASIC DRAWING TOOLS

Drawing board
Any flat surface with one true, straight edge and with a vinyl cover to keep the surface smooth. Can be homemade from a vinyl sheet (available at art supply stores) fastened to a board with double-faced tape.

Drafting brush
Keeps board and drawings clean.

T-square
Used to draw horizontal lines if you don't have a parallel rule; head sits flush against the edge of the board.

Architect's scale
Flat or triangular scale rule. Flat type is easier to read, but triangular models have more scales.

Triangles
Laid on top of T-square or rule to draw vertical and angled lines. Buy a 45° and a 30°/60° model. Can be combined to mark 15°, 75°, or 105°.

Templates
Patterns for most common sizes of circles, arcs, and other geometrical figures; found at art or drafting supply stores.

Protractor
Measures and marks angles.

Compass
For drawing circles and arcs.

Erasing shield
Exposes line to be erased, protecting lines to be saved.

Eraser
Type intended for pencil.

Parallel rule
Used to draw horizontal lines; rides on wires attached to the drawing board.

Pencils
Wood or mechanical type. Choose medium lead between HB and 3H; have several different leads on hand for different weights of line or lettering.

DEVELOPING A SITE PLAN

Mapping your lot can be a way to make some interesting discoveries about what you thought was familiar territory. Use your observations about your site and its setting to produce a site plan like the one shown below. If you can locate the architect's drawings or deed maps that show the actual dimensions and orientation of your property, you'll save yourself considerable work. These may be available at your city hall, county office, title company, bank, mortgage company, or through the former owner.

You'll gradually be covering a good deal of your paper with written and sketched details, so make each entry as neat and concise as possible. The following information should appear in one form or another on the site plan.

Boundary lines and dimensions: Outline your property accurately and to scale, and mark its dimensions on the site plan. Indicate any required setback allowances from your lot lines *(page 53)*. Also note the relation of the street to your house.

The house: Show your house precisely and to scale within the property. Note all exterior doors (and the direction each one opens), and all overhangs. You may also want to note the height of lower-story windows.

Exposure: Use a compass to determine North, and mark it on your plan; then note on your site plan the shaded and sunlit areas of your landscape. Indicate the direction of the prevailing winds and mark any spots that are windy enough to require shielding.

Utilities and easements: Map the location of outdoor faucets and show the locations of all underground lines, including the sewage line or septic tank. If you're contemplating a tall overhead or elevated deck, identify any overhead lines. If your deed map shows any easements *(page 53)*, note them on your site plan and check legal restrictions limiting development of those areas.

Downspouts and drainage: Mark the locations of all downspouts and any drainage tiles, drainpipes, or catch basins. Note the direction of drainage, any point where drainage is impeded (leaving soil soggy), and any place where runoff from a steep hillside could cause erosion.

Existing plantings: If you're remodeling an old landscape, note any established plantings that you want to retain or that would require a major effort or expense to remove or replace.

Views: Note all views, attractive or unattractive, from every side of your property. You can use a ladder to check views from different elevations. Also take into account views into your yard from neighboring houses or streets.

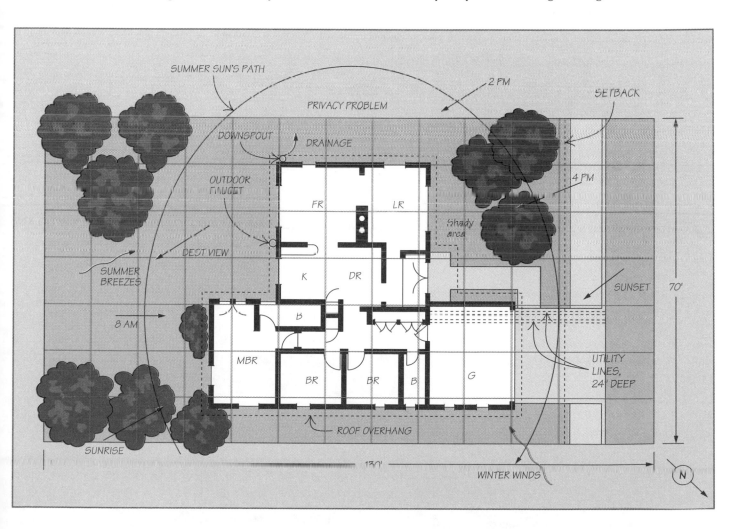

SKETCHING DECK CONFIGURATIONS

When you're ready to plan the shape of the deck itself, arm yourself with a good supply of tracing paper and a sharp pencil. Place a sheet of tracing paper over your site plan—you may want to enlarge the plan to make your work easier. Start by sketching some circles to indicate the basic use areas. As you work, consider such issues such as whether a children's play area is in full view of your living area, or whether the private sunning spot you envision is accessible from the master bedroom. Once you've established how you'd like to use the space, start testing possible deck configurations. Try placing scale cutouts of outdoor furniture on your sketch. If you're not pleased, just start over again with a fresh piece of paper—correcting mistakes costs nothing at this point.

Once you've created a shape that seems to work, figure the deck's actual size and confirm its shape and placement at the site. Then refine your scale drawing. Finally, using a dark, felt-tip pen, draw in the permanent background —house and landscaping—on the tracing paper. Don't worry about capturing every detail—your eye will compensate for features that you've suggested with just a few lines.

DEVELOPING WORKING PLANS

Once you've sketched in the overall shape of the deck, you're ready to create the working plans. To do this, you'll also have to take into account the information given in the next chapter on how a deck is put together, and you'll need to make sure the construction methods conform to any local code (*page 53*).

Working plans must be drawn to scale, as described below, and they should include the types of views shown opposite: plan, elevation, and details. A deck's basic surface pattern and substructure should both be drawn in plan view. Arrangement of the substructure should also be drawn in an elevation view. To simplify confusing portions of the deck, you may need to draw them in a section view as well. Railings and other vertical members are best drawn in elevation view. Attachments and other details should be drawn from the view that most clearly shows their construction; three-dimensional detail drawings such as the one shown on page 48 sometimes work best.

READING PLANS

Even if you don't draw up your own plans, you'll need to know how to read existing plans, such as those shown later in this book, or those provided by a designer. Plans typically include the views shown opposite: plan views, elevations, and details. Remember that if you're using plans not specifically designed for your lot, you may need to adjust them; turn to page 183 for information on how to do this.

DRAWING TO SCALE

To reduce the actual dimensions of your future deck to paper size accurately, you must draw it to scale. The tools shown on page 54 will be useful for this task. To draw your site plan, you'll need to measure the existing landscape. For a large lot, you may want to choose a tape measure as long as 50 to 100 feet. A long tape will reduce inaccuracies and exasperation.

For your site plan, reduce each foot of your lot to 1/4 inch, or 1/8 inch for a large lot. A typical scale for plan and elevation views of the actual deck is 1/4 inch or 1/2 inch, depending upon the deck's size. Use 1/2 inch to 1 foot for details. To make the drawing job easier, you can use an architectural scale ruler. A triangular ruler such as the one shown below has markings for a variety of scales.

Another way to draw to scale is to use graph paper. The most common size has 1/4-inch squares. For a site plan, one square would be 2 feet. For plan and elevation views, one square would equal 1 foot. And for details, one square would equal 6 inches. If you need a larger drawing area than one sheet provides, tape several pieces of graph paper together.

*Lower numbers are 1/4"
scale from right to left.*

*Upper numbers are 1/8"
scale from left to right.*

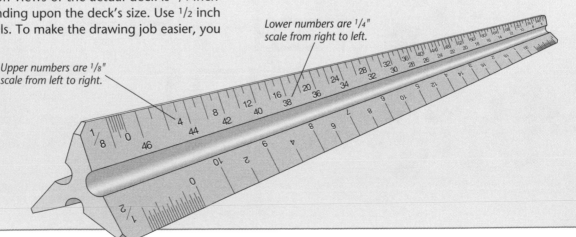

DIFFERENT POINTS OF VIEW

Shown are the working plans for the deck illustrated on page 48.

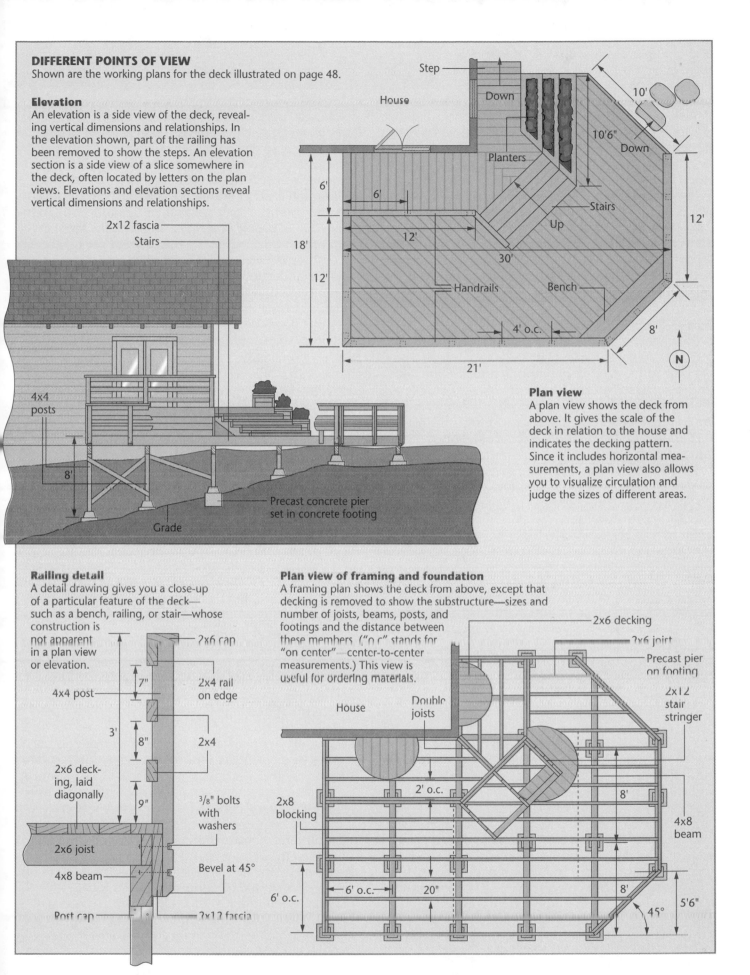

Elevation

An elevation is a side view of the deck, revealing vertical dimensions and relationships. In the elevation shown, part of the railing has been removed to show the steps. An elevation section is a side view of a slice somewhere in the deck, often located by letters on the plan views. Elevations and elevation sections reveal vertical dimensions and relationships.

2x12 fascia
Stairs
4x4 posts
8'
Precast concrete pier set in concrete footing
Grade

Step
House
Down
Planters
Down
Stairs
Up
Handrails
Bench
30'
4' o.c.
21'
8'
N
6'
6'
18'
12'
12'
10'
10'6"
12'

Plan view

A plan view shows the deck from above. It gives the scale of the deck in relation to the house and indicates the decking pattern. Since it includes horizontal measurements, a plan view also allows you to visualize circulation and judge the sizes of different areas.

Railing detail

A detail drawing gives you a close-up of a particular feature of the deck—such as a bench, railing, or stair—whose construction is not apparent in a plan view or elevation.

2x6 cap
4x4 post
7"
2x4 rail on edge
3'
8"
2x4
2x6 decking, laid diagonally
9"
3/8" bolts with washers
2x6 joist
4x8 beam
Bevel at 45°
Post cap
2x12 fascia

Plan view of framing and foundation

A framing plan shows the deck from above, except that decking is removed to show the substructure—sizes and number of joists, beams, posts, and footings and the distance between these members. ("o.c." stands for "on center"—center-to-center measurements.) This view is useful for ordering materials.

2x6 decking
2x6 joist
Precast pier on footing
2x12 stair stringer
House
Double joists
2x8 blocking
6' o.c.
6' o.c.
2' o.c.
20"
8'
8'
8'
4x8 beam
45°
5'6"

PLANNING THE WORK

There are a number of ways to tackle a deck-building project. You can design and build the deck yourself; design it, then have it built by a contractor; have it designed by a professional and build it yourself; or explore some type of work-share arrangement with a builder. What part of the task you decide to take on yourself will depend on your design and construction skills, the tools you own, your available time and energy, and the project's complexity. If you decide to hire a professional it pays to know as much as possible about deck construction so you can participate in decisions on how your deck will be designed and built.

WHEN TO BUILD IT YOURSELF

If you have a knack for design, there's no reason why you can't develop a working plan for your deck, although it's wise to have at least an hour's consultation with a professional landscape architect or designer. Even if you decide to leave the working plans to a professional, you'll probably want to produce your own site plan and sketch in the configuration of the deck. This will help you communicate your ideas more clearly.

Whether or not you intend to do your own work, it's helpful to invite two or three contractors to bid on the job. Their bids will help you estimate the potential savings of doing your own work, and the pros may offer invaluable input regarding your deck's design or construction.

Because labor represents 40% or more of a professionally built deck, you can save significantly by doing your own work. Of course, the job will probably take you longer than it would take a contractor. Don't forget to factor in the cost of any tools you'll have to buy or rent and expect to absorb the cost of any errors. On the other hand, besides the financial savings, doing your own work gives you more control over the noise and disruption, as well as the satisfaction and pride inherent in a successful result.

To decide whether to do the job yourself, think realistically about your skills. Can you handle a power saw? Are you willing and able to mix and cast concrete footings? Can you swing a hammer for hours on end? To build a deck, you'll have to be fairly adept with tools and willing to work hard.

The tools you'll need are discussed on page 104. Don't be discouraged if you're missing a few; the money you'll save by doing your own work will more than cover a few additions to your toolkit. And, if you don't own the specialty tools, you can probably rent or borrow them.

In most cases, the critical factors that determine whether or not you should do the work yourself are a deck's complexity and its site conditions. Decks on relatively flat sites are easier than decks on slopes, and single-level decks are far easier to design and build than decks that have multiple levels or stairs. Decks with simple, rectangular shapes are much easier to design and build than decks with angled or curved shapes. A house-attached deck is usually easier than a freestanding one because less foundation work is needed. Simple railings and benches are manageable, but complex amenities and overhead structures can add significantly to the task. And, of course, the larger the deck, the more labor it will require. In evaluating the scope of the job, take all of these factors into consideration.

With moderate skills, a few tools, and this book as a reference, you should be able to design and build a rectangular, low-level deck on a relatively flat site—a small deck that doesn't involve multiple levels or have attached amenities such as railings, benches, or an overhead. If you're fairly handy, you can probably tackle a deck that has a couple of level changes, steps, railings, benches, an overhead, and the like. These additions just take a little more understanding of construction practices and more time, energy, and materials.

WHEN TO HIRE A PROFESSIONAL

What projects should you avoid? Strongly consider hiring a professional designer and/or builder if the deck you want involves any of these conditions:

• **High levels:** The higher the deck, the harder it normally is to build. With decks higher than about 6 feet, it's difficult to position posts, beams, and other framing. Such decks may also require structural reinforcement to protect them from lateral loads caused by wind or earthquakes.

• **Sites over sand, mud, or water:** Decks perched above water or marshy ground, at lakeside or beach locations require special pilings for support.

• **Steep or unstable sites:** A steep site, particularly where slides may occur, must be checked by a soils engineer. A deck over such a site generally requires structural engineering and special building department approval.

• **Waterproof decking:** A deck that must be waterproof —that is, one on a roof, or one that must keep an area below it dry—requires a leak-proof barrier that's normally applied by a roofing contractor. Concrete, tile, or slate surfaces are tricky to install and best left to a masonry contractor. The added weight of such materials may require a stronger-than-normal deck structure; on a roof it may call for strengthening the roof structure.

• **Cantilevered construction:** A cantilevered deck is supported by joists or beams that extend into and are anchored by the house structure. Calculating loads for such a deck should be done by a professional.

• **Special amenities:** If your deck building project will include electrical wiring or plumbing, or require home remodeling skills—to open up a wall, for example—you may need licensed professionals.

CHOOSING THE RIGHT PROFESSIONAL

Regardless of how much work you wish to handle yourself, you can choose from a variety of professionals for advice or help. Here is a brief look at some of the people who can help you and what they do.

Architects and landscape architects: These state-licensed professionals can work with you to help set objectives, analyze the site, and produce detailed working plans; they can also select and estimate materials. In addition to providing design services, some architects will negotiate bids from contractors and supervise the actual work.

Landscape architects are specialized in outdoor structures; however, if your deck poses particular engineering problems, you may want to consult a building architect. Building architects, often referred to simply as architects, design houses and have more engineering expertise than most landscape architects.

Landscape and building designers: Landscape designers often have a landscape architect's education and training, but not a state license. They can generally offer the same services as a landscape architect, and they are often more experienced with residential projects than many architects. Designers may be certified by their professional association.

Draftspersons: Drafters may be members of a skilled trade or unlicensed architects' apprentices. They can make the working plans (from which you or your contractor can work) needed for building permits.

Structural and soils engineers: Before approving your plans, your building department may require that you (or your designer) consult with a structural or soils engineer. An engineer's stamp may be required if the structure will be on an unstable or steep lot, or if strong winds or heavy loads might come into play.

General and landscape contractors: Licensed general and landscape contractors specialize in construction (landscape contractors specialize in garden construction), although some have design skills and experience as well. They usually charge less for design work than landscape architects do, but some contractors may make design decisions based on ease of construction rather than aesthetics.

ASK A PRO

WHAT ARE MY RESPONSIBILITIES IF I HIRE WORKERS DIRECTLY?

Even if you do the work on your own, you may want to hire workers on an hourly basis. As an employer, you're expected to withhold state and federal income taxes; to withhold, remit, and contribute to Social Security; and to pay state unemployment insurance. For more information about your responsibilities as an employer, talk to a building department official, or call your state's tax department.

Contractors hired to build a small project may do all the work themselves; on a large project, they assume the responsibility for hiring qualified subcontractors, ordering construction materials, and seeing that the job is completed according to contract.

Subcontractors: If you act as your own general contractor, it's up to you to hire, coordinate, and supervise any subcontractors—specialists in grading, carpentry, plumbing, etc. Aside from following the working plans you provide, subcontractors can often supply you with current product information and sell hardware and supplies.

HIRING A DESIGNER

If you're looking for a designer, friends and neighbors are usually the best sources of information—most top-quality professionals gain much of their work by word-of-mouth from satisfied clients. Also contact offices of the American Institute of Architects (AIA), American Institute of Building Designers (AIBD), the American Society of Landscape Architects (ASLA), or the Association of Professional Landscape Designers (APLD), for referrals to a professional in your area. Professionals on these lists have met the standards of their respective associations. Make sure the professional has experience with small-scale residential projects. For a small project, you may also be able to entice an apprentice or draftsperson working in an architect or designer's office to draw plans for you; expect to pay by the hour.

If you include an architect or designer in your project, there are at least three working arrangements:

Retained on a consultation basis, an architect or designer will review your plans, suggest ideas for a more effective design, and perhaps provide a couple of rough conceptual sketches. After that, it will be up to you to prepare the working plans for the building department.

You may also hire a professional to design or modify your project and provide working plans, with the understanding that you yourself will oversee the construction. For the design and working plans, you may be charged either a flat fee or an hourly rate.

Finally, you can retain an architect or designer on a planning-through-construction basis. Besides designing your project and providing working plans and specifications, the professional will supervise the construction process. It will cost you more (usually 10% to 15% of the cost of the work) to have your project designed and built this way, but you'll also be free from the plethora of details you'd have to handle otherwise.

HIRING A CONTRACTOR

In looking for a contractor, start by asking for referrals from people you know who have had similar work done—nothing beats a personal recommendation. You can also ask architects and designers, local real estate brokers and lenders, or even your building inspector for names of qualified builders. Experienced lumber dealers are another good source of names.

Call several contractors: First find out whether each handles your type of job and can work within the constraints of your schedule. Arrange meetings with about three of them; ask them to be prepared with photos of their work and references. Discuss your ideas or plans and ask whether they can give you a rough estimate; if you have complete plans and specifications, you should be able to get firm bids. The contractor with the lowest bid will not necessarily be your best bet; look for a reasonable bid and the best credentials, references, and terms. Make sure the contractor has experience specifically with deck-building. Don't hesitate to probe for advice or suggestions that might make building your deck less expensive.

Narrow down the field to one or two contractors. Call their former clients and ask questions about quality of workmanship, communication, promptness, and follow-up. If possible, visit former clients to check the contractors' work firsthand. You can also contact the Better Business Bureau to find out whether there are existing complaints about the contractors you're considering.

Be sure your final candidate is licensed, bonded, and insured for worker's compensation, public liability, and property damage. Also try to determine how financially solvent he or she is (you can call their bank and credit references for information).

THE BUILDING CONTRACT

A building contract binds and protects both you and your contractor. You can minimize the possibility of misunderstandings later by writing down every possible detail. (If you're acting as your own contractor, agreements with subcontractors should be put in writing.) You might want to get a model contract from the American Homeowners Foundation in Arlington, Virginia.

The contract should clearly indicate all work to be done, including specific materials and work descriptions, the time schedule, and payment plan, as discussed below. If you will be responsible for any aspects of the job, be sure they are spelled out clearly. The contract should be keyed to the working plans and should include all of the following:

• **The project and participants:** It should include a general description of the project, its address, and the names and addresses of both you and the builder.

• **Construction materials:** Identify grade and species of lumber and quality of fasteners. Indicate brand and model number of any accessories, such as lighting systems. Avoid the clause "or equal" that will allow the builder to substitute materials for your choices.

• **Work to be performed:** All work you expect the contractor to do should be clearly stated in the contract. Specify all major jobs from grading to finishing.

• **Time schedule:** Though a contractor cannot be responsible for construction delays caused by strikes and material shortages, he or she should assume responsibility for completing the project within a reasonable period of time. The contract should include both start and completion dates.

• **Method of payment:** Though some contractors may want a fee based on a percentage of the cost of materials and labor, it's usually wiser to insist on a fixed-price bid. The contract should specify how payments are to be made. This is usually done in installments as particular phases of the work are completed. Many states limit the amount of money that contractors can request before work begins. The final payment is withheld until the job receives its final inspection and is cleared of all liens.

• **Waiver of liens:** If subcontractors are not paid for materials or services delivered to your home, in some states they can place a "mechanic's lien" on your property, tying up the title. This may happen even if the contractor is negligent. Protect yourself with a waiver of liens. Have the general contractor, subcontractors, and major materials suppliers sign it.

OVERSEEING THE PROJECT

Even when you rely upon professionals to design and build a new deck, you should oversee the process and keep an eye on quality. If something isn't being done according to your wishes or the terms of the contract, talk to the designer or contractor.

It pays to know the order of events so you can discuss progress with your builder and prepare for important decisions you may need to make along the way. Once construction begins, the carpenters and any subcontractors must work steadily. If you haven't made a key decision, it can bring the work to a frustrating and expensive halt. By studying the checklist that follows, and understanding the building process, as described in this book, you can anticipate potential problems.

PLANNING AND BUILDING CHECKLIST
- ☑ Choose site.
- ☑ Gather ideas, sketches.
- ☑ Draw or obtain site plan.
- ☑ Hire designer (optional).
- ☑ Develop working plans.
- ☑ Estimate costs.
- ☑ Finalize design.
- ☑ Get contractor bids and select contractor (optional).
- ☑ Obtain (or have contractor get) permits.
- ☑ Arrange financing and insurance if needed.
- ☑ Price and purchase materials.
- ☑ Prepare site and build foundation.
- ☑ Request building inspection (if required).
- ☑ Complete deck and apply any finishes.

DECK COMPONENTS

In this chapter we'll break down a deck into each major component—the decking, substructure, stairs, railings, and screens—and show you how they all fit together. You'll see both simple designs and some more complex ones, to give you the range of possibilities. There are building instructions for the simplest type of freestanding or attached deck in the chapter beginning on page 102, and if you want to dress up your deck, amenities such as benches and planters are discussed beginning on page 153.

In mixing and matching the components shown in this chapter, try to maintain a unified look to your deck. It's also important to balance the look you would like to achieve with ease of construction, depending upon your abilities. Once you've made these decisions, you'll be ready to develop your final working plans as described in the previous chapter.

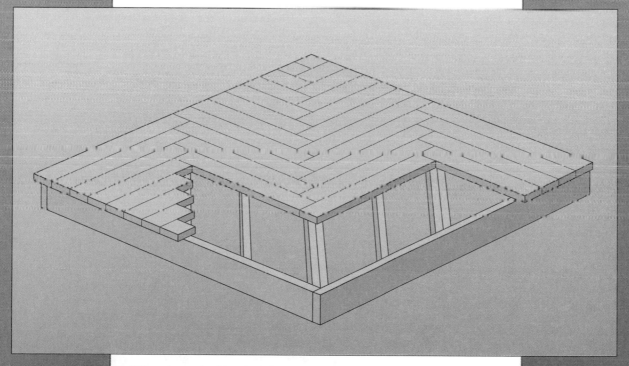

Although you build a deck from the ground up, it's usually best to design it from the decking surface down. That way, you can first develop the part you see and use, then figure out how to support it. Shown here is a herringbone decking pattern requiring diagonal joists.

DECK STRUCTURE

In their basic structure, most decks resemble the deck shown below. Footings support piers, which hold posts. Beams run from post to post; joists span from beam to beam, either running across the tops of beams or hanging between them for a lower profile. A deck attached to a house is connected to a ledger mounted on a wall, as shown, while on a freestanding deck, the ledger is replaced with another row of posts and piers. Decking spans across the tops of the joists, and railings are required on elevated decks. Finally, fascia boards and other trim details help dress up the structure.

The basic design shown can be varied in many ways, including changes in the shape of the supporting structure, the direction of the decking, and the location and direction of the stairs. You can also add more complex railings—or for more privacy, screens.

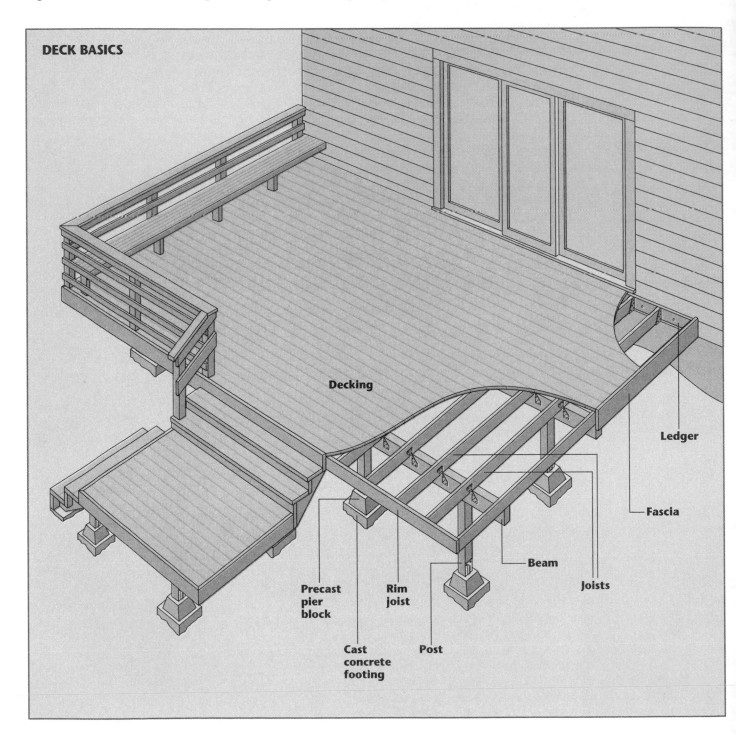

DECK BASICS

Decking

Ledger

Fascia

Beam

Joists

Precast pier block

Rim joist

Post

Cast concrete footing

DECKING

The pattern you choose for your deck surface will establish your deck's character, much as a wallpaper design gives ambiance to a room. In many cases, a simple arrangement is the best choice: decking lumber set parallel, perpendicular, or diagonal to the deck's long axis. These simple patterns create an illusion of size because the eye is drawn beyond the deck rather than encouraged to focus on design detail. More elaborate patterns such as those shown on page 65 can be effective if you coordinate them with other surface textures or if they relate to architectural features of your house. A basketweave deck pattern, for example, might be a logical outdoor extension of an indoor parquet floor. A deck tucked into a corner of a house could employ opposing diagonal units that come together to form a square "bull's-eye." However, there are some instances where a complex pattern wouldn't work; for example, between a shingled house and a flagstone walkway, anything but a simple pattern of parallel boards would introduce an unsettling distraction. To evaluate possible decking patterns, sketch them on tracing paper laid on top of your scale drawing of the deck's shape.

Generally speaking, the more complex the decking pattern, the more complicated the substructure must be to support it. A diagonal pattern requires setting joists closer together; more elaborate designs call for doubling joists at regular intervals to permit nailing of abutting lumber. (Examples of the framework required for various decking patterns are illustrated on the next page.) Spacing between supports is also affected by the lumber's thickness, grade, and species. For information on the correct spacing of supports, refer to the span charts on page 73.

You can minimize waste by designing your deck to take standard lumber lengths—from 8 to 16 feet, in 2-foot increments. (Lumber up to 20 feet long is available, although it may have to be special-ordered.) If the length of your deck will exceed 20 feet, you must plan how to handle end joints. Three possibilities are shown at left. Random or alternating joints are the strongest, while grouped joints create a pattern that calls attention to itself. For maximum strength, deck boards should span at least three joists without a joint.

Redwood and cedar boards should be spaced about $1/8$ to $3/16$ inch apart to allow for drainage, ventilation, and the natural expansion and contraction of the wood. Most pressure-treated wood, however, has not been dried after treatment and will tend to shrink as it dries. With this wood, butt the edges. With pressure-treated wood that has been dried after treatment, leave $1/8$- to $3/16$-inch gaps. In all cases, butt the ends of the boards.

Most decks are surfaced with standard sizes of dimension lumber: surfaced 2x6s, 2x4s, or 2x3s. You'll find that 2x2s tend to twist and warp easily unless they are redwood or cedar; 2x8s (and anything larger) tend to cup and drain poorly. The most common choice is 2x6s—they can be laid faster than narrower boards, offer more room for fastening, and warp less.

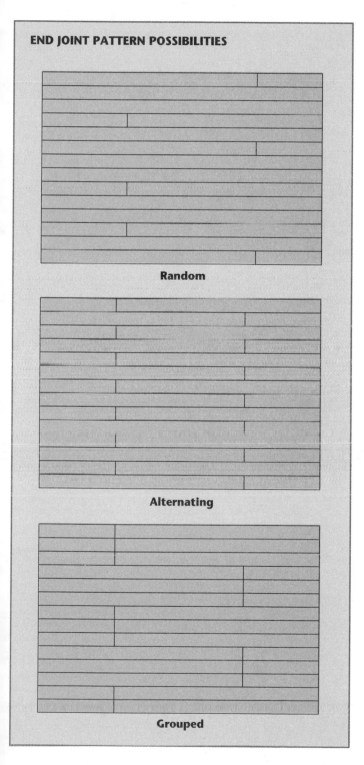

END JOINT PATTERN POSSIBILITIES

Random

Alternating

Grouped

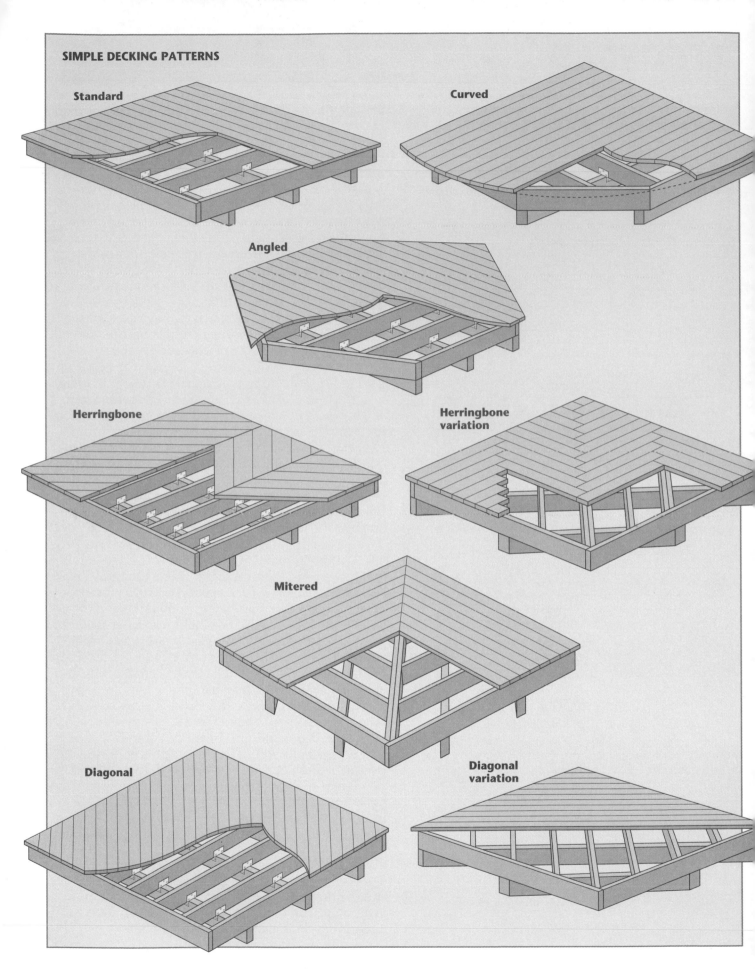

SIMPLE DECKING PATTERNS

Standard

Curved

Angled

Herringbone

Herringbone variation

Mitered

Diagonal

Diagonal variation

INTRICATE DECKING PATTERNS

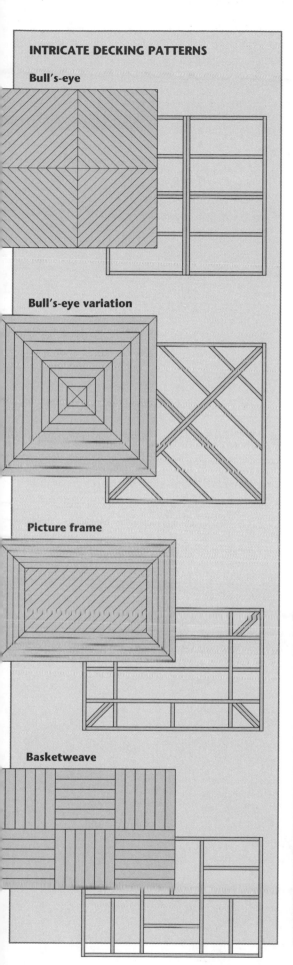

Bull's-eye

Bull's-eye variation

Picture frame

Basketweave

The simplest, soundest, and most economical decking patterns are those in which 2x6s or 2x4s are laid parallel and running the deck's full length or width, but lumber can also be arranged in many other patterns, as shown below. For example, you might mix lumber of two or more different widths, such as 2x4s and 2x6s.

An alternative to the standard flat decking is patterns created by laying 2x3s or 2x4s on their edges, usually directly on beams (without joists). On-edge decking is heavy and expensive, but it can span longer distances between supports—an advantage if you want to pare down the substructure. Be aware, though, that the added expense of this sort of decking pattern generally isn't offset by the substructure savings. Fastening the ends of on-edge decking requires more nailing surface than flat decking; if the joints don't fall over a large beam, locate them over a double joist, or attach cleats to the sides of the joists to increase the nailing surface. On-edge decking should be separated with spacers as shown below, both over the supports and in the middle of the spans. Spacers should be made of $1/8$"x3"x$3^1/2$" tempered hardboard. Coat the spacers in waterproof construction adhesive and face-nail the boards together through the spacers.

Whether you're planning to lay the deck boards flat or on edge, turn to page 96 for information on estimating how much decking lumber you'll need for your design.

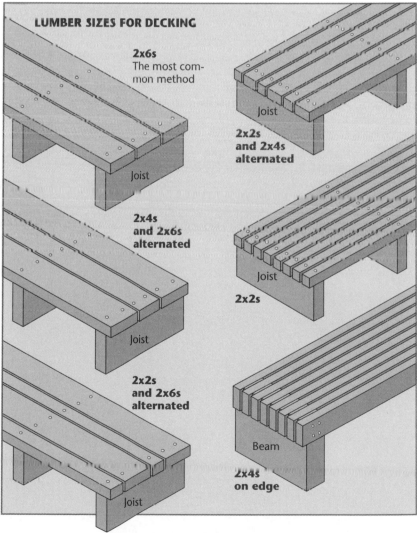

LUMBER SIZES FOR DECKING

2x6s
The most common method

Joist

2x2s and 2x4s alternated

Joist

2x4s and 2x6s alternated

Joist

2x2s

Joist

2x2s and 2x6s alternated

Joist

Beam

2x4s on edge

ASK A PRO

HOW CAN I SPEED UP DECKING INSTALLATION?

Decking modules like the one shown can be put together away from the construction site and then installed as a unit. Create the modules by fastening lengths of 2x4 to the back of the deck boards. The unit can then be fastened to joists, or directly to beams spaced 4 feet apart.

The ready-made parquet decking modules available from some lumber retailers are a quick way to create a basket-weave pattern like the one shown on page 65. They need to be supported by a grid of joists.

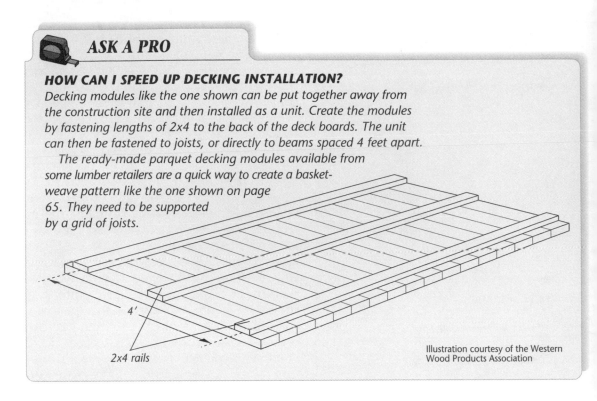

4'

2x4 rails

Illustration courtesy of the Western Wood Products Association

---

ACCOMMODATING NATURE

Think twice before you remove an intrusive boulder or cut down a tree that happens to be in your planned deck-building area. Instead, consider how your deck might be enhanced by including such natural features as elements in your plan.

There are two approaches to building around a tree or rock. In both cases, you first build a frame of bracing around the object. Then, either lay decking to the edge of the frame, or make a custom-fitted cutout (turn to page 128 for instructions on scribing the decking).

Whenever you surround a tree with decking, remember to allow space for the trunk to enlarge as the tree ages. And never attach lumber to the trunk: This is bad for the tree, and the tree's movement in wind will damage the deck. If you allow a generous opening, consider incorporating a bench into the plan, providing shaded seating.

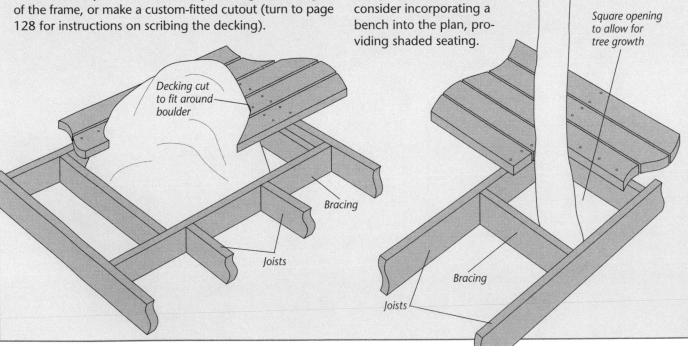

Decking cut to fit around boulder

Bracing

Joists

Square opening to allow for tree growth

Bracing

Joists

SUBSTRUCTURE

Once you've decided on your decking pattern, design the substructure—joists, beams, posts, ledgers and foundation—to support it; a discussion of each element follows. The spacing between these elements is critical; to determine acceptable spacing and spans, turn to page 72.

Don't forget that any structural members that will be in contact with concrete, or within 6 inches of the ground, should be made of decay-resistant wood.

JOISTS

Deck joists—typically 2x6s, 2x8s, 2x10s, or 2x12s on edge—spread decking loads across beams, making it possible to use decking materials that otherwise couldn't span the distances between beams. (Some designs eliminate joists, using only beams and on-edge 2x3 or 2x4 decking.) Joists either sit on top of beams and ledgers or are connected to the faces of these supports; both options are shown below. The two approaches can also be combined with joists hanging from a ledger at one end and sitting on top of a beam at the other end *(page 62)*. You'll get a more finished look if the outside joists hanging off the ledger overlap the ends of the ledger.

You can cap the ends of joists resting on top of a beam with rim joists as shown below. When figuring joist lengths from the overall dimensions of your plan, be sure to allow for the added thickness of the rim joist.

Joists that support standard deck boards are mounted level, but those supporting solid, watertight materials must slope to allow for rain runoff. For more on this subject, see page 134.

BEAMS

Beams may be solid lumber—commonly 4x6s or 4x8s—or built up from lengths of 2-by dimension lumber fastened together. Large beams are usually easiest to handle if they're built up, since they can be carried to their final destination in pieces. However, a single, solid beam is generally favored for a highly visible location.

Wood beams usually rest on or mesh with posts using one of the methods shown on the next page. (Turn to page 100 for a selection of connectors used to attach beams to posts.) For low-level decks, beams can rest directly on pier blocks. Any beam within 6 inches of the ground or pier block should be pressure-treated.

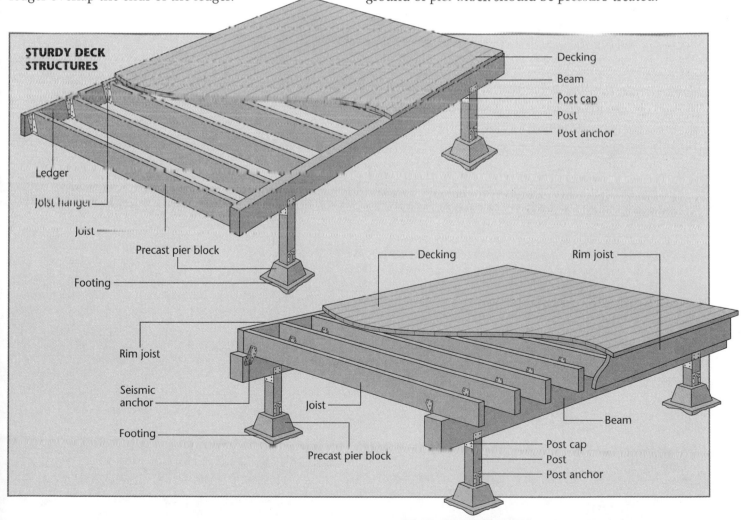

STURDY DECK STRUCTURES

Decking
Beam
Post cap
Post
Post anchor

Ledger
Joist hanger
Joist
Precast pier block
Footing

Decking
Rim joist

Rim joist
Seismic anchor
Footing
Joist
Precast pier block
Beam
Post cap
Post
Post anchor

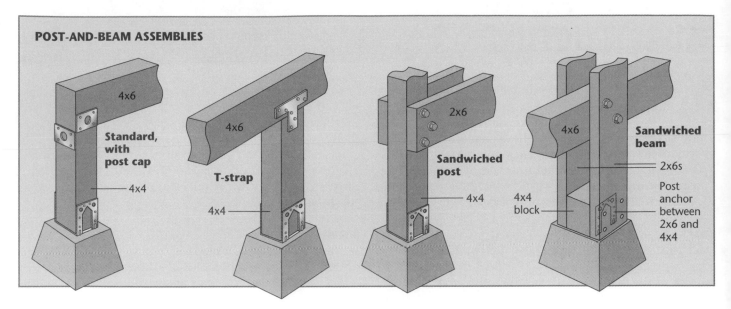

POST-AND-BEAM ASSEMBLIES

Standard, with post cap — 4x6 — 4x4

T-strap — 4x6 — 4x4

Sandwiched post — 2x6 — 4x4

Sandwiched beam — 4x6 — 2x6s — Post anchor between 2x6 and 4x4 — 4x4 block

POSTS

Although most deck posts are made of 4x4s, various other materials can be used: larger sizes of dimension lumber, built-up lumber, steel, or a combination of these. (For more on post materials, see page 91.) Posts and beams often mesh—for example, posts can be designed to sandwich beams, as shown above. Sandwiched beams or posts allow the post to extend upward; this is the sturdiest way to provide support for railings, screens, overheads, and benches.

Posts are anchored to the pier with post anchors or metal straps. However, for a sandwiched beam, you'll have to insert a block in the post anchor and attach 2-by lumber to each side.

The proper spacing of posts depends upon the distances the deck's beams can span; see the table on page 74 to determine this.

LEDGERS

A ledger is a plank or beam mounted to a house wall, an adjoining deck, or any similar structure; it supports one end of a deck's joists. Joists can rest on top of the ledger or hang in joist hangers as shown at right. To support the weight of the deck, a ledger must be fastened with lag screws or bolts to a solid masonry wall or to the house framing. In some cases, this may mean placing the ledger quite low. Although the strongest way to attach joists to the ledger is with joist hangers, resting the joists on top of the ledger allows you to raise the surface of the deck.

When a ledger is placed within about 36 inches of the ground, it is often made of a 2x6 or 2x8—ledgers are generally the same width or one size larger than the joists. Because taller decks require more support, their ledgers are usually best made from a 4x8 or 4x10. If a ledger is within 6 inches of earth, or in contact with masonry, pressure-treated lumber is best.

To prevent water from collecting where the ledger contacts the house wall, cover the joint with flashing

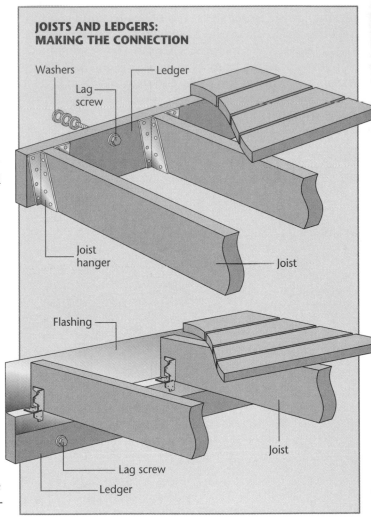

JOISTS AND LEDGERS: MAKING THE CONNECTION

Washers — Lag screw — Ledger — Joist hanger — Joist

Flashing — Lag screw — Ledger — Joist

as shown above *(bottom)*, or use washers to provide a drainage gap between the ledger and the wall as shown *(top)*. If you use flashing and hang the joists from the ledger, you'll have to nail the joist hangers through the flashing (not shown).

FOUNDATIONS

Almost all decks are supported by a basic foundation that anchors the substructure against settling, slippage, and wind lift; distributes loads into the ground; and protects posts or beams from direct contact with the earth. A typical foundation has two parts: concrete piers and footings (or their equivalents), as shown below.

Building codes govern the size and spacing of foundations and specify how deep into the ground they must go. Typical footings are 18 inches square and should extend 6 inches below the frost line. In a cold climate with a deep frost line, you'll need to cast a concrete column to extend the buried footing to the surface. Fiber tube forms can be purchased to cast the column; they can extend above the surface to take the place of a pier.

In general, footings are cast on undisturbed soil, although in some areas gravel is recommended for drainage.

Concrete pier blocks can be purchased, or can be formed and cast at the same time the footings are cast. They may be cylindrical, rectangular, or pyramidal with flat tops. The top surface must be large enough to hold metal post anchors. Once in place, piers should be exposed at least 6 inches above ground to protect the post end from rot and termites. A selection of precast pier blocks is shown below; for adequate hold-down strength, choose one with a cast-in metal strap or anchor. If casting your own piers, choose from the post anchors on page 100.

An alternative to footings and piers is to embed the end of a pressure-treated post in the footing. This reinforces the post against lateral movement, but even a pressure-treated post will rot eventually if in contact with the concrete. Also, repairs will be more difficult.

A FIRM FOUNDATION

Treated post
Post anchor
6" above grade
Asphalt shingle
Concrete pier block
Concrete footing
6" below frost line

ASK A PRO

HOW DO I PREVENT POST ENDS FROM ROTTING?

Wood will tend to decay with time, especially when in contact with either earth or concrete, since both retain moisture. The best insurance against rotten post ends is to use pressure-treated lumber.

Whether or not you're using a treated post, you can increase the life of the post by placing an asphalt roof shingle under the post end; the shingle will mold to the end texture of the post and help protect it from moisture. If you choose to use untreated lumber, you can further protect the post by using a post anchor that provides 1 inch of clearance between the post and the concrete (page 100).

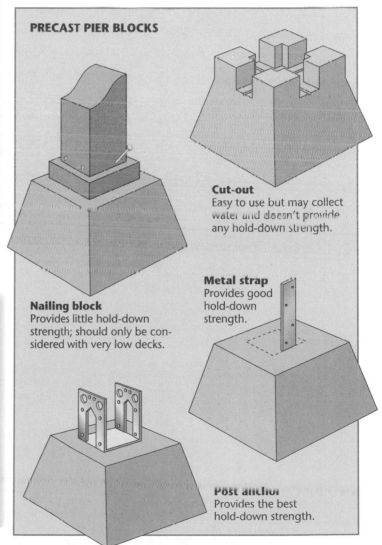

PRECAST PIER BLOCKS

Cut-out
Easy to use but may collect water and doesn't provide any hold-down strength.

Nailing block
Provides little hold-down strength; should only be considered with very low decks.

Metal strap
Provides good hold-down strength.

Post anchor
Provides the best hold-down strength.

BRACING AND BLOCKING

Despite the inherent strength in a deck's structural members, reinforcing may be needed for maximum stability. Bracing provides lateral stability for tall posts; bridging or blocking installed between the joists keeps them from twisting or moving.

Bracing posts: To determine the need for bracing, you must consult local building codes. In general, you can count on bracing posts that support any of the following:
• Freestanding decks over 36 inches above ground;
• Attached decks taller than 8 feet;
• Any attached deck (regardless of height) projecting farther than 20 feet from the house (or projecting for more than twice the length of the attached side);
• Decks exposed to high winds, earthquakes, or big loads.

If a deck attached to a house is less than 8 feet high, only perimeter posts will normally need cross bracing. Plan to use 2x4s for distances less than 8 feet, and 2x6s

for greater distances. Fasten the cross braces to the posts with bolts or lag screws. Various bracing methods are illustrated below; when using Y-bracing, a 90° angle between the pieces of bracing gives the strongest support. If installing a decorative skirt around the posts, choose a type of bracing that won't interfere with it. NOTE: A structural engineer may be able to modify your design to eliminate the need for bracing.

Bridging or blocking joists: Long spans and wide spacing may allow joists to twist or buckle unless they're cross braced with bridging or blocking, as shown on the next page. The joist width is also a consideration; 2x8 joists and wider require more blocking than 2x6s.

Local codes determine the need for blocking. It's good to block between joists directly over any beams or load-bearing members. Joists spanning more than 8 feet need an extra row of blocking in the middle of the span.

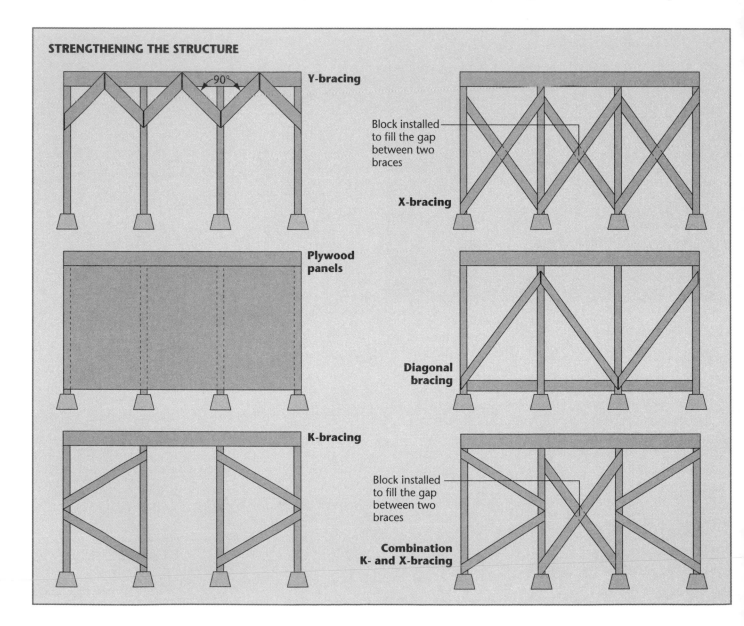

STRENGTHENING THE STRUCTURE

Y-bracing

90°

Block installed to fill the gap between two braces

X-bracing

Plywood panels

Diagonal bracing

K-bracing

Block installed to fill the gap between two braces

Combination K- and X-bracing

KEEPING BRACING DRY

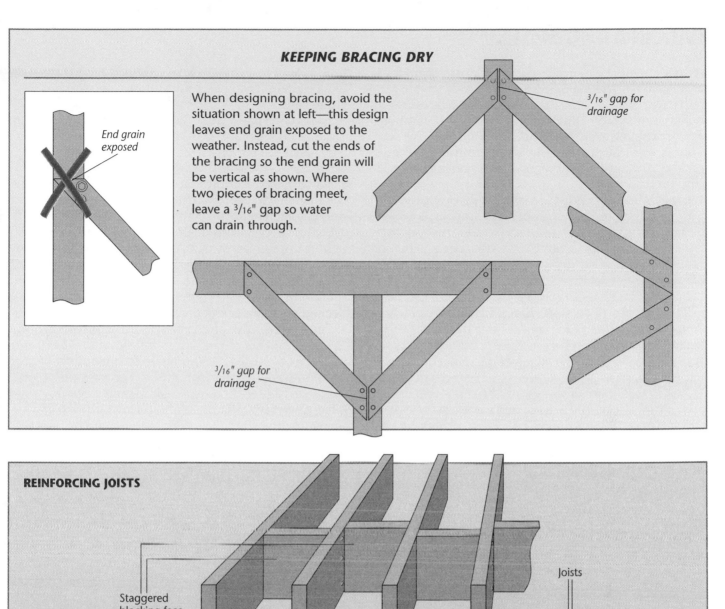

End grain exposed

When designing bracing, avoid the situation shown at left—this design leaves end grain exposed to the weather. Instead, cut the ends of the bracing so the end grain will be vertical as shown. Where two pieces of bracing meet, leave a ³/₁₆" gap so water can drain through.

³/₁₆" gap for drainage

³/₁₆" gap for drainage

REINFORCING JOISTS

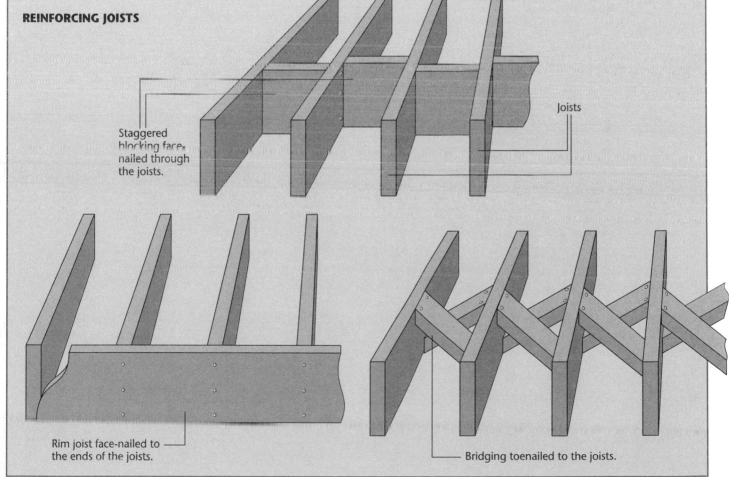

Staggered blocking face-nailed through the joists.

Joists

Rim joist face-nailed to the ends of the joists.

Bridging toenailed to the joists.

CALCULATING SPANS

A deck's framework must be designed to withstand loads, as specified by the building code applicable to your area. Otherwise, under pressure from unusual stresses—a heavy snowfall or a large number of people at an outdoor party, for example—the structure may give way. The strength of the structure is determined by the size and type of lumber used and by the spacing between structural members.

Loads: Though building codes vary, many areas require that a substructure be strong enough to support 40 pounds of live load plus 10 pounds of dead load (the weight of the construction materials themselves) per square foot. The tables and other design information given on the following pages are based on this "40 plus 10 p.s.f." loading at deck heights of up to 12 feet.

If your deck will be more than 8 feet above grade (even if only at one post), or if it must bear abnormally weighty loads, such as firewood or a very large planter, make sure you have your plans checked by an engineer; special reinforcement may be required.

NOTE: Generally, a spa should be supported on its own structure, with the deck built around it—unless the spa manufacturer gives specific instructions on how to reinforce your deck to handle the added weight. It is best to check with your building department in either case.

Spans and spacings: As illustrated below, a span is the distance bridged by deck boards, joists, or beams; spacing is the distance between adjacent joists, beams, or posts. Thus, the joist span is the same as the beam-to-beam spacing. Keep in mind that span refers to the distance the member spans from one support to the next, and not its total length.

Because they determine the ultimate strength or weakness of the support system, carefully figured spans and spacings are critical to proper substructure design.

As indicated in the tables opposite, the maximum safe spans and spacings for lumber of different dimensions depend on the species of wood and the grade you use.

Cantilever: Joists that extend unsupported beyond the last beam are referred to as cantilevered. The unsupported part of the joist can be up to one fourth of the span indicated in the span tables. For example, a joist that spans 12 feet between beams could be cantilevered 3 feet at each end. Thus, cantilevering joists is a way of increasing the size of the deck without adding another

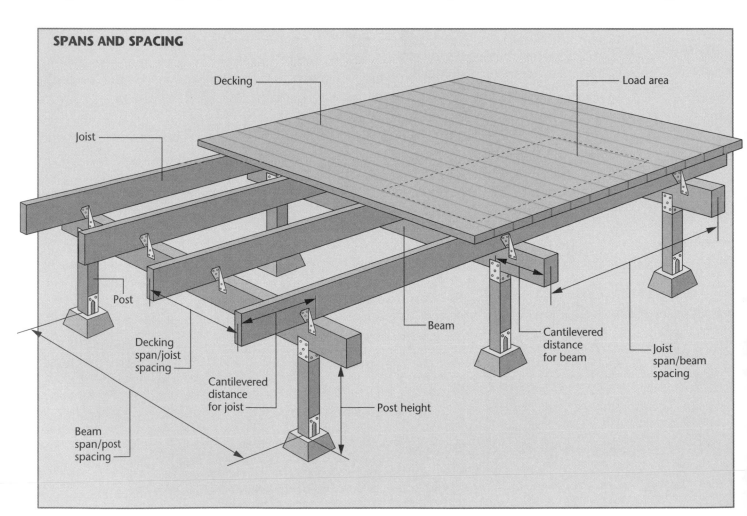

SPANS AND SPACING

Decking

Load area

Joist

Post

Decking span/joist spacing

Cantilevered distance for joist

Post height

Beam span/post spacing

Beam

Cantilevered distance for beam

Joist span/beam spacing

beam. Make sure that cantilevered joists are secured to the beams or ledger with metal framing anchors to avoid a seesaw effect when someone steps on the unsupported ends.

Similarly, beams can be cantilevered past the last post to one-fourth their post-to-post span. Deck boards should not be cantilevered more than a couple of inches.

USING SIZE, SPAN, AND SPACING TABLES

Use the five tables given here to calculate the proper sizes, spans, and heights for your deck's structural elements. The figures given are recommended maximums; you can always choose shorter spans, closer spacings, or larger lumber for a more rigid structure. All lumber sizes are based on nominal sizes. Spacings are measured "on center," that is from the center of one member to the center of the next.

As you work through the tables, you'll see that any of several joist-beam-post combinations will work for a given situation. For example, 4x8 beams spaced 10 feet apart may call for supporting posts every 6 feet; if spaced just 4 feet apart, the same beams would only require posts every 10 feet along their length.

The information in the tables conforms to the recommendations of the Council of American Building Officials (CABO). However, code requirements vary from one locale to another; they also change over time to adapt to changes in the composition of the wood supply. Use these tables for planning and design, but be sure to check with your building department as well.

TABLE 1: SOFTWOOD STRENGTH GROUPINGS
(Based on No. 2 and Better)

Group A	Douglas-fir, western hemlock, western larch, southern pine
Group B	Western cedar, Douglas-fir (South), hem/fir, Alpine white fir, eastern mountain hemlock, pine (all but southern), redwood (Clear and Better), spruce (eastern, Engelmann, Sitka)
Group C	Northern white cedar, redwood (Construction Common and Better)

Table 1—Softwood strength groupings: Lumber strength varies with species. This table groups species with comparable strength. Before using the span tables, check the strength grouping of your wood. The table assumes the use of No. 2 and better grade lumber. Pressure-treated wood falls into the same strength groupings as untreated wood of the same species and grade.

TABLE 2: DECKING SIZES AND SPANS
(On center measurements)

Maximum Spans for Species Group	A	B	C
1-by lumber laid flat	16"	14"	12"
Radius-edge decking	16"	16"	16"
2-by lumber laid flat	24"	24"	24"
2x3s laid on edge	48"	36"	32"
2x4s laid on edge	60"	60"	60"

Table 2—Decking spans: Now select the size of decking boards. Then, using the Table 1 strength group, calculate the maximum distance your decking should span between joists—or between beams, if you plan to place on-edge boards directly on the beams. The table is applicable for any lumber of a grade appropriate for decking—grading systems vary depending on the type of wood (page 94). The spans indicated assume normal loads, distributed evenly; if the loads will be concentrated, such as with a very large planter, the spans must be reduced. Greater spans are allowable with some decking materials, but be careful; this may result in an overly springy deck.

NOTE: For joists supporting diagonal boards, the allowed spacing in the table corresponds to the distance between the joists measured on the diagonal.

TABLE 3: MAXIMUM JOIST SPACINGS AND SPANS
(Maximum on center measurements based on No. 2 and Better joists placed on edge)

	Maximum Spans for Species Group		
	A	B	C
16" joist spacings			
2x6	9'9"	8'7"	7'9"
2x8	12'10"	11'4"	10'2"
2x10	16'5"	14'6"	13'
24" joist spacings			
2x6	8'6"	7'6"	6'9"
2x8	11'3"	9'11"	8'11"
2x10	14'4"	12'8"	11'4"
32" joist spacings			
2x6	7'9"	6'10"	6'2"
2x8	10'2"	9'	8'1"
2x10	13'	11'6"	10'4"

Table 3—Joist sizes and spans: Next, use this table to determine the correct size and beam-to-beam span of joists for the spacings determined in Table 2. You can start with either your joist size or your joist span—the chart will provide the other one. The figures are based on joists placed on edge.

Remember that joists can be cantilevered up to one fourth their span.

TABLE 4: BEAM SPACINGS AND SPANS

(Maximum on center measurements based on No. 2 and Better beams placed on edge)

Species Group	Beam Size	4'	5'	6'	7'	8'	9'	10'	11'	12'
A	4x6	6' spans →								
	3x8	8' →		7'	6' →					
	4x8	10'	9'	8'	7' →		6' →			
	3x10	11'	10'	9'	8' →		7' →	6' →		
	4x10	12'	11'	10'	9' →		8' →		7'	
	3x12		12'	11'	10'	9' →		8'		
	4x12			12' →		11'	10' →		9'	
	6x10						12'	11'	10' →	
B	4x6	6' →								
	3x8	7' →		6' →						
	4x8	9'	8'	7' →		6' →				
	3x10	10'	9'	8'	7' →		6' →			
	4x10	11'	10'	9'	8' →		7' →			6'
	3x12	12'	11'	10'	9'	8' →		7'		
	4x12		12'	11'	10' →		9' →		8'	
	6x10			12'	11'	10' →		9'		
C	4x6	6'								
	3x8	7'	6'							
	4x8	8'	7'	6' →						
	3x10	9'	8'	7'	6' →					
	4x10	10'	9'	8' →		7' →		6' →		
	3x12	11'	10'	9'	8'	7' →			6' →	
	4x12	12'	11'	10'	9' →		8' →		7' →	
	6x10		12'	11'	10'	9' →		8' →		

Table 4—Beam sizes and spans: Again, use the strength groupings to determine which size beams will span from post to post when set various distances apart. You may be limited by the beam sizes available. For this table, round the beam spacing down to the nearest whole foot before looking up the span. The figures apply to solid beams only, placed on edge. For laminated or built-up beams, consult your building department.

Remember that beams can be cantilevered up to one-fourth their span.

Table 5—Minimum post sizes: To determine post size, you need to know the wood grouping (Table 1), the joist span (Table 3), and the beam span (Table 4). Multiply the joist span (in feet) by the beam span (in feet) to determine the load area (in square feet) that each post supports—round up to the next largest load area listed. Then, from Table 5, select a post size that meets your height requirements. In order to make construction simpler, try to use posts and beams of the same thickness.

If you'll be designing your deck with continuous posts to support an overhead, consult a professional for the best size of post for the height and load.

TABLE 5: MINIMUM POST SIZES

(Maximum on center measurements based on Standard and Better for 4x4 posts, No. 1 and Better for larger sizes.)

Species Group	Post Size	36	48	60	72	84	96	108	120	132	144
A	4x4	12' high →				10' high →			8' high →		
	4x6					12' →				10' →	
	6x6									12' →	
B	4x4	12' →		10' →			8' →				
	4x6				12' →			10' →			
	6x6							12' →			
C	4x4	12'	10' →		8' →			6' →			
	4x6			12' →			10' →		8' →		
	6x6				12' →						

If you want the distance between levels to be only one step—thus avoiding a flight of stairs—you can accomplish this most easily by constructing the upper level with joists resting on top of beams, then using joist hangers for the lower level (A). This way, the lower joists are at the same level as the tops of the beams and only the width of the joists below the upper level.

For a greater change in levels, you can attach a ledger along the posts of the higher level and use it to support the lower deck's joists (B). Of course, you'll also have to add steps if the difference between deck levels is more than 8 inches. This can be done with standard stairs with stringers as described on page 76, or with a series of independent pads as shown on page 79.

If the upper deck will be very small, create multiple levels by building the framing of the deck as though it were for one level, then adding a second layer of joists (at right angles) on top of the first (C). This setup offers the advantage of reversing the decking on the two levels, creating a safer visual separation.

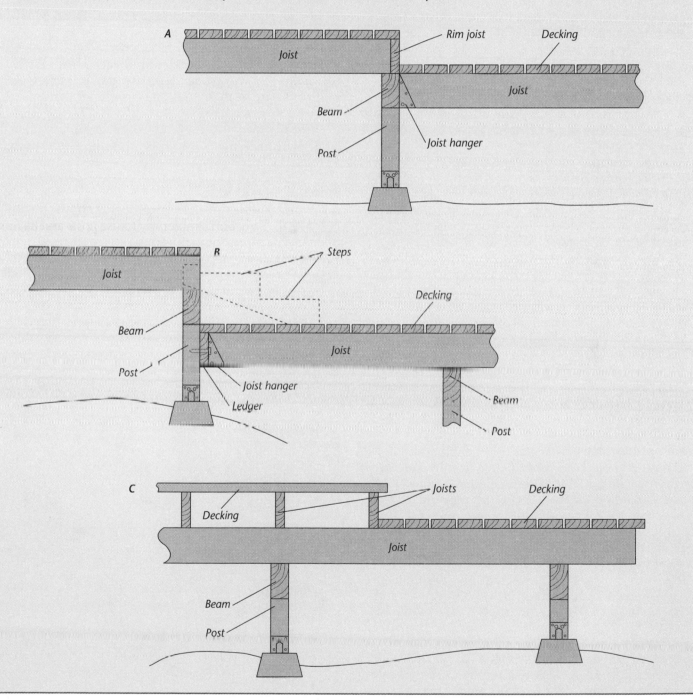

STAIRS AND RAMPS

Any deck too high to step up onto comfortably (above about 10 inches) should have steps or a ramp leading up to it. In addition to offering access to your deck, stairs and ramps guide foot traffic, help the deck follow ground contours, and provide visual interest. Steps or a ramp running the full length or width of the deck also serve to hide views of the support structure. And steps can provide extra seating.

STAIRS

The basic construction of a flight of stairs consists of treads (the flat surface on which you step) and risers (the vertical surface). Both are fastened to a support structure of angled stringers. The following are guidelines for designing safe, convenient stairs.

STAIR DIMENSIONS
The comfort and safety of a flight of stairs depends on the passage width, the total run, and the relationship between the risers and treads. For illustrations of these terms, see below.

Passage width: Decide how much traffic you expect, then base your stairs' passage width on the following minimums for general access: Provide at least 4 feet for one person, or 5 feet for two abreast; add 2 feet per person for greater numbers of side-by-side users. Service stairs or other deliberately restricted access may have a minimum passage width of 2 feet.

Length of run: Steps and stairs for elevation changes up to about 8 feet can generally be handled in a single straight, uninterrupted run stretching directly from one level to another. For a higher total rise, a landing makes climbing easier, and a change in direction makes the stairs less imposing. L-shaped or U-shaped runs with landings are recommended in these situations.

Step proportions: For steps to be safe and comfortable to use, the tread width and riser height must maintain a particular relationship: As risers become shorter, treads should grow wider.

For outdoor steps, twice the riser height added to the tread width should equal 24 to 26 inches. The ideal riser height for standard stairs is considered to be 6 to 7 inches. If you're building very wide stairs, this may feel too steep; instead you may want as little as a 4½-inch rise. Keep in mind that shallower stairs will have a longer total run, making them impractical for climbing up to a high deck. Typical tread-to-riser ratios are shown opposite.

Measuring for stairs: To determine the number of steps you need, measure the vertical distance (total rise) from the deck to the ground; then divide by the riser height you intend to use. For example, if the deck is 45½ inches above grade and you plan on using 6½-inch risers, you need 7 steps exactly—45½ divided by 6½. If this formula gives you a number of steps ending in a fraction, divide the whole number into the vertical distance to learn the exact riser measurements. That is, if the deck is 54 inches above grade, 54 divided by 6½ inches per riser equals 8+ steps; 54 divided by 8 equals 6¾ inches rise per step.

Next, subtract twice the exact riser height from 26 inches to find the proper depth of each tread. For a 6½-inch riser, the proper tread depth is 13 inches—26 minus 13. The tread dimension is from riser to riser, not counting any overhang.

The risers' heights must be as close as possible to identical—within ¼ inch—to avoid tripping. If you must have an odd-sized riser, it should be at the bottom.

CONSTRUCTION BASICS
A number of different stairway styles are shown starting on page 78. For outdoor stairways, risers are typically left open. Stringers can be notched to receive the treads, or the treads can rest on wooden cleats or metal connectors fastened to the inside of the stringers. Pre-cut notched stringers can be purchased.

Stringers are generally made of 2x12 lumber. For narrow stairways, you'll need one stringer supporting each end of the treads. For stairways over 4 feet wide, add a third stringer down the center. For extremely wide steps, plan a stringer every 4 feet.

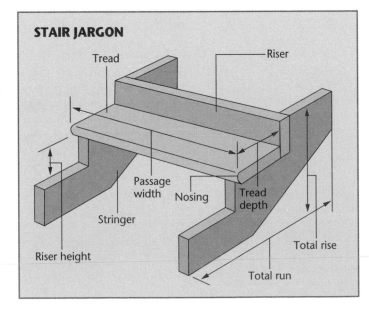

STAIR JARGON

Tread · Riser · Passage width · Nosing · Tread depth · Stringer · Riser height · Total rise · Total run

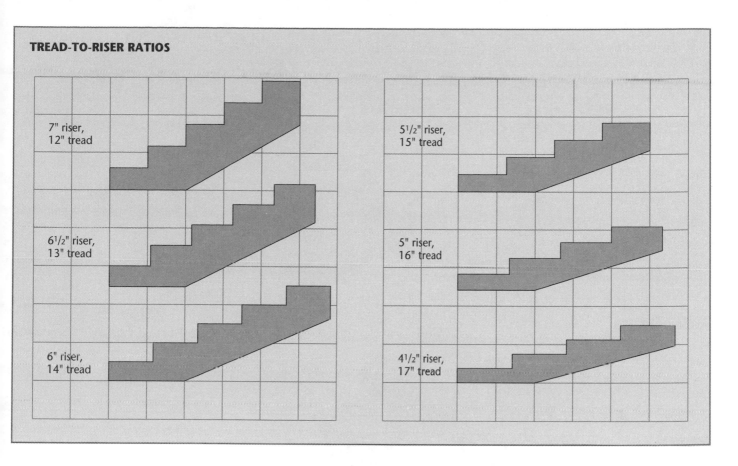

7" riser, 12" tread

6¹/₂" riser, 13" tread

6" riser, 14" tread

5¹/₂" riser, 15" tread

5" riser, 16" tread

4¹/₂" riser, 17" tread

The choice of lumber for the treads depends on the depth of tread you want to achieve. Two 2x6s with a ¹/₈-inch gap give a tread of 11¹/₈ inches—you'll then want a rise of 7³/₈ inches. For a shallower stairway, you can use three 2x6s to give a tread of about 17 inches. You can visually tie the steps to the deck if you use the same material for both treads and decking.

RAILINGS

Hand railings are seldom required for passage widths of 8 feet or more, even though the total rise may be several feet. But stairs and ramps with passage widths of 4 or 5 feet should have hand railings regardless of the total rise, for a feeling of security.

Railings on stairs must meet the same design requirements as the deck perimeter railings described on page 81. Most codes allow only 4 inches between rails (6 inches is acceptable for the triangle under the lowest rail). Measured from the top of the railing to the top front edges of the treads as shown at right, the railing height must be at least 30 inches, at most 34 inches (check your building code). Posts should be bolted or lag screwed to the stringers, never to the stair treads. Cap the tops of the posts.

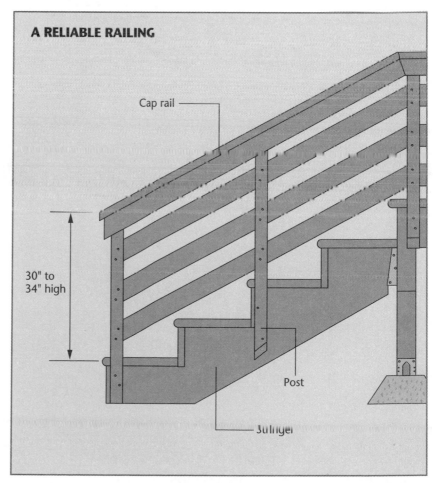

A RELIABLE RAILING

Cap rail

30" to 34" high

Post

Stringer

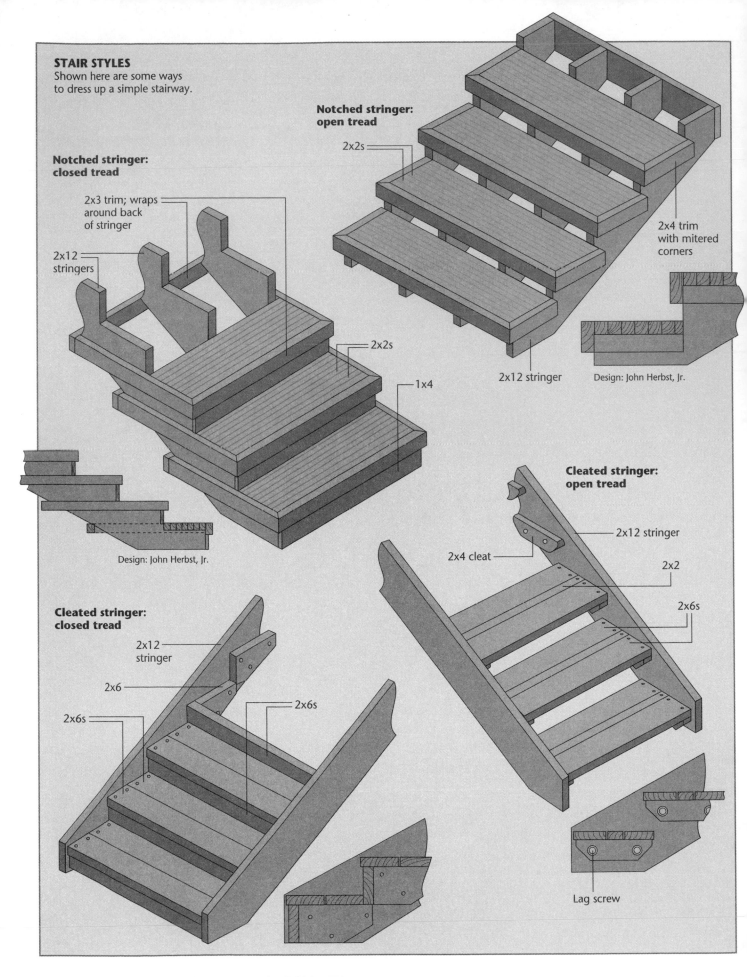

STAIR STYLES
Shown here are some ways
to dress up a simple stairway.

**Notched stringer:
open tread**

2x2s

2x4 trim
with mitered
corners

**Notched stringer:
closed tread**

2x3 trim; wraps
around back
of stringer

2x12
stringers

2x2s

1x4

2x12 stringer

Design: John Herbst, Jr.

Design: John Herbst, Jr.

**Cleated stringer:
open tread**

2x12 stringer

2x4 cleat

2x2

2x6s

**Cleated stringer:
closed tread**

2x12
stringer

2x6

2x6s

2x6s

Lag screw

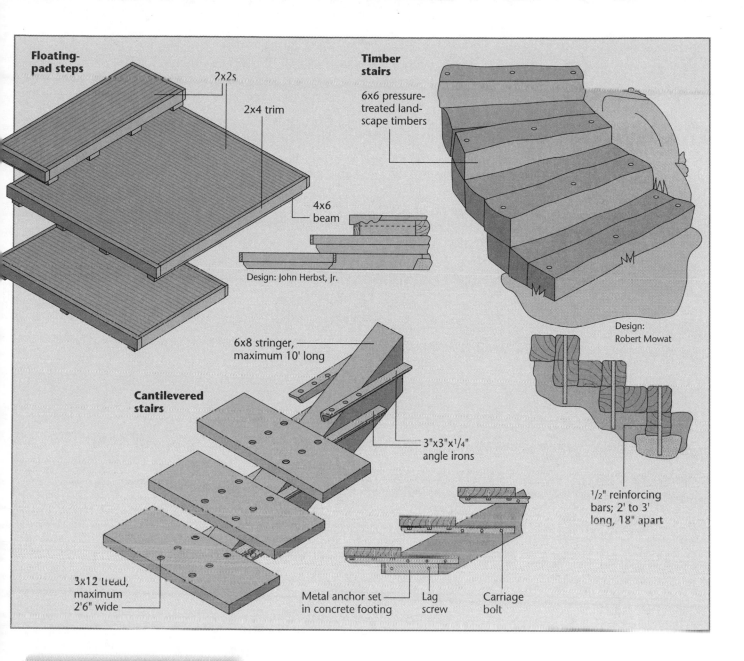

Floating-pad steps

2x2s

2x4 trim

4x6 beam

Design: John Herbst, Jr.

Timber stairs

6x6 pressure-treated land-scape timbers

Design: Robert Mowat

6x8 stringer, maximum 10' long

Cantilevered stairs

3"x3"x¹/₄" angle irons

½" reinforcing bars; 2' to 3' long, 18" apart

3x12 tread, maximum 2'6" wide

Metal anchor set in concrete footing

Lag screw

Carriage bolt

ASK A PRO

SHOULD I USE CLEATED OR NOTCHED STRINGERS?

Notched stringers are the more conventional stair-building method—the stringers are hidden underneath, giving the stairway a neater look. On the other hand, cleated stringers can be made of narrower lumber because no material is cut away. Cleated stringers also give a more secure feeling to the steps since your feet can't slip off sideways.

If you decide to fasten the treads to the stringers with cleats, your fastest method is to use metal stair angles like those shown at right. These are positioned in the same way as wooden cleats, and fastened in place with lag screws.

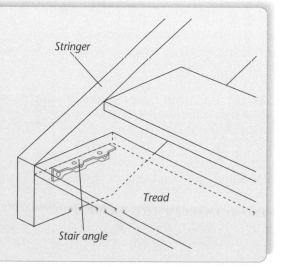

Stringer

Tread

Stair angle

STAIR ATTACHMENT

Both ends of the stair stringers must be firmly anchored. Some typical methods of attachment are shown below.

The bottom of the stringer can be anchored to a concrete pad using an angle iron, or by face-nailing to a pressure-treated kicker plate rated for ground contact. NOTE: Stringers should never be in direct contact with the ground. The top of the stringer can be fastened to a joist or rim joist using bolts or framing anchors. In the example shown below *(left)*, the top of the uppermost tread should be on the same level as the decking. In the attachment method shown below *(right)*, the final tread is one riser below the deck's surface. Stringers can also be hung from a beam, with the rim joist forming the top riser.

Cleated stringers can be fastened to the deck structure in the same way as a notched stringer; the final tread will be the distance of one riser below the deck surface.

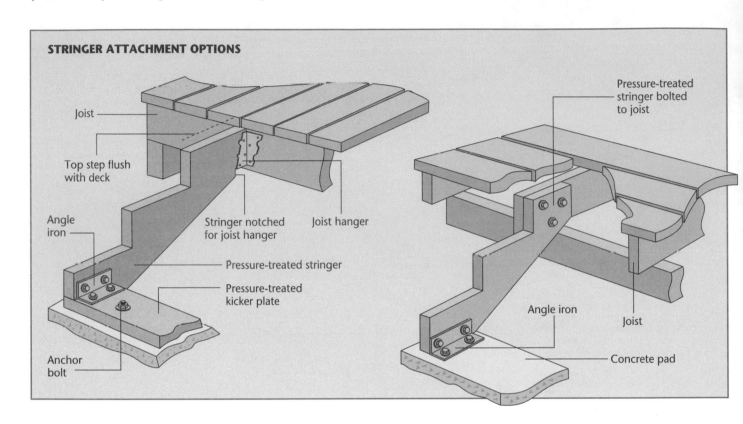

STRINGER ATTACHMENT OPTIONS

Joist

Top step flush with deck

Angle iron

Stringer notched for joist hanger

Joist hanger

Pressure-treated stringer

Pressure-treated kicker plate

Anchor bolt

Pressure-treated stringer bolted to joist

Angle iron

Joist

Concrete pad

RAMPS

The most obvious use for ramps is, of course, for wheelchair access, but they're also useful for maneuvering baby carriages and wheelbarrows.

In designing a ramp, ease of ascent is critical. A ramp's slope is measured in inches of vertical rise per foot of linear distance, a lower rise allowing an easier ascent. For wheelchair access, construct a ramp with a slope no greater than 1 in 12; for a utility ramp, 1 in 8 will do.

As in step design, the length of the run is part of what makes climbing a ramp pleasant or threatening. Be sure that no straight run makes an elevation change greater than 36 inches. For a higher rise, break the run with a level landing where the user can pause. Try to allow for some change in direction—although you needn't have dramatic switchbacks—at each landing.

To build a ramp, begin by constructing your deck as though you were going to build stairs. The ramp itself is essentially a narrow deck on an incline. Use stringers that are not notched, and run decking crosswise.

Anchor the bottom of the ramp to a concrete pad as shown below. Check local codes to see if a handrail is required.

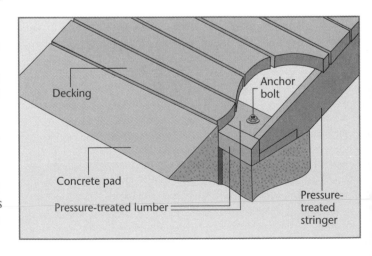

Decking

Anchor bolt

Concrete pad

Pressure-treated lumber

Pressure-treated stringer

RAILINGS

ailings are generally required for decks over 30 inches high and for flights of stairs 5 feet or narrower. However, rails are a good addition to any deck above ground level, especially if it will be used by small children. Multilevel decks can sometimes go without railings if each level is at least 36 inches deep from front to back (so that each level becomes a deck unto itself), but even in these cases, railings are strongly recommended.

Railings are generally a minimum of 36 inches high; however, a higher railing—up to 42 inches—feels safer. Code generally requires that there be no gaps in the structure big enough to accept a 4-inch sphere (some codes allow 6 inches); this will prevent babies from slipping through. (If you have active small children, try to design a railing that will be difficult to climb.) Railings must be built strongly enough to resist a hefty horizontal force (up to 20 pounds per square foot). Be sure to consult your building department for any local requirements.

Regardless of design, railings have the same basic structure: vertical posts capped and joined by a cross member laid flat, with the space between the post filled in with horizontal rails, vertical balusters, or both. The strongest railings are those connecting to posts that extend up from the deck's substructure. This will require designing your deck with sandwiched beams or posts as shown on page 68. Independent railing posts can be fastened to the deck structure after it is completed. Typical attachment methods are shown on the next page.

The top cross member (the cap) may be the same width or wider than the posts. The size of the cap rail is related to post spacing: A 2x4 cap can span 4 feet between 4x4 posts; a 2x6 cap can span up to 6 feet.

The simplest, sturdiest railings have horizontal members screwed or bolted to the faces of posts as shown in the simple designs below; however, you can create a cleaner, more streamlined railing by placing horizontals between the posts (page 130). Balusters are generally fastened to the outside faces of the horizontal railings.

Well-designed railings provide safety and enhance a deck's appearance. You can coordinate railings with the house by using similar materials and detailing. Turn to page 83 for sample railing styles, from simple to intricate.

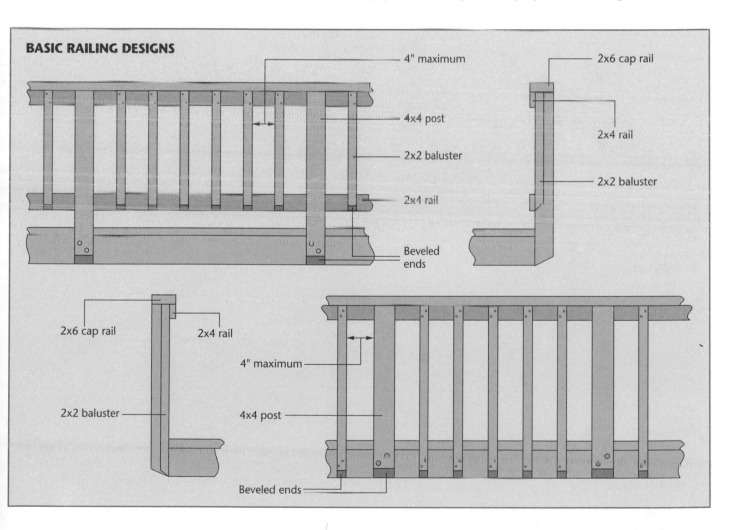

BASIC RAILING DESIGNS

4" maximum
4x4 post
2x2 baluster
2x4 rail
Beveled ends

2x6 cap rail
2x4 rail
2x2 baluster

2x6 cap rail
2x4 rail
2x2 baluster
4" maximum
4x4 post
Beveled ends

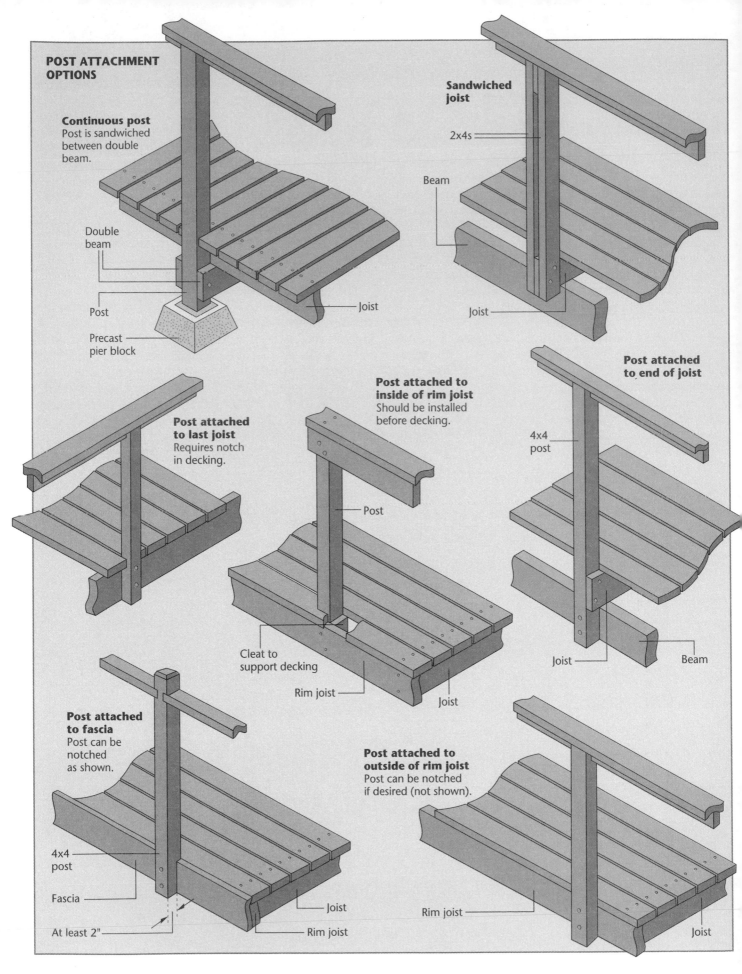

POST ATTACHMENT OPTIONS

Continuous post
Post is sandwiched between double beam.

Double beam

Post

Precast pier block

Joist

Sandwiched joist

2x4s

Beam

Joist

Post attached to last joist
Requires notch in decking.

Post attached to inside of rim joist
Should be installed before decking.

Post

Cleat to support decking

Rim joist

Joist

Post attached to end of joist

4x4 post

Joist

Beam

Post attached to fascia
Post can be notched as shown.

4x4 post

Fascia

At least 2"

Rim joist

Joist

Post attached to outside of rim joist
Post can be notched if desired (not shown).

Rim joist

Joist

STYLISH RAILING POSSIBILITIES

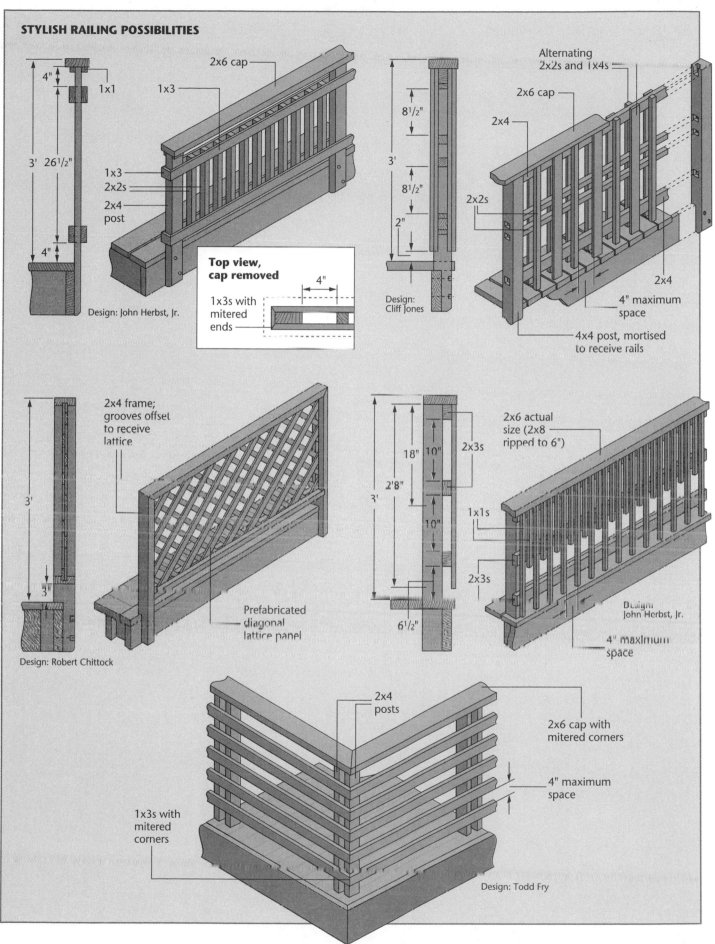

4"

1x1

3' 26½"

4"

2x6 cap

1x3

1x3

2x2s

2x4 post

Design: John Herbst, Jr.

Top view, cap removed

4"

1x3s with mitered ends

8½"

3'

8½"

2"

Design: Cliff Jones

Alternating 2x2s and 1x4s

2x6 cap

2x4

2x2s

2x4

4" maximum space

4x4 post, mortised to receive rails

2x4 frame; grooves offset to receive lattice

3'

3"

Prefabricated diagonal lattice panel

Design: Robert Chittock

18" 10"

2'8"

10"

3'

6½"

2x3s

2x6 actual size (2x8 ripped to 6")

1x1s

2x3s

Design: John Herbst, Jr.

4" maximum space

2x4 posts

2x6 cap with mitered corners

4" maximum space

1x3s with mitered corners

Design: Todd Fry

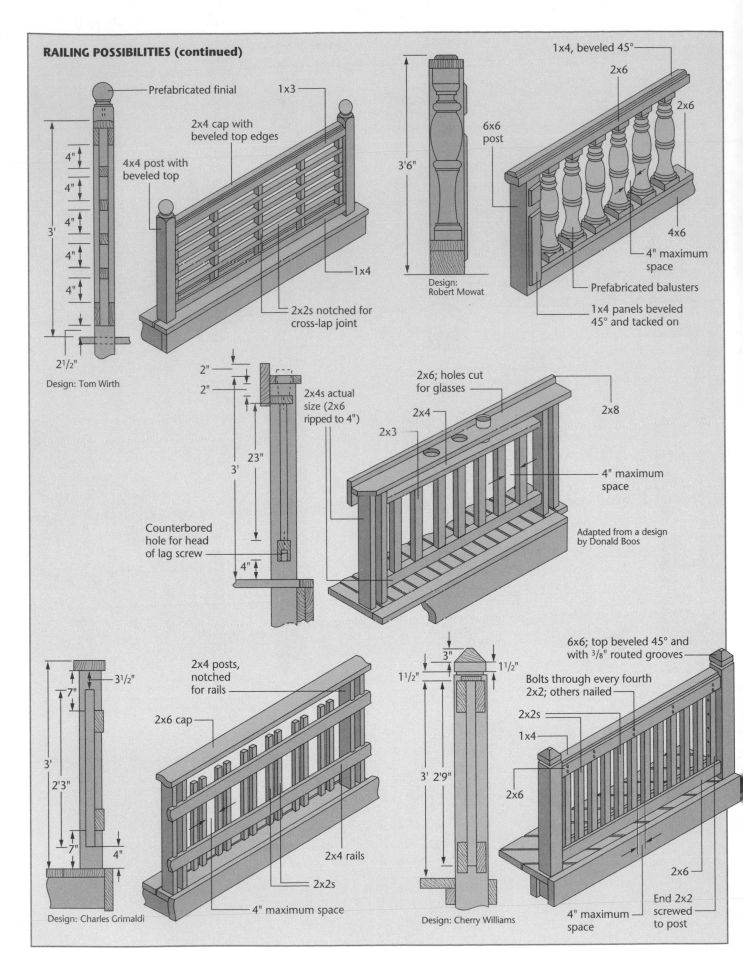

Prefabricated finial

1x3

2x4 cap with beveled top edges

4x4 post with beveled top

1x4

2x2s notched for cross-lap joint

4"
4"
4"
4"
4"
3'
2 1/2"

Design: Tom Wirth

1x4, beveled 45°

2x6

2x6

6x6 post

3'6"

4x6

4" maximum space

Prefabricated balusters

1x4 panels beveled 45° and tacked on

Design: Robert Mowat

2"
2"
3'
23"
4"

2x4s actual size (2x6 ripped to 4")

Counterbored hole for head of lag screw

2x6; holes cut for glasses

2x4

2x3

2x8

4" maximum space

Adapted from a design by Donald Boos

3 1/2"
7"
3'
2'3"
7"
4"

2x4 posts, notched for rails

2x6 cap

2x4 rails

2x2s

4" maximum space

Design: Charles Grimaldi

3"
1 1/2"
1 1/2"
3'
2'9"

6x6; top beveled 45° and with 3/8" routed grooves

Bolts through every fourth 2x2; others nailed

2x2s

1x4

2x6

2x6

End 2x2 screwed to post

4" maximum space

Design: Cherry Williams

You may want to incorporate materials other than wood into your railing design, either to contrast with the rest of the deck or to match your house. Some possibilities are shown here.

Code requirements don't allow more than 4-inch or 6-inch openings in your railings; this means spacing balusters and horizontal railings quite close together. If you want your railing to have a more open look, space the wooden elements further apart, and fill in between them with tempered glass, metal pipe, or wire mesh. If you want your railings to look more solid, choose among facings such as plywood siding, shingles, stucco, or opaque plastic panels.

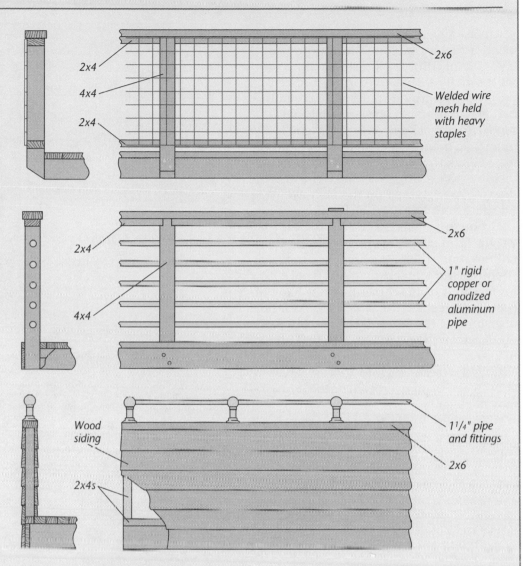

2x4
4x4
2x4
2x6
Welded wire mesh held with heavy staples

2x4
4x4
2x6
1" rigid copper or anodized aluminum pipe

Wood siding
2x4s
1¼" pipe and fittings
2x6

ASK A PRO

HOW CAN I ADD A GATE TO MY RAILING?

To build a gate, you'll need a post at each edge of the gate, firmly attached to the deck structure. Build a frame for the gate, rabbeting the vertical pieces into the horizontal rails; screw the joints together. The gate should be braced with a 2x4 running from the bottom of the hinge side to the top of the latch side. Make sure that the gate opens into the deck, away from the stairs and that the latch is childproof.

Add balusters or additional horizontal rails. You'll get a seamless appearance by repeating the railing design in the gate, as shown. As with railings, if you have small children, design a gate that is difficult to climb.

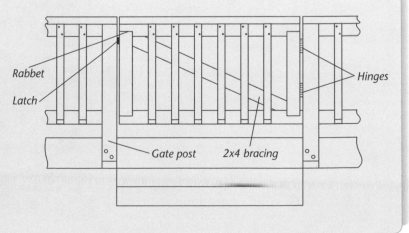

Rabbet
Latch
Hinges
Gate post
2x4 bracing

SCREENS

Structurally, screens are essentially tall railings, but the functions of the two components differ. Whereas a railing provides chiefly a physical barrier, a screen's purpose is to provide a visual or climatic barrier—to block an objectionable view or moderate or filter winds. Screens tend to be more solid or intricate than railings. However, like railings, the most attractive screens coordinate with existing structural elements. The drawings at right and on the next two pages illustrate both basic and elaborate patterns.

Although screens don't need to bear the weight from people leaning or sitting that railings must, their attachment to the deck should be no less secure; refer to page 82 for methods of attachment. The spacing of posts for screens is the same as that for railings: up to 4 feet apart if the cap is a 2x4, up to 6 feet if the cap is a 2x6. Maximum height for freestanding screens is 8 feet, although screens tied into another structure at both ends—an overhead, or the house—may be taller.

Hillside and upper-story decks may have a long-legged look because of the exposed support posts. You can construct a decorative "skirt" to mask them and, at the same time, visually anchor the deck to the ground and provide a hidden spot for storage. Such skirts are really screens that extend below, rather than above, deck level. Follow the same design guidelines as for screens, but anchor the skirt to the posts, a beam, and a support board attached to the posts near the ground. To avoid a buildup of humidity under the deck, leave a gap below the bottom of the skirt.

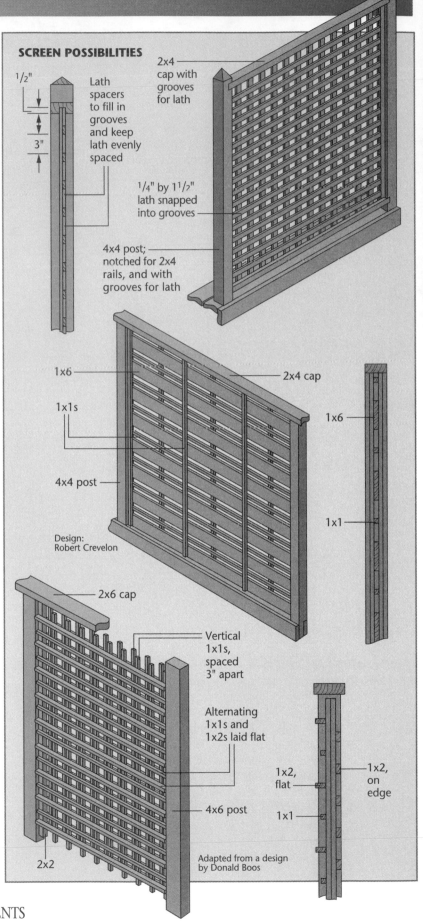

SCREEN POSSIBILITIES

1/2"

3"

Lath spacers to fill in grooves and keep lath evenly spaced

2x4 cap with grooves for lath

1/4" by 1 1/2" lath snapped into grooves

4x4 post; notched for 2x4 rails, and with grooves for lath

1x6

1x1s

4x4 post

2x4 cap

1x6

1x1

Design: Robert Crevelon

2x6 cap

Vertical 1x1s, spaced 3" apart

Alternating 1x1s and 1x2s laid flat

4x6 post

2x2

1x2, flat

1x1

1x2, on edge

Adapted from a design by Donald Boos

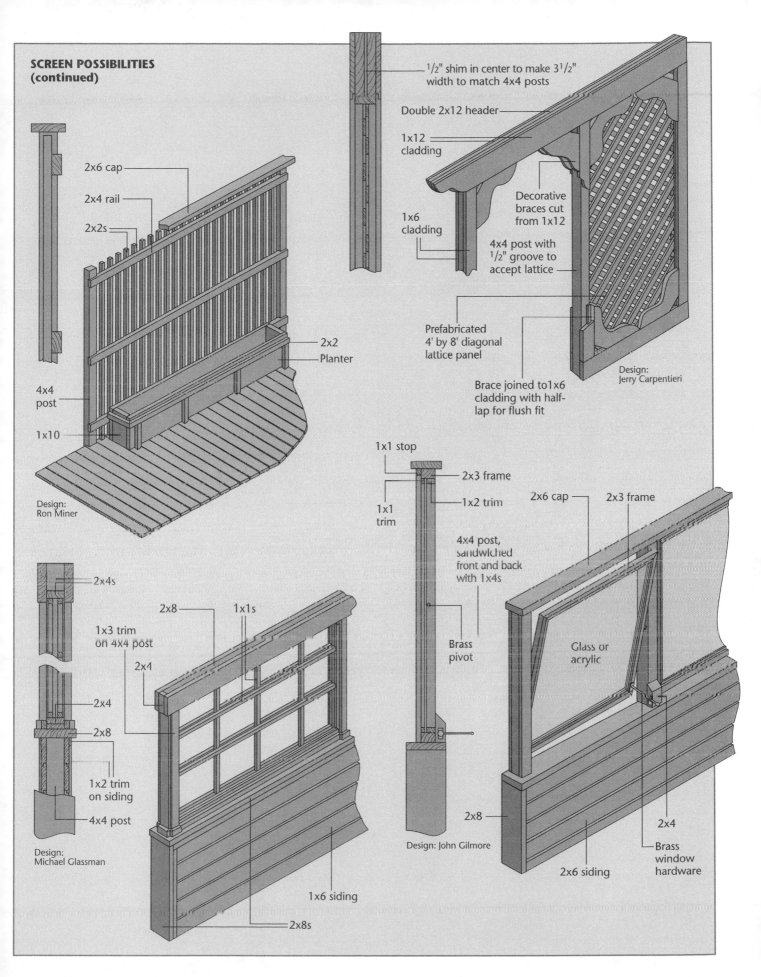

SCREEN POSSIBILITIES
(continued)

2x6 cap

2x4 rail

2x2s

2x2

Planter

4x4 post

1x10

Design:
Ron Miner

½" shim in center to make 3½"
width to match 4x4 posts

Double 2x12 header

1x12
cladding

1x6
cladding

Decorative
braces cut
from 1x12

4x4 post with
½" groove to
accept lattice

Prefabricated
4' by 8' diagonal
lattice panel

Brace joined to 1x6
cladding with half-
lap for flush fit

Design:
Jerry Carpentieri

2x4s

1x3 trim
on 4x4 post

2x4

2x4

2x8

1x2 trim
on siding

4x4 post

Design:
Michael Glassman

2x8

1x1s

2x4

1x6 siding

2x8s

1x1 stop

2x3 frame

1x1
trim

1x2 trim

4x4 post,
sandwiched
front and back
with 1x4s

Brass
pivot

Design: John Gilmore

2x6 cap

2x3 frame

Glass or
acrylic

2x8

2x4

Brass
window
hardware

2x6 siding

DECK COMPONENTS   87

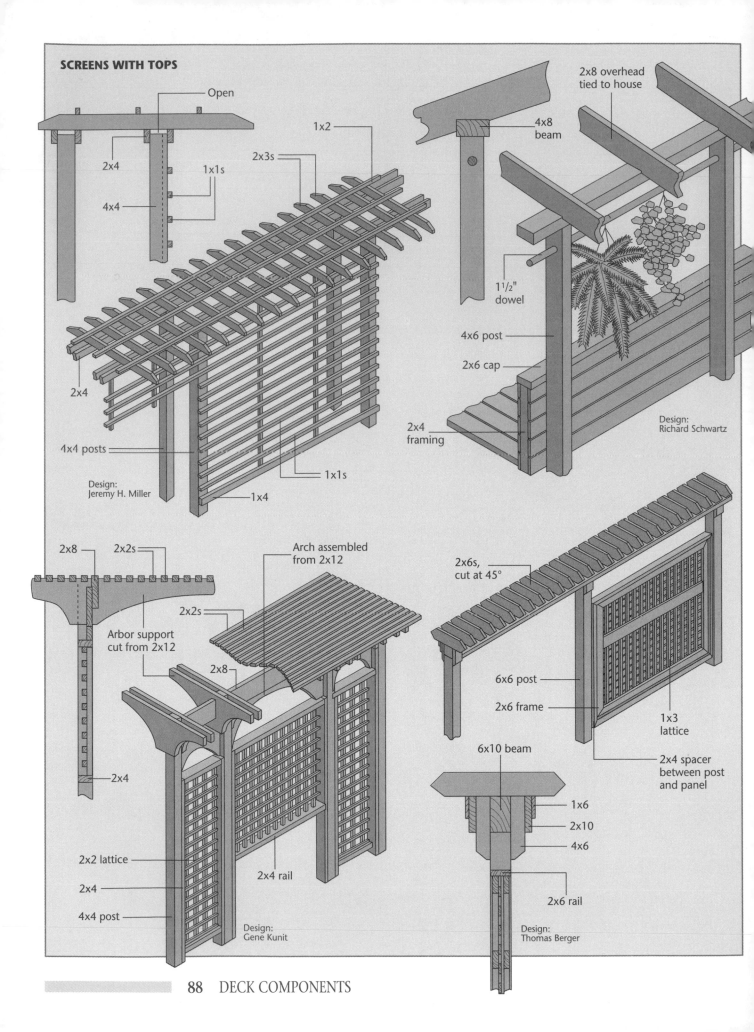

SCREENS WITH TOPS

Open

2x4

1x1s

4x4

2x4

4x4 posts

Design:
Jeremy H. Miller

1x4

1x2

2x3s

1x1s

2x8 overhead
tied to house

4x8
beam

1½"
dowel

4x6 post

2x6 cap

2x4
framing

Design:
Richard Schwartz

2x8

2x2s

Arbor support
cut from 2x12

2x4

2x2 lattice

2x4

4x4 post

2x2s

Arch assembled
from 2x12

2x8

2x4 rail

Design:
Gene Kunit

2x6s,
cut at 45°

6x6 post

2x6 frame

6x10 beam

1x3
lattice

2x4 spacer
between post
and panel

1x6

2x10

4x6

2x6 rail

Design:
Thomas Berger

DECK MATERIALS

The materials you choose for your deck will determine not only its looks, but also its function, durability, and cost. For this reason, it's important to be aware of your options, and to acquaint yourself with the characteristics of the various materials and the differences between them.

This chapter offers information on materials that can be used for the decking as well as those for the substructure and foundation; you'll find descriptions of the many products available—other than traditional wood and concrete. In the section beginning on page 92 we'll show you how to choose the species and grade of lumber appropriate for your project, and we'll help you out with lumberyard parlance—terms such as "heartwood," "vertical grain," and "S-DRY," for instance. On page 97, we introduce you to the fasteners and connectors you'll need for building your deck. Finishing materials such as water repellents and stains are covered in the chapter starting on page 153.

As you compare materials, balance the cost of each item against its appearance, durability, and suitability for your particular design.

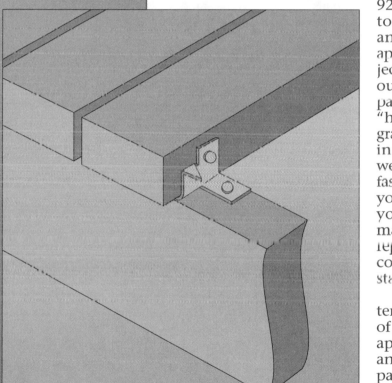

These handy deck clips allow you to fasten deck boards to the substructure with no visible nails or screws, giving your deck the look of a hardwood floor. A wide variety of metal connectors are available for assembling other parts of your deck, from hanging joists to attaching stair treads.

AN OVERVIEW OF DECK MATERIALS

In the next chapter, we'll show you how to build a deck that has concrete footings, a wood substructure, and wood decking. These are the most common materials used in deck building, and the simplest choices for the do-it-yourselfer. In this section we'll explain the advantages of these materials and we'll also describe some of the other, more unusual alternatives that you might want to consider.

SURFACE MATERIALS

The vast majority of decks are surfaced with wood, and for good reason: Wood is affordable, versatile, relatively lightweight, and easy to work with standard tools. But it's far from the only choice. You can choose from a variety of other excellent deck materials, each with its own pros and cons.

Decks requiring watertight surfaces call for special materials. Some materials—fiberglass or elastomerics—provide their own watertight membrane. Masonry materials, on the other hand, must go on top of a watertight roof. The installation of most watertight surfacing materials is best left to professionals; you'll need the help of a roofer and possibly a mason. If you plan to use heavy masonry, weight will be a major concern—reinforcing the structure may require the advice of an engineer or architect. For more information on waterproof decks, turn to page 133.

WOOD DECKING

In addition to the advantages noted above, wood offers natural warmth and beauty. Because it comes in a variety of species, grades, sizes, and textures, lumber allows you to create many decking styles and patterns (*page 63*). Since the deck surface will be exposed to rain, it's advisable to select a decay-resistant species such as redwood or cedar heartwood, or pressure-treated wood, especially in a climate subject to dampness or termites. See page 92 for information on choosing lumber.

NONWOOD BOARDS

Deck boards are available in a variety of materials other than wood. These include vinyl, fiberglass composites, and recycled plastic, all of which are durable and maintenance free.

Vinyl and fiberglass composite boards come in a variety of colors; they are usually fastened from underneath, with no nails or screws visible on the surface. Boards made from recycled plastic are generally installed with nails or screws in the same way as wood decking. Some of these boards also contain wood shavings, making them resemble wood.

OUTDOOR CARPETING

Synthetic outdoor carpeting is highly durable and resistant to fading, soil, stain, mildew, fire, and insects. As a deck covering, it offers good traction, deadens sound, and remains cool underfoot on hot days. This carpeting isn't watertight, though, and requires a base of pressure-treated plywood. Carpeting requires more upkeep than the other varieties of surface materials.

CONCRETE

A deck may be covered with concrete that's troweled smooth and, if desired, tinted or seeded with exposed aggregate gravel. Concrete is highly durable, relatively low in cost, fire resistant, and maintenance free. But it's heavy—a 3-inch-thick slab of "lightweight" concrete weighs about 30 pounds per square foot. Because of their weight, concrete decks must be professionally engineered; to be watertight, they require an underlying roof membrane.

TILE AND PAVERS

Tile, brick, and concrete pavers are often expensive, but they're hard to surpass for beautiful, elegant-looking surfaces. You'll find a wide range of colors, patterns, and textures. Choose pavers that will stand up well to rugged outdoor use and that don't create glare or heat buildup.

To create a watertight surface, tile and pavers must go on top of a waterproof membrane such as hot-mopped asphalt. Because tile and pavers are comparable in weight to concrete, the supporting structure should be professionally designed to ensure adequate strength.

 PLAY IT SAFE

ENSURING A NONSLIP SURFACE

If you're choosing a nonwood surface for your deck, you'll need to make sure it's not too slick when wet. This is a particular concern for a poolside deck. If you decide to go with tile, opt for an unglazed type; you may want to investigate tiles with a special nonslip surface, primarily used in commercial applications.

Fiberglass coatings are dusted with an aggregate sand for traction, and elastomeric coatings usually contain a nonskid texturing agent. Exterior carpeting is another good choice for improving traction.

FIBERGLASS

"Glassing" is another way to obtain a watertight deck. This fiberglass surface actually costs about the same as all-wood decking; to install it, you first put down a special fiberglass mat (called roving) over plywood subflooring, and then you apply coats of polyester resin. The clear resin is often pigmented.

Installing fiberglass is generally considered to be a do-it-yourself project, but make sure you follow the manufacturer's instructions carefully. Otherwise, you may end up with a lumpy mess.

On the positive side, a fiberglass deck is durable, termite proof and rot free (though the subflooring is not); on the downside, it may strongly reflect heat and light (depending upon its color and location), and it must be recoated with resin every four to five years.

ELASTOMERIC SURFACE COATINGS

Various kinds of rubberlike surface coatings, either painted or troweled on, are used as both waterproof membranes and finished walking surfaces. These substances come in a variety of colors. Though it's possible for homeowners to install these membranes themselves, opt for professional application if you want the job to be guaranteed.

SUBSTRUCTURE MATERIALS

Beneath a deck's surface, you're likely to find a framework of joists, beams, and posts made of dimension lumber and standing on concrete piers. Special conditions—a need for exceptional strength or durability, for example —call for other materials, such as timber, treated poles, steel, or concrete columns.

DIMENSION LUMBER

Wood is the most common substructure material. For most decks, you'll use dimension lumber, which is lumber up to 4 inches thick. Any structural members within 6 inches of the ground should be made of pressure-treated wood.

To increase the lifespan of your deck, you may choose to build the entire structure from pressure-treated wood, although this wood is more expensive and often less attractive than regular lumber. For a discussion of lumber species, grades, sizes, and other pertinent information, turn to the next page.

TIMBERS

Especially large framing members call for timber—lumber with both a width and a thickness of 5 inches or more. Timber is the usual choice for a beam that spans a long distance or a post subject to severe loads.

In place of single-piece timbers, it's possible to use laminated wood structural beams, custom manufactured in straight, arched, or curved shapes; some can span 30 feet or more. Such beams are expensive and generally limited to professionally designed decks.

POLES AND PILINGS

Natural poles make particularly attractive, functional posts for decks belonging to rustic cabins and beach houses. Such poles are usually treated with preservatives, but if local codes allow, they may be left untreated or used with the bark attached. Building codes also specify the weights various pole diameters can support.

Decks over sand, mud, or water should be supported with pilings—large-diameter steel or specially treated wooden poles driven into the ground. These are designed and installed by professionals, but once the pilings are in place, a do-it-yourselfer can usually complete the rest of the deck.

STEEL

Impervious to rot and termites, steel posts and beams also offer exceptional strength in small dimensions. Because they can cover longer spans than lumber, they're ideal for strong, uncluttered substructures. However, due to its high cost, structural steel is usually used only for carrying extreme loads or crossing unusually long spans. In addition, steel structures must be professionally engineered; installation requires welding and often the use of special lifts or even a crane.

Remember that steel isn't maintenance free; it must be painted periodically to prevent rust.

NOTE: Although steel doesn't burn, it can collapse in the event of a fire.

CONCRETE

Most decks stand on concrete footings and piers. In some cases—when a deck is perched on a steep hillside, for example—concrete columns take the place of footings, piers, and posts. These columns are strong, fireproof, and impervious to termites and decay.

Concrete columns are generally cylindrical, and special fiber tubes, available at some masonry yards and home improvement centers, are usually used for forming them. The columns are reinforced with steel bars.

Though working with concrete does involve hard physical labor, fairly small jobs are usually manageable. As a rule, do-it-yourselfers shouldn't attempt to cast concrete columns taller than 5 feet above grade. For information on estimating and working with concrete, turn to page 113.

CHOOSING LUMBER

Because the lumber you use strongly influences your deck's strength and appearance, and takes the largest bite out of your project budget, it pays to learn the basics of lumber types and terminology before you visit your lumberyard. In this section we'll introduce you to the characteristics of different kinds of lumber and the way lumber is sized, graded, and priced.

LUMBER CHARACTERISTICS

The use you can make of a particular piece of lumber depends on the species, the moisture content, the way the piece is cut, and any existing defects.

Softwood and hardwood: These terms don't refer to a wood's relative hardness, but rather to the kind of tree from which it comes: Softwoods come from evergreens (conifers), hardwoods from broadleaf (deciduous) trees. Because hardwoods are generally costlier and more difficult to work with, and more prone to rotting outdoors, they're rarely used for deck construction.

Species, heartwood, and sapwood: Wood is defined by its species, or the particular tree that it comes from— Douglas-fir, redwood, or pine, for example. Woods of different species have different characteristics, as shown in the chart below. Douglas-fir/larch, southern pine, and hem/fir are good choices for the deck substructure. Redwood and cedar are common choices for decking and railings, due to their decay-resistant properties *(page 95)*.

Even within a species, a wood's properties will vary depending upon which part of the tree it came from. The inactive wood nearest the center of a living tree is called heartwood. Sapwood, next to the bark, contains the growth cells. Heartwood is more resistant to decay; sapwood is more porous and absorbs preservatives and other chemicals more efficiently.

Moisture content: Lumber is either air-dried in stacks or kiln-dried to a certain percentage moisture content. The moisture content dramatically affects the wood's shrinkage, ability to hold nails, and other important properties. If wood is very damp, it's likely to split, warp, or cup as it dries. S-GRN designates "green" (unseasoned) lumber with a moisture content of 20% or more; S-DRY means the moisture content is 19% or less; MC 15 lumber is dried to a moisture content of 15% or less. S-DRY is adequate for deck-building. Pressure-treatment introduces a lot of moisture into the wood. Some pressure-treated wood is available that has been dried again after treatment. Redwood and cedar are very stable woods and can be used green.

MAJOR SOFTWOODS		
Species or species group	**Growing range**	**Characteristics**
Cedar, western red	Pacific Northwest from southern Alaska to northern California; Washington east to Montana	Heartwood is similar to redwood in decay-resistance, but not as resistant to termites; coarser than redwood. High resistance to warping, weathering. Strongly aromatic. Somewhat weak and brittle; moderate nail-holding ability; very easy to work.
Douglas-fir/ western larch	Western states (Rocky Mountains and Pacific Coast ranges)	Very heavy, strong, and stiff; good nail-holding ability. Somewhat difficult to work with hand tools. Good choice for structural applications. Resistant to decay and termites only if pressure-treated with preservatives.
Hem/fir (eastern and western hemlock; true firs)	Western hemlock and firs: Rocky Mountains and Pacific Coast ranges; eastern hemlock: northeastern U.S. and Appalachians	Firs are generally lightweight, soft to moderately soft, with average strength. Hemlocks are fairly strong and stiff; below-average nailing ability. Firs are easy to work; hemlocks are somewhat more difficult. Shrinkage can be substantial. Resistant to decay and termites only if pressure-treated with preservatives.
Pine, ponderosa	Western states	Moderately strong and stiff; high resistance to warping. Good nail-holding ability. Not as strong as southern pine, but easier to work. Resistant to decay and termites only when pressure-treated.
Pine, red	New England, New York, Pennsylvania, and lake states	Strong and stiff. Good nail-holding ability. Not quite as strong as southern pine but easier to work. Resistant to decay and termites only if pressure-treated.
Pine, southern yellow (longleaf, slash, shortleaf, loblolly)	Southeastern U.S. from Maryland to Florida; Atlantic Coast to East Texas	Like Douglas-fir, very strong and stiff, hard, good nail-holding ability. Moderately easy to work. Resistant to decay and termites only if pressure-treated with preservatives.
Redwood	Northwestern California, extreme southwestern Oregon	Heartwood known for its durability and resistance to decay, disease, termites. Moderately light with limited structural strength (but strong for its weight). Good workability, but brittle; splits easily. Medium nail-holding ability.

COMMON LUMBER DEFECTS

Defect	Description	What to do
Crook	Warp along the edge line; also known as crown.	Straighten with a circular saw and a clamped-on guide.
Bow	Warp on the face of a board from end to end.	Cut the piece into smaller, unbowed pieces, or remove the bow by planing the face.
Cup	Hollow across the face of a board.	Dry the piece until both faces have equal moisture content, or cut the piece to eliminate the cupped part.
Twist	Multiple bends in a board.	Cut off the twisted part, or plane the face to remove the twist.
Knot or knothole	A tight knot is not usually a problem; a loose or dead knot, surrounded by a dark ring, may fall out later, or may already have left a hole.	Cut off the part with a knot or knothole; sound knots may be kept if a knotty look is desired. CAUTION: Remove any loose knots before cutting the lumber.
Check	Crack along the length of the board, not passing through the entire thickness of the wood.	Cut off the checked portion.
Split	Crack going all the way through the piece of wood, commonly at the ends.	Cut off the split part of the board.
Shake	Separation of grain between the growth rings, often extending along the board's face, and sometimes below its surface.	Cut off the shake.
Wane	Missing wood or untrimmed bark along the edge or corner of the piece.	Cut off the affected part.

Rough and surfaced lumber: Surfaced lumber, which has been planed smooth, is the standard for most construction and a must for decking. It is available in a range of grades, as discussed on the next page. Some lumberyards also carry rough lumber, but it tends to be available only in lower grades, with a correspondingly greater number of defects and higher moisture content.

Vertical and flat grain: Depending on the cut of the millsaw, lumber will have either parallel grain lines running the length of the boards (vertical grain), a marbled appearance (flat grain), or a combination of the two. Vertical-grain lumber is less likely than flat-grain lumber to cup, and you may prefer its appearance, but it usually costs more. (Vertical- and flat-grain boards are illustrated below.)

Defects: Lumber is subject to a number of possible defects due to weathering and the way the piece was milled. When choosing lumber, lift each piece and sight down the face and edges for any defects. The most common defects are shown at left, along with some suggestions for salvaging affected boards. In addition, be on the lookout for problems such as rotting, staining, insect holes, and pitch pockets (reservoirs of sap).

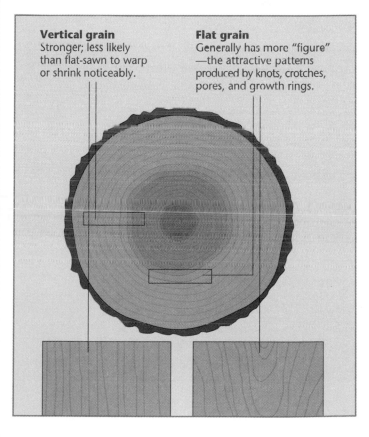

Vertical grain
Stronger; less likely than flat-sawn to warp or shrink noticeably.

Flat grain
Generally has more "figure" —the attractive patterns produced by knots, crotches, pores, and growth rings.

SIZING

Lumber is divided into categories based on size. **Dimension lumber** is intended for structural applications and is used for both decking and the deck substructure. Sizes range from 2 to 4 inches thick and at least 2 inches wide. **Timbers** are heavy structural lumber 5 inches thick or more used for large posts or beams. **Boards** are normally not more than 2 inches thick, and are 4 to 12 inches wide. They are not as strong as dimension lumber and are used for nonstructural applications, such as planters.

Wood specifically intended for decking is available, referred to as radius-edge patio decking. These boards have rounded edges and are available in thicknesses of 1 inch or 1⁵/₃₂ inch. Patio decking can also be used for amenities such as benches and planters.

Be aware that a typical "2x4" is not actually 2 inches by 4 inches. The nominal size of lumber is designated before the piece is dried and surfaced; the finished size is less. Rough lumber is actually closer to the stated dimensions. For real sizes of surfaced lumber, consult the chart below.

Lumber is normally stocked in even lengths from 6 to 16 feet, in 2-foot increments. You may want to special-order longer pieces; for instance, to avoid end joints in your decking.

STANDARD DIMENSIONS OF SOFTWOODS

Nominal size	Surfaced (actual) size
1x2	³/₄"x1¹/₂"
1x3	³/₄"x2¹/₂"
1x4	³/₄"x3¹/₂"
1x6	³/₄"x5¹/₂"
1x8	³/₄"x7¹/₄"
1x10	³/₄"x9¹/₄"
1x12	³/₄"x11¹/₄"
2x3	1¹/₂"x2¹/₂"
2x4	1¹/₂"x3¹/₂"
2x6	1¹/₂"x5¹/₂"
2x8	1¹/₂"x7¹/₄"
2x10	1¹/₂"x9¹/₄"
2x12	1¹/₂"x11¹/₄"
4x4	3¹/₂"x3¹/₂"
4x10	3¹/₂"x9¹/₄"
6x8	5¹/₂"x7¹/₄"

GRADING

Lumber is sorted and graded at the mill. Generally, lumber grades depend on several factors: natural growth characteristics (such as knots), defects resulting from milling errors, and commercial drying and preserving techniques that affect each piece's strength, durability, and appearance. A stamp on the lumber identifies moisture content, grade name, and species, as well as the producing mill and the grading agency, such as WWP for the Western Wood Products Association stamp shown below.

Dimension lumber and timbers are graded for strength. The most common grading system includes the grades Select Structural, No. 1, No. 2, and No. 3, with Select Structural being the highest grade. Often, lumberyards sell a mix of grades called "No. 2 and Better." A second grading system exists for some lumber: Construction, Standard, and Utility. A mixture of grades called "Standard and Better" is commonly available; it is less strong than No. 2 and Better. In the case of No. 2 and Better, and Standard and Better, you may be able to look through the pile to select lumber with a higher grade stamp.

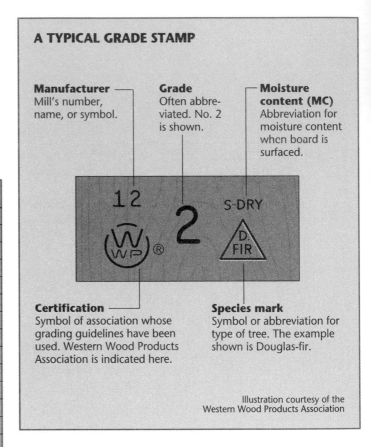

A TYPICAL GRADE STAMP

Manufacturer Mill's number, name, or symbol.

Grade Often abbreviated. No. 2 is shown.

Moisture content (MC) Abbreviation for moisture content when board is surfaced.

Certification Symbol of association whose grading guidelines have been used. Western Wood Products Association is indicated here.

Species mark Symbol or abbreviation for type of tree. The example shown is Douglas-fir.

Illustration courtesy of the Western Wood Products Association

No. 2 and Better is the minimum grade required for a deck's substructure, but you may want to choose a higher grade for a better appearance. For decking, either No. 2 and Better, or Standard and Better are adequate; for appearance you may want to invest in a higher grade, such as Select Structural.

"Boards" are graded for appearance. For outdoor applications, you should choose 2 and Better Common, or if you want to economize, 3 Common.

Western red cedar and redwood decking are generally graded for appearance. Each has its own grading system. The cedar grades, starting with the highest quality, are: Architect Clear, Custom Clear, Architect Knotty, and

Custom Knotty. The lower grades have more knots, but don't rule them out—you may decide you like the knotty look. Cedar grades don't indicate whether the wood is heartwood or sapwood. Cedar heartwood is a rich orange color, while the sapwood is a creamy white; for maximum decay-resistance, pick out pieces with as much heartwood as possible.

The top grades of redwood are the "architectural grades": Clear All Heart, Clear, B Heart, and B Grade. A more economical choice—with a rougher look—is one of the "garden grades." Of these, Construction Heart and Construction Common are suitable for decking. The lower quality garden grades—Merchantable Heart and Merchantable—are suitable for benches and planters. The grades with the word "heart" in the name are those with the highest proportion of heartwood and are therefore the most decay resistant.

PRICING

The price of lumber is calculated either by the lineal foot or by the board foot. The lineal foot refers to only the length of a piece. For example, if you ask for "20 2x4s, 8 feet long" you'll be charged for 160 lineal feet of 2x4.

The board foot, on the other hand, takes all the board's dimensions into account: A piece of wood 1 inch thick by 12 inches wide by 12 inches long equals one board foot. The board foot is the most common unit for volume orders and allows you to compare pricing of different sizes of lumber. To compute board feet, use this formula: nominal thickness in inches, multiplied by nominal width in feet, multiplied by length in feet. For example, a 2x6 board 10 feet long would be computed: $2" \times 1/2' \times 10' = 10$ board feet. Of course, you still need to list the exact dimensions of the lumber you need so your order can be filled correctly.

PLAY IT SAFE

WORKING WITH PRESSURE-TREATED WOOD

Wood can be preserved with a number of different chemicals; the wood you find at a lumberyard has most likely been treated with inorganic arsenicals. This wood should never be burned. Dispose of it by burying it or by including it with your ordinary trash collection.

When cutting this type of lumber, always wear respiratory protection (dust mask or respirator) and safety goggles. Wash your hands before eating and launder work clothes separately from other clothing.

Some salvaged wood, such as railway ties, has been treated with creosote, a more toxic chemical not usually used in residential applications. This wood is not recommended for deck construction because it is harmful when in prolonged contact with the skin—this is a particular hazard for animals and small children

DECAY-RESISTANT WOOD

Parts of the deck that trap water or are close to the ground should be made of decay-resistant wood. Redwood and cedar heartwood is naturally resistant to decay and termites, although redwood is more termite resistant than cedar. (Some exotic Central American hardwoods such as Ipé are also decay resistant—consult your local hardwood dealer.) Other woods can be pressure-treated with chemicals to make them resistant to both decay and termites. Although redwood and cedar are attractive options, these species tend to be softer and weaker than woods such as hem/fir or southern pine, which are available pressure-treated. The decay-resistant cedar or redwood hardwood is also more expensive than pressure-treated wood and generally is not available in large sizes. To get the best of both worlds, most professional designers favor pressure-treated woods for a deck's substructure, but then opt for decking, benches, and railings of cedar or redwood heartwood.

Any structural members that are within 6 inches of the ground or are in contact with concrete should be made of decay-resistant wood. Decking on a low-level deck, within 1 foot of the ground, should be made of decay-resistant wood—either cedar or redwood heartwood, or pressure-treated wood. Structural members or decking not near the ground can be made of ordinary lumber, but making your entire deck of decay-resistant wood will increase its life, particularly in an area subject to dampness or termites.

Pressure treatment: The pressure-treating process forces chemicals into the wood to protect it against rot, insects, and other sources of decay. Pressure treating is much more effective than do-it-yourself brush-on products. (Although you'll also need some brush-on preservative on hand to treat sawcuts and drilled openings in the pressure treated lumber.) The preservatives most commonly used for pressure-treating are inorganic arsenicals such as chromated copper arsenate (CCA) and ammoniacal copper arsenate (ACA), also known as water-borne preservatives.

Pressure-treated wood is available in two exposures, depending on the amount of preservative: Ground Contact is required for lumber that will be close to the ground. For other applications, such as decking, you can choose Above Ground.

Working with treated lumber isn't always a pleasure. Unlike redwood and cedar, which are easy to cut and nail, treated wood is hard and prone to splitting; it also warps and twists more readily. Moreover, some people object to its typically brown or greenish cast. Pressure-treated wood is often covered with staplelike treatment incisions, but certain species are available without the incisions. Finally, special safety precautions are required for working with treated wood, as outlined at left.

PLYWOOD

In outdoor construction, plywood is used for solid decking under a waterproof surface (page 134) or under outdoor carpet. It's also useful for making forms to cast concrete piers. Plywood is available in two common types of panels: performance-rated and sanded.

For solid decking, you'll want performance-rated panels. These are graded for particular applications such as sheathing or subflooring. A good choice for decks is combination subfloor and underlayment panels.

Performance-rated panels are rated for exposure to the weather—either Exposure 1 or Exterior. Exposure 1 panels can tolerate some moisture during construction but should then be covered; they are adequate for solid decking that will be covered with a waterproof surface. Plywood decking that is to be covered with a nonwaterproof surface, such as outdoor carpet, should be rated Exterior and pressure-treated.

In addition to the grade and the exposure rating, grade stamps on performance panels indicate the thickness of the panels, the spacing between supports, and an association trademark that assures quality (such as APA-The Engineered Wood Association). A sample grade stamp is shown at right.

For building forms to cast concrete piers, any plywood will do—buy the cheapest available. You may be able to find "shop grade" panels—inexpensive panels that fail to meet standard grades. Some lumberyards also stock leftover, odd-sized pieces called "cutting panels."

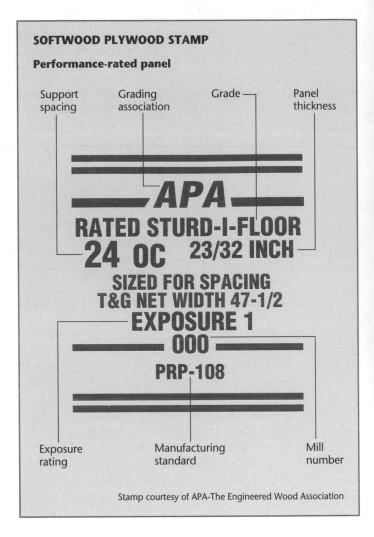

SOFTWOOD PLYWOOD STAMP

Performance-rated panel

Support spacing — Grading association — Grade — Panel thickness

APA
RATED STURD-I-FLOOR
24 OC   23/32 INCH
SIZED FOR SPACING
T&G NET WIDTH 47-1/2
EXPOSURE 1
000
PRP-108

Exposure rating — Manufacturing standard — Mill number

Stamp courtesy of APA-The Engineered Wood Association

ESTIMATING AND ORDERING LUMBER

Estimating is primarily a matter of measuring and counting the number of pieces necessary for your particular project. Ballpark estimates made early in the planning stage will help you compare the costs of different surface and substructure arrangements; a detailed estimate of your final plan provides a basis for ordering materials. Always order 5% to 10% more than your estimated needs to allow for waste.

For decking, the following formula will help you calculate how many boards of a specific width will cover the deck's width, assuming a standard $^3/_{16}$-inch spacing between planks:

Number of 2x4s laid flat = 3.3 x width of deck in feet

Number of 2x6s laid flat = 2.1 x width of deck in feet

Number of 2x2s or edge-laid 2x3s or 2x4s = 7.1 x width of deck in feet

In estimating, round your result to the next highest foot. For example, if you want to cover a 12-foot-wide deck with 2x4s, you'll need 3.3 x 12 = 39.6 boards—so you would order at least 40 boards.

No handy rules are available for estimating the amounts needed for a deck's substructure; you'll have to make your estimates by counting the pieces in your drawings.

Remember these basic rules that will help you cut the cost of materials:
1) Order as many materials as possible at a single time from a single supplier;
2) Choose your supplier on the basis of competitive bids from several retailers;
3) Order your lumber in the regularly available, standard dimensions.

Keep in mind that if all or part of your construction is being done by a licensed contractor, the contractor may arrange to purchase materials for you at a professional discount.

FASTENERS AND CONNECTORS

The strength and durability of your deck will largely be determined by the choice of appropriate fasteners. For installing the decking you'll probably use nails or screws, but for the substructure, choose from the many available metal connectors to make stronger joints.

Corrosion is a major concern for outdoor building. Always use corrosion-resistant fasteners—galvanized, aluminum, or stainless steel.

NAILS

The fastest, least expensive way to fasten wooden decking to joists or beams is, of course, nailing. You can use common or box nails, shown below. Although box nails are the easiest to drive through soft woods such as redwood and cedar, they tend to ease upward as the wood

swells and shrinks. To avoid nail-popping, use deformed shank nails such as spiral or ring shank. The one drawback to this type of nail is that they are hard to remove if bent; however, the increased holding power more than compensates for this inconvenience.

Use common nails to assemble your substructure. For more cosmetic connections, where you don't want a nail's head to show (and where strength isn't required), choose casing nails. After driving the nails nearly flush, sink the slightly rounded heads with a nailset.

Buy galvanized, aluminum, or stainless steel nails; other types will rust. Hot-dipped nails are the best quality galvanized nails; others such as electroplated nails have a thinner coating and are more likely to stain the decking. In fact, even the best hot-dipped nail will rust in time, particularly at the exposed head, where the coating has been battered by your hammer. Stainless steel and aluminum nails won't rust, but they're hard to find (you'll probably have to special-order them) and cost about three times as much as galvanized nails. Aluminum nails are softer than the other types and have more of a tendency to bend or pop.

Nails are sold in boxes (1, 5, or 50 pounds) or loose in bins. A nail's length is indicated by a "penny" designation (abbreviated as "d"). The equivalents in inches are shown on the next page. To fasten decking, use 3¼-inch or 3½-inch nails.

To order nails, estimate how many you'll need from your plans and then convert to pounds, using the chart below. In some cases, a hardware staffperson may be able to make the estimate for you from your plans. For the nailing pattern for decking, turn to page 125.

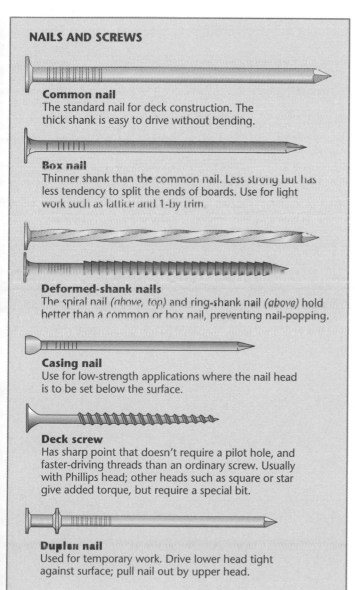

NAILS AND SCREWS

Common nail
The standard nail for deck construction. The thick shank is easy to drive without bending.

Box nail
Thinner shank than the common nail. Less strong but has less tendency to split the ends of boards. Use for light work such as lattice and 1-by trim.

Deformed-shank nails
The spiral nail (above, top) and ring-shank nail (above) hold better than a common or box nail, preventing nail-popping.

Casing nail
Use for low-strength applications where the nail head is to be set below the surface.

Deck screw
Has sharp point that doesn't require a pilot hole, and faster-driving threads than an ordinary screw. Usually with Phillips head; other heads such as square or star give added torque, but require a special bit.

Duplex nail
Used for temporary work. Drive lower head tight against surface; pull nail out by upper head.

HOW MANY NAILS PER POUND?			
	Common	Box	Casing
2½"	106	145	147
2¾"	96	132	-
3"	69	121	108
3¼"	64	94	-
3½"	49	71	71

SCREWS

Although more expensive than nails, galvanized deck screws (similar to drywall screws) provide secure, high-quality fastening for decking. Screws have several advantages over nails: they hold very securely, their galvanized coating is less likely to be damaged during installation, and they eliminate the problem of hammer dents.

Screws are sold by the pound or, at a substantial savings, by the 25-pound box. Be sure to choose galvanized screws (some even better coatings such as ceramic are also available at greater cost). The screws should be long enough to penetrate joists at least as deep as the decking is thick (for 2x4 or 2x6 decking, buy 3-inch screws.)

ADHESIVES

To prevent deck boards from working loose, you can use adhesive in addition to nails or screws. However, the disadvantage of doing this is that the boards will be very difficult to remove later, for repairs.

There are some adhesives designed specifically for decking, but you can choose any construction adhesive that is appropriate for outdoor use. If you are using pressure-treated wood, make sure the adhesive is compatible with this type of wood.

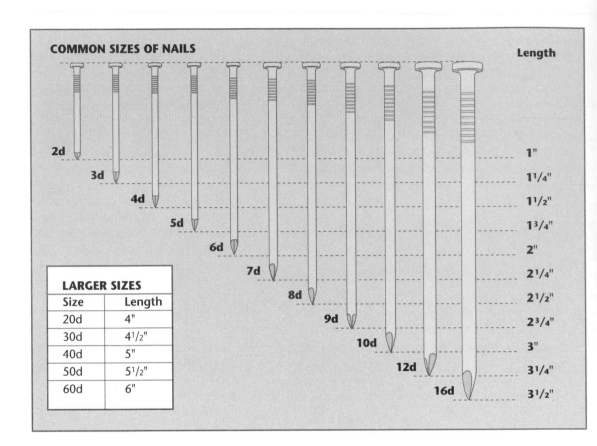

COMMON SIZES OF NAILS

Length: 2d — 1", 3d — 1¼", 4d — 1½", 5d — 1¾", 6d — 2", 7d — 2¼", 8d — 2½", 9d — 2¾", 10d — 3", 12d — 3¼", 16d — 3½"

LARGER SIZES	
Size	Length
20d	4"
30d	4¹/₂"
40d	5"
50d	5¹/₂"
60d	6"

ASK A PRO

HOW CAN I AVOID VISIBLE NAILS AND SCREWS?

While decking is usually nailed or screwed through the surface, these methods leave fasteners visible from above. The two systems shown at right leave no visible fasteners. Although both systems are more time-consuming to install than ordinary nails or screws, the result is a beautiful deck with an unmarred surface. There are no nail holes or hammer dents, and no popped nails to trip on.

The deck clips secure each board to the joist before the next one is added. With the deck track system, the track is nailed to the side of the joist near the top; the underside of each decking board is then screwed to the track.

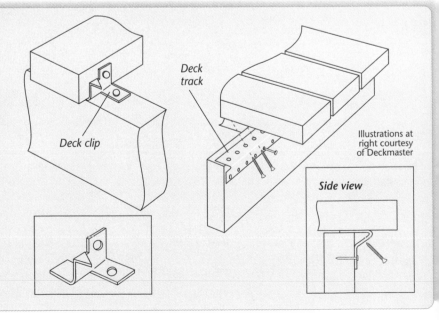

Deck clip

Deck track

Illustrations at right courtesy of Deckmaster

Side view

BOLTS AND LAG SCREWS

For connections where strength is vital (beam-to-post, ledger-to-house, etc.), the fasteners of choice are bolts or lag screws.

For decks, you'll be using 3- to 12-inch-long fasteners with diameters from 1/4 to 3/4 inch (diameter increases in 1/16-inch increments). To accommodate the necessary washers and nuts, bolts should be about 1 inch longer than the combined thickness of the pieces to be bolted together. Drill holes for bolts with a bit the same diameter as the bolt. Use washers under all nuts and under the heads of machine bolts; don't use them under carriage bolt heads, since the shoulder of this type of bolt bites into the wood, keeping the bolt from turning as you turn the nut.

Lag screws come in equivalent sizes to bolts, and are useful if only one side of the connection is accessible. Drill a pilot hole about two-thirds the length of the lag screw, using a bit 1/8 inch smaller in diameter than the lag screw shank. Place a washer under the head of each lag screw.

The number and size of bolts or lag screws depend upon the width of the lumber; typical combinations are shown at right. Remember: It's better to form a connection with several small-diameter bolts or lag screws than with fewer fasteners of greater diameter.

For securing ledgers to a masonry wall or a post anchor to a concrete slab, use either expanding anchor bolts or expansion shields.

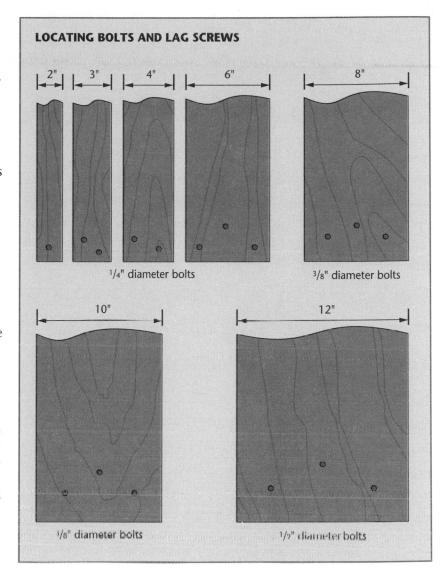

LOCATING BOLTS AND LAG SCREWS

2"   3"   4"   6"   8"

1/4" diameter bolts   3/8" diameter bolts

10"   12"

3/8" diameter bolts   1/2" diameter bolts

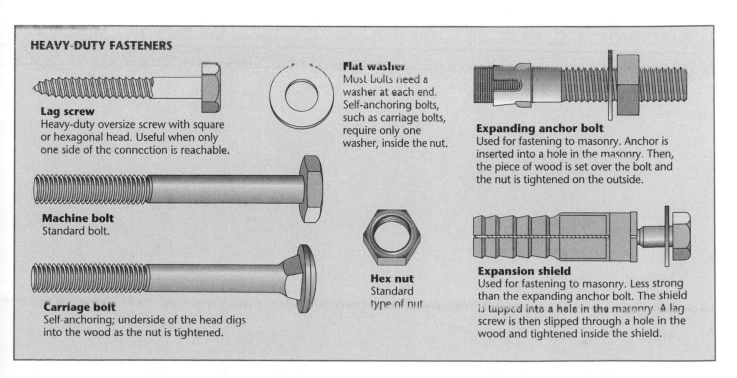

HEAVY-DUTY FASTENERS

Lag screw
Heavy-duty oversize screw with square or hexagonal head. Useful when only one side of the connection is reachable.

Machine bolt
Standard bolt.

Carriage bolt
Self-anchoring; underside of the head digs into the wood as the nut is tightened.

Flat washer
Most bolts need a washer at each end. Self-anchoring bolts, such as carriage bolts, require only one washer, inside the nut.

Hex nut
Standard type of nut.

Expanding anchor bolt
Used for fastening to masonry. Anchor is inserted into a hole in the masonry. Then, the piece of wood is set over the bolt and the nut is tightened on the outside.

Expansion shield
Used for fastening to masonry. Less strong than the expanding anchor bolt. The shield is tapped into a hole in the masonry. A lag screw is then slipped through a hole in the wood and tightened inside the shield.

FRAMING CONNECTORS

Although metal framing connectors add an extra cost element to your project, they will pay off in the end by making your work easier and the result stronger. They strengthen joints by allowing you to avoid the toenailing that leads to weak connections. Connectors also make it much simpler to join two pieces of wood,

and they prevent splitting the ends of the lumber. Almost any home center offers most of the types of framing connectors shown below (and probably several others) in sizes to fit most standard dimensions of surfaced lumber. Connectors intended for outdoor use are galvanized.

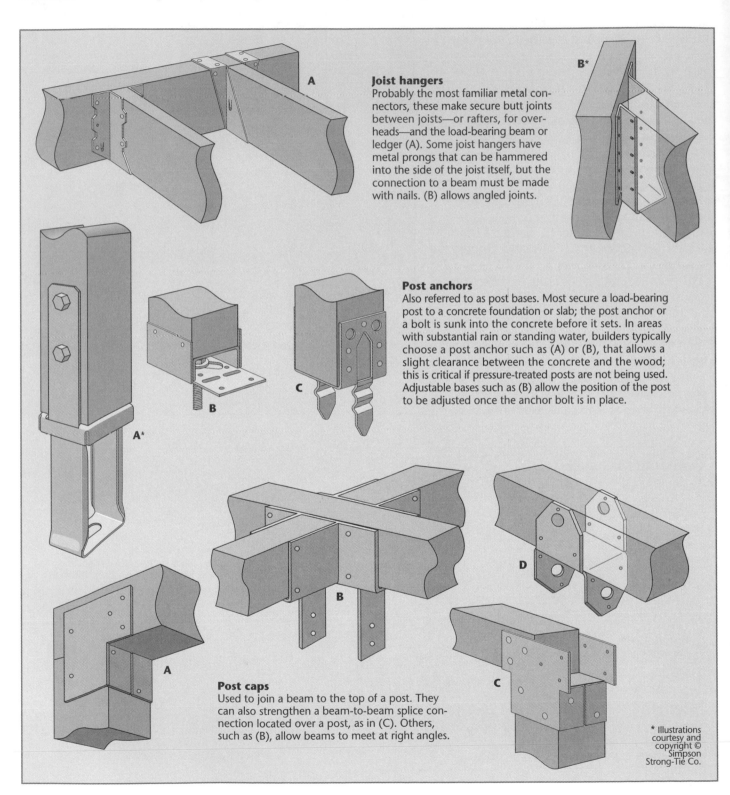

Joist hangers
Probably the most familiar metal connectors, these make secure butt joints between joists—or rafters, for overheads—and the load-bearing beam or ledger (A). Some joist hangers have metal prongs that can be hammered into the side of the joist itself, but the connection to a beam must be made with nails. (B) allows angled joints.

Post anchors
Also referred to as post bases. Most secure a load-bearing post to a concrete foundation or slab; the post anchor or a bolt is sunk into the concrete before it sets. In areas with substantial rain or standing water, builders typically choose a post anchor such as (A) or (B), that allows a slight clearance between the concrete and the wood; this is critical if pressure-treated posts are not being used. Adjustable bases such as (B) allow the position of the post to be adjusted once the anchor bolt is in place.

Post caps
Used to join a beam to the top of a post. They can also strengthen a beam-to-beam splice connection located over a post, as in (C). Others, such as (B), allow beams to meet at right angles.

* Illustrations courtesy and copyright © Simpson Strong-Tie Co.

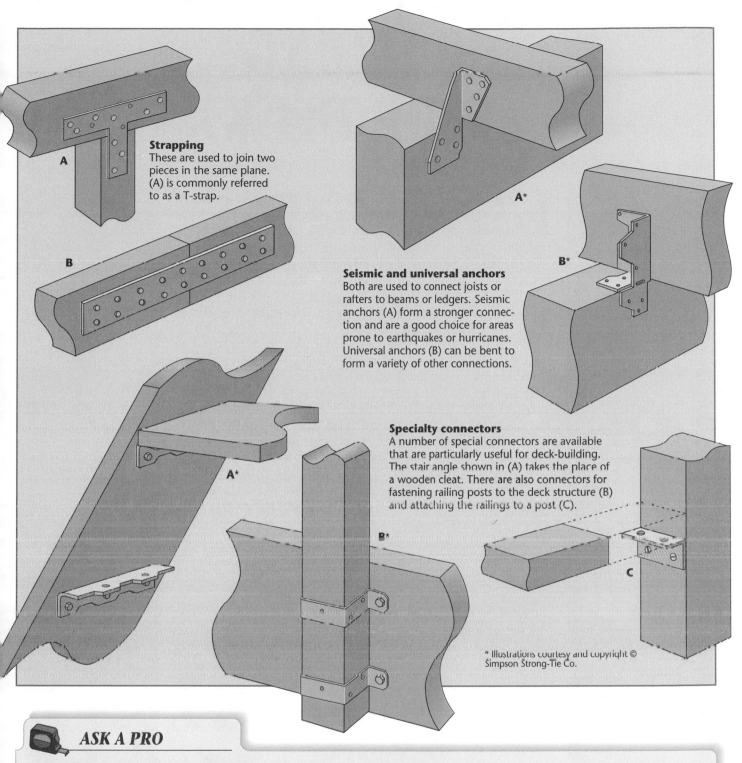

Strapping
These are used to join two pieces in the same plane. (A) is commonly referred to as a T-strap.

A

B

A*

Seismic and universal anchors
Both are used to connect joists or rafters to beams or ledgers. Seismic anchors (A) form a stronger connection and are a good choice for areas prone to earthquakes or hurricanes. Universal anchors (B) can be bent to form a variety of other connections.

B*

Specialty connectors
A number of special connectors are available that are particularly useful for deck-building. The stair angle shown in (A) takes the place of a wooden cleat. There are also connectors for fastening railing posts to the deck structure (B) and attaching the railings to a post (C).

A*

B*

C

* Illustrations courtesy and copyright © Simpson Strong-Tie Co.

ASK A PRO

WHAT KIND OF FASTENERS SHOULD I USE WITH FRAMING CONNECTORS?

Always use the fasteners recommended by the connector manufacturer. These are usually nails 1¹/₄ or 1¹/₂ inches long to avoid complete penetration of 2-by lumber. The special short nails intended for use with framing connectors are thicker than ordinary nails of that length; they are usually available where the connectors are sold. The nails can be smooth-shank or ring-shank, and should be hot-dipped galvanized. In general, use all the available nail holes in the connector.

Wood screws can also be used, of the same diameter as the recommended nails.

In some cases, connectors come with large holes for through bolts in addition to the small holes for nails—use one or the other. Nails are faster to install and ultimately stronger, but you may prefer the look of through-bolts. With certain connectors, such as the stair angle shown above, lag screws can be used instead of through-bolts.

BUILDING YOUR DECK

In this chapter, we'll show you how to build a straight-forward, one-level, attached deck with simple stairs and railings. For more complex variations on the basic components, see the chapter beginning on page 61.

Whether the deck you're building is simple or complex, you'll follow the same basic steps: preparing the site for construction; mounting a ledger on the house; building a foundation of footings and piers; installing posts, beams, joists, and decking; and finally, adding stairs and railings. The sequence will be the same if you're building a freestanding deck, but a beam will take the place of the ledger.

If you're an inexperienced carpenter or are planning a very complicated deck, you may want to enlist the help of a professional. For tips on making this decision and on working with professionals, turn to page 58.

Before you begin, you'll want to make sure you have the tools for the job; starting opposite, we'll show you those you'll be most likely to need, as well as the necessary safety gear.

The simplest deck to build is one that is low to the ground. For higher decks, you may need to lift heavy beams above your head as shown here. In this chapter, we'll explain how to do this safely.

TOOLS AND SAFETY

Pictured on the next two pages are the tools you'll find most useful for your deck-building project. Most are standard tools that you may already have. If you decide to add tools to your collection, buy the best quality you can afford. They will pay for themselves in accuracy and durability, and are also safer than the bargain-basement variety. Some specialized tools can be rented, such as a power digger for footing holes or a power miter saw for making angled cuts.

Before you begin, make sure you have the necessary safety equipment on hand. Working with pressure-treated wood requires special precautions—be sure to read the safety information on page 95.

 PLAY IT SAFE

WORKING WITH POWER TOOLS

When using a new power tool, always read the owner's manual carefully and follow all the safety directions.

To guard against shock, power tools must be either double-insulated or grounded. Double-insulated tools offer the best protection. These tools contain a built-in second barrier of protective insulation; they are clearly marked and should not be grounded (they'll have two-prong plugs only).

Since most of your work will take place outdoors, you'll have to take special precautions against shock. A ground-fault circuit interrupter (GFCI)—either built into the outlet or the portable type—is essential. A GFCI will cut the power within 1/40 of a second after a leak in current.

Always use the shortest extension cord you can for the job. A very long cord can overheat, causing a fire hazard.

SAFETY EQUIPMENT

Protective headgear
Wear a hard hat when working under the deck and when working with others in close quarters.

Eye protection
Wear goggles, safety glasses, or a face mask to operate power tools and any striking tool. They should be made of scratch-resistant, shatterproof plastic that won't fog, and must fit comfortably. Glasses with side-guards are best for heavy-duty work; goggles are good for dust, but may scratch more easily.

Protective footwear
Sturdy work boots or shoes—especially models with steel toes—protect your feet from dropped blades, tools, or lumber; puncture-proof insole protects from stepped-on nails.

Respiratory protection
Wear a respirator to prevent breathing harmful vapors such as from finishes or preservatives. Interchangeable cartridges and filters are rated for special requirements. Disposable painter's dust mask can protect you from heavy sawdust; essential when cutting pressure-treated wood.

Hearing protection
Wear earmuff protectors (most effective) or earplugs when operating a power tool for any length of time; high noise levels can be painful and can cause permanent damage.

Hand protection
Wear all-leather or leather-reinforced cotton work gloves to handle wood. Wear rubber gloves when applying wood preservatives and other caustic products.

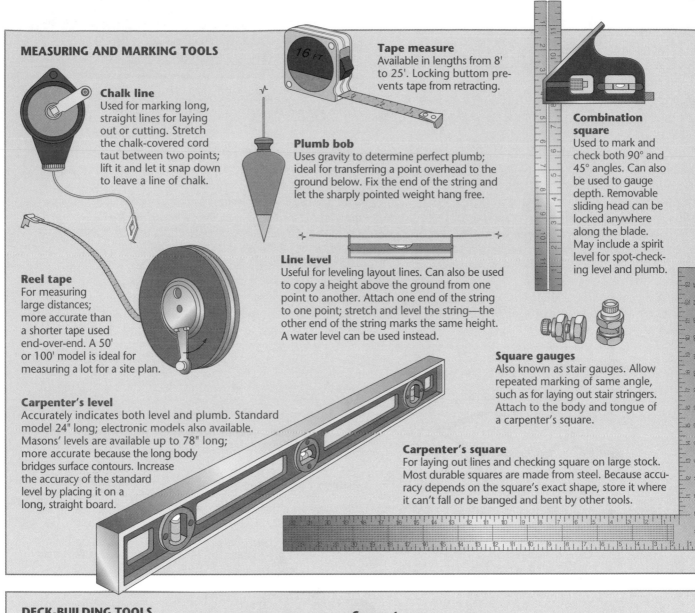

MEASURING AND MARKING TOOLS

Chalk line
Used for marking long, straight lines for laying out or cutting. Stretch the chalk-covered cord taut between two points; lift it and let it snap down to leave a line of chalk.

Reel tape
For measuring large distances; more accurate than a shorter tape used end-over-end. A 50' or 100' model is ideal for measuring a lot for a site plan.

Carpenter's level
Accurately indicates both level and plumb. Standard model 24" long; electronic models also available. Masons' levels are available up to 78" long; more accurate because the long body bridges surface contours. Increase the accuracy of the standard level by placing it on a long, straight board.

Tape measure
Available in lengths from 8' to 25'. Locking buttom prevents tape from retracting.

Plumb bob
Uses gravity to determine perfect plumb; ideal for transferring a point overhead to the ground below. Fix the end of the string and let the sharply pointed weight hang free.

Line level
Useful for leveling layout lines. Can also be used to copy a height above the ground from one point to another. Attach one end of the string to one point; stretch and level the string—the other end of the string marks the same height. A water level can be used instead.

Combination square
Used to mark and check both 90° and 45° angles. Can also be used to gauge depth. Removable sliding head can be locked anywhere along the blade. May include a spirit level for spot-checking level and plumb.

Square gauges
Also known as stair gauges. Allow repeated marking of same angle, such as for laying out stair stringers. Attach to the body and tongue of a carpenter's square.

Carpenter's square
For laying out lines and checking square on large stock. Most durable squares are made from steel. Because accuracy depends on the square's exact shape, store it where it can't fall or be banged and bent by other tools.

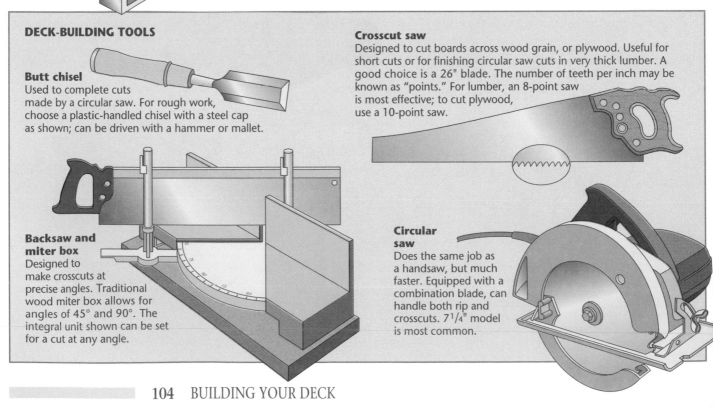

DECK-BUILDING TOOLS

Butt chisel
Used to complete cuts made by a circular saw. For rough work, choose a plastic-handled chisel with a steel cap as shown; can be driven with a hammer or mallet.

Backsaw and miter box
Designed to make crosscuts at precise angles. Traditional wood miter box allows for angles of 45° and 90°. The integral unit shown can be set for a cut at any angle.

Crosscut saw
Designed to cut boards across wood grain, or plywood. Useful for short cuts or for finishing circular saw cuts in very thick lumber. A good choice is a 26" blade. The number of teeth per inch may be known as "points." For lumber, an 8-point saw is most effective; to cut plywood, use a 10-point saw.

Circular saw
Does the same job as a handsaw, but much faster. Equipped with a combination blade, can handle both rip and crosscuts. 7 1/4" model is most common.

DECK-BUILDING TOOLS (continued)

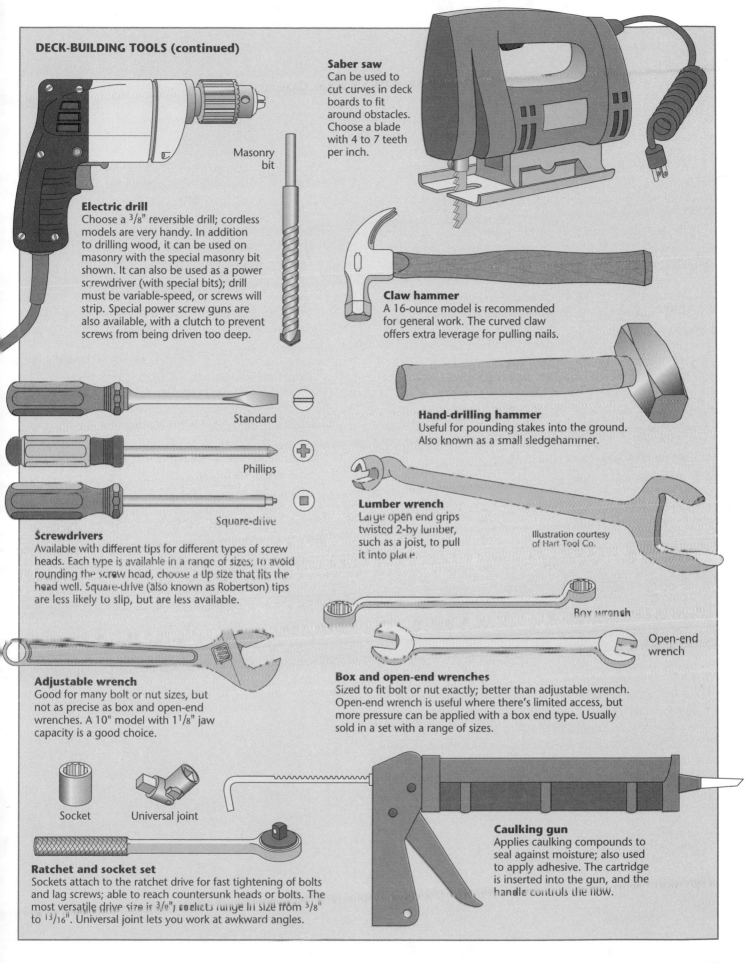

Electric drill
Choose a $3/8$" reversible drill; cordless models are very handy. In addition to drilling wood, it can be used on masonry with the special masonry bit shown. It can also be used as a power screwdriver (with special bits); drill must be variable-speed, or screws will strip. Special power screw guns are also available, with a clutch to prevent screws from being driven too deep.

Masonry bit

Saber saw
Can be used to cut curves in deck boards to fit around obstacles. Choose a blade with 4 to 7 teeth per inch.

Claw hammer
A 16-ounce model is recommended for general work. The curved claw offers extra leverage for pulling nails.

Standard

Phillips

Square-drive

Screwdrivers
Available with different tips for different types of screw heads. Each type is available in a range of sizes; to avoid rounding the screw head, choose a tip size that fits the head well. Square-drive (also known as Robertson) tips are less likely to slip, but are less available.

Hand-drilling hammer
Useful for pounding stakes into the ground. Also known as a small sledgehammer.

Lumber wrench
Large open end grips twisted 2-by lumber, such as a joist, to pull it into place.

Illustration courtesy of Hart Tool Co.

Box wrench

Open-end wrench

Adjustable wrench
Good for many bolt or nut sizes, but not as precise as box and open-end wrenches. A 10" model with $1\,1/8$" jaw capacity is a good choice.

Box and open-end wrenches
Sized to fit bolt or nut exactly; better than adjustable wrench. Open-end wrench is useful where there's limited access, but more pressure can be applied with a box end type. Usually sold in a set with a range of sizes.

Socket

Universal joint

Ratchet and socket set
Sockets attach to the ratchet drive for fast tightening of bolts and lag screws; able to reach countersunk heads or bolts. The most versatile drive size is $3/8$"; sockets range in size from $3/8$" to $13/16$". Universal joint lets you work at awkward angles.

Caulking gun
Applies caulking compounds to seal against moisture; also used to apply adhesive. The cartridge is inserted into the gun, and the handle controls the flow.

PREPARING THE SITE

Before you begin to build, you should take care of any drainage problem in the area where you plan to build your deck, and undertake any required grading of your lot. These tasks may be impossible once the deck is in place. In addition, a very severe drainage problem can undermine the stability of your deck. Now is also the time to take steps to prevent any future weed growth under the deck.

Drainage: To determine whether you have a drainage problem, check your site for permanent wet spots or standing water, particularly around downspouts. If you think there may be a problem, it would be wise to get advice from your building department or a professional landscape architect or designer. A professional can help you decide what kind of drainage system is in order, where to locate it, and where to direct the water. A proper drainage system should carry water away from the house and the deck's substructure, particularly the footings. A drainage ditch dug in the direction of the runoff is generally best for diverting unwanted water. However, you have to take care not to direct the water onto a neighbor's property. Instead, direct it into a dry well or into the city's storm sewer system.

Where runoff is slight, a ditch filled with gravel alone is sufficient. Otherwise a ditch with a bed of gravel and a drainage pipe *(opposite page)* might be needed.

On a hillside site, your concern won't be so much getting rid of standing water as channeling surface runoff to minimize erosion. To take care of this job, you can call on a professional to build a concrete trough or spillway running downhill from a collection point, as shown below. If runoff is heavy, a flare at the downhill end of the trough will make the water flow more slowly and spread it over a wider area; the area should be planted to hold the soil in place. In extreme cases, a pile of large rocks may be needed at the outlet of the trough to prevent erosion.

If your site has a severe drainage problem, consult a soils engineer.

Grading: The ground around your house should slope away from the house at about 1 inch in 10 feet. If your lot is improperly graded, you'll want to correct the problem before you build your deck. Though decks typically bridge a yard's bumps and dips, it may be necessary to knock down a high spot or two to control the deck's height. In most situations, this is just a matter of shifting earth from a higher area to a lower one. Remember that footings should always go on undisturbed soil; soil that has been filled and repacked will tend to settle.

ASK A PRO

HOW CAN I CONTROL WEEDS UNDER MY DECK?

Most low-level decks naturally prohibit weed growth by blocking out the light and air the plants need to grow. However, you may want to take extra precautions to prevent weeds. Many commercial weed killers are harmful for the environment, and pose a hazard for small children or pets who may crawl around under the deck. Instead, you can cover the ground with black 6- to 10-mil polyethylene sheeting or landscape fabric (available at gardening centers). Hold sheeting down with bricks or stones and poke some holes in it to allow for drainage. To hold down landscape fabric, cover it with a layer of gravel.

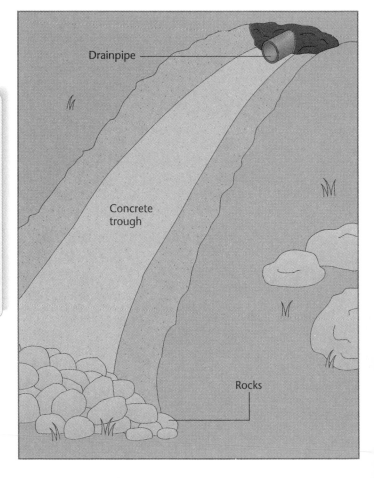

Drainpipe

Concrete trough

Rocks

Creating a drainage ditch

TOOLKIT
• Pointed shovel

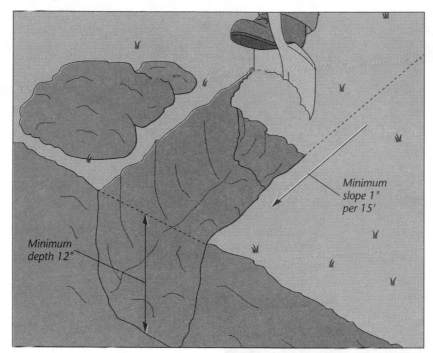

1 ▶ Digging the trench

Shovel out the earth in your chosen location, digging at least 1' deep. The trench should slope in the direction you want the water to run, at a minimum of 1" for every 15'.

Minimum slope 1" per 15'

Minimum depth 12"

2 ▶ Setting the pipe

Shovel a 1" bed of drain rock into the trench (the rock should be smooth and rounded and about 1½" in diameter). Then lay 4" perforated drainpipe on top of the gravel, with the holes pointing down.

You may want to line the ditch with landscape fabric before placing the rock to keep dirt from clogging the pipe.

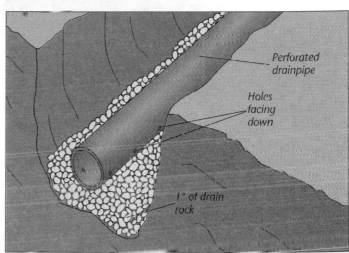

Perforated drainpipe

Holes facing down

1" of drain rock

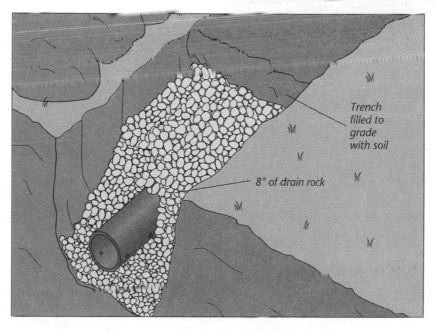

Trench filled to grade with soil

8" of drain rock

3 ▶ Filling in the trench

Cover the pipe with drain rock to within 2" of grade (if you've used landscape fabric, fold it over top of the rock). Then, fill in with soil up to grade level. Pack the soil lightly with the back of your shovel.

MOUNTING A LEDGER

Unless a deck is freestanding, a ledger connects it to the house or some other solid structure. To bear the weight of the deck, the ledger must be attached to something very solid—either masonry or wood fram-ing. In the case of a wood frame house (including a stuc-coed house), fasten either to the foundation wall or to framing members inside the house wall. If the ledger is at about the same level as the interior floor, attach it to the house's band joist as shown at left, or to the blocking between the joists. In a situation where the ledger will be between floors, you can fasten it to wall studs.

A ledger can be fastened to a brick wall with masonry anchors if the brick is solid and well attached. (Note that a thin brick facade does not offer enough support, and you'll have to go right through it into solid framing.) If your brick wall is crumbling or the bricks are loose, you'd be well-advised to opt for a freestanding deck, supported by another beam rather than by a ledger.

When you determine a ledger's height outside a door, allow for the decking's thickness and, if joists will rest on top of the ledger, the joist height. Also be sure to drop the deck's surface 1 inch below the interior floor level to keep water and snow out.

Nails alone are never sufficient for securing a ledger. Always use either lag screws or bolts.

If you're attaching the ledger to a wood frame house, you'll have to protect the house wall from water that could collect between it and the ledger. Either space the ledger out from the wall with washers as shown, or cover the joint with flashing as explained on page 110. Washers should not be used with stucco because they will tend to sink into the surface of the wall.

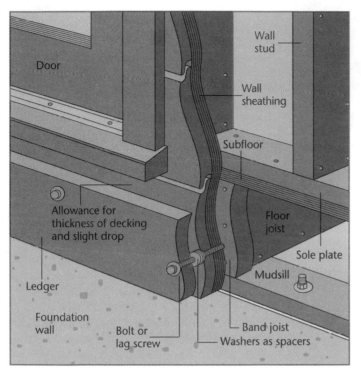

Labels: Door; Wall stud; Wall sheathing; Subfloor; Allowance for thickness of decking and slight drop; Floor joist; Sole plate; Mudsill; Ledger; Foundation wall; Bolt or lag screw; Band joist; Washers as spacers

ASK A PRO

SHOULD I REMOVE THE SIDING TO INSTALL A LEDGER?

Siding should be removed if it is a type that doesn't rest flat against the house sheathing or framing. An example would be the clapboard siding shown near right. The pressure of the ledger will crush the siding, resulting in a less solid and attractive joint. Wood shingle, vinyl, and aluminum siding should also be removed.

If the siding does rest flat against the sheathing, as in the case of the rabbeted-bevel siding shown at far right, it can be left in place. If the outside surface of the siding is not smooth, add a shim as shown to provide a smooth surface for the ledger; the shim can be made of a piece of siding turned upside down.

NOTE: If you're removing siding and you want the joists to sit on top of the ledger, you'll have to use a 4-by ledger so it will stick out far enough past the siding to support the joists.

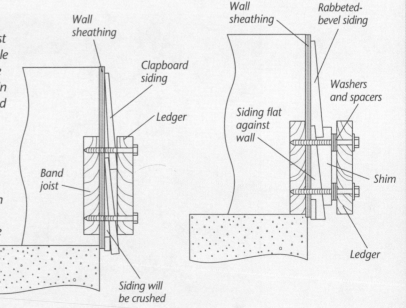

Labels: Wall sheathing; Clapboard siding; Ledger; Band joist; Siding will be crushed; Wall sheathing; Rabbeted-bevel siding; Washers and spacers; Siding flat against wall; Shim; Ledger

Attaching a ledger to framing

TOOLKIT

- Tape measure
- Carpenter's level
- Water level and chalk line (optional)
- Carpenter's square
- Circular saw
- Chisel and hammer or mallet
- Hand-drilling hammer or claw hammer
- Electric drill
- Caulking gun
- Socket wrench

1 Marking and removing siding

Measure down the correct distance from the door threshold. Outline the section of siding to be removed. The top line should be the thickness of the decking plus 1/2" above the top of the ledger. If the end joists are going to overlap the ledger, allow for the thickness of the joists at each end of the ledger. To draw the top and bottom line, use a long carpenter's level. Alternatively, mark two points along each line with a water level and join them with a chalk line. Use a square to mark the end lines.

Cut the siding along the lines using a circular saw. Adjust the depth of the blade to cut through the siding only. For making vertical cuts in clapboard siding, rest the saw on a 2x4 guide. Finish the corners of the cut with a chisel.

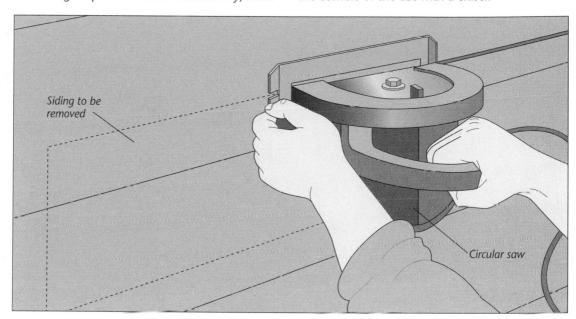

Siding to be removed

Circular saw

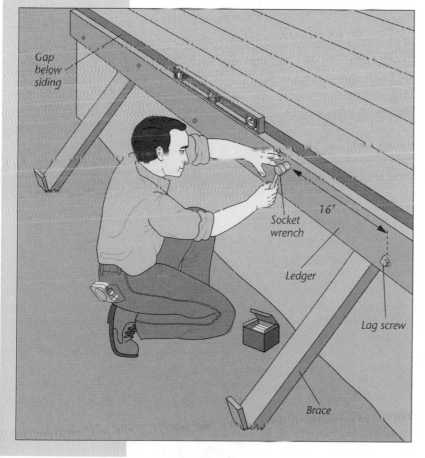

Gap below siding

Socket wrench

16"

Ledger

Lag screw

Brace

2 Fastening the ledger

First, brace or nail the ledger in place as shown. Then, if you can reach the inside of the house framing to add washers and nuts, drill all the way through the framing and fasten the ledger with 1/2" carriage bolts. Otherwise, drill a clearance hole for a lag screw through the ledger and then a pilot hole into the framing. For a stucco house, you'll need to switch to a masonry bit between the two steps. In any case, plan to set 1/2" lag screws at each end of the ledger and stagger the rest up and down every 16" as shown.

Remove the ledger and pack each pilot hole with silicone caulk for moisture protection. Run lag screws into the ledger until the points protrude about 1/2". (The lag screws you use should be long enough to penetrate the framing to a minimum of 1 1/2", or as specified by local codes.) If you're not planning to use flashing, slip several large washers onto each lag screw, to leave a space of about 3/8" between the house wall and ledger. Working with a helper, line up the lag screws with the holes in the wall and then tighten them in place using a socket wrench.

Attaching a ledger to masonry

TOOLKIT
- Carpenter's level, or water level and chalk line
- Tape measure
- Electric drill
- Claw hammer
- Socket wrench

Drilling and fastening

A ledger hung from a concrete or brick wall should be made of treated lumber. To anchor the ledger, you must use special masonry fasteners *(page 99)*. Your best choice is expanding anchor bolts.

First, mark a level line indicating the top of the ledger. Use a long level, or mark two points with a water level and join them with a chalk line. Drill holes for the expanding anchor bolts, staggering them every 16" as shown.

Tap in the anchor bolts with a hammer. Then, with a helper, hold the ledger in place, making sure it's level, and tap it with a hammer to indent the bolt locations on it. Remove the ledger and drill holes through it at the marks made by the bolt tips. Or, you can measure and transfer the bolt locations to the ledger.

Push (or hammer) the ledger onto the bolts; add washers and nuts, and tighten.

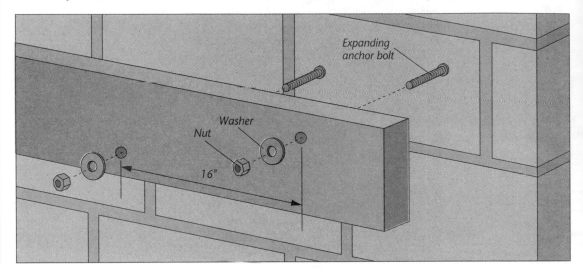

Flashing the ledger

TOOLKIT
- Tin snips
- Circular saw for stucco
- Prybar (optional)
- Caulking gun

Installing the flashing

For a wood frame house, you'll have to keep moisture from penetrating the space between the ledger and the house wall. If you haven't spaced the ledger out with washers, you'll need to flash the ledger. This should be done before you fasten the joists in place. You can use either aluminum or galvanized sheet metal Z-flashing. Cut the flashing to length with tin snips.

If the wall is finished with wood siding or shingles, slip the flashing up under the edge of the siding and then pull it down to rest on the top of the ledger *(right, above)*. You may need to pry up the siding a bit to get the flashing in. You don't have to fasten the flashing—the siding will hold it in place. If you've removed a section of siding, caulk the ends of the flashing where they butt up against the adjoining siding. Use silicone rubber sealant.

For a stucco wall, use flashing with a crimped top edge (you'll have to have it made at a sheet metal shop). Cut a groove in the siding with a circular saw equipped with a masonry blade. Fit the crimped edge of the flashing into the groove *(right, below)*. Caulk the edge of the flashing where it enters the groove.

Be sure to caulk any end joints between adjacent pieces of flashing as well as the edge where the flashing butts up against the bottom of the door threshold.

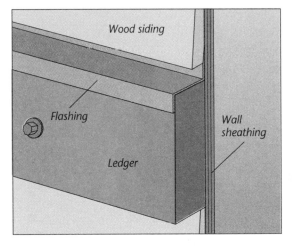

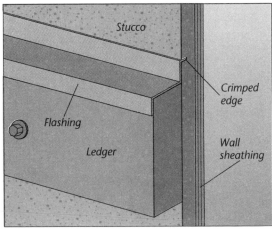

BUILDING THE FOUNDATION

The weight of the deck must be supported on a solid foundation. This is usually a series of concrete piers and footings. First you'll lay out the location of each footing and dig the holes. Then, the next step is to mix the concrete, cast each footing, and put the piers in place. The depth of footings is governed by code; refer to the information on page 69 and double-check with your local building department.

LAYING OUT THE FOUNDATION

Because each pier holds a post (or a beam), pier placement is governed by post locations which are in turn determined by beam and joist spans. When you designed your deck you will have worked out all these measurements using the span tables (*page 73*); now you can simply transfer them to the ground.

A rectangular or square deck should have corners that are truly square—at precise 90° angles. And if such a deck is attached to the house with ledgers, its sides should be perpendicular to the house wall. To be sure the corners are square you should lay out a triangle with sides 3 feet, 4 feet, and 5 feet. Keep in mind that this triangulation method works with any multiple of 3-4-5, such as 6-8-10 (as illustrated below), 9-12-15, or even 12-16-20. For maximum accuracy, use the largest multiple possible.

1 **Setting up string lines perpendicular to the house**

Hammer a nail into the top of the ledger board at a point in line with the center of the corner post, and then set up a batterboard about 18" past the location of this post. Stretch a string from the ledger to the batterboard, using a carpenter's square to check that it is about 90° to the ledger.

To check for exact square, measure 6' along the ledger and mark the point. Then put a mark on the string with a piece of tape 8' away from the ledger. Move the string back and forth along the batterboard until the diagonal is exactly 10', as shown below; hammer a nail into the top of the batterboard at the spot you've established. Leave the nail sticking out a couple of inches, and attach the string to it.

Repeat this procedure at the other end of the deck to set up a second string line.

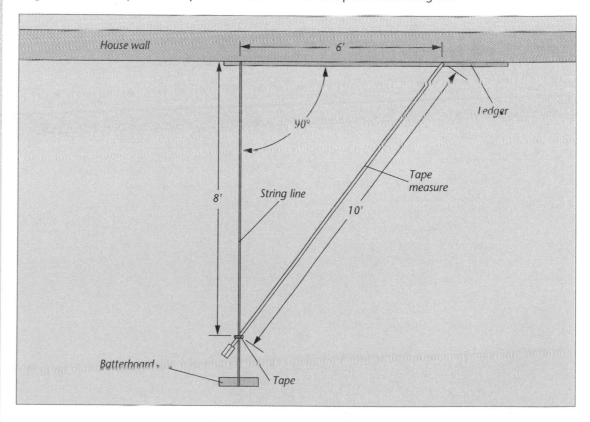

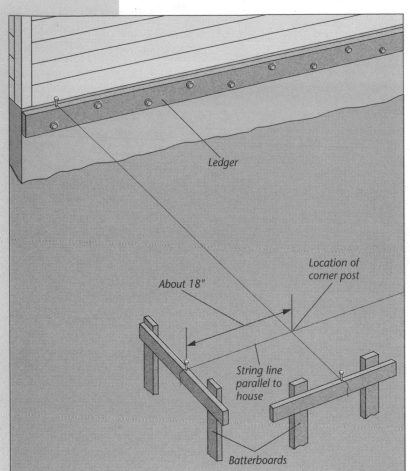

Ledger

About 18"

Location of corner post

String line parallel to house

Batterboards

2 ► Setting up a string line parallel to the house

Measure away from the house along each string line and use tape to mark a point corresponding to the center of each corner post; make sure the tape measure is level. Set up two more batterboards near the ones set up in the previous step and stretch a string between them parallel to the ledger board, crossing the original strings *(left)*. Make sure to keep the batterboards about 18" away from the post locations so they don't get in the way when you're digging. You should now have a complete rectangle formed of string lines and the house wall.

The point where the strings cross indicates the center of each corner post. To make sure everything is exactly square, measure both diagonals and adjust the strings until the diagonal distances are identical *(below)*.

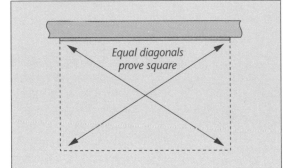

Equal diagonals prove square

3 ► Marking post locations

Use a plumb bob to transfer the point where the strings cross to the ground; mark the point with a small flag (drive a large nail through a piece of colored tape), a stake, or lime. Then, measure along the strings and plumb down to mark all the other post locations as shown; make sure your tape measure is level.

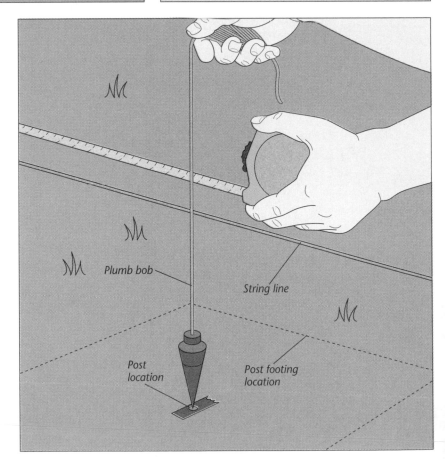

Plumb bob

String line

Post location

Post footing location

WORKING WITH CONCRETE

To build your deck's foundation, you'll need to mix and cast concrete. Be prepared for a day of hard work and a night of sound sleep; there's nothing like working with concrete to test your stamina.

You'll need a large container to mix your concrete. Mortar boxes can be purchased, but you can substitute a large plastic bin, a wheelbarrow, or even a sheet of plywood. You'll want a square shovel to measure the concrete ingredients. The best tool for the actual mixing is a mortar hoe, but you can use a shovel instead. A mason's trowel, or other small trowel, is needed to test the consistency of your concrete mixture.

BUYING CONCRETE

How you buy your concrete will depend on the size of your project and how much time and energy you have. You can choose among the following options:

Bulk dry ingredients: If your project is large, you can save money by mixing your own concrete from dry ingredients—a formula is given at right. You'll find that this method is even more economical if you haul the materials yourself.

Dry prepackaged mix: This is by far the most convenient option for a small job. The dry ingredients come premixed and require only the addition of water.

Haul-it-yourself plastic mix: Some dealers provide trailers you can haul with your car. These trailers contain about 1 cubic yard of concrete with the water already added. They may have a revolving drum that mixes the concrete as you go. CAUTION: Be sure the tires and brakes on your vehicle are in good condition and that both your vehicle and trailer hitch are capable of taking the weight.

Ready-mix: Commercial ready-mix trucks can deliver a large quantity all at once. This is the best choice for a very large job. NOTE: Many concrete suppliers require that you buy a certain minimum amount.

MIXING AND CASTING CONCRETE

For a small project, the simplest method is to mix the concrete by hand. For jobs that require casting 3 cubic feet or more at once, you may want to rent an electric mixer. Instructions are given for both methods on the next page.

When mixing your own concrete, start by making a trial batch. Work a sample of this batch with a trowel. The concrete should slide off the trowel, but not run freely. You should be able to smooth the surface of the concrete with your trowel so that the large pieces of aggregate are submerged. All the aggregate at the edges of the sample should be evenly coated with cement. If your mix is too stiff and crumbly, add a little water. If it's too wet and soupy, add some cement-sand mixture, in the proportions required by your recipe. Once you've made the adjustments necessary to achieve the

---

A CONCRETE FORMULA

All proportions are by volume. The sand should be clean concrete sand (never beach sand); the aggregate should range in size from quite small to about $3/4$ inch in size. The water should be drinkable—neither excessively alkaline nor acidic, nor containing organic matter. The following is a good formula to use for concrete footings:

- 1 part portland cement
- $2^1/2$ parts sand
- $2^1/2$ parts stone or gravel aggregate
- $1/2$ part water

To know how much concrete to buy, refer to the table below. The figures given are for 10 cubic feet of finished concrete and include 10% extra for waste. Note that the final volume is less than the sum of the ingredients because the smaller particles fit in among the larger ones. If you order bulk materials sold by the cubic yard, remember that each cubic yard contains 27 cubic feet.

INGREDIENTS FOR 10 CUBIC FEET OF CONCRETE	
Bulk dry materials	Portland cement: 2.6 sacks Sand: 5.8 sacks Aggregate: 6.5 cubic feet
Dry prepackaged mix	20 60-pound bags
Ready-mix	.41 cubic yards

---

right consistency, record how much extra water or cement-sand mix you've added and maintain these proportions for the other batches.

Each footing must be cast at once—one batch of concrete should not be allowed to dry before the next one is placed. So, for large footings, you'll probably want to have one person mixing while other people push the loaded wheelbarrows and place the concrete. If you're working with a ready-mix truck, you'll need extra hands to move the concrete from the truck to the site.

Mixing concrete by hand

TOOLKIT
• Square shovel
• Mortar hoe

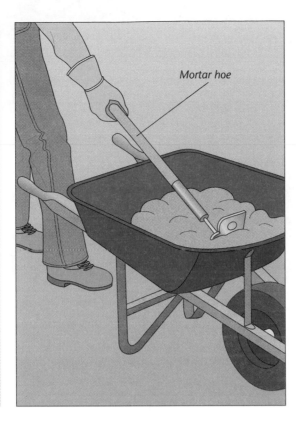

Mortar hoe

Using a mortar hoe

To mix by hand, you can put the materials in a wheelbarrow or mortar box—for small batches —or on a piece of plywood—for large batches— and use a mortar hoe or shovel as your mixing tool. To measure out the ingredients, use shovelfuls for the dry ingredients. Use a pail for the water after finding out how many shovelfuls it takes to fill your pail.

First, spread the sand and cement on the mixing surface. Using a rolling motion, mix these ingredients until the color is even. Add the aggregate; again, mix until the color is even. Finally, scoop out a hole in the middle of the dry ingredients and add the water.

Work around the edges of the puddle with the hoe or shovel, slowly rolling the dry ingredients into the water. Take particular care not to slop the water out of the wheelbarrow (or off the platform), since escaping water may weaken the batch by carrying particles of cement with it.

Work in small batches; this will make mixing easier and give you more control over proportions.

Mixing concrete by machine

TOOLKIT
• Carpenter's level
• Square shovel

Using a concrete mixer

Set up the mixer close to your supplies of sand and aggregate so you can feed the machine directly from the piles. Wedge the machine firmly in place and make sure that it is level. CAUTION: Concrete mixers can be dangerous—be sure to read the safety information opposite.

First, with the mixer off, add the coarse aggregate and half the water. Then, turn on the machine to scour the drum. (If the machine is gas-powered, you'll need to warm it up.) Next, add the sand, and all but about 10% of the water. Then, add the portland cement. When the mixture is an even color and consistency, add the rest of the water. Mix for at least two minutes or until the mixture has reached a uniform appearance.

Measure the dry ingredients by equal shovelfuls as you add them; never put the shovel inside the mixer while it's in operation.

Concrete mixer

WORKING WITH A CONCRETE MIXER

Be sure to follow all the safety measures for the concrete mixer you're using. Never reach into a rotating mixer drum with your hands or tools. Wear tight-fitting clothes, a dust mask, and goggles, and keep away from the moving parts. Do not look into the mixer while it's running—check the mix by dumping some out.

Mixers are either electric or gas-powered. To avoid shock hazard, an electric mixer must be plugged into a ground-fault circuit interrupter (GFCI) outlet. The mixer should have a three-prong grounding-type plug; use only an outdoor-rated three-prong extension cord.

Do not run an electric mixer in wet or damp conditions and be sure to cover it with a tarpaulin when not in use.

The engine on a gasoline-powered mixer should be fueled from the proper type of can for storing and pouring flammable fuel. Add fuel only when the engine is off and has cooled down; close the fuel container tightly after fueling. Any fuel spills should be wiped up immediately. While the engine is running, don't work or stand where you must breathe the exhaust fumes. And never run the mixer in an enclosed space.

CASTING FOOTINGS AND PIERS

The simplest method for building foundations is to cast a footing and set a precast concrete pier block on top of it *(below, left)*; a selection of pier blocks is shown on page 69. However, you can also cast your own piers *(below, right)*. This will give you a greater choice of post anchors—a selection is shown on page 100.

If you live in a cold climate, it's very important to sink the footings deep in the ground, so that the bottom of the footing is about 6 inches below the frost line. Then you'll need a way to connect this concrete footing to the surface. The easiest way to do this is to use commercial fiber form tubes. The tubes can reach down to the footing, and extend at least 6 inches up above grade to form a pier.

When casting concrete footings and piers, you may need to add steel bars for reinforcement. Requirements for steel reinforcements are governed by local codes.

In general, footings must be cast on solid, undisturbed soil, but in some areas gravel is required below the footing for drainage—check your building code. Before mixing the concrete, remove the string lines and dig the postholes to the depth required by code—usually 6 inches below the frost line. Cast the concrete, then replace the string lines to align the pier blocks or post anchors.

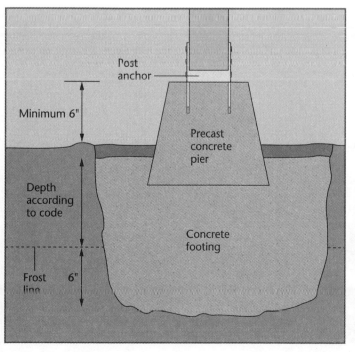

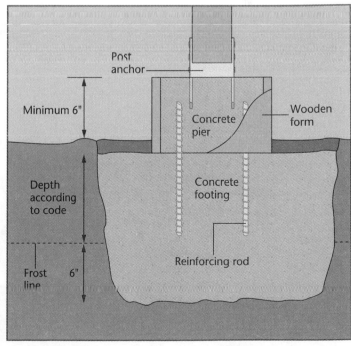

Casting footings and adding piers

TOOLKIT
- Mortar hoe or shovel for placing concrete
- Carpenter's level
- Shovel

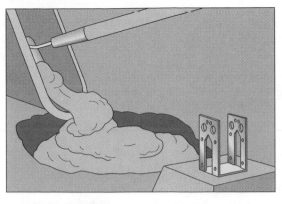 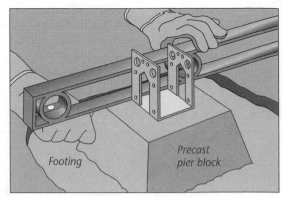

Footing

Precast pier block

Using precast piers

First soak the pier blocks with a hose. Then, cast the footings to the depth and size required by the local building code (above, left); the top of the footing should be about 1" below grade. Wait a few minutes—until the concrete has stiffened enough to support the piers—then position the pier blocks and level them in both directions (above, right). Cover the exposed part of the footings with earth.

Casting footings and piers together

TOOLKIT
- Tape measure
- Mortar hoe or shovel for placing concrete
- Claw hammer
- Carpenter's level
- Shovel

For wooden forms:
- Screwdriver for assembling forms (optional)

For fiber form tubes:
- Crosscut saw for cutting tubes
- Hand-drilling hammer for driving stakes

Using wooden forms

Use plywood or scrap lumber for forms. If you will be casting several piers over a period of weeks, hinge the forms so they can be opened and reused. Otherwise, use duplex nails for easy disassembly. Reinforce large forms with wire.

First, cast all the footings to the depth and size required by local codes; their tops should be about 1" below grade. Wait a few minutes, then set and level the piers' forms over the wet concrete footings, inserting steel reinforcing rods, if required, to strengthen the link between the footings and the piers. Fill the pier forms with concrete; use a straight board to level the concrete flush with the tops of the forms. Immediately embed a metal post anchor (page 100) in each wet concrete pier. Before the concrete begins to stiffen, check for plumb: Hold a carpenter's level against two adjacent sides of a short length of post material placed in the post anchor. Use your string line to make sure the anchor is in line with or at right angles to the direction the beam will run.

After the concrete has begun to set, cover the top of the footings with earth. Leave the forms on the new piers while the concrete cures. To protect curing piers from direct sun or hot, dry weather, cover with newspapers, straw, or burlap sacks; keep the covering moist for at least a week so the piers will dry slowly.

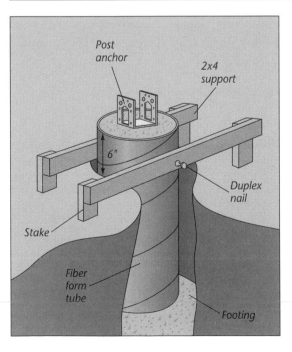

Post anchor

2x4 support

6"

Duplex nail

Stake

Fiber form tube

Footing

Using fiber form tubes

The hole for the fiber form tube must be splayed at the bottom to allow the concrete to spread out to form a footing. Cut the tube to length and suspend it; it should be about 6" above the bottom of the hole and extend at least 6" above grade. Hold the tube at the right height by nailing a staked 2x4 laid on edge to each side of the tube using duplex nails as shown. For taller columns, also brace the tubes as you would brace a post (page 118).

Insert steel rods if necessary and place the concrete. Smooth off the top with a piece of wood and immediately insert a metal post anchor; align it using the string lines. Make sure the anchor is level by inserting a piece of post material in the anchor and checking it for plumb with a carpenter's level.

Fill in the hole around the tube with earth. Cover the top of the tube with newspaper, straw, or burlap and keep it damp for at least a week. Then peel off the part of the tube that sticks up above the ground.

INSTALLING POSTS AND BEAMS

Once the concrete footings have cured for at least a week, you can begin to erect posts and beams. The following directions assume a standard beam-on-post configuration; if you're building a deck with railings, benches, or overheads, consider the extended-post assemblies illustrated on page 68. For a low-level deck, 4-by beams can be placed directly on the piers and held in place with post anchors.

For a stable, level substructure, posts must be measured accurately and cut squarely. If your deck is house-attached, start with the posts farthest from the house. For a free-standing deck, begin with the posts supporting two opposite edges; then do any intermediate posts.

To measure posts, remember: An attached deck's height is defined at the ledger line along the wall, while for a freestanding deck, you mark the height on one post first and then use it to establish the height of the other posts.

A solid deck must slope slightly for surface drainage; drop the otherwise level marks away from the house about 1 inch for every 10 feet.

Tall posts may need bracing; to determine whether this is required for your deck, turn to page 70.

ASK A PRO

HOW DO I PROTECT THE CUT ENDS OF LUMBER FROM ROT?

If you're working with pressure-treated wood, you'll need to apply wood preservative to any cut ends and drilled holes. This is because the preservatives used in pressure treatment don't always penetrate all the way through the wood.

The most common wood preservative you can apply yourself is copper naphthanate; it has a bright green color. There are also clear preservatives available, but these generally protect against rot only, and not against termites. You may want to choose a preservative that also contains a water repellent. (For a discussion of water repellents and other wood finishing products, turn to page 166.)

Apply the preservative with a brush, or by dipping the end of the wood directly into the preservative. Continue to apply preservative until the wood is saturated. Always wear rubber gloves when working with preservatives.

Cutting and setting posts

TOOLKIT
- Tape measure
- Combination square
- Circular saw
- Crosscut saw
- Carpenter's level
- Water level or line level
- Hand-drilling hammer for driving in stakes
- Claw hammer
- Electric drill and wrenches if using bolts

1 ▸ Plumbing and marking the post

First cut a post 6" to 12" longer than the estimated finished length. Have a helper hold the post firmly in place on its anchor; then plumb it, using a carpenter's level—check two adjacent sides. Use a line level *(page 104)* or a water level to mark the post at the same height as the bottom of the joists; this will usually be at the bottom of the ledger, but if you're using a ledger that is wider than the joist, you'll need to measure down from the top of the ledger to find where the bottom of the joists will fall.

To use the water level, make sure the tube is free from air bubbles. Tape one end of the tube to the ledger and adjust the other end against the post until the level of the water at the taped end is at the right height. The water at the post will be at the same level: Mark this point on the post. Repeat for all the posts.

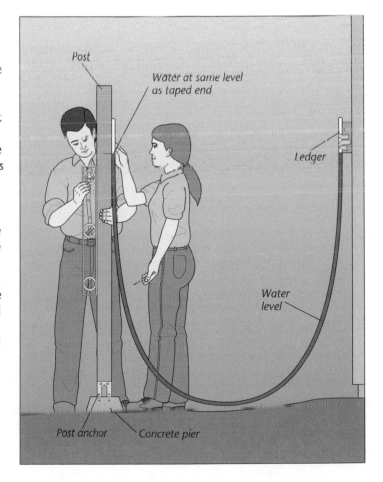

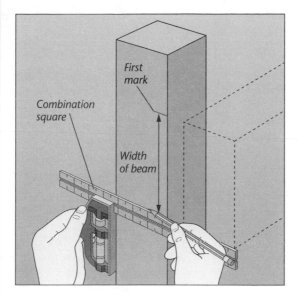

2 **Marking the cutting line**

If the joists will sit on top of the beam, subtract the width of the beam from the post height, as shown. Measure down the actual height of the beam from your first mark. Using a combination square, mark this new height on all four sides of the post.

If the joists will butt against the beam, extend the first mark all around the post using a combination square. If the beam is wider than the joists, first move the mark down to where the bottom of the beam will fall.

3 **Cutting the post**

First, take the post down. Cut around all four sides of the post with a circular saw, following the lines that you marked. Finish the cut with a crosscut saw, as shown. Repeat for each post.

If you're using pressure-treated wood, you must treat the cut ends as described on the previous page—the uncut end of the post should face down in order to take full advantage of the pressure treatment. Fasten a post cap to the top of each post.

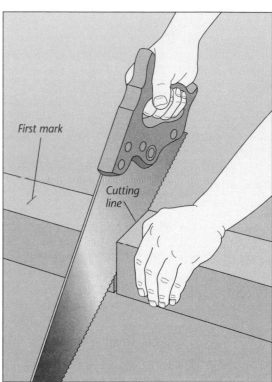

4 **Setting the posts**

Before moving the first post into position, drive stakes into the ground to hold two braces on adjacent sides of the post. Use 1x2s or 1x3s for the braces, and set the stakes far enough from the end of the post to allow the braces to reach midway up the post at a 45° angle (be sure you cut the braces long enough). Nail the braces to each stake; to allow the brace to pivot, use only one nail.

Seat the post squarely in its anchor and check for plumb, using a carpenter's level on two adjacent sides. Nail the braces to the post, keeping the post plumb. Then nail or bolt the post to its anchor. Finally, drive additional nails into each brace to secure the posts until the beams are seated.

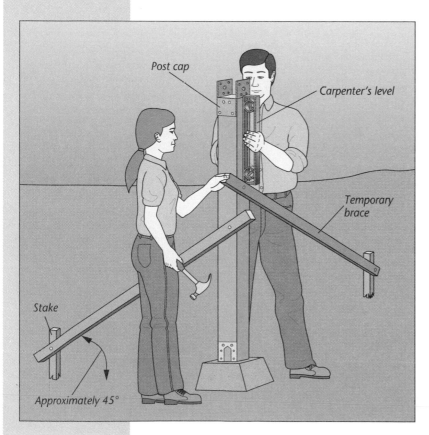

Installing beams

TOOLKIT
- Claw hammer if using nails

OR

- Electric drill and wrenches if using bolts

1 ▶ **Seating the beam**

Beams that sit directly on piers are nailed or bolted to the metal post anchors. Beams seated on low posts can be lifted into position easily, but raising heavy beams onto fairly tall posts is another story.

Before seating a beam, sight down it to find the crown, if any. When you mount the beam on the posts, place it crown side up unless the beam is cantilevered at one or both ends, in which case the crown side should face down.

To seat a heavy beam, drag it beside the posts, then slip a short length of 2x4 under one of its ends. With a helper, lift the 2x4 to raise that end of the beam into the post cap *(right)*. Temporarily nail the beam with one nail through one of the top holes in the post cap, then lift and place the other end. (With four people, you can lift both ends of the beam into position at once.) This is heavy work—be sure of your footing, and always wear a hard hat.

Nail the beam to the post cap. If you're using bolts, mark the bolt positions through the holes in the anchor; then, lift the beam out of the cap and set it on a piece of wood on top of the cap. Drill from one side until the drill tip shows on the other side; then finish the hole from the other direction.

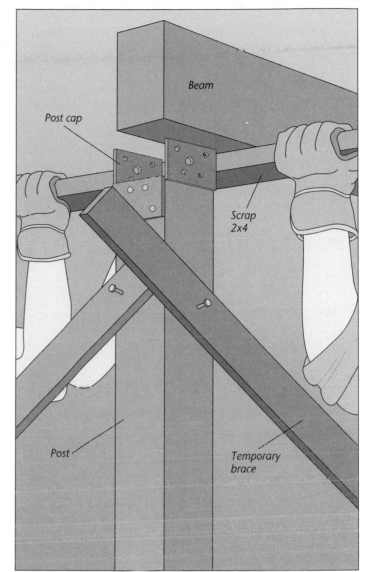

Beam

Post cap

Scrap 2x4

Post

Temporary brace

ASK A PRO

HOW CAN I MAKE A BUILT-UP BEAM?

A typical built-up beam consists of 2-by lumber nailed together with ¹/₂-inch pressure-treated plywood spacers in between. The total thickness of the beam will work out to 3¹/₂ inches—the same as the actual size of a 4-by post. Place the spacers 24 inches apart on center and nail the beam together with four nails through each spacer from each side as shown. The spacers should be pointed at the top to prevent water from collecting.

If you must make a long beam from shorter lengths, stagger the end joints; each joint should fall over a post. Sight along each piece to find the crown; align the crowns on the same side.

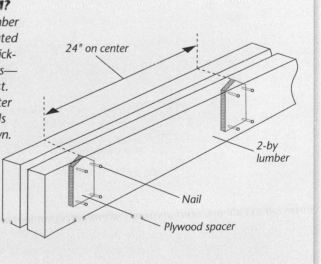

24" on center

2-by lumber

Nail

Plywood spacer

2 Splicing beams

If you must join two beams end to end, be sure the joint falls over a post. You can make the splice with metal straps or gusset plates that can be purchased, or with cleats made of 2-by stock. You can also make the splice with special post caps such as the one shown below *(right)*.

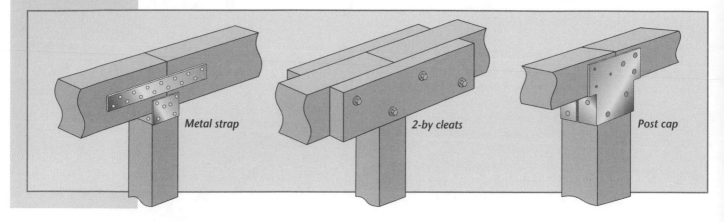

Metal strap

2-by cleats

Post cap

Bracing posts

TOOLKIT
- Combination square
- Circular saw or crosscut saw
- Claw hammer
- Electric drill
- Wrenches

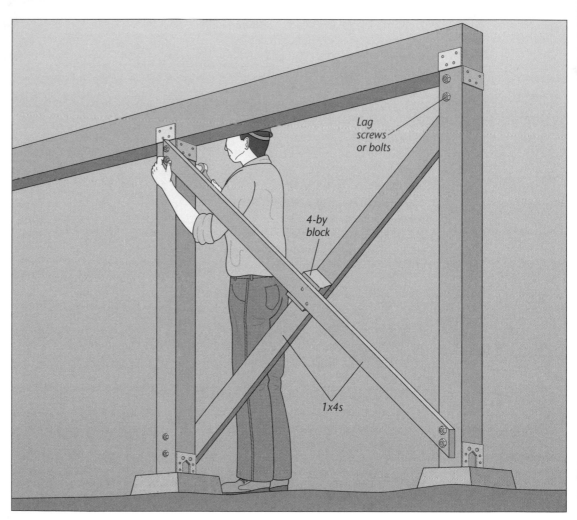

Lag screws or bolts

4-by block

1x4s

Attaching the brace

If your deck's posts will require bracing, the bracing should be installed before you add any more weight to the structure. Mark the individual cross braces in position, then cut them on the ground.

Temporarily nail the braces in place and then drill pilot holes for bolts or lag screws and fasten the ends of the bracing. To provide support and fill the space between the braces, insert a 4-by block where they cross as shown above and nail it in place.

If you're using pressure-treated wood, don't forget to treat the cut ends and drilled holes with wood preservative.

INSTALLING JOISTS

nce the posts and beams are in place, you're ready to lay out the joist positions and attach the joists to the ledger and beams.

Joist locations can be marked on the ledger and opposite beam using a storyboard as explained below. Or, you can lay out the joist locations on both members at once before the ledger is installed. The most secure method for fastening joists is to use metal framing connectors *(page 100)*—joist hangers when the joists hang off the beam or ledger and seismic anchors when they sit on top.

Laying out joist locations

TOOLKIT
- Tape measure
- Combination square

1 ▶ Marking the ledger
Starting at one outside corner of the ledger (or of one beam for a freestanding deck), mark the location of the first joist with an X. For standard 16" centers, hook your tape measure over the end of the beam or ledger and measure 16" to the edge of the next joist; draw a line with a combination square *(right)* and then an X to indicate which side of the line the joist will fall on. The last interval may be less than 16".

Plan to double up joists around deck openings. To do this, continue to space the joists every 16" but add an extra joist next to one of the regular ones.

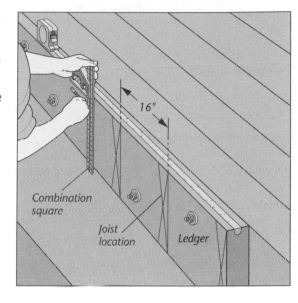

Combination square

Joist location

Ledger

16"

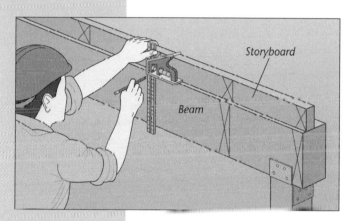

Storyboard

Beam

◀ 2 Marking the opposite beam
Once the layout is complete, transfer the same spacing to the opposite beam, using a storyboard—a marked length of scrap lumber *(left)*.

If you're splicing joists by overlapping them, as described on the next page, the layout on the opposite beam must be offset 1½" to allow for the overlap. Mark the edge of the first joist in from the end at 14½"; then mark every 16".

Installing joists

TOOLKIT
- Claw hammer
- Tape measure
- Combination square
- Circular saw

1 ▶ Installing joist hangers
If you're mounting the joists in metal joist hangers, it saves time to get all the hangers in place before mounting any of the joists: Position each hanger so that one side of the opening falls on your layout line and so the joist's top edge will sit flush with the top edge of the ledger or beam (insert a scrap piece of lumber the same size as the joist to align the hanger). Nail this first side to the ledger or beam. Then, squeeze the hanger so it is snug around the scrap of wood, and nail the other side to the ledger or beam. Remove the wood and repeat with each hanger.

NOTE: If the end joist will come flush to the end of the ledger or beam, you won't have room to put a joist hanger. Instead, use an all-purpose framing anchor such as the one shown on page 101.

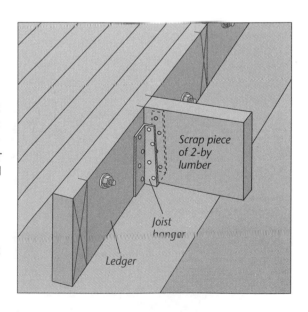

Scrap piece of 2-by lumber

Joist hanger

Ledger

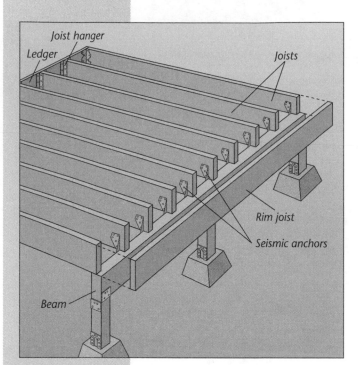

Joist hanger

Ledger

Joists

Rim joist

Seismic anchors

Beam

2 ▎ Fastening joists

Measure the exact distance each joist must span between the beam and the ledger. If the joists will sit in joist hangers, they can be 1/2" short of the proper measurement and still fit. If you find greater discrepancies in distance, you'll have to measure and cut each joist individually; otherwise, you can cut them all to the same length.

If the joists will sit in joist hangers at both ends, simply lift them into place and nail through the hangers into the joists. For joists over 8' long, work with a helper, each lifting one end of the joist. If the joists will sit on top of the ledger or beam, line them up with your marks, and fasten each joist with one seismic or universal anchor. Joists should also be fastened to any intermediate beams.

If you're installing a rim joist, face-nail it through the ends of the joists using three or four 3 1/2" nails at each joist. Any joints in the rim joist must fall at a joist end.

3 ▎ Splicing joists

Where looks aren't important, joists can be spliced together end to end. A splice must be supported by a beam; be sure each joist end bears a full inch on the beam. If several spliced joists are needed, plan to stagger the splices over different beams to avoid weakening the substructure.

The overlap method of splicing (right, above) is the easiest, but it breaks up uniform spacing—throwing off the alignment of decking end joints later on. If you use this method and more than one splice is needed on a full joist length, alternate overlapped sides. For standard 2-by lumber, nail both faces of each splice with six 3" common nails.

To maintain uniform spacing, use wood cleats (right, below) or metal straps or gusset plates.

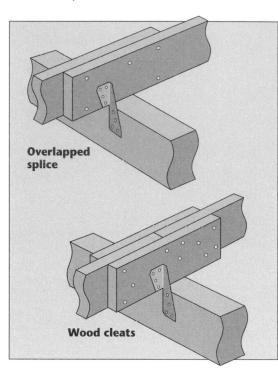

Overlapped splice

Wood cleats

Blocking joists

TOOLKIT
• Tape measure
• Chalk line
• Combination square
• Circular saw
• Claw hammer

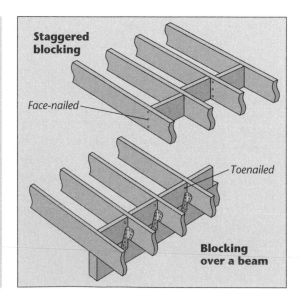

Staggered blocking

Face-nailed

Toenailed

Blocking over a beam

Fastening the blocking

Locations and requirements for blocking are discussed on page 70. Snap a chalk line across the joists at the relevant points, then work your way across the joists, measuring and listing the lengths of blocking you'll need to cut from the joist material. Cut and code all the blocks to correspond to their locations.

It's easiest to alternate the blocks, staggering them from one side of the chalk line to the other (left, above). By using this technique, you'll be able to face-nail the blocks—use 3 1/2" nails.

When you install blocks over beams (left, below) you can face-nail one end of each block, but the other end will have to be toenailed—use 2 1/2" nails.

CONSTRUCTING STAIRS

Stairs can be attached to the deck before or after the decking is laid. However, it's usually more convenient to build the stairs first, so you can use them to get up to work on top of the deck.

Specifications for stairs as well as a number of designs are shown starting on page 76. In this section, we will show you how to build the traditional style of outdoor stairway, which is one supported by stringers with sawtooth notches for steps. Stringers should be made of knot-free, split-free 2x12s, and this lumber should be pressure treated.

To assemble the stairway, you'll need to lay out and cut the stringers and then fasten them securely both to a foundation and to the deck's substructure. The final steps are to add treads, and if you wish, risers—but remember that traditional outdoor steps have open risers.

Building the stairway

TOOLKIT
- Shovel
- Mortar hoe (optional)
- Electric drill
- Wrench
- Carpenter's square and stair gauges
- Circular saw
- Crosscut saw
- Tape measure
- Combination square
- Claw hammer

1 ▶ Casting the foundation

To support the bottom of the stringers, cast a concrete pad about 4" deep. First dig a trench, then fill it with concrete, taking care to place the concrete on undisturbed soil. (Turn to page 113 for information on working with concrete.) Cover the concrete with burlap, straw, or newspaper, and keep the covering moist for about a week.

If you're using a kicker plate, as shown at right, set J-bolts in the concrete while it's still wet, leaving about 2½" exposed. When the concrete has cured, drill holes for the bolts in a pressure-treated 2-by board. Place this kicker plate over the exposed bolts, add washers, and tighten the nuts on the outside.

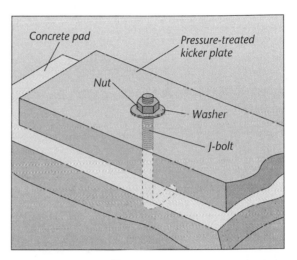

Concrete pad
Pressure-treated kicker plate
Nut
Washer
J-bolt

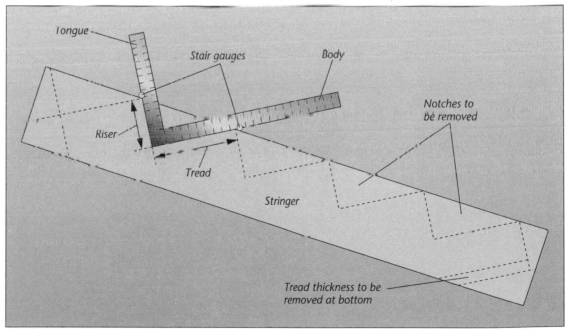

Tongue
Stair gauges
Body
Riser
Tread
Notches to be removed
Stringer
Tread thickness to be removed at bottom

2 ▶ Marking the first stringer

Using stair gauges, mark the riser dimension on the tongue of a carpenter's square; then mark the tread dimension on the square's body. Line up the gauges with the top edge of the stringer, as shown above, and trace the outline of the riser and tread onto the stringer. Move the square along to mark the rest of the notches. Because the tread's thickness will add to the height of the first step, you'll need to subtract this amount from the bottom of the stringer (above).

If you're using a kicker plate, notch the bottom of the stringer to fit around it (page 80).

3 ▶ Cutting the stringer

Cut out the notches with a circular saw, finishing each cut with the crosscut saw. Once your pattern is cut, hold it in position against the deck to check the alignment; if it's satisfactory, use the stringer you've just cut as a template for marking the others, as shown at right.

First stringer as template

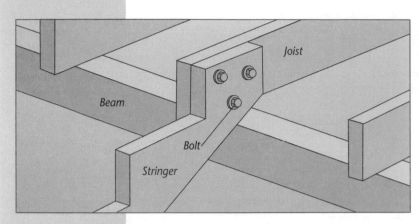

Joist
Beam
Bolt
Stringer

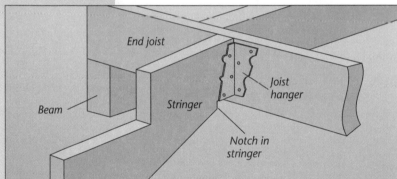

End joist
Joist hanger
Beam
Stringer
Notch in stringer

4 ▶ Fastening the stringers

If the ends of the joists are exposed on the side of the deck where you want to install the stairs, bolt the tops of the stringers to them as shown *(left, above)*. Otherwise, attach the stringers to the end joist or rim joist using joist hangers—the stringers will have to be notched to accommodate the connector *(left, below)*.

Next, you have to attach the bottom of the stringers to the concrete pad. If you have installed a kicker plate, fasten the stringers to it with universal anchors or angle irons. If you haven't used a kicker plate, attach the stringers to the pad with angle irons. Using a masonry bit, drill holes for expanding anchor bolts or expansion shields *(page 99)* and tap the bolts or shields into the concrete. Fasten the angle irons to the pad and then to the stringer with lag screws.

5 ▶ Adding treads and risers

When measuring and cutting risers and treads, remember that the bottom edge of a riser tucks behind the back of the tread, and the forward edge of the tread overlaps the riser below it. Giving each tread a 1" nosing (a projection beyond the front of the riser) lends a more finished appearance to the stairway.

Nail risers to the stringers first, using 3$\frac{1}{4}$" nails, then nail the treads to the stringers; use two nails at each end of the boards. Use a nail to space the tread boards $\frac{1}{8}$" to $\frac{3}{16}$" apart (use the same spacing as you will use for the decking). Finally, working under the stairway, fasten the bottom edges of the risers to the backs of the treads.

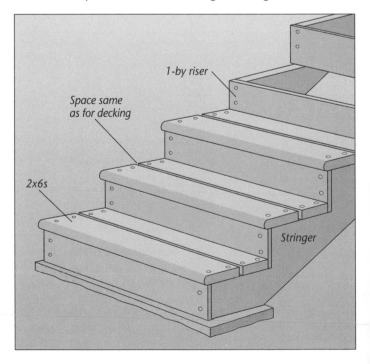

1-by riser
Space same as for decking
2x6s
Stringer

LAYING DECKING

A deck's surface is the most visible part of a deck and often the easiest part to build. Laying the decking usually involves simply measuring, cutting, and nailing, but knowing a few tricks will ensure a quality job.

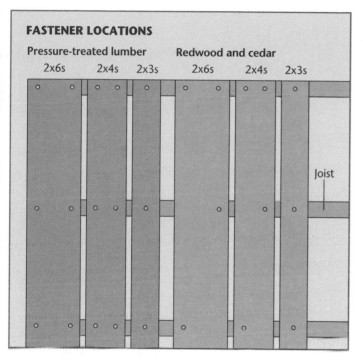

FASTENER LOCATIONS

Pressure-treated lumber			Redwood and cedar		
2x6s	2x4s	2x3s	2x6s	2x4s	2x3s

Joist

Both ends of every length of decking must be supported by a joist or beam. If the decking won't reach across the deck's full length, butt-join the ends of the pieces over joists using one of the joint patterns shown on page 63. Each board should span at least three joists.

Decking can be fastened to joists with nails, screws, or special clips. Nailing is the cheapest and quickest method, but screws hold better. For information on choosing the right fastener, turn to page 97. For extra holding power, you can apply construction adhesive in addition to the nails or screws—it is applied to the joists with a caulking gun before the deck boards are laid down. Keep in mind that the boards will be nearly impossible to remove once the adhesive sets up—a potential problem if you must make repairs later.

Fasten deck boards at every support point (joist or beam). Fastening requirements depend on whether you are using pressure-treated lumber, or redwood or cedar, since redwood and cedar are less prone to warping. Consult the illustration at left for the correct pattern for your lumber.

If you intend to apply a finish to your deck boards, it's a good idea to do this before you install them. This allows you to get at all sides of the boards. For information on finishing, turn to page 166. If you're using pressure-treated lumber, be sure to brush the cut ends with wood preservative.

Installing the decking

TOOLKIT
• Tape measure
• Combination square
• Circular saw
• Caulking gun for adhesive (optional)
• Claw hammer, screw gun, electric drill with screwdriver bit, or pneumatic nailer
• Nailset
• Chalk line

1 ▶ Preparing the substructure

Before you lay the decking, finish any remaining work on the substructure. Now is the time to apply a protective finish to the substructure (page 166). You can cover the joists with roll flashing to protect them even more.

If you'll be installing any support posts for railings, benches, or overheads that will come up through the middle of the decking, it's simplest to install these posts first (right) and then fit the decking around them; you may need to install cleats on the sides of the posts to support the ends of the decking. Make sure to add extra joist blocking around openings for trees or anything else that penetrates the deck's surface, as shown on page 66.

On a low-level deck, install any wiring (page 151) or plumbing (page 156) now, before the area under the deck becomes inaccessible.

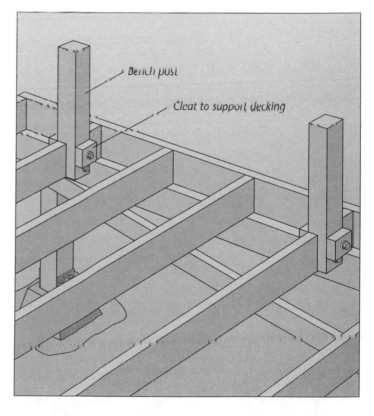

Bench post

Cleat to support decking

2 Laying the first board

Decide on the joint pattern *(page 63)* and cut the deck boards to length. Then start by laying one length of decking across the joists, beginning at the wall if the deck is attached to the house. Align the board parallel to and about ⅛" from the house wall. It's fine to let the decking boards run long, since you'll be cutting them off later. If the appearance of the lumber permits, lay the boards bark side up to minimize checking and cupping. (The bark side is the convex side of the board, the outer side of the tree's growth rings.)

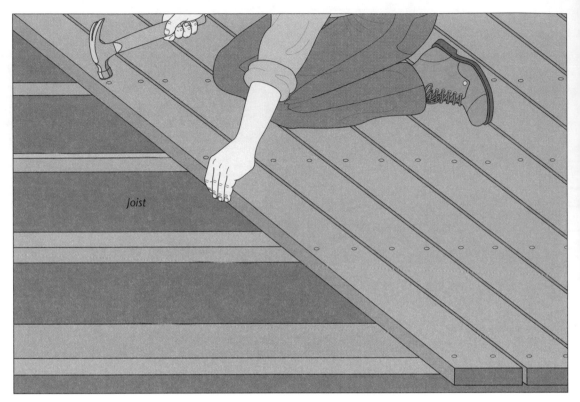

Joist

3 Fastening the boards

Fasten the boards over each joist, following the pattern given on the previous page. If you're using adhesive in addition to the nails or screws, apply it to each joist with a caulking gun before setting the boards in place.

If you're using nails, hand-nailing is favored for a top-quality job. While an air-powered nail gun (pneumatic nailer) fastens down decking much more quickly than a person wielding a hammer, the nails it shoots tend to sink into the wood a little too far, especially in the softer woods such as redwood and cedar.

As you hammer in each nail, be careful not to crush the wood's surface with the final blows. Stop hammering as soon as the nail is flush with the decking; then, when the deck is completely nailed, set the head of each nail slightly below the surface with a large nailset.

To drive screws, use a screw gun or an electric drill with the appropriate bit.

 ASK A PRO

HOW DO I AVOID SPLITTING THE BOARDS?

To keep from splitting boards when nailing, try this carpenter's trick: Blunt each nail's tip with a light tap of the hammer, then angle the nails slightly toward the board's center. If this doesn't prevent splitting, you may have to drill pilot holes three-quarters of the diameter of the nail shanks.

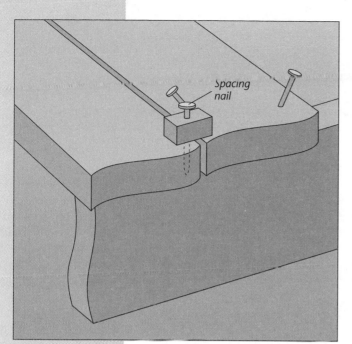

Spacing nail

4 Spacing the boards

Some types of decking require ⅛" to ³/₁₆" spaces between the edges of the deck board to allow for proper drainage and the natural expansion and contraction of the wood—turn to page 63 to determine whether your decking requires spaces. (The ends of boards should be butted in all cases.) Measure the deck precisely and, if possible, pick the spacing that will allow you to fit the boards without needing to rip any to fit.

You can use 3½" nails to space decking quickly and uniformly. Use two nails, one at each end of the board already secured; set the nails snugly against the board and push their tips into the joist. Push the next board against the nails, then secure it. Pull out the two spacing nails and repeat the process with the remaining boards.

To keep the nail from slipping down, you can nail it through a small block of wood as shown at left. For different spacing, use a larger or smaller nail or cut a spacer from wood. Commercial plastic spacers designed for decking are also available.

ASK A PRO

CAN I USE A BOWED BOARD?

When you're laying decking, you'll find that some boards are too bowed to align properly. To correct the problem, first nail each end of the board to the joists. Then start the nails at their proper locations in the bowed area, over the joists. If the board bows away from the neighboring board, drive the chisel into the joist at the bow's apex (angle the chisel slightly), then pry the board into place and nail (right, above). If it bows toward an adjoining length of decking, force a chisel between the two and pry the bowed board outward, then nail.

Special tools are available to lever bowed boards into place. The tool shown at right (below) has a jaw that grips the joist; a cam butts up against the board. To use the tool you pull the handle until it's parallel to the joist. The tool then locks in place, leaving both hands free to fasten the board down.

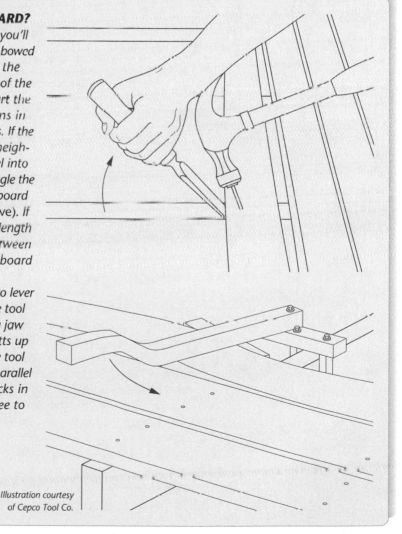

Illustration courtesy of Cepco Tool Co.

5 Placing the last boards

As you fasten decking over the joists, occasionally check the remaining distance to be covered, measuring from both ends of the decking. If possible, readjust the spacing slightly to be able to fit the last board. If a large adjustment will be required, rip the last board to fit—you may need to use a board that is wider than the others in order to fill the space. The last board should fit flush with the rim joist or, if there is none, the ends of the joists.

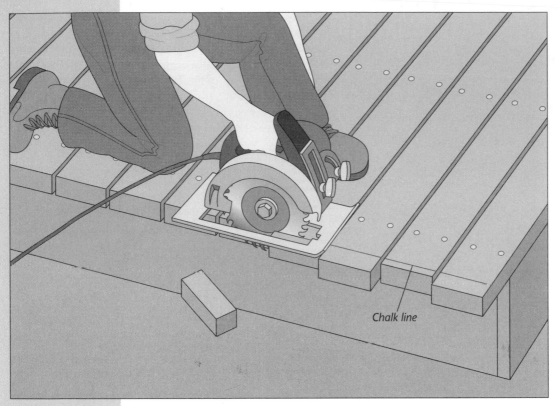

Chalk line

6 Trimming the boards

Once all the boards are nailed down, snap a chalk line carefully along the deck edges and saw along it (you can leave the deck boards cantilevered a couple of inches if you wish). Skilled hands can saw freehand along a chalk line; less experienced builders will want to guide the saw with a length of wood tacked to the deck.

FITTING DECKING AROUND OBSTACLES

Use a compass to copy the contours of the obstacle onto the ends of the deck boards placed right against the obstacle, such as a rock, as shown. Make sure to keep the compass parallel to the deck boards; don't pivot the pencil end as you move along the obstacle. Then cut along your marks with a saber saw. Set the cut ends in place and then mark and cut the other end of each board to fit.

If you have to trim a board along its edge, set it directly on top of the last complete board. Then adjust the compass to the width of the board plus the space between boards (e.g. for a 2x6, $5\frac{1}{2}$ inches plus $\frac{1}{8}$ inch). Copy the contour of the obstacle onto the top board. Cut along the line and fit the board in place.

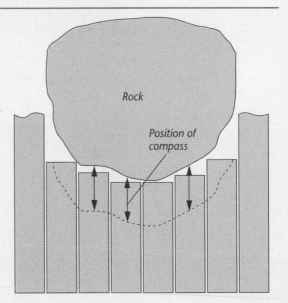

Rock

Position of compass

BUILDING RAILINGS

R ailings that go through the decking are best installed before the decking is laid. Railings attached to the outside of the structure can be installed before or after the decking; depending on your method of attachment, you may need to notch the decking to fit the posts. Make sure your railings meet the local building code requirements for height and maximum space between railings.

Stair railings *(page 77)* are built in the same way as the deck railings.

ASK A PRO

HOW DO I MAKE SURE THE RAILING POSTS ARE ALL NOTCHED IN THE SAME SPOT?

If your railing design calls for fitting rails into dadoes in the posts, it's best to cut all the dadoes at once. Align the ends of the posts and mark them all using a combination square or carpenter's square. Then outline the depth of cut on the outside pieces. Measure the distance from the saw blade to each side of the base plate and clamp a straightedge at this distance to one side of your marks.

Make a cut along one edge of the notch; keep the blade to the waste side of the cut. Reposition the straightedge and make another cut along the other edge of the notch. Then make a series of cuts between the first two. Use a chisel to remove the waste, holding it bevel side down and tapping it lightly with a hammer. You can also use a router to cut the dadoes.

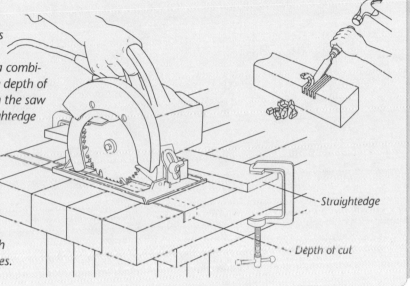

Straightedge

Depth of cut

Assembling the railings

TOOLKIT
• Tape measure
• Combination square
• Circular saw
• Crosscut saw
• Butt chisel
• Electric drill
• Wrenches
• Hammer or screwdriver
• Power miter saw or table saw
• Hand-drilling hammer

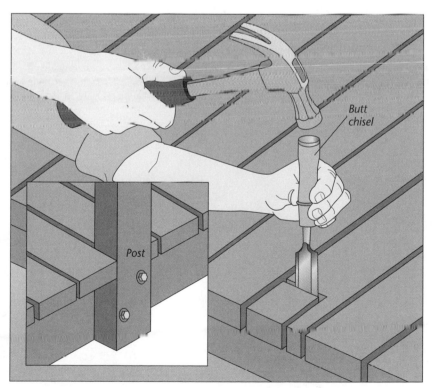

Butt chisel

Post

1 Attaching the posts

Cut the posts to length using a circular saw—for 4x4 posts you may have to finish the cuts with a crosscut saw. If you have to notch the decking, mark the notch and then make the cuts with a butt chisel *(left)*.

Drill holes for bolts and bolt the posts to the deck substructure *(inset)*; you can use any of the attachment methods shown on page 82.

NOTE: If the end of a deck board will be left unsupported, install a cleat on the post for the board to rest on.

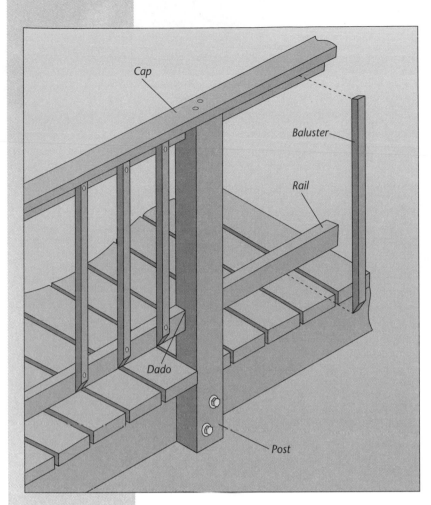

Cap

Baluster

Rail

Dado

Post

2 Completing the railing

First, add the cap, fastening it to each post with two 3" screws, or 3¼" or 3½" nails. Use the longest lumber available so that the cap will be supported by as many posts as possible. At corners, miter the cap (below).

If the rails are set into dadoes in the posts as shown at left, tap them into place and secure them with two 3¼" or 3½" nails. As with the cap, use the longest lumber available.

Use a power miter saw or table saw to cut the balusters to length; you can also bevel the ends as shown. Fasten the balusters with one 3" nail or screw at each end. To avoid knocking the rails off as you hammer, hold them in place with a hand-drilling hammer.

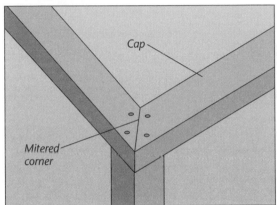

Cap

Mitered corner

ATTACHING RAILS BETWEEN POSTS

Some railing designs require the horizontal rails to be placed between the posts rather than attached to the outside of the posts. To do this, you can use one of the methods illustrated below: angle irons, wooden cleats, or dadoes. Dadoes provide the most elegant results; notch all the posts at once as explained on the previous page. If you set the rails in dadoes, toenail them with one 2½-inch casing nail at each joint to keep them from sliding out.

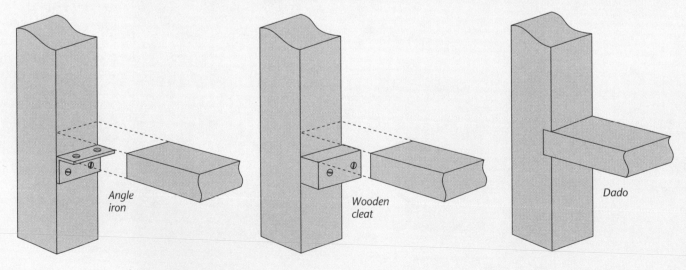

Angle iron

Wooden cleat

Dado

DECKING OVER A PATIO

If you have a damaged or unsightly patio, the easiest and least expensive way to update it may be to cover it with a new deck. As long as you use approved materials and practices, most building codes will allow a simple, low-level deck to be laid directly on a concrete patio. You can also build a deck over a brick patio if the bricks are firmly bonded to a concrete base.

Make sure the patio slopes away from the house, since the deck will follow this slope. The patio must be clean and dry; remove any loose material. Support for the decking is provided by sleepers—typically 2x4s laid flat—fastened directly to the patio. To ensure decay resistance, the sleepers must be made from lumber treated for ground contact.

Building the deck

TOOLKIT
- Tape measure
- Combination square
- Circular saw
- Claw hammer
- Caulking gun or powder-actuated nailer
- Screw gun (optional)
- Electric drill and wrench (optional)

Covering a patio

Begin by laying the sleepers every 24". If the patio is sloped for runoff, be sure to run the sleepers in the direction of the slope, so water won't pool behind them. If your patio has low spots, shim the sleepers with small redwood wedges or cedar shingles. Place the shims about 24" apart and tap one in from each side of the sleeper.

If the sleepers are in contact with the slab along most of their length, you can fasten them with adhesive. Take the sleepers up and glue the shims in place. Then run a bead along any part of the sleeper that will contact the slab, as well as at the points that will contact the shims. Set the sleepers back in place. If the slab is very uneven, fasten

the sleepers with expanding anchor bolts *(page 99)* spaced about every 4'.

You can also fasten sleepers by "shooting" them down with a powder-actuated tool, a gunlike device that blasts concrete nails into the concrete or brick—be sure to read the safety information on the next page. These tools are available from tool rental centers.

Fasten decking to sleepers just as you would attach the boards to joists *(page 125)*. Joints must fall over sleepers, and each deck board should span at least three sleepers *(below)*. If you wish, add a 1x6 or 1x8 fascia to cover the ends of the sleepers.

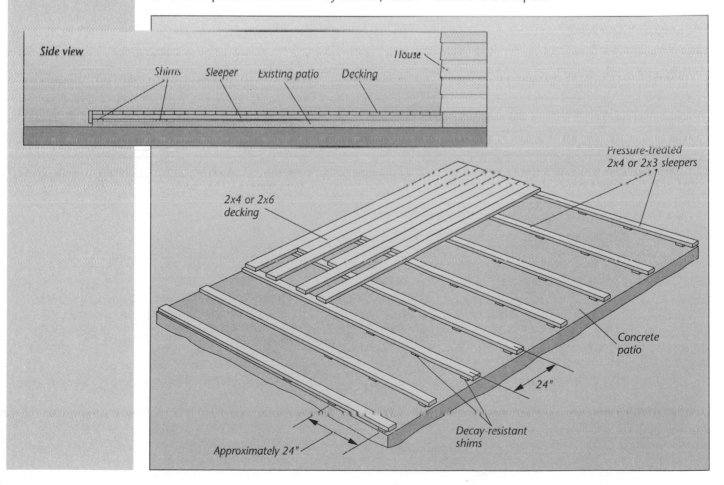

Side view

Shims   Sleeper   Existing patio   Decking   House

Pressure-treated 2x4 or 2x3 sleepers

2x4 or 2x6 decking

Concrete patio

24"

Decay-resistant shims

Approximately 24"

Extending past a patio

If you want to run your deck beyond the perimeter of the patio slab, the sleepers must be 4x4s supported by a typical arrangement of footings and piers. If you use precast pier blocks *(page 69)*, you'll have to bury them so their top surfaces will be level with the patio. Secure the sleepers directly to the piers, and then to the slab with angle irons *(shown below)*, adhesive, or expanding anchor bolts.

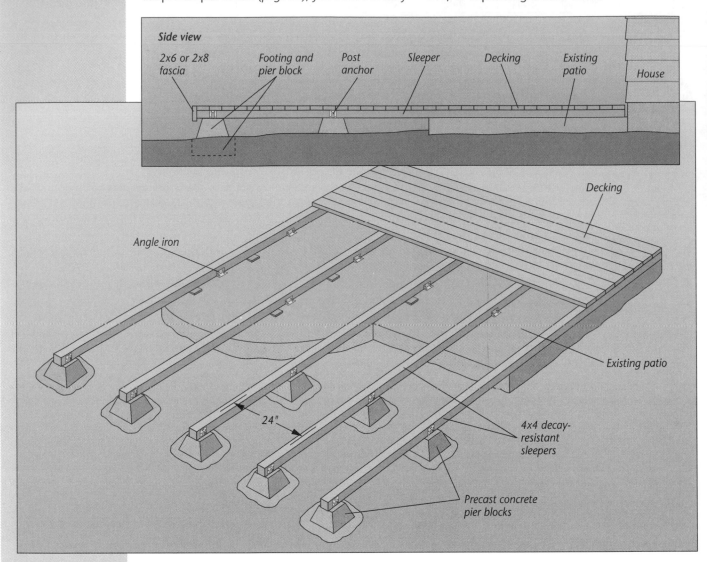

Side view

2x6 or 2x8 fascia

Footing and pier block

Post anchor

Sleeper

Decking

Existing patio

House

Angle iron

Decking

Existing patio

24"

4x4 decay-resistant sleepers

Precast concrete pier blocks

PLAY IT SAFE

WORKING WITH A POWDER-ACTUATED TOOL

Powder-actuated tools are used to fasten into concrete. They use a cased "load" (blank cartridge with gunpowder) as an energy source and they fire a special nail-like fastener. The type of tool available from rental centers is fired with a trigger. Another type, available for purchase from hardware stores, must be hit with a hammer to work.

Misuse of these tools can lead to serious injury. By law, training is required to operate them. This training is provided either by the tool rental center or the local tool distributor. Always follow all safety information provided with the tool; this will include information on safe loading, operation, and storage.

Fragments of the concrete slab might fly up into your face when you're using a powder-actuated tool—be sure to wear safety goggles or a face shield. Hearing protection is also highly recommended.

BUILDING A WATERPROOF DECK

There are two special situations that call for waterproof decks: rooftop locations, and second-story decks that must shelter the area below.

ROOFTOP DECKS

If your roof is flat, you can build a deck directly on it. An attached garage or single-story wing provides a perfect opportunity to build a deck adjacent to an existing room. If you need a stairway or ladder for access, be sure it meets local codes.

Because a roof deck places additional loads on your house roof, walls, and foundation, you'll need to consult an architect or engineer to see if the framing will have to be reinforced. You'll also want to hire a professional to install the waterproof surface—typically felt with hot-mopped asphalt. You may then be able to install the walking surface yourself; some options are shown at right—wooden deck modules, concrete pavers (you can use brick instead), or an elastomeric coating.

Wood deck modules rest on 2x4 or 2x3 pressure-treated sleepers. To avoid penetrating the roofing materials these modules are left unfastened. This also allows you to remove them to repair or clean the roof. Make sure roof drainage isn't obstructed; if necessary, cut or drill slots in the sleepers.

If you decide to install pavers or bricks on the waterproof surface, you may want to hire a professional to do the job.

Bitumen rubber or elastomeric coatings such as silicone rubber provide both the waterproof membrane and the walking surface; they can generally be installed by the do-it-yourselfer. Some roofs are surrounded by a low parapet. Regardless of whether there is a parapet, your roof deck must have railings. These can be tricky to attach securely—consult a professional.

SECOND-STORY DECKS

Waterproof second-story decks are built on a plywood base. You can install the plywood yourself (next page), but hire a professional roofer to waterproof the surface. You can then install any of the walking surfaces described above for rooftop decks. If you plan on installing masonry, check with an architect or engineer to make sure your deck structure can handle the extra weight.

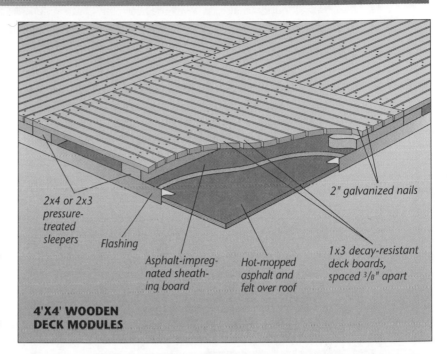

2x4 or 2x3 pressure-treated sleepers

Flashing

Asphalt-impregnated sheathing board

Hot-mopped asphalt and felt over roof

2" galvanized nails

1x3 decay-resistant deck boards, spaced 3/8" apart

4'X4' WOODEN DECK MODULES

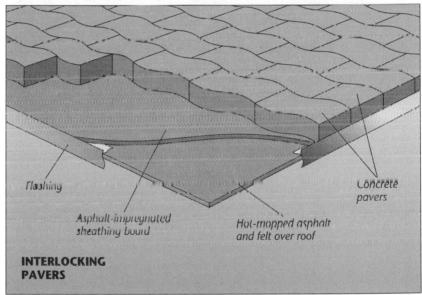

Flashing

Asphalt-impregnated sheathing board

Hot-mopped asphalt and felt over roof

Concrete pavers

INTERLOCKING PAVERS

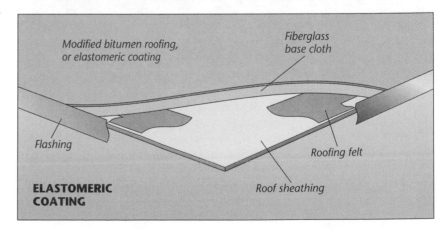

Modified bitumen roofing, or elastomeric coating

Fiberglass base cloth

Flashing

Roofing felt

Roof sheathing

ELASTOMERIC COATING

1 Providing for drainage

Solid-surface decks must be designed for proper rain runoff: The surface must slope toward gutters that carry away the rainwater. Create a slope (typically 1/4" per foot) as shown below.

If your design calls for joists that run in line with the planned runoff, you can rip each one to a taper to create the proper pitch. Because this method leaves the undersides of joists level, it's often the best technique to use if you think you'll attach a ceiling below some day. If you decide to rip joists in this way, be sure that the narrowest part of the joist won't be less than the minimum size specified in the span tables *(page 73)*. Another way to keep the lower edges of joists level is to nail thin, tapered boards, angled toward the planned runoff, on top of the joists. Where there won't be a ceiling below, simply slope the joists and angle-cut their ends.

If joists run perpendicular to the direction of runoff, you can mount each one about 1/2" lower than its neighbor to create the proper slope; the undersides will have to be furred down if you want to mount a level ceiling below.

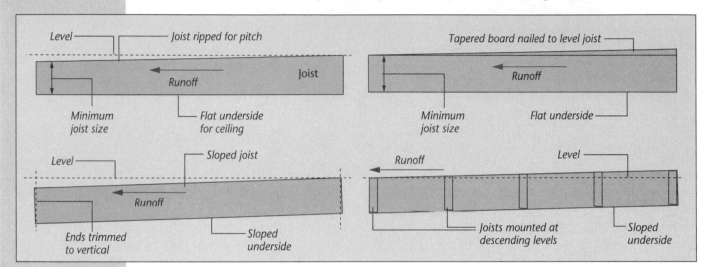

2 Fastening the plywood

As a base for watertight decking, nail a solid deck of plywood sheathing to the joists. Choose tongue-and-groove plywood or plan to block between joists. Stagger 5/8" plywood sheets (or 3/4" sheets for tile or concrete) as shown above, centering the panel ends on joists. To allow for expansion, leave 1/8" between the edges and ends of adjoining panels. Before installing the plywood, brush the edges of each sheet with a water repellent.

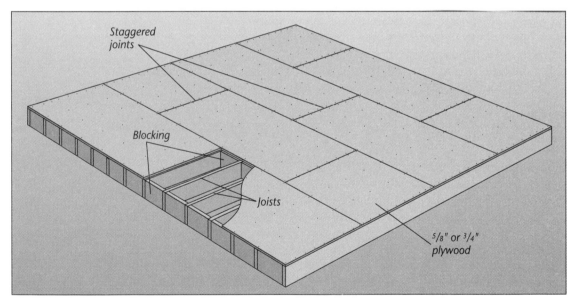

Attach the plywood by nailing it to each bearing surface. To prevent the plywood from bowing, begin by nailing two adjacent sides, starting from a corner (preferably a corner that butts against other sheets).

When nailing plywood to joists, choose 2 1/2" nails for 5/8" and thicker plywood. Space nails every 6" along the sides of each panel and every 12" at intermediate supports.

BUILDING OVERHEADS

Sometimes the difference between a deck that's inviting and one that's seldom used is nothing more than an overhead structure. The suggestion of a roof can transform an open space into a cozy enclosure, giving you an outdoor "room" on fair-weather days.

Of course, there are also purely practical reasons for installing an overhead: to ensure sun control and provide privacy. Depending on its design, an overhead can cast varying degrees of shade, cooling a hot deck and perhaps increasing the number of days it can be used. An overhead can also create instant privacy where none existed—especially significant if the upper-story windows from a neighboring house overlook your deck.

In this chapter, we'll show you a number of overhead designs *(page 137)*, introduce you to the basic structure of an overhead *(page 140)*, and help you choose cover materials *(page 148)*. Detailed plans for a few overheads are included in the chapter beginning on page 182.

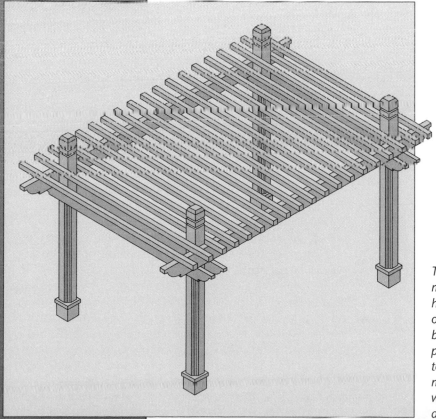

The elements that make up this overhead mirror those of a deck: posts, beams, rafters in place of joists, and to top it all off, cover materials, which would be the equivalent of decking.

DESIGNING OVERHEADS

The steps for designing an overhead are essentially the same as those for designing a deck. You'll start by choosing a site, working from a scale drawing of your house and lot. Your choice of site will likely be an obvious one—you'll want the overhead to shelter an existing deck. However, you may not want to cover the entire deck. The placement of an overhead can serve to define use areas, such as a shady area for children to play or an area for dining or entertaining. When choosing the area the overhead will shelter, consider existing traffic patterns and the accessibility of the area to both the house and yard.

When situating your overhead, consider how your family's needs are likely to change over time, and think about any outdoor additions you may want to make in the future. Consider integrating your deck and overhead into an overall landscaping plan. For example, a series of overheads can serve to unify several landscaping features, such as a deck, a pool, and a patio.

Start designing your overhead by sketching in cover designs on tracing paper set over the scale drawing of your property. Then decide on the type of structure that will support it. Once you've settled on an overall design, you're ready to develop the working drawings—typically an elevation view of the structure and a plan view of the cover. For more details on the planning and design process, turn to the chapter on planning a deck, beginning on page 44.

Be sure to check with the local building department for any code restrictions that apply to the overhead you want to build. You'll also need to check zoning ordinances and your deed for any restrictions on the design and location of your overhead. For more information on legal restrictions, turn to page 53.

Construction of most overheads is within the reach of a do-it-yourselfer. Make sure you have a helper if you'll need to raise heavy beams. Even if you're considering hiring a professional for some or all of the design and construction, it's a good idea to come up with a preliminary design yourself. (You'll find information on working with professionals on page 59.)

A variety of overhead designs are shown on the pages that follow; you may be able to adapt one of these to meet your needs. When selecting a design or creating your own, keep the following factors in mind:

Sun and shade: An overhead cuts glare from the sun, and can shade not only your deck, but also the house. The amount of shade provided by an overhead can be controlled through the spacing, size, and angle of the roofing materials. Be careful not to create more shade than you really want. An overhead in a shady north-facing location should be kept as light and open as possible. It helps to know the sun's path through the sky in your locale so you can judge when and at what angle the sun will strike your overhead at different times of year. See page 50 for information on determining sun angles.

Wind and rain: If you want to shield your deck from rain, you'll need to select solid materials for your overhead cover. These materials are discussed on page 149. To protect your deck from wind, you can combine the overhead with screens *(page 86)*.

Views: You'll want to be sure your overhead doesn't block desirable views from the deck underneath or from inside the house. When you're standing inside looking out, beams that are too low will pull down your viewable horizon. Generally, it's best never to place the lowest beam less than 6 feet 8 inches from the finished floor surface.

Matching your house: A good design should take its cue from your home's architectural style. If your house is Victorian, for example, classic crisscrossed lattice would be an appropriate material for an overhead. If your home has a feeling of openness, so should a trellis that's part of its outdoor space. Though it's not essential that an overhead near the house be built from the same materials as the house, the new structure should blend harmoniously with it, rather than create a jarring contrast. Use complementary colors, and try to design the lines of the overhead so the structure appears to flow from the inside space. An overhead can dramatically improve your home's appearance, giving a new dimension to a nondescript roofline.

ASK A PRO

HOW CAN I GET MORE SHADE IN THE SUMMER THAN IN THE WINTER?

You can cover your overhead with leafy vines by training them up the supporting structure. The leaves will provide shade in the summer. When the leaves fall in the winter, more light will be allowed through. Another way to vary the amount of shade provided by an overhead is to use removable modules for the cover.

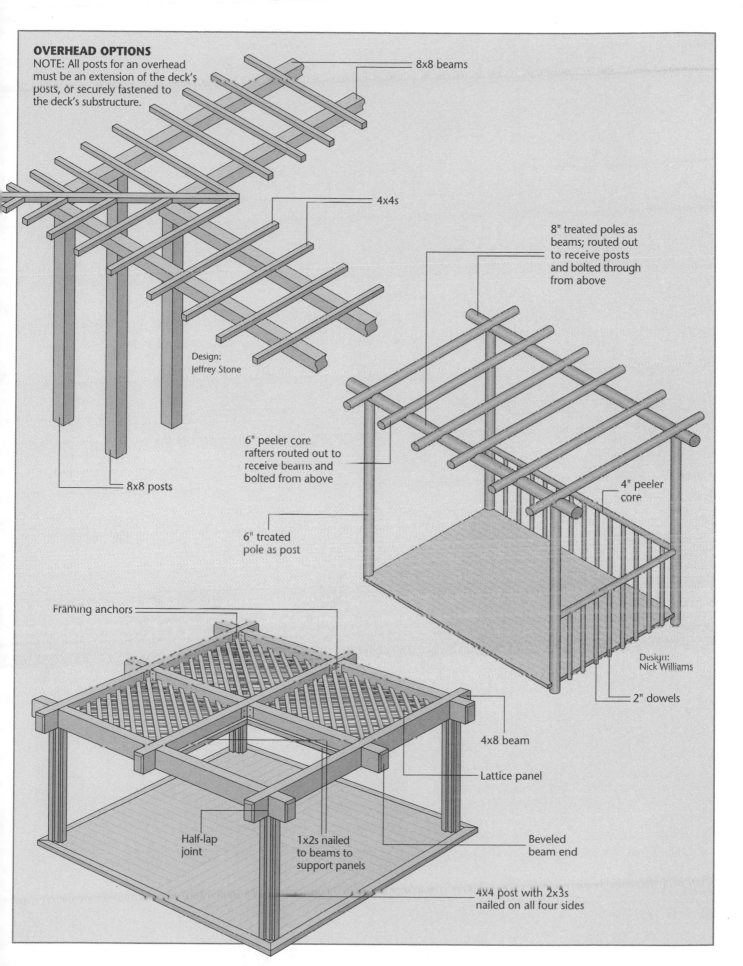

OVERHEAD OPTIONS
NOTE: All posts for an overhead must be an extension of the deck's posts, or securely fastened to the deck's substructure.

8x8 beams

4x4s

Design:
Jeffrey Stone

8x8 posts

8" treated poles as beams; routed out to receive posts and bolted through from above

6" peeler core rafters routed out to receive beams and bolted from above

6" treated pole as post

4" peeler core

Design:
Nick Williams

2" dowels

Framing anchors

4x8 beam

Lattice panel

Half-lap joint

1x2s nailed to beams to support panels

Beveled beam end

4x4 post with 2x3s nailed on all four sides

BUILDING OVERHEADS   **137**

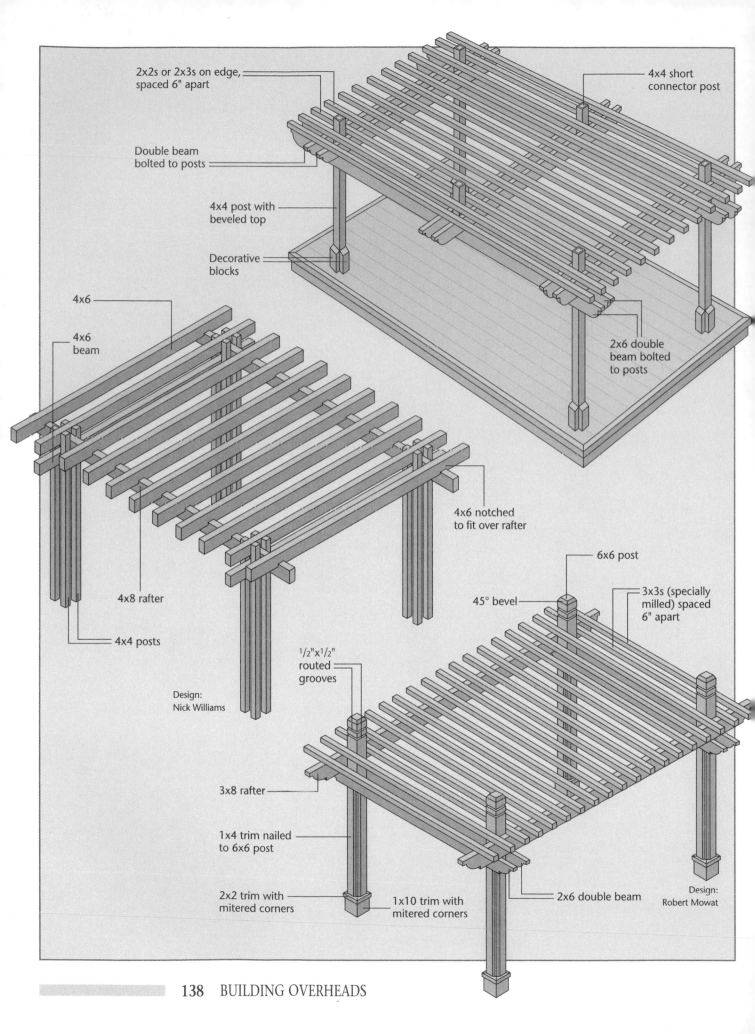

2x2s or 2x3s on edge, spaced 6" apart

4x4 short connector post

Double beam bolted to posts

4x4 post with beveled top

Decorative blocks

4x6

4x6 beam

2x6 double beam bolted to posts

4x6 notched to fit over rafter

4x8 rafter

6x6 post

3x3s (specially milled) spaced 6" apart

45° bevel

4x4 posts

Design: Nick Williams

1/2"x1/2" routed grooves

3x8 rafter

1x4 trim nailed to 6x6 post

2x2 trim with mitered corners

1x10 trim with mitered corners

2x6 double beam

Design: Robert Mowat

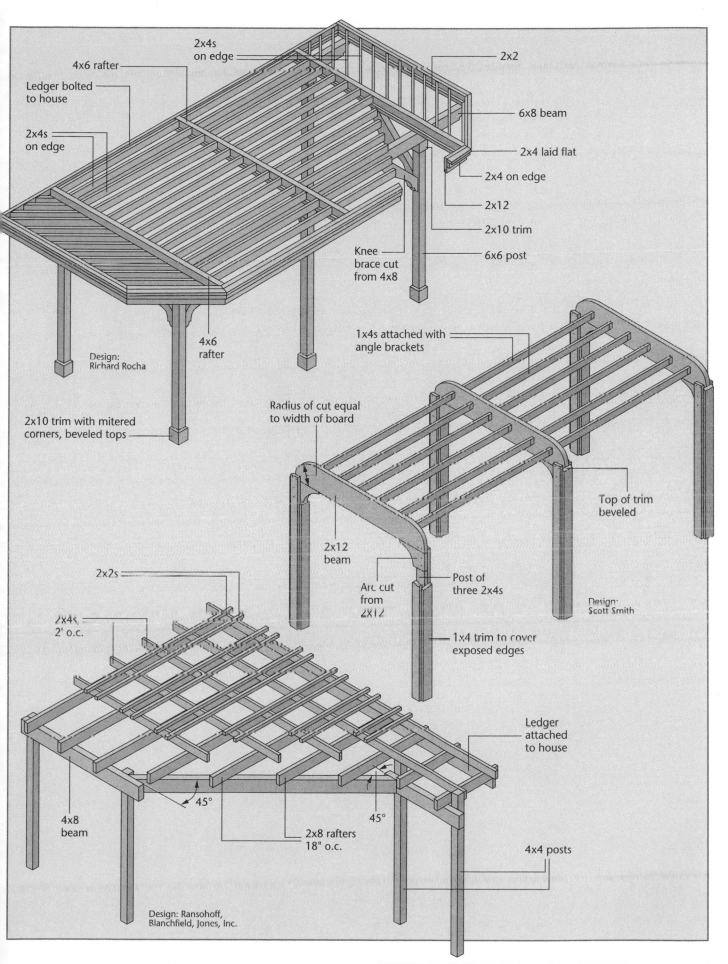

4x6 rafter

2x4s on edge

2x2

Ledger bolted to house

2x4s on edge

6x8 beam

2x4 laid flat

2x4 on edge

2x12

2x10 trim

Knee brace cut from 4x8

6x6 post

Design: Richard Rocha

4x6 rafter

2x10 trim with mitered corners, beveled tops

1x4s attached with angle brackets

Radius of cut equal to width of board

Top of trim beveled

2x12 beam

Arc cut from 2x12

Post of three 2x4s

Design: Scott Smith

1x4 trim to cover exposed edges

2x2s

2x4s 2' o.c.

Ledger attached to house

45°

45°

4x8 beam

2x8 rafters 18" o.c.

4x4 posts

Design: Ransohoff, Blanchfield, Jones, Inc.

OVERHEAD STRUCTURE

The structure of an overhead is essentially the same as that of a deck. The overhead can be attached to the house with a ledger, as shown below *(bottom)*, or it can be freestanding *(below, top)*. In either case the overhead is supported by a series of posts. These can be attached to the deck substructure or be a continuation of the deck posts. The posts support beams, which in turn support rafters (the equivalent of deck joists). In a house-attached overhead the ledger takes the place of a beam, supporting the rafters directly. The rafters can be left

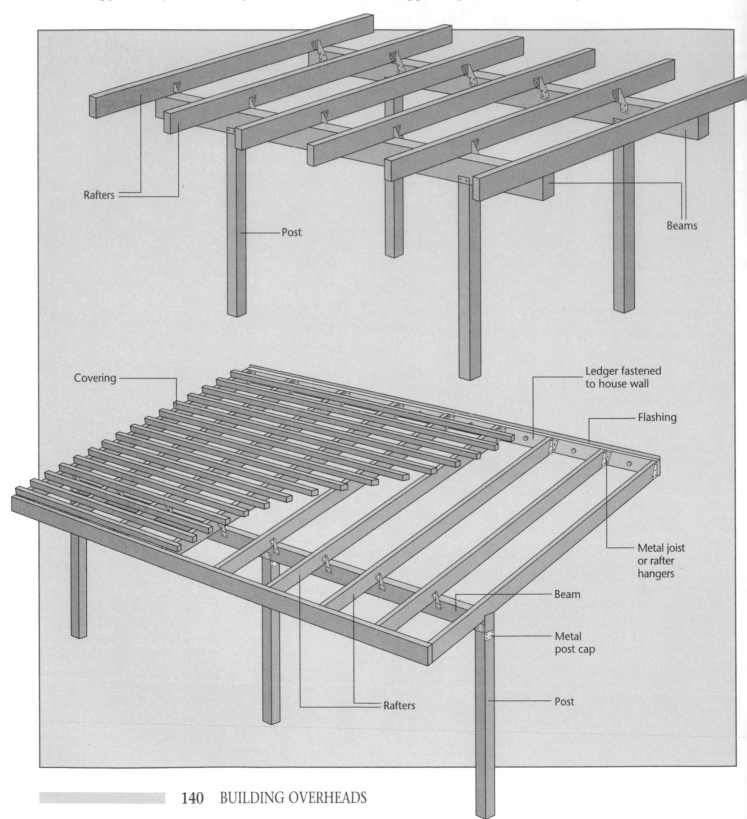

Rafters

Post

Beams

Covering

Ledger fastened to house wall

Flashing

Metal joist or rafter hangers

Beam

Metal post cap

Rafters

Post

uncovered as shown opposite, or they can be covered with one of a number of cover materials.

Each structural element of an overhead is discussed on the pages that follow. Like the elements that make up a deck, these must conform to spans and spacings determined by local building codes. Consult the span charts given below.

In most cases you will construct your overhead structure from standard dimension lumber or timbers; for information on choosing lumber, turn to page 92. For the covering, you can choose from a variety of materials, such as lath or lattice; these are discussed on page 148. To increase the life of your overhead, it is wise to construct it from pressure-treated or naturally decay-resistant wood *(page 95)*.

ASK A PRO

CAN I BUILD AN OVERHEAD WITHOUT SUPPORT POSTS?

Short, lightweight overheads can sometimes be cantilevered from a house wall, eliminating the need for posts. This involves extending the house eaves by attaching the overhead to the rafter tails—this is only possible if the overhead reaches to just below the house roof. Because of the loads exerted by cantilevered overheads, the design and construction should be left to professionals.

CALCULATING SPANS

The number, size, and spacing of rafters, beams, and posts needed for an overhead are determined by the loads they must carry. Unlike decks, overheads don't have to bear the load of people and furniture. In addition, open overheads don't collect much snow, so all they have to support is the weight of the materials themselves. This generally works out to about 5 pounds per square foot (psf). Solid roofs, such as those with shingles, must be built to withstand considerably more weight—the roofing materials are heavy and, in addition, the roof will collect snow. Thus, overheads with solid roofs should be designed by a professional.

The tables here give maximum recommended spans for rafters and beams, assuming a 5 psf load. These spans are from the center of one supporting member to the center of the next; thus, rafter spans are the same as beam spacings. The distance rafters or beams can span is dependent on how far apart they are spaced and the dimension of the lumber. For example, if you want your rafters to span a greater distance from beam to beam, you'll need to either space the rafters closer together or increase their size.

The figures given in the tables at right are based on quality materials, for example No. 2 and better. For lesser grades, spans will be shorter. Keep in mind that these are maximums—you may want to shorten them slightly for a more solid structure.

The main restriction on your design will be the placement of the posts; this will be critical to the look of the overhead and to traffic flow on the deck below. Once you've decided on the position of the posts, this will determine the distance the beams must span. Then use table 2 to figure out how far apart you can space the beams and what size lumber to use. The beam spacing will determine the rafter spans. Working from the rafter spans, you can use table 1 to figure out the size and spacing of the rafters (rafter spacing will be limited by

the cover materials you choose, although most materials will allow at least 2-foot spacings).

You can use 4x4 posts for most overheads. Exceptions are very tall structures—those over 12 feet.

TABLE 1: MAXIMUM RECOMMENDED RAFTER SPANS

The following spans are based on a load of 5 psf and No. 2 and Better lumber

Rafter size	Maximum Rafter Spacing		
	12"	16"	24"
2x4	10'	9'	8'
2x6	16'	14'	12'
2x8	20'	18'	16'

TABLE 2: MAXIMUM RECOMMENDED BEAM SPANS

The following spans are based on a load of 5 psf and No. 2 and Better lumber

Beam size	Maximum spacing between beams (or between beam and ledger)	
	12'	16'
2x10	10'	8'
2x12	14'	12'
3x6	8'	6'
3x8	10'	8'
3x10	12'	10'
3x12	16'	14'
4x4	6'	4'
4x6	8'	6'
4x8	12'	10'
4x10	14'	12'
4x12	18'	16'

LEDGERS

A ledger is fastened to the house and supports one end of the rafters. It must be fastened to a masonry wall or to the framing of a wood frame house. If you have a one-story house, you'll fasten the ledger to wall studs, or if the overhead falls just under the house roof, you can attach the ledger to the roof rafters. On a two-story house, you can attach the ledger to the floor framing as shown at right. Locate the middle of the ledger about 6 inches below the interior floor level. To transfer this measurement to the exterior wall, use a window or door sill as a reference point.

Fasten the ledger to the house as you would a deck ledger *(page 108)*. First you'll need to brace or nail the ledger temporarily at the desired height; make sure it's level. For a wood frame house, drill lag screw holes into the framing every 16 inches as shown and screw the ledger in place. For a masonry wall, use expanding anchor bolts at the same intervals. Unless the ledger is protected from the rain by the eaves or by its own solid cover material and flashing, you'll have to prevent water from accumulating in the joint between the ledger and the house wall. To do this, either space the ledger out from the wall with washers, or cover the joint with Z-flashing after the ledger is in place *(page 110)*.

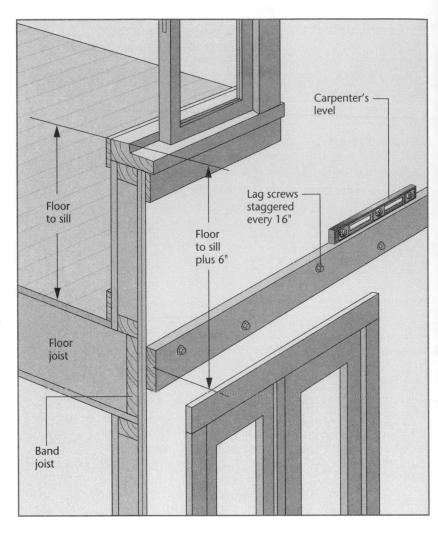

Floor to sill

Carpenter's level

Lag screws staggered every 16"

Floor to sill plus 6"

Floor joist

Band joist

POSTS

Overheads are most commonly supported by posts of solid or built-up lumber, steel, or a combination of the two. A variety of post styles is shown opposite.

Wood posts are made of dimension lumber or timbers—for information on choosing lumber turn to page 92. In addition to surfaced lumber, you may also want to consider rough or resawn lumber *(page 148)* for a different surface texture. Another alternative to standard lumber is treated poles, available from your lumber or landscaping center. Wood posts that will be within 6 inches of the ground or in contact with concrete should be made of pressure-treated lumber. Wood posts can be decorated with trim or shaped with a router.

Because structural steel is a costly substructure material, it's often reserved for use where extreme loads must be carried.

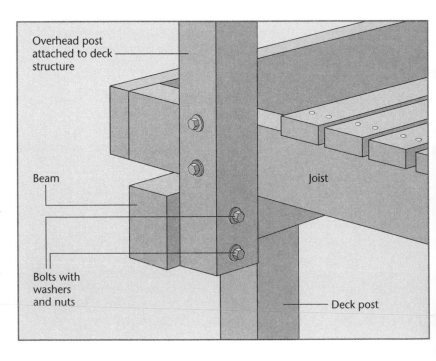

Overhead post attached to deck structure

Beam

Joist

Bolts with washers and nuts

Deck post

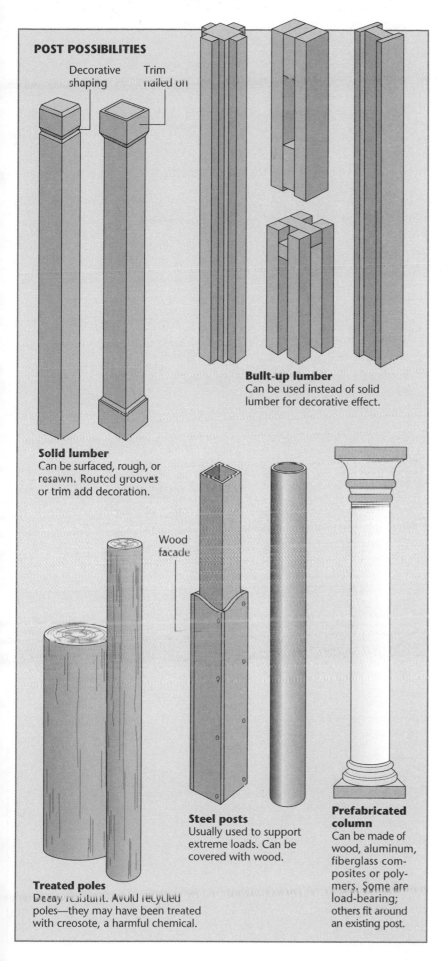

POST POSSIBILITIES

Decorative shaping

Trim nailed on

Solid lumber
Can be surfaced, rough, or resawn. Routed grooves or trim add decoration.

Built-up lumber
Can be used instead of solid lumber for decorative effect.

Wood facade

Treated poles
Decay resistant. Avoid recycled poles—they may have been treated with creosote, a harmful chemical.

Steel posts
Usually used to support extreme loads. Can be covered with wood.

Prefabricated column
Can be made of wood, aluminum, fiberglass composites or polymers. Some are load-bearing; others fit around an existing post.

Most steel structures must be professionally engineered. In addition, flanges for attaching the post to the foundation and the beam must be welded to the ends, and the posts must be cut to exact length. Often, steel posts are hidden under a facade of wood; this gives the look of wood while eliminating the need for knee braces and increasing overall strength.

If you're designing the deck and overhead at the same time, the best system of support for the overhead is to continue the posts supporting the deck upward to support the overhead as well *(page 68)*. Overheads can also be attached to the substructure of an existing deck; however, this may put strain on the deck structure that it was not designed to handle. In order to transfer the weight of the overhead directly to the ground, design it so that the overhead posts fall directly over or adjacent to the deck posts below; one such arrangement is shown on page 142. (If the overhead posts penetrate through the decking, attach cleats to the sides of the posts to support the ends of the deck boards.) If the design of your overhead does not allow you to position the posts in this way, you should consult a professional to determine whether the beams or joists can support the weight of the overhead in the middle of their spans.

When attaching overhead posts to the deck substructure, drill holes for through bolts and use four ½-inch bolts.

BEAMS

Beams can be made of solid lumber or built up from lengths of 2-by lumber *(page 119)*. While a solid beam is more attractive, a built-up beam is easier to handle.

Beams generally sit on top of posts, but they can also mesh with them in any of the ways shown on page 68. To fasten the beam to the post, use a metal post cap *(page 100)*, or one of the decorative methods shown at right.

Hoisting a large beam atop a post over your head may demand more strength and agility than you possess; be sure to get help for this stage of the construction. Seat the beam in the same way as you would seat a deck beam; for directions, turn to page 119.

 PLAY IT SAFE

WORKING ON A LADDER

You'll need a stepladder to raise the beams of your overhead (as well as to install the covering). Make sure the ladder doesn't rock, placing boards under its front or back feet if necessary. The legs should be opened all the way and the spreader braces pushed down into the locked position. When climbing the ladder, face toward it and hold onto the steps, not the side rails. Never stand higher than the third rail from the top; lean into the ladder. If you can't reach comfortably from where the ladder is set up, reposition the ladder rather than stretching away from it.

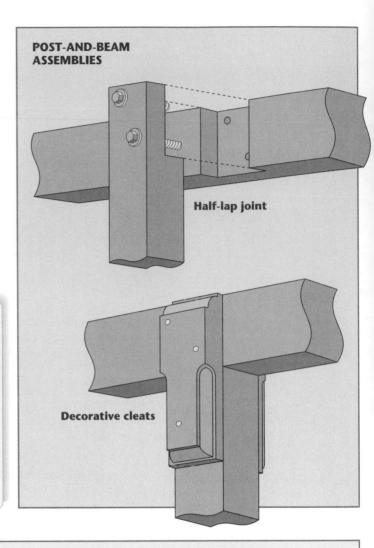

POST-AND-BEAM ASSEMBLIES

Half-lap joint

Decorative cleats

BRACING POSTS

Unless they have a steel structure, overheads normally require knee-bracing for lateral stability; this is particularly important for freestanding overheads. The exceptions are very lightweight overheads or those where the beams mesh with the posts, providing the posts with support in more than one direction.

If the design you're working from doesn't include knee-bracing, you can start by building the overhead without the bracing; then, check the stability of the structure and, if necessary, add bracing. Mark individual braces in position and cut them on the ground. Nail them in place temporarily. Then drill pilot holes for lag screws or bolts into the posts and beams and fasten the braces permanently.

Shown are the simplest type of knee-bracing and a couple of decorative options. To prevent rot, braces should be designed to avoid placing the end grain of the boards in a horizontal position and thus exposed to the rain.

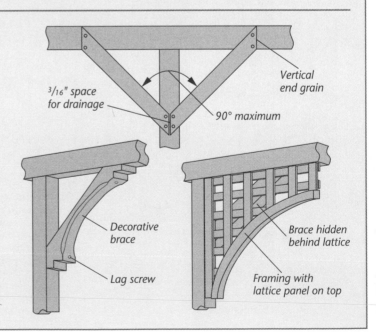

3/16" space for drainage

Vertical end grain

90° maximum

Decorative brace

Lag screw

Brace hidden behind lattice

Framing with lattice panel on top

RAFTERS

Most overheads have rafters of one kind or another. These are the equivalent of the joists in a deck design; they can be either level or sloping. Rafters spread the load of the cover materials across beams, making it possible to use thin materials that otherwise couldn't span the distances between the beams. Rafters must support their own weight over the open space without sagging or twisting, and they must also support the added weight of the covering. They must be a suitable dimension for the distance they have to span—consult the span table on page 141.

In an attached overhead, the rafters are fastened to the house at one end. This can be accomplished in any of the ways shown below. The most common method is to fasten the rafter ends to a ledger on the house wall, but they can also be attached to the roof of the house or can rest on the top plate. Some light overheads can be attached to the house rafter tails—check with an engineer to be sure. The best connections are made with metal framing connectors. You can use joist hangers to hang the rafters from the ledger, but for sloping rafters you would have to notch the rafters; instead

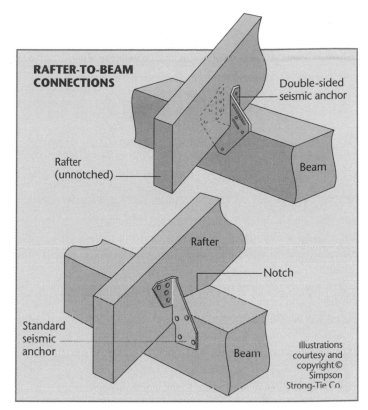

RAFTER-TO-BEAM CONNECTIONS

Double-sided seismic anchor

Rafter (unnotched)

Beam

Rafter

Notch

Standard seismic anchor

Beam

Illustrations courtesy and copyright© Simpson Strong-Tie Co.

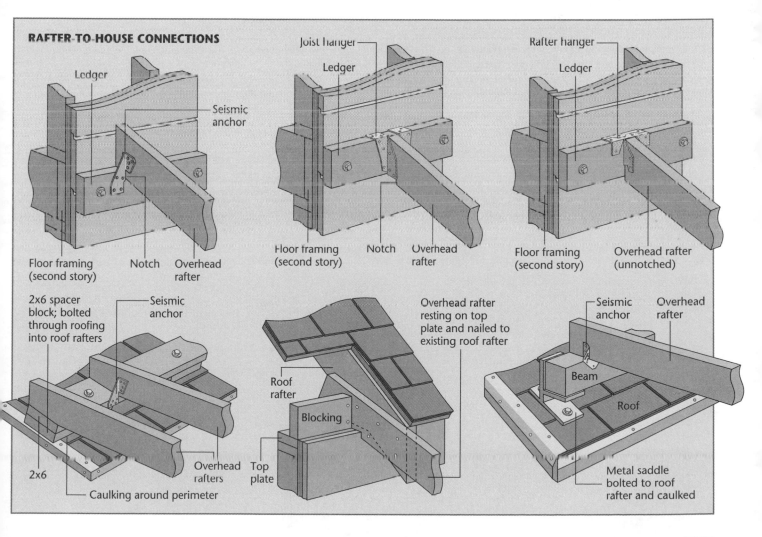

RAFTER-TO-HOUSE CONNECTIONS

Ledger

Seismic anchor

Floor framing (second story)

Notch

Overhead rafter

Joist hanger

Ledger

Floor framing (second story)

Notch

Overhead rafter

Rafter hanger

Ledger

Floor framing (second story)

Overhead rafter (unnotched)

2x6 spacer block; bolted through roofing into roof rafters

Seismic anchor

2x6

Caulking around perimeter

Overhead rafters

Overhead rafter resting on top plate and nailed to existing roof rafter

Roof rafter

Blocking

Top plate

Seismic anchor

Overhead rafter

Beam

Roof

Metal saddle bolted to roof rafter and caulked

you can use special rafter hangers as shown on the previous page. (If the rafters will sit on top of the ledger, attach them with seismic anchors in the same way as you would attach rafters to a beam.)

Opposite the ledger, rafters are typically supported by a beam. If the rafters are sloped, use seismic anchors, as shown on the previous page. In most cases, one standard anchor is adequate. However, in high wind or seismic areas, a second one may be required diagonally across from the first one—consult your building department. If you choose the standard anchors, you'll need to notch the rafters to fit; this can be avoided by using a double-sided anchor. Fitting sloping rafters that sit on top of the ledger and beam can be tricky—the rafters must be angle-cut at both ends *(below)*.

For a level overhead, attach the rafters to the ledger and beam—or to both beams if the overhead is freestanding—the same way you would attach joists to beams *(page 122)*.

Rafters can be spliced over beams in the same way as deck joists *(page 122)*; make sure each rafter end bears a full inch on the beam. Long rafters usually need blocking to prevent twisting or buckling; blocking requirements are typically determined by local codes. For rafters longer than 8 feet, install staggered blocking in the middle of the span in the same way as for joists *(page 122)*. For rafters shorter than 8 feet, a 1-by fascia nailed across rafter ends is adequate.

RAFTER DETAILS

Since the overhead's rafters are visible from below, cutting their ends in a decorative way gives your overhead a distinctive style. A number of possible treatments are shown below.

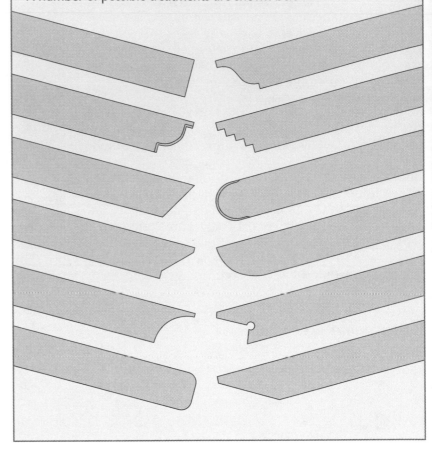

Fitting sloping rafters

TOOLKIT
• Circular saw
• Crosscut saw
• Claw hammer

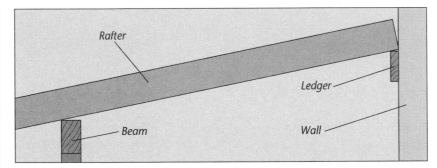

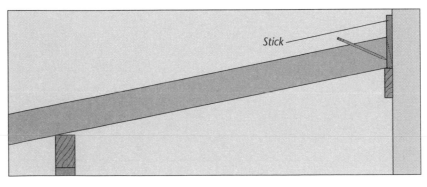

1 Marking the rafter

For rafters sitting on top of the ledger, lay a rafter so it rests on edge on both the beam and ledger. Force the tip snugly against the house wall *(left, above)*; then, using a straight stick, mark the end for cutting *(left, below)*.

For a rafter that will hang from the ledger, rest one end on the beam and hold the other end in position against the ledger to mark it.

2 Cutting the rafter

For a rafter that will sit on the ledger, cut the triangular piece off the end of the rafter that will go against the house *(inset)*. Then, use this triangle as a template to trim the beam end as shown below. Notch the bottom of the rafter where it will sit on the beam and ledger. NOTE: If you use double-sided seismic anchors of the type shown at the top of page 145, you won't need to make these notches.

If the rafter will hang off the ledger, trim a triangle off both ends in the same way as described above. If you're using standard joist hangers, you'll need to notch the rafter to fit the hanger; special rafter hangers do not require notching.

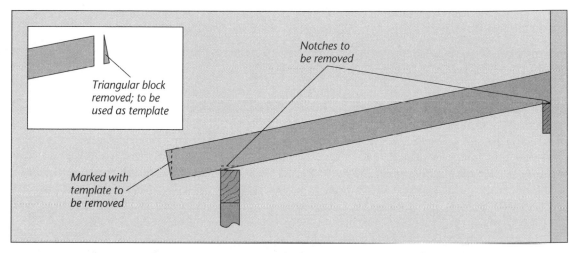

Triangular block removed; to be used as template

Notches to be removed

Marked with template to be removed

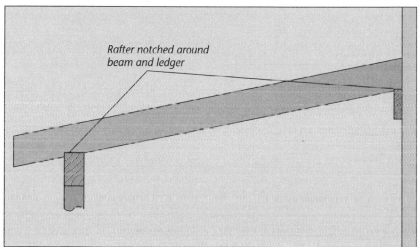

Rafter notched around beam and ledger

3 Checking the fit

Set the rafter in position to see if it fits. Check the fit in several other positions along the length of the beam and ledger. If the rafter doesn't fit all the way along, you'll have to mark and cut each rafter individually.

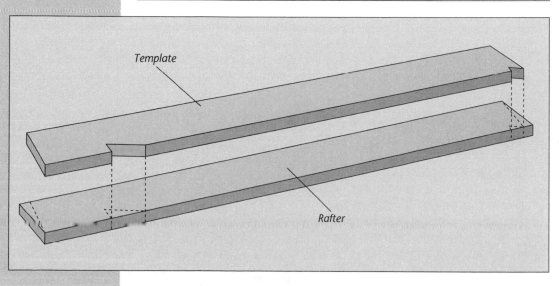

Template

Rafter

4 Cutting the other rafters

Use the first rafter as a template to mark each of the other rafters. Cut the rafters individually and fasten them in place with metal framing connectors.

OVERHEAD COVERS

Cover materials are applied over the overhead structure of posts, beams, and rafters. Overhead covers can be of two types: open or solid. There are a broad range of styles of open covers—designs that block the sun, frame a view, or create a feeling of enclosure, but that don't shed rain or snow. Directions for constructing two common styles—lath or boards, or louvers—are given starting on page 150. Open covers can be made of a number of types of materials, as discussed below.

Solid roofs shelter the area below from rain and snow; the appropriate materials are discussed opposite.

OPEN-STYLE OVERHEAD COVERS

Open-style covers are generally made of wood, but the wood used can range from thin lath to standard lumber sizes, or you can choose less common wood products such as tree stakes or woven reed. Your most common options are discussed below; additional products may be available from your lumberyard or garden-supply center.

Standard lumber: Information on choosing lumber is given starting on page 92. For overhead covers, you will commonly use 1-by boards. In addition to the standard surfaced milling, lumber is available rough or resawn, or may be sandblasted on site.

Rough lumber has been milled but not planed. Although rough lumber can be used to achieve a very rustic look, its splintery texture makes it unpleasant to touch. Rough lumber is generally only available in the lowest grades. When choosing rough lumber, shop carefully—pieces with excessive knots, flat grain, or too high a moisture content can warp and twist. Rough lumber can be stained but has a poor surface for painting.

Resawn lumber is preferred by many landscape professionals because of its rustic—but not too rough—texture. It generally must be special-ordered, but unlike rough lumber, is available in a variety of grades.

Sandblasted lumber has a rustic appearance similar to resawn wood. Sandblasting surfaced lumber is generally not cost-effective unless you're having other sandblasting work done.

Lath: Common outdoor lath is rough-surfaced redwood or cedar that's about 3/8 inch by 1 1/2 inches in size and is sold in bundles of 50. The term "lath" can also be used to refer to any open-work slat cover where lengths run parallel. Look for high-quality lath that's free of excessive knots or other defects. Relatively straight grain is also important to minimize warping and twisting.

Stakes and poles: Available at garden supply outlets, stakes and poles can be used for rustic, open-style overhead covers. These products include grapestakes, tree stakes, and lodgepoles. Grapestakes, favorites of fence-builders, offer a hand-hewn look. Made from redwood or cedar, grapestakes are roughly 2x2 inches and are usually available in up to 6-foot lengths. Split grapestakes, more the size of 1x2s, also make a satisfactory, rustic-looking cover.

Tree stakes are redwood and are 1/2 inch to 2 inches square and up to about 5 feet long. Lodgepoles are generally pressure treated and are about 2 inches thick; they are available in lengths up to 10 feet.

Peeler cores: These rustic, inexpensive landscape timbers can be used for nonstructural purposes. They come round or with two flat sides and are typically about 6 inches in diameter and 8 feet long. Though most have been pressure treated with preservatives; they may not be treated to the same standards as regular pressure-treated lumber and therefore may be more susceptible to decay. Peeler cores don't take a finish well, and tend to warp.

Reed, bamboo, and other woven woods: These woods are available in rolls at many nurseries and garden supply centers; they are inexpensive, lightweight, and easy to handle. However, most are not very durable. To increase their life, remove them and bring them under cover in the rainy season.

Woven reed comes in 15- and 25-foot rolls that measure 6 feet wide. The reed is woven with a stainless steel wire to help withstand the elements. The wire can be easily cut and retwisted if you want to trim the roll. Because constant flexing of the wire strands causes them to fail easily, woven reed cannot be easily rolled up and down; instead it should be nailed or stapled to a rigid frame.

ASK A PRO

HOW CAN I PROTECT OVERHEAD COVERS FROM DECAY?

Because cover materials are exposed to the rain, they are prone to decay with time. To give the maximum life to your overhead roofing, choose products that are pressure treated, such as lodgepoles, or products made from cedar or redwood heartwood, such as grapestakes or outdoor lattice panels.

Woven bamboo, which is manufactured primarily for vertical shade use, comes in rolls that vary in width from 3 to 12 feet; standard length is 6 feet. Bamboo is available woven with wire or string; if it is woven with string, it can be readily rolled up and down.

Bamboo is available in two main grades—split and matchstick. Split bamboo is coarser and less regular than matchstick but it is preferable for most installations since it's stiffer than matchstick. For a covering that will be rolled out of the way, matchstick bamboo is often used because of its flexibility.

Woven spruce and basswood are similar to woven bamboo. They're generally woven with heavy twine.

Preassembled lattice panels: Wood lattice panels are manufactured in 4x8-foot, 2x8-foot and 4x6-foot sizes. Several grades are available depending on the quality, thickness, and spacing of the wood lath, and the quality of the manufacturing. Only redwood and cedar panels are durable enough for outdoor use. Patterns vary—the most common are diagonal or checkerboard designs.

Another type of lattice panel you can buy is made not from wood but from PVC (polyvinyl chloride). Resembling carefully painted wood lattice, these panels are smooth, very tough, and never require refinishing. They are available in white and several earth tones. You can buy panels with diagonal or rectangular patterns of different weights and spacings. These vinyl lattice panels are generally more expensive than wood.

SOLID ROOFING

Solid roofs are designed to shed rain and snow. Materials you can install yourself include asphalt shingles, wood shingles and shakes, siding, asphalt roll roofing, aluminum panels, and aluminum shingles. Clay and concrete tiles, tar and gravel, and polyurethane foam are options that should be installed by a professional.

The pitch of the roof will depend on the materials chosen, as will the base that is installed under the roofing material. A typical solid roof of asphalt shingles is shown below. The shingles are installed over a base of plywood sheathing and a layer of roofing felt.

Another option for a solid roof is plastic or glass. These materials can maximize light, view, and shelter. However, when improperly designed, a plastic or glass roof can act as a heat trap or create a condensation and drip problem.

Because of the weight of solid roofing materials and the snow they collect, solid roofs should be designed by a professional.

For a colorful and lightweight roof, you may want to consider outdoor fabrics. A number of types are available including acrylic, cotton duck, vinyl-coated canvas, and vinyl-laminated polyester. You can design a fabric roof yourself, but be sure to take in the covering in the winter so it doesn't become loaded with snow.

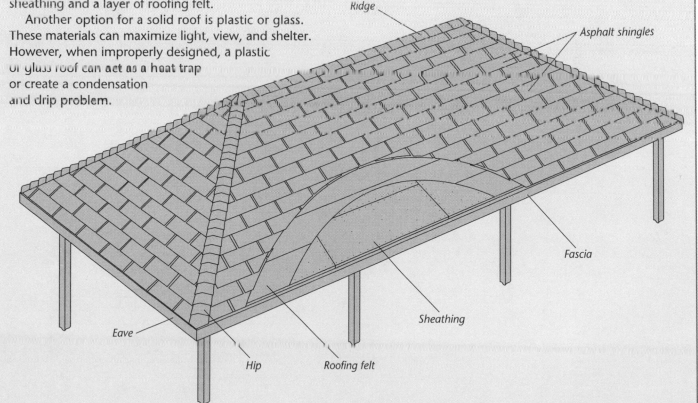

Ridge

Asphalt shingles

Fascia

Sheathing

Eave

Hip

Roofing felt

COVERS OF LATH OR BOARDS

When designing an overhead cover of lath or boards, you'll have to determine the right spacing and direction for the lath or boards to create the amount of shade you're trying to achieve. You'll also have to be sure not to exceed the allowable spans for the materials you're using.

CREATING SHADE

Wood thickness and spacing can vary enormously. Thin lath laid flat won't cast as much shade as thicker stock. Lath or boards can be laid flat or set on edge as shown below. Laid flat, they will allow in more sun in the early morning or late afternoon but block more of the midday sun.

The direction you should choose to run the lath or boards depends on what time of day you need maximum shade. If you want the greatest relief from the sun at noon, plan to run the material east-west; if you want more shade in the early morning and late afternoon, run it north-south.

The height of the overhead affects the amount of light that falls on your deck. The higher the overhead, the more diffused the light becomes. The lower the overhead, the sharper the striped shadows will be on the deck surface.

SUITABLE SPANS

To avoid sagging and warping, be conservative on the distance your cover material must span. For common lath, 2 feet is the maximum; with 1-by boards, you can span up to 3 feet, but 2 feet is better; with 1x2 or 1x3 stock laid on edge and with 2x2s, you can span 4 feet without objectionable sagging, but boards may warp or curve a bit. Don't exceed 4 feet with any size.

 ASK A PRO

HOW CAN I BE SURE OF THE RIGHT LATH OR BOARD LAYOUT FOR MY SITUATION?

Since there are a number of variables involved in the amount of shade cast by an overhead cover, the surest way to decide on the best width, spacing, and direction of the wood is to experiment. Temporarily nail several different sizes to the rafters using various spacings and study the effects of each configuration at different times during the day. Be aware that the resulting effects will vary from one season to the next.

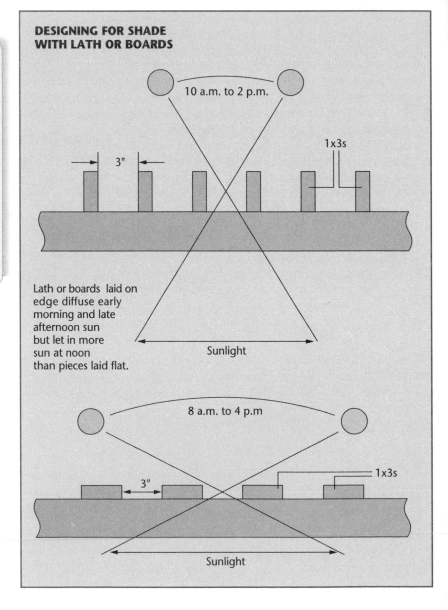

DESIGNING FOR SHADE WITH LATH OR BOARDS

10 a.m. to 2 p.m.

1x3s

3"

Lath or boards laid on edge diffuse early morning and late afternoon sun but let in more sun at noon than pieces laid flat.

Sunlight

8 a.m. to 4 p.m

1x3s

3"

Sunlight

Fastening individual boards

Sight down the lumber to check for any crown; when possible, place the board with the crown facing upward.

Cut the boards to length, making sure each board spans at least three rafters. Join cut ends directly over a rafter; leave about 1/8" between board ends. Make sure that the boards are aligned and evenly spaced before nailing; a little bit of twisting or bending is acceptable.

Always use corrosion-resistant nails to secure the wood to the framework. With 3/8" or 1/2" thick lath, use 1 1/4 " or 1 1/2" galvanized common or box nails—box nails will tend to split the wood less. For 3/4" batten or 1-by boards, choose 2 1/2" nails. Use 3 1/4" or 3 1/2" nails for thicker materials.

Nail twice at each rafter. If your nails split the wood, drill pilot holes before nailing.

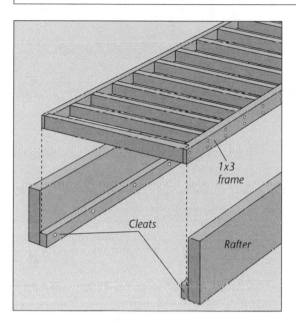

1x3 frame

Cleats

Rafter

Making preassembled panels

To reduce the time you need to spend on the rooftop, you may want to assemble panels on the ground and then fasten them in place as a unit— just be sure the rafters are straight enough to receive the panels without a struggle. You can make the panels in practically any size, but about 3x6 feet is the optimum for lightweight material.

Face-nail the roofing material to a frame of 1x3s. Attach cleats to the faces of the rafters and fit the panels in place. You can face-nail the panels to the inside of the rafters, or you can leave the panels unfastened for easy removal and cleaning.

COVERS OF LOUVERED SLATS

Angled louvers made from 1-by boards offer an extra element of sun control. Adjustable types can give you almost any degree of light or shade you want throughout the day; fixed louvers can block the sun during the part of the day when it's unwanted.

Generally speaking, if you run louvers east-west, slanting the boards away from the sun, you'll block the midday sun and admit morning and afternoon sun. If you run them north-south, you'll admit either morning or afternoon sun, depending on the louvers' slant.

Since the louvered overhead is designed to block direct light for part of the day, you'll have to take into account the height of the sun at that time *(page 50)*.

As shown at right, the more you tilt the boards, the fewer pieces you'll need. But if you try to spread them too far, you'll diminish the amount of reflected light that can shine through. NOTE: For a pitched roof, don't forget to add the angle of the pitch to the angle of the sun's altitude when figuring louvers.

Louvers are generally made of 1x3s, 1x4s, or 1x6s not more than 4 feet long. The narrower the pieces, the closer they'll have to be spaced.

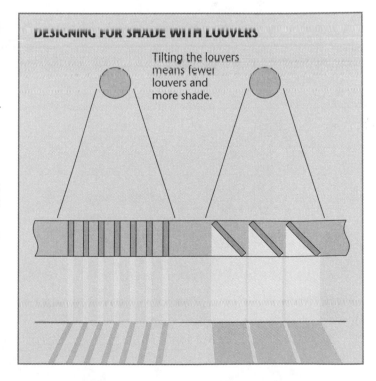

DESIGNING FOR SHADE WITH LOUVERS

Tilting the louvers means fewer louvers and more shade.

Installing louvers

TOOLKIT
- Tape measure
- Combination square
- Adjustable T-bevel for copying angles
- Carpenter's square and stair gauges for stepped rafter or cleat
- Circular saw
- Crosscut saw to complete stepped cuts
- Claw hammer

Fastening fixed louvers

Fixed louvers can be built in place—nailed directly to rafters—or they can be built in modular sections and then fastened in place in the same way as the vertical boards shown on the previous page. Shown at right are three different ways of fastening louvers to their supports. NOTE: If you make stepped cuts in the rafters, be sure the width of the rafter at its narrowest point is not less than that specified for the span.

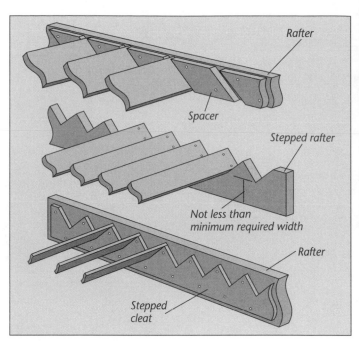

Rafter

Spacer

Stepped rafter

Not less than minimum required width

Rafter

Stepped cleat

Metal pin and washer

1x6 frame nailed between rafters

1x6 louver

Rafter

Hole for pin

Constructing adjustable louvers

Though adjustable louvers can be exacting to build, they offer excellent sun control. If you don't want to attempt the precision work involved, consider buying a ready-made system.

Shown at left is one home-built design. Louvers fit into a frame fastened between the rafters. They pivot on metal pins and washers. A 1x2 attached to the bottom of the louvers with eye screws controls the angle.

Build the modules separately and then fasten them between rafters. Cut the louvers slightly shorter than the spacing between the sides of the frame to allow them to pivot, while remaining tight enough to stay in place. For metal pins, aluminum nails with the heads clipped off work well.

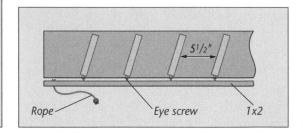

$5\,1/2"$

Rope

Eye screw

1x2

ASK A PRO

SHOULD I FINISH MY OVERHEAD COVER?

Regardless of the kind of wood you've chosen, it's a good idea to apply a finish (page 166). You can use the same finish that you've used for your decking, or paint the covering a light color to reflect light.

The best time to finish your cover materials is before you install them, while you can get at all the sides easily. In order to touch up the cut ends as you work, keep a brush and a container of the finish you're using on hand.

FINISHING TOUCHES

For a deck that offers maximum enjoyment and usefulness, you'll want to consider a variety of amenities and finishing touches, such as lighting, plumbing, benches or tables, built-in storage compartments, or planters. You may also want to look into radiant heating panels for greater comfort at cooler temperatures, or a mist cooling system if you live in a hot, dry climate.

Although your need for one or more of these amenities may be clearer once you've had a chance to use the deck, some of them must be thought out at the planning or building stages. For instance, certain benches are tied into the understructure, and built-in storage will affect the placement of the deck boards. If you're planning to add wiring or plumbing to a low-level deck, do it as the substructure is being built. (On a raised deck, however, it's generally easier to run wires and pipes after the deck is finished.) Furthermore, since permits may be required for plumbing or wiring work, it pays to plan ahead. More information on wiring and plumbing starts on page 154.

Several ideas for deck furnishings, such as benches, tables, and planters, are shown in this chapter. You'll also find suggestions for integrated storage, either under the surface of the deck or inside a bench. For other ideas, look through the Deck Plans chapter *(page 182)*.

The most common "finishing touch" is the deck finish itself. Properly applied, it should keep your deck looking beautiful for years to come. You'll find tips on finishing techniques, including information about the types of products available and the application tools you may need, on pages 166 and 167.

Benches are just one of the many finishing touches you'll find in this chapter. You can build them freestanding, like this one, or attached to the deck. On some, you can even add a handy storage compartment.

LIGHTING YOUR DECK

Lighting is a welcome addition to many decks, increasing the number of hours you can spend outdoors. You can choose to install low-voltage (12-volt) lighting fixtures yourself or have your home's 120-volt system extended to the deck. Home improvement centers and hardware stores offer low-voltage deck lighting kits, including post-style lights, a transformer, and cable. Many kits also include a timer, which you can set to turn the lights on and off automatically.

A 12-volt lighting system is more energy efficient and much easier to install than a 120-volt system, and it carries far less risk of harmful shock; in fact, in most areas, no electrical permit is required for installing a system extending from a low-voltage plug-in transformer (the most common kind). Installation is easy, following the manufacturer's instructions, but you'll need an outlet equipped with a ground fault circuit interrupter (GFCI): This device cuts off power within 1/40 of a second if current begins leaking anywhere along the circuit. You simply plug the transformer into the GFCI-protected outlet and run the two-wire outdoor cable to the fixtures (most transformers can handle several fixtures).

Most transformers for outdoor lights are encased in watertight boxes, but it's still wise to install them in a sheltered location at least one foot off the deck or ground. The cable can be laid on the ground or fastened to wooden support members below the decking. Most fixtures connect to cables without requiring you to strip the insulation and splice the wires, although some do require a connector. No grounding connections are required.

If you want a 120-volt wiring system, you'll need an electrician to install it, although it may be worth considering. Not only can light can be projected a greater distance than with a low-voltage system, but outlets can be added, enabling you to plug in power tools, radios, or outdoor heaters. With this type of system, the wires are run underground, and all boxes, switches, and fixtures must be sealed from the weather.

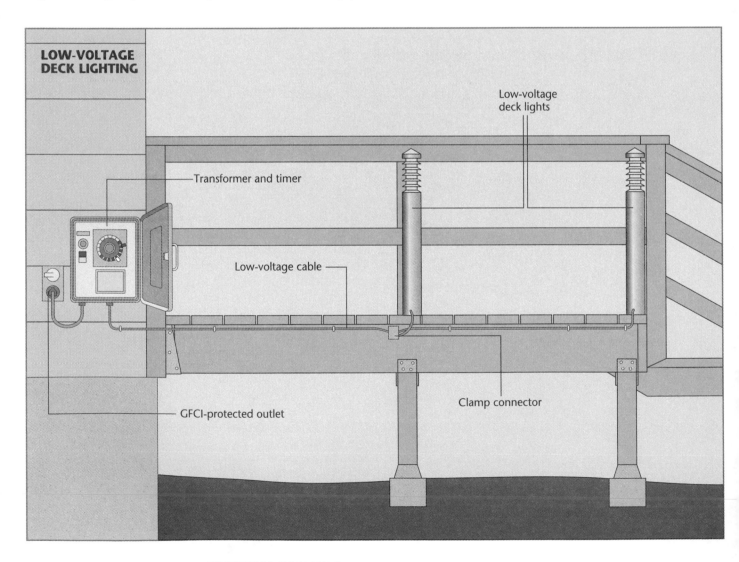

LOW-VOLTAGE DECK LIGHTING

Low-voltage deck lights

Transformer and timer

Low-voltage cable

GFCI-protected outlet

Clamp connector

Most outdoor fixtures are made of bronze, cast or extruded aluminum, copper, or plastic. But you can also find decorative stone, concrete, and wood fixtures (choose a naturally decay-resistant wood, such as redwood, cedar, or teak). When evaluating fixtures, look for solid gaskets, high-quality components at joints and pivot points, and locking devices for aiming the fixtures.

A low level of light is often enough for outdoor dining or quiet conversation. Several low-wattage fixtures placed around the deck create a softer effect than one high-wattage bulb. But you'll probably want stronger light where you do your outdoor cooking or serving. Downlights (lights focused down from above) and indirect lighting (diffused through plastic or another translucent material) are both good choices. To improve safety at night and add charm to your deck, light up the steps, railings, or benches, either directly with strings of minilights or indirectly with low-voltage lights hidden underneath.

Whatever system you plan to install, check with your local building department to see if you need a permit for the electrical work.

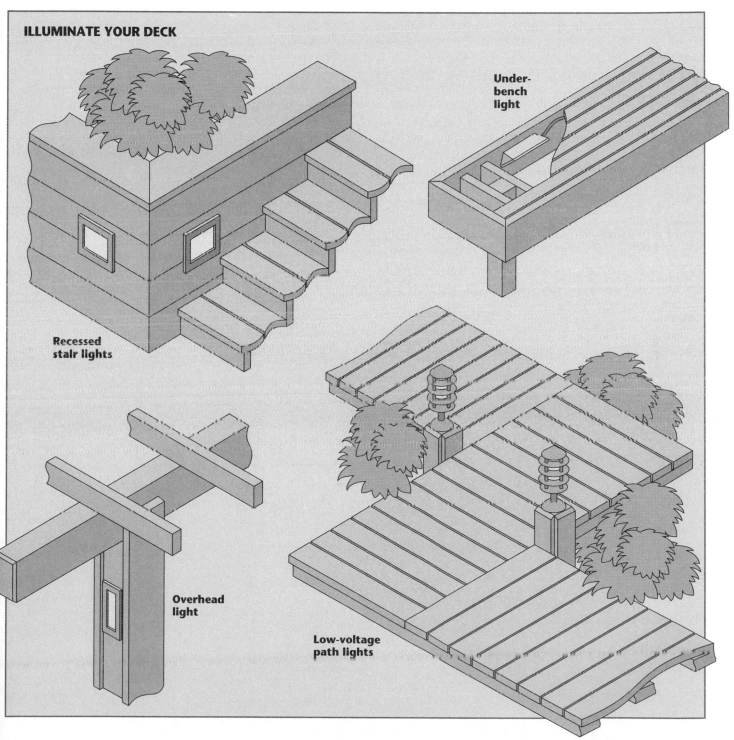

ILLUMINATE YOUR DECK

Under-bench light

Recessed stair lights

Overhead light

Low-voltage path lights

ADDING PLUMBING TO YOUR DECK

Piping water to your deck will provide increased comfort and convenience. For easy deck maintenance, it's important to provide at least one hose connection; you may also want garden sprinklers, a shower or outdoor sink, or a fountain, pool, or spa.

Outdoor faucets (hose bibbs) and hoses can be effectively camouflaged in storage boxes recessed below the deck, as shown on page 163; a 3x5-foot chamber makes a handy container for 50 to 100 feet of hose. You can also conceal an outdoor faucet and hose in a bench with solid sides and a hinged seat, or in a workbench with vertical doors. For other deck storage ideas, see page 162.

Water supply systems for decks are subject to building code regulations in most areas, and any modifications you want to make may require a permit. If you're short on plumbing experience, plan on getting professional help; if you're handy—and particularly if you choose plastic pipe—you should find that installing a couple of outdoor faucets is quite an easy job. A typical plumbing configuration is shown below.

When to install plumbing: If you have a high-level deck with access to the substructure, you can install pipes after completing your deck. This allows you to live with the new deck long enough to know just where and how you'll want to use water. Putting in an entire system at once costs less than developing it bit by bit. However, for a low-level deck with limited or no access to the underside, plumbing must usually be installed before the deck surface is laid.

Protecting the pipes in cold climates: Deck pipes are especially vulnerable to bursting during freezing weather. Main pipes buried beneath the frost line are adequately protected, but short lengths of exposed pipe leading up to faucets will freeze if not protected. Insulation alone merely slows down the cooling of the water in the pipe; eventually the water will freeze. Keep pipes from freezing with heating cable, insulating them to conserve heat, or drain the pipes for the winter.

If there's extensive piping attached to beams or joists, drain it completely in winter; a good plan is to equip the system with a main shutoff valve inside the house and a drain valve (or threaded plug) at the lowest point in the deck plumbing. During winter, close the main valve and keep the drain valve open (or remove the plug). Also open all faucets or other fixtures and drain any sink traps.

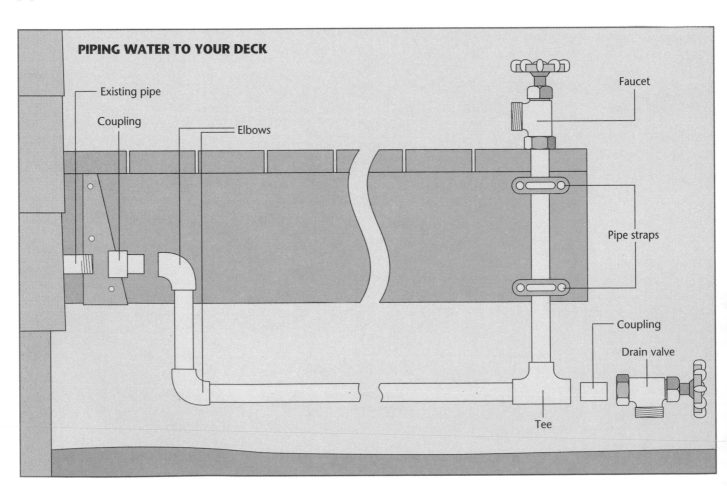

PIPING WATER TO YOUR DECK

Existing pipe

Coupling

Elbows

Faucet

Pipe straps

Coupling

Drain valve

Tee

BENCHES

TYPICAL BENCH DIMENSIONS

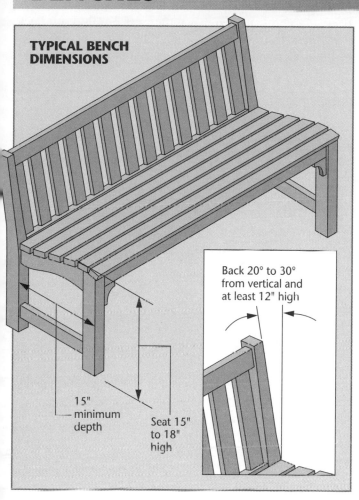

Back 20° to 30° from vertical and at least 12" high

15" minimum depth

Seat 15" to 18" high

Benches serve primarily as hardy, multipurpose deck furniture. In addition, they can funnel foot traffic, separate areas for different activities, and double as railings for both low- and high-level decks (for high-level decks, use benches with backs).

In designing benches for your deck, take cues from the railings, screens, even the deck's surface pattern; such planning helps achieve an integrated design. But you can also design a bench to stand out and serve as a focal point.

For conventional seating, a bench should stand between 15 and 18 inches high; sunbathing platforms may be as low as 6 to 8 inches. Backs on chair-height benches should offer support at least 12 inches above the seat; the seat itself should be at least 15 inches deep. For an inclined back, you'll probably find that the most comfortable angle is between 20° and 30°. Backs of built-in deck benches can be capped like railings: The caps protect the post ends from decay and, when level, provide a surface to hold food and drinks.

You can construct benches so that they're an integral part of your deck, build them independently and then attach them when completed, or leave them unattached and movable—but sturdy enough not to topple. You can even build a combination bench and overhead, as shown on page 160.

Bench legs or supporting members should be big enough to provide solid support, yet still be in scale with the bench design. Pairs of legs made from 4x4s (or a material of similar strength) should be spaced 3 to 5

BENCH AND RAILING COMBINATIONS

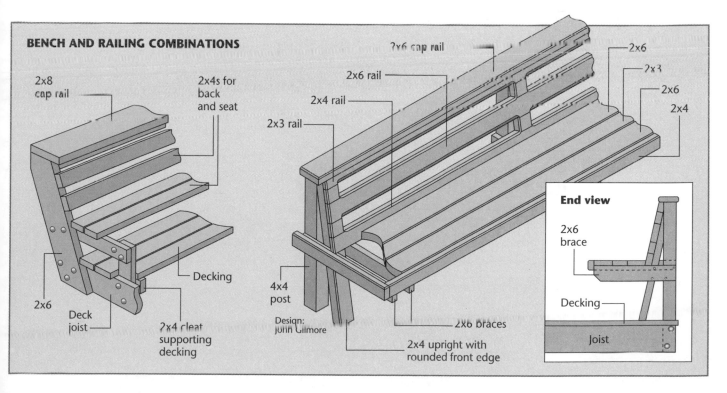

2x8 cap rail

2x4s for back and seat

2x6

Deck joist

2x4 cleat supporting decking

Decking

2x6 cap rail

2x6 rail

2x4 rail

2x3 rail

2x6

2x3

2x6

2x4

4x4 post

Design: John Gilmore

2x6 braces

2x4 upright with rounded front edge

End view

2x6 brace

Decking

Joist

feet apart; if you're using 2x4s or other lightweight materials, or if the seat top needs additional support, the legs should be spaced more closely. Always choose surfaced lumber for the seat boards.

As illustrated on the facing page, built-in benches can be connected to posts extended from the deck's founda-tion up through the decking, or to vertical members bolted to joists. These uprights can form pedestal supports for bench seats, or become the frame for a bench's back. Plan built-in benches when you design your deck; if you build a freestanding bench but want to attach it to the deck later, use brackets or cleats.

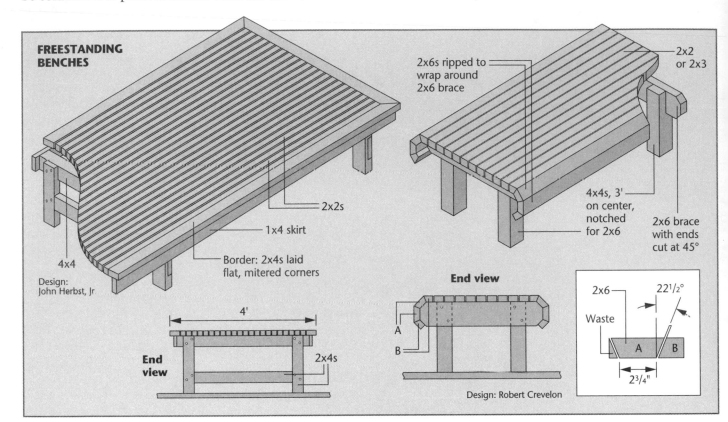

FREESTANDING BENCHES

2x6s ripped to wrap around 2x6 brace

2x2 or 2x3

2x2s

1x4 skirt

Border: 2x4s laid flat, mitered corners

4x4

Design: John Herbst, Jr.

4x4s, 3' on center, notched for 2x6

2x6 brace with ends cut at 45°

End view

End view

4'

End view

2x4s

A

B

2x6

22½°

Waste

A

B

2¾"

Design: Robert Crevelon

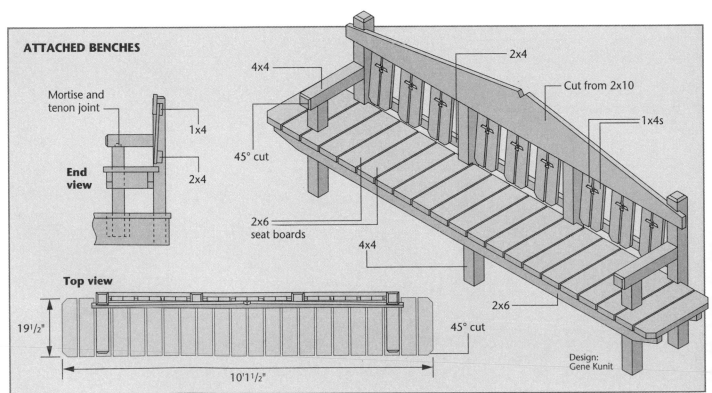

ATTACHED BENCHES

Mortise and tenon joint

1x4

2x4

End view

4x4

45° cut

2x6 seat boards

4x4

2x4

Cut from 2x10

1x4s

2x6

Top view

19½"

45° cut

10'1½"

Design: Gene Kunit

ATTACHED BENCHES
(continued)

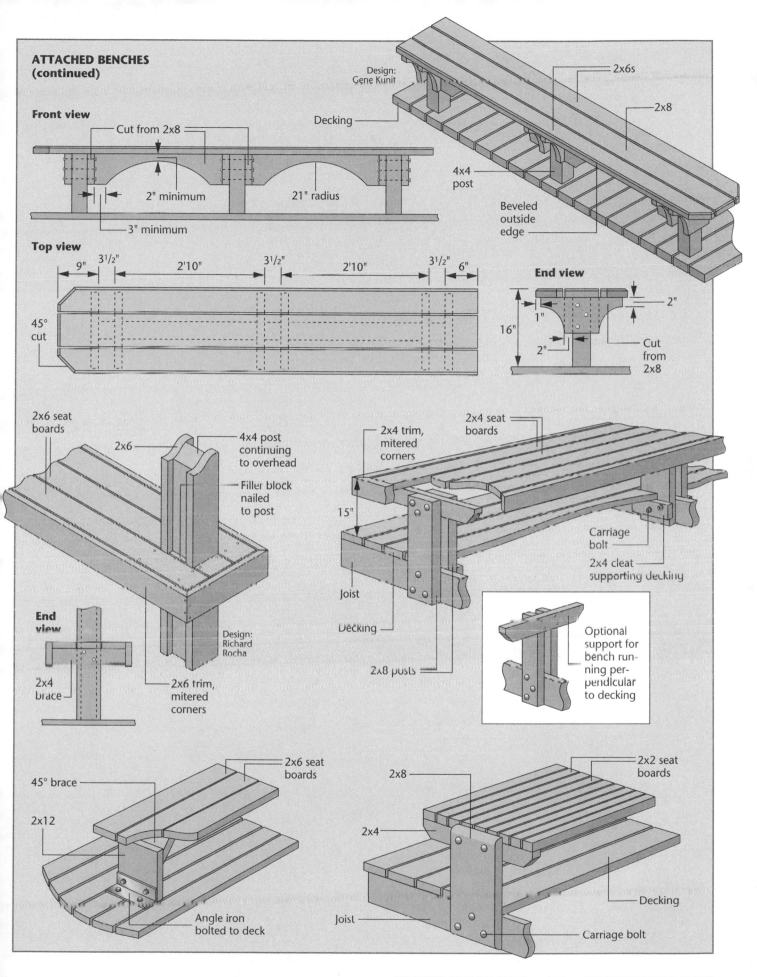

Design: Gene Kunit

Front view

Cut from 2x8

2" minimum

3" minimum

21" radius

Decking

2x6s

2x8

4x4 post

Beveled outside edge

Top view

9"   3½"   2'10"   3½"   2'10"   3½"   6"

45° cut

End view

16"

1"

2"

2"

Cut from 2x8

2x6 seat boards

2x6

4x4 post continuing to overhead

Filler block nailed to post

End view

2x4 brace

2x6 trim, mitered corners

Design: Richard Rocha

2x4 trim, mitered corners

2x4 seat boards

15"

Joist

Decking

2x8 posts

Carriage bolt

2x4 cleat supporting decking

Optional support for bench running perpendicular to decking

45° brace

2x12

2x6 seat boards

Angle iron bolted to deck

2x8

2x4

Joist

2x2 seat boards

Decking

Carriage bolt

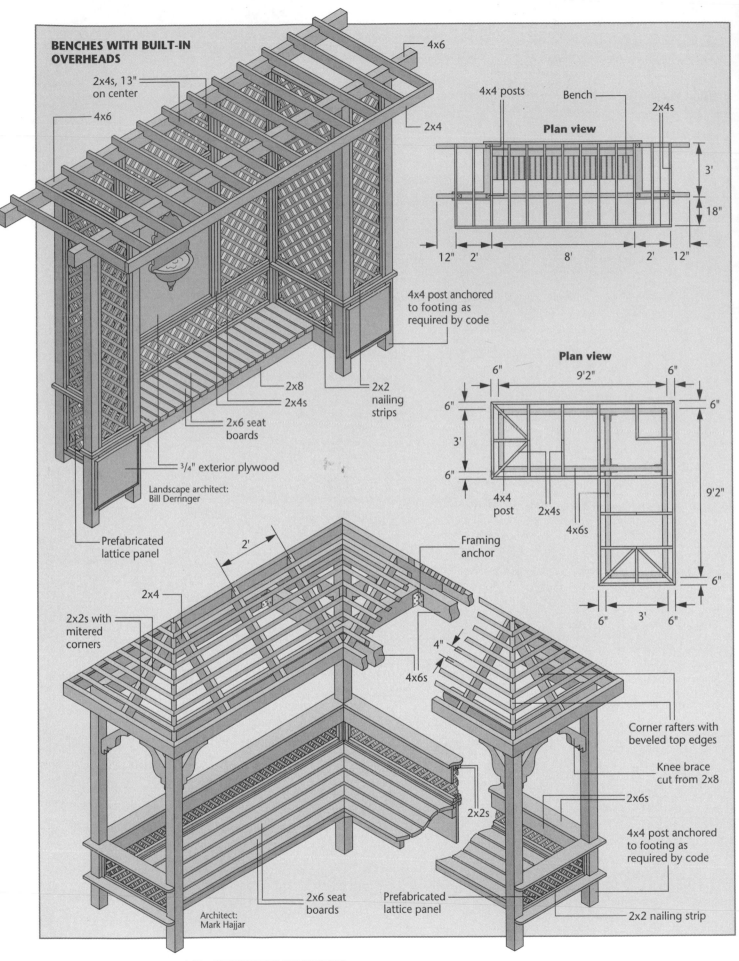

BENCHES WITH BUILT-IN OVERHEADS

2x4s, 13" on center

4x6

4x6

2x4

Plan view

4x4 posts

Bench

2x4s

3'

18"

12"   2'   8'   2'   12"

4x4 post anchored to footing as required by code

2x8

2x4s

2x2 nailing strips

2x6 seat boards

3/4" exterior plywood

Landscape architect: Bill Derringer

Prefabricated lattice panel

Plan view

6"   9'2"   6"

6"   6"

3'

6"

9'2"

4x4 post

2x4s

4x6s

6"

6"   3'   6"

2'

2x4

2x2s with mitered corners

Framing anchor

4"

4x6s

4x6s

Corner rafters with beveled top edges

Knee brace cut from 2x8

2x6s

4x4 post anchored to footing as required by code

2x2s

2x6 seat boards

Prefabricated lattice panel

2x2 nailing strip

Architect: Mark Hajjar

TABLES

If you plan to use your deck for outdoor entertaining, you'll find that a table is an essential addition. You can, of course, purchase ready-made tables. However, if you prefer one that is custom-tailored to your deck and its other amenities, you'll want to build the table yourself.

The simplest tables, as shown below *(top left)*, are constructed like four-legged, backless benches *(page 158)*. A slightly more elaborate table is also shown

(bottom). It's a variation of the traditional four-legged style, which was designed to fit into a conversation nook. You can also choose a double-pedestal style (also called a refectory table).

Whatever style you choose, plan the table's height to suit its intended purpose: 16 to 18 inches for a coffee table or children's play surface, 28 inches for dining or games.

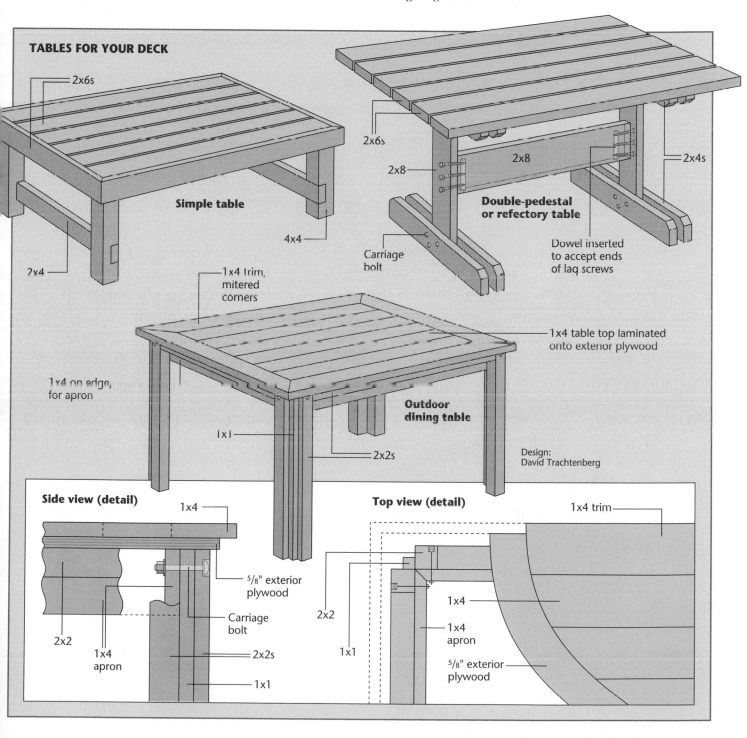

TABLES FOR YOUR DECK

2x6s

Simple table

4x4

2x4

2x6s

2x8

2x8

**Double-pedestal
or refectory table**

Carriage
bolt

2x4s

Dowel inserted
to accept ends
of lag screws

1x4 trim,
mitered
corners

1x4 table top laminated
onto exterior plywood

1x4 on edge,
for apron

1x1

2x2s

**Outdoor
dining table**

Design:
David Trachtenberg

Side view (detail)

1x4

5/8" exterior
plywood

Carriage
bolt

2x2

1x4
apron

2x2s

1x1

Top view (detail)

1x4 trim

1x4

1x4
apron

5/8" exterior
plywood

2x2

1x1

STORAGE COMPARTMENTS

There's great potential for outdoor storage right on your deck. You can create storage space by hinging the seat of a bench that has enclosed sides (two possibilities are shown below). Or by hinging a section of decking—in essence, making a trapdoor—you can gain access to a perfect storage area for hoses, outdoor equipment, toys, or even a sandbox.

For storage in a bench, you can hinge the whole seat, or just a section of it (install 2x4 supports on each side of the section). Use either brass or galvanized hinges; both are weather resistant, but galvanized hinges are less expensive. Add battens (1x3s or 2x4s) perpendicular to the seat boards for bracing. If your bench seat will open against a railing, you can hold it open with a hook and eye.

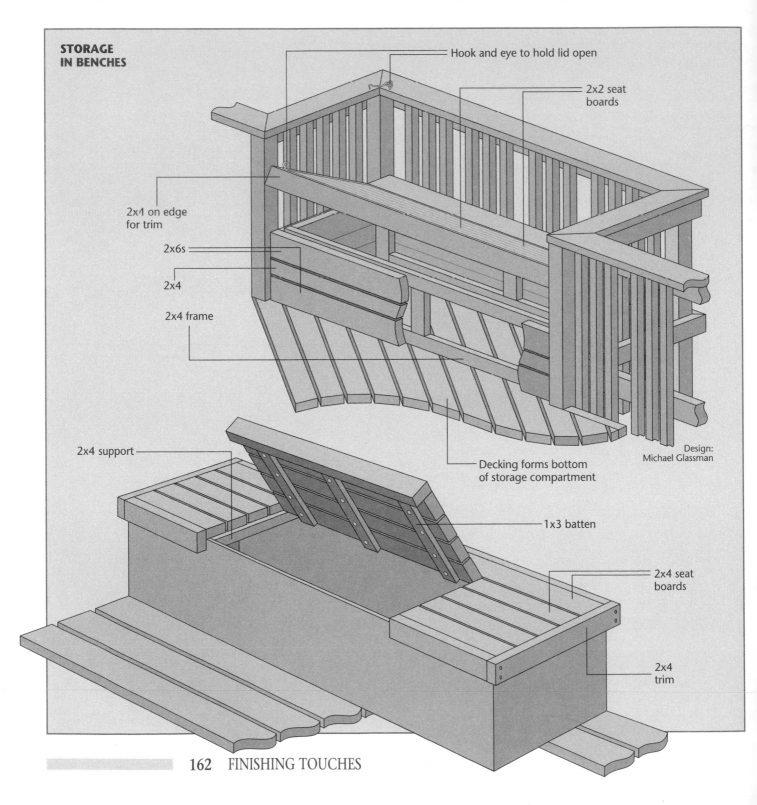

STORAGE IN BENCHES

Hook and eye to hold lid open

2x2 seat boards

2x4 on edge for trim

2x6s

2x4

2x4 frame

Decking forms bottom of storage compartment

Design: Michael Glassman

2x4 support

1x3 batten

2x4 seat boards

2x4 trim

For any below-deck compartment, construction is similar—and simple; some examples are shown below. Cut the decking for the door so each end rests on the center of a joist or beam. On the door's underside, fasten a batten (such as a 1x3 or 2x2) to hold the door together. Fasten these strips into the deck boards from beneath with nails or screws that penetrate about two-thirds of the way into the decking. For extra support or for large doors, fasten strap metal or an extra batten diagonally across the underside of the door.

Doors can be set in place and simply lifted out for access, or hinged for greater convenience. If you opt for hinges, use the leaf type. To create a finger pull, just drill a hole. You can add a handle, but make sure it's recessed into the decking so that no one will trip over it.

For the sides and bottom of your storage compartment, make a five-sided box of exterior-grade plywood to fit between the joists, and secure it to the joists with galvanized wood screws or, for extra strength, carriage bolts or lag screws. Drill holes in the bottom for drainage.

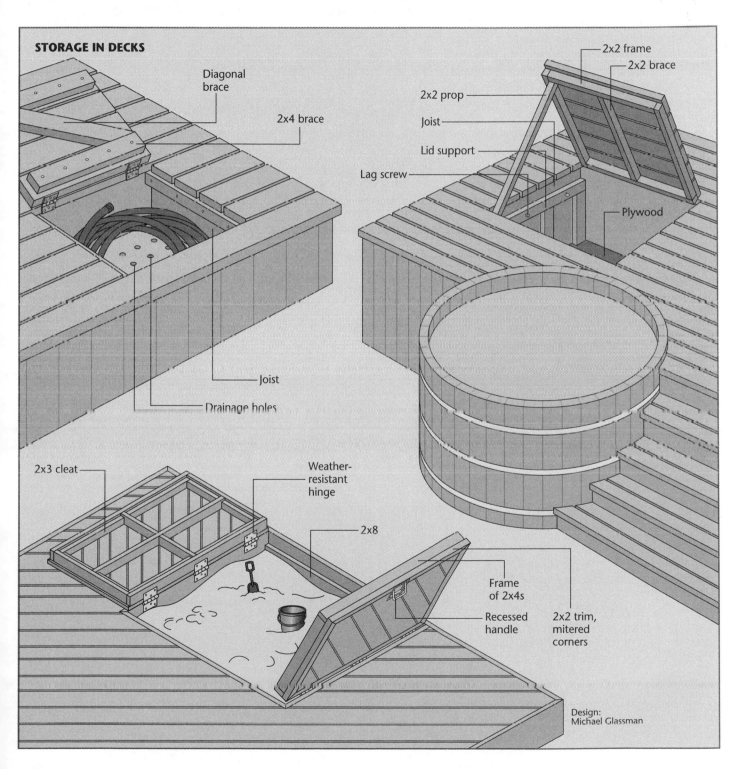

STORAGE IN DECKS

Diagonal brace

2x4 brace

2x2 frame

2x2 brace

2x2 prop

Joist

Lid support

Lag screw

Plywood

Joist

Drainage holes

2x3 cleat

Weather-resistant hinge

2x8

Frame of 2x4s

Recessed handle

2x2 trim, mitered corners

Design: Michael Glassman

PLANTERS

Plants help to soften the look of a deck: A custom-built planter can unite the deck with an adjacent garden, or if there's no garden nearby, a planter can provide a miniature garden right on the deck.

Most planters are variations on the basic box. Yet there are seemingly infinite ways to vary the surface ornamentation. No matter what design you devise, there are some construction guidelines you should follow.

Use decay-resistant wood, such as cedar or redwood heartwood. You can use pressure-treated wood instead, but not if it's treated with creosote, which is toxic to plants. If a design calls for plywood, exterior-rated pressure-treated plywood is recommended. If you're designing a planter entirely of dimension lumber, use boards that are nominally 2 inches thick—actually 1$\frac{1}{2}$ inches thick—for all but small planters.

To build a basic box, simply screw the corners together—if they'll be covered by trim. For additional sturdiness, use waterproof glue as well. To avoid unsightly rust stains, make sure all nails, screws, or bolts are corrosion resistant (*page 97*).

ASK A PRO

SHOULD I WATERPROOF A PLANTER?

To give your custom-crafted planter the longest possible life, line its interior with a waterproof barrier to separate the soil from the wood. Two easy-to-use materials are heavy-duty plastic sheeting and roofing felt (tar paper). Completely cover the bottom and sides, staple the material in place around the top margin—the soil will hold the rest snug to the sides—then make slits over the planter's drainage holes. Or, you could paint the planter's interior with a waterproof, bituminous roof coating or roofing cement.

For longest-lasting protection, use a more solid liner fabricated to fit the planter's inside dimensions. You can make a fiberglass liner with materials from an auto-body or boat repair kit, or you can have a liner made—galvanized steel from a sheet metal shop or vinyl from a waterbed manufacturer. Remember to include drainage holes.

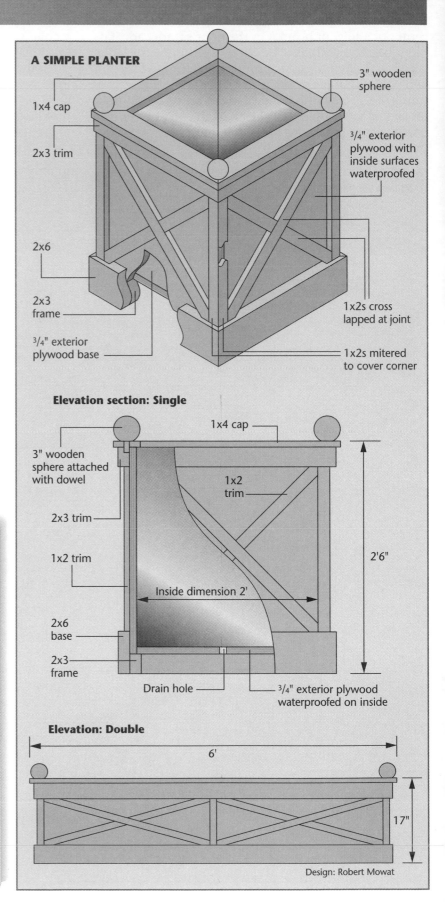

A SIMPLE PLANTER

1x4 cap

3" wooden sphere

2x3 trim

$\frac{3}{4}$" exterior plywood with inside surfaces waterproofed

2x6

1x2s cross lapped at joint

2x3 frame

$\frac{3}{4}$" exterior plywood base

1x2s mitered to cover corner

Elevation section: Single

3" wooden sphere attached with dowel

1x4 cap

1x2 trim

2x3 trim

1x2 trim

Inside dimension 2'

2'6"

2x6 base

2x3 frame

Drain hole

$\frac{3}{4}$" exterior plywood waterproofed on inside

Elevation: Double

6'

17"

Design: Robert Mowat

Bore drainage holes in the bottom of each planter, or leave space between the boards in the bottom to allow for drainage.

Because you'll be watering the plants in your containers, you should take a few precautions to safeguard your deck from decay. Always provide air space between planters and decking by setting the planters on 1/2-inch-high decay-resistant spacers. If possible, avoid placing planters over the deck's supporting members; ongoing drainage could lead to structural rot in areas that will be difficult to replace later on.

MAINTENANCE TIP

SHIFT YOUR DECK ACCESSORIES

A deck that is given a chance to dry out completely is less likely to rot. If possible, you should regularly change the position of your deck accessories, such as planters, tables, and benches, to give your deck a chance to dry out. Also, never place a bottomless planter directly on a deck.

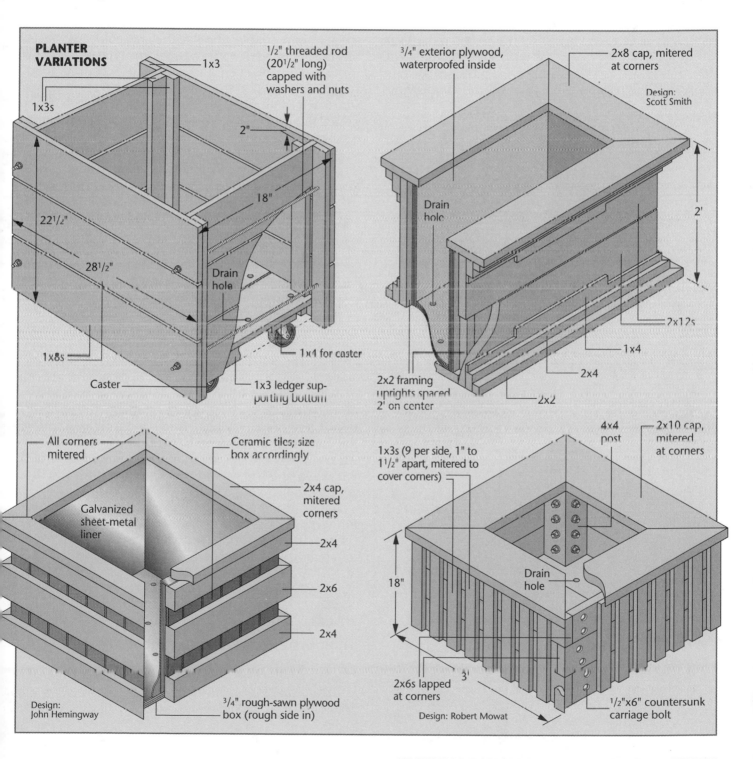

PLANTER VARIATIONS

1x3

1x3s

1x3s

22 1/2"

28 1/2"

1x8s

Caster

1/2" threaded rod (20 1/2" long) capped with washers and nuts

2"

18"

Drain hole

1x4 for caster

1x3 ledger supporting bottom

3/4" exterior plywood, waterproofed inside

2x8 cap, mitered at corners

Design: Scott Smith

Drain hole

2'

2x12s

1x4

2x2

2x4

2x2 framing uprights spaced 2' on center

All corners mitered

Galvanized sheet-metal liner

Ceramic tiles; size box accordingly

2x4 cap, mitered corners

2x4

2x6

2x4

Design: John Hemingway

3/4" rough-sawn plywood box (rough side in)

1x3s (9 per side, 1" to 1 1/2" apart, mitered to cover corners)

4x4 post

2x10 cap, mitered at corners

Drain hole

18"

2x6s lapped at corners

3'

Design: Robert Mowat

1/2"x6" countersunk carriage bolt

FINISHING YOUR DECK

The type of finish with the right degree of protection for your deck depends on the climate, grade and species of wood, and the look you want to achieve. Possible choices include clear water repellents, stains, and paints. Water repellents and stains may include a mildewcide (to protect the deck against surface mildew), or a stronger preservative (sometimes listed as a fungicide) that will prevent decay as well as mildew.

Different species of wood vary in their resistance to natural damage. Some types—redwood and cedar heartwood, for example—are decay resistant by nature, while pressure-treated woods are chemically treated to resist decay. But because no wood is completely impervious to damaging environmental effects, all types benefit from a finish.

Exposed unfinished wood will turn gray from the effects of the sun's UV rays. It also has a tendency to warp, crack, and split from seasonal wet and dry periods, and it may rot.

The heartwood of cedar and redwood is resistant to rot, but it will turn gray from UV rays. It may also crack and split over time, although not as much as some other species. Some people who like the gray color that develops over time may want to leave this type of decking unfinished. However, a finish is still recommended, to protect the wood from the physical effects of exposure (such as warping) and from surface mildew. If you prefer the gray color, you can choose a clear water repellent without UV protection.

If your cedar or redwood decking contains any sapwood, apply a finish containing a preservative, since the sapwood of cedar and redwood is no more resistant to decay than any other species of wood.

If you're using pressure-treated lumber for the substructure of your deck, it's not essential to finish it; the wood won't rot, and as long as the effects of weathering aren't visible, they won't detract from the beauty of your deck. However, the substructure will withstand the effects of weather better if it's finished. If you are going to apply a finish to the substructure, it's easiest to do so before you fasten the decking in place.

Regardless of the kind of wood you're using in your deck, or the finish treatment you choose, it's best to apply the finish as soon as possible, to reduce the effects of exposure to weather. Leaving lumber untreated for more than four weeks is not recommended. For best results, treat the decking before you install it. Coating the ends is especially important because they absorb water much more quickly than the surface of the board. But make sure the wood is dry if required for the finishing product you're using.

The finishing product you choose must be suitable for decks, for the type of lumber you're using, and for the specific application. For example, you may need a different finish for the decking than for the vertical sur-

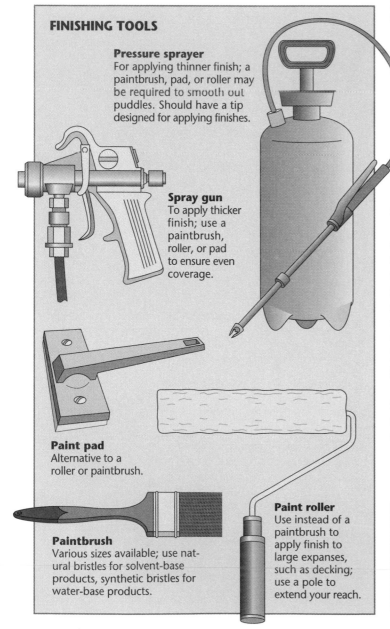

FINISHING TOOLS

Pressure sprayer
For applying thinner finish; a paintbrush, pad, or roller may be required to smooth out puddles. Should have a tip designed for applying finishes.

Spray gun
To apply thicker finish; use a paintbrush, roller, or pad to ensure even coverage.

Paint pad
Alternative to a roller or paintbrush.

Paintbrush
Various sizes available; use natural bristles for solvent-base products, synthetic bristles for water-base products.

Paint roller
Use instead of a paintbrush to apply finish to large expanses, such as decking; use a pole to extend your reach.

ASK A PRO

SHOULD I ROUND BOARD EDGES?
The exposed edge of a deck board may split; rounding over this edge with a router will help prevent this. This will also give a decorative touch to the deck, and can be done on stairs, railings, and benches.

faces, because the decking is subject to more wear. To help you choose between water repellents, stains, and paints, some details follow.

Clear water repellents: Also known as water sealers, these products protect wood and help prolong its beauty, although only those water repellents with UV protection prevent the natural graying of wood. Water repellents don't color wood (unless you buy a pigmented type), but they do darken it slightly.

A water repellent with a mildewcide is recommended, especially if the product is oil-base, to discourage the growth of surface mildew. Water repellents with a mildewcide or fungicide are often called water repellent preservatives.

Stains: Stains come in two color intensities. Semitransparent types contain enough pigment to tint the wood, but not enough to hide the natural grain. Solid-color stains (also called heavy-bodied stains) contain more pigment; many are almost as opaque as paint.

With stains, the final color is a combination of the color of the wood and the color of the stain. A darker-colored stain will help mask the green tinge of some pressure-treated lumber.

A semitransparent stain is a good choice for a new deck. When the deck has weathered and needs to be refinished, you'll then have the choice of cleaning the deck *(page 172)* and refinishing it with a semitransparent stain, or covering it with a solid-color stain. Semitransparent stains will last up to nine years, while solid-color stains require reapplication every two or three years.

Paints: Deck paints can mask defects in lower grades of lumber. However, they're harder to apply and maintain than stains; to keep your deck looking good, you may have to repaint it nearly every year. A primer is not recommended for decking, but may be used on the substructure. Paints are not recommended for naturally decay-resistant woods, since they tend to trap water inside the wood.

You can either construct the deck first and paint afterward, or paint the substructure before laying the decking. Depending on what product you're applying, you may need to leave the lumber some time to dry before applying paint; follow the manufacturer's instructions.

QUICK FIX

REPAIRING HAMMER DENTS

If you dent the wood when you're nailing decking in place, there are two ways to fix it. You can splash a little wood sealer on the indentations—the sealer will cause the bruised wood to swell back to its normal size. Or, you can treat the bruised wood with a rag soaked with warm water. If you plan to stain the deck, choose the second option since the sealer may have a tendency to repel the stain.

NOTE: Some states have laws requiring lower levels of volatile organic compounds (VOCs) in finishes. Solvent- or oil-base products contain high levels of VOCs; water-base products also contain VOCs, but at much lower levels. In areas with strict VOC regulations, you'll only find products that comply; elsewhere, you may have a choice. Water-base finishes can be applied to wood previously treated with an oil-base finish, but for best results, use products from the same manufacturer.

FINISHING TIPS

Before you apply a finish, the boards must be free of mill glaze and sufficiently dry. Mill glaze is an impervious layer on the wood's surface created by the polishing effect of power tool blades when the wood is cut or planed. To remove it, sand the surface (try using a drywall pole), or use a mill-glaze removal product. Once this is done, apply the finish in a hidden area or to a scrap board (also treated for mill glaze). If it doesn't penetrate, allow the wood more time to dry (usually not more than one month), unless the finishing product is designed to be applied directly to damp lumber. Finally, sweep or dust any debris off all the surfaces.

Semitransparent stains can be brushed on, or applied with a roller or sprayer and then brushed smooth. Solid-color stains may be brushed, rolled, or sprayed on. For either type, follow the label instructions for specific application tools or procedures.

Apply paint with either a brush, roller, or spray gun, unless the manufacturer recommends otherwise. Try to paint on a cool, windless day. Paint often dries so quickly in hot weather that it fails to bond properly—and if conditions are dusty as well as hot, the deck's surface may be marred or roughened. If you must paint on a hot, dry day, work only after the sun is low so the paint will dry slowly.

Pay special attention to the chemical compatibility of the primer (if you're using one), and the top coat. Be sure that the manufacturer's recommendations apply to the treatment and finish you're using, and that these materials are suitable for decks. Using materials from the same manufacturer will give you a head start on compatibility, but even so, check labels.

Be sure to use the type of brush recommended for the product: natural bristle brushes for solvent-base finishes, synthetic bristle brushes for water-base ones. If the deck is raised, use drop cloths to protect the surrounding area from drips and overspray.

CAUTION: Wear goggles and a respirator to protect your eyes and lungs when applying a finish.

MAINTENANCE AND REPAIR

It's no wonder that a deck may begin to show its age after a few years—just consider what it has to endure. Sun beats down on it, breaking down wood fibers; rain may make the deck boards swell and twist; debris can fill the cracks between the boards, restricting air circulation and encouraging rot; mildew can develop under potted plants; and the surface of the decking typically gets stained, scraped by furniture, and has dirt ground in as people walk over it.

If your deck looks the worse for wear, consider restoring it. You may be surprised at how new you can make it look, even down to the color.

In this chapter, you'll find tips on regular deck maintenance *(page 171)*. Beginning on page 172, you'll learn how to remove dirt, mildew, and discoloration and how to prepare your deck for refinishing. Information on how to repair the various parts of your deck—the decking, railings, and stairs, as well as the substructure—begins on page 174.

You may need to fix the structural supports of your deck; the repairs shown in this chapter include replacing a beam (above), *reinforcing a joist, and installing a ledger support for extra strength.*

BEFORE YOU BEGIN

The best way to keep your deck looking beautiful is to develop the habit of regular maintenance and inspection. Tips on what to look for are given on page 171.

Repairs to the substructure of the deck—replacing a joist, for example—are easiest to do from below, as shown in the illustrations further along in this chapter. However, if your deck is too low to permit you to work from underneath, you'll have to remove some deck boards to get at the area that needs repair. Remove decking carefully if it's in good condition, because you'll probably want to reinstall the same pieces when your repairs to the substructure are completed.

You may want to apply preservative or the same finish as the existing deck to any new pieces you need

PLAY IT SAFE

SET UP A BARRIER TO ACCIDENTS

To keep accidents from happening while you're repairing your deck, set up a temporary barrier around any potentially dangerous areas. Keep the area well lit at night, and put up signs to indicate that there's a hazard.

Cover any opening (in the decking or in the ground) with a sheet of plywood. Position sawhorses and boards or a rope, or a row of outdoor furniture around any hazard, such as a hole or a missing section of railing. Tie colored rags to the barrier to help draw attention to it.

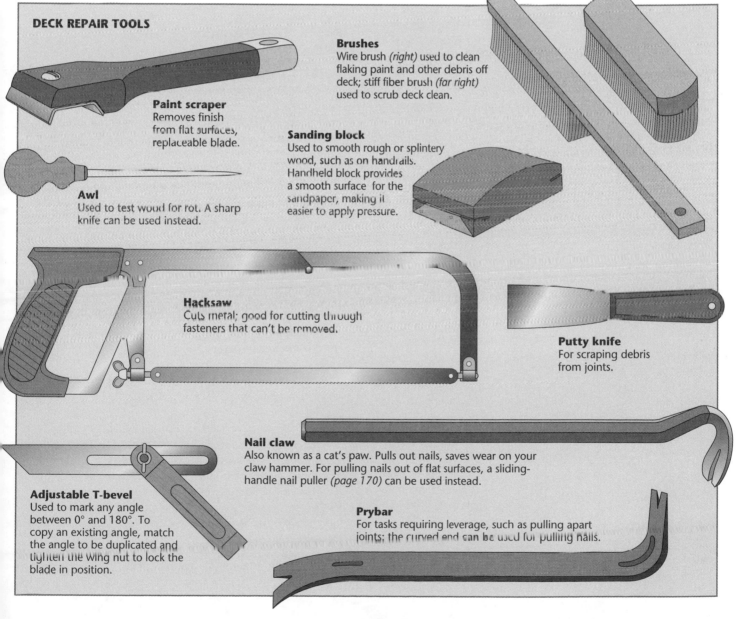

DECK REPAIR TOOLS

Paint scraper
Removes finish from flat surfaces, replaceable blade.

Brushes
Wire brush *(right)* used to clean flaking paint and other debris off deck; stiff fiber brush *(far right)* used to scrub deck clean.

Awl
Used to test wood for rot. A sharp knife can be used instead.

Sanding block
Used to smooth rough or splintery wood, such as on handrails. Handheld block provides a smooth surface for the sandpaper, making it easier to apply pressure.

Hacksaw
Cuts metal; good for cutting through fasteners that can't be removed.

Putty knife
For scraping debris from joints.

Nail claw
Also known as a cat's paw. Pulls out nails, saves wear on your claw hammer. For pulling nails out of flat surfaces, a sliding-handle nail puller *(page 170)* can be used instead.

Adjustable T-bevel
Used to mark any angle between 0° and 180°. To copy an existing angle, match the angle to be duplicated and tighten the wing nut to lock the blade in position.

Prybar
For tasks requiring leverage, such as pulling apart joints; the curved end can be used for pulling nails.

to install before you install them. If you have to replace some of the deck boards, take the time to coat the joists or beams underneath with a wood preservative before nailing on the new wood.

Depending on the age of your deck, you may find that you have to refinish the entire surface of the deck after the new pieces are installed, so that the new boards aren't so obvious.

In addition to the tools shown on the previous page, you'll need some or all of the following tools: claw hammer, screwdriver, screw gun (or a variable-speed electric drill equipped to drive screws), wrench or socket wrench, and circular saw. (Turn to page 104 for illustrations and further details on these tools.) You can rent a power washer to wash the deck. You may also want a power miter box if you've got a lot of angles to cut, or a router to smooth over the edges of new deck boards; both of these tools can be rented.

The finishing tools that you may need to use are shown on page 166, along with information on the available finishing products and tips on their application. Also shown is a pressure sprayer, very handy for applying deck-cleaning products.

Repairs to decks rarely require a permit, but significant new work does have to conform to local codes. Keep in mind that these codes may have changed from those in effect when the deck was originally built. For example, the spacing between the rails of a new railing will have to meet current code requirements, even if the railing you're replacing didn't.

GEARED FOR SAFETY

When you're repairing your deck, always wear the appropriate safety gear. Protect your eyes with goggles, safety glasses, or a face mask when using any striking tool, such as a hammer, or power tools. Protect your ears from the noise of power tools by wearing earplugs or the earmuff type of hearing protectors. Respiratory protection is also important: To avoid breathing harmful chemicals, wear a respirator; a dust mask is considered adequate protection from sawdust.

To protect your hands, wear the appropriate type of gloves: all-leather or leather-reinforced cotton work gloves for handling rough or sharp objects; disposable rubber or plastic gloves when working with solvents, wood preservatives, or adhesives. Wear sturdy work-boots or shoes—models with steel toes and soles are recommended—and if you're working under the deck or with others, put on a hardhat.

 ### ASK A PRO

WHAT'S THE BEST WAY TO REMOVE FASTENERS?
Different fasteners are removed in different ways. To remove nails, first, if possible, loosen them by hammering on the back of the wood near the joint or by prying apart the joint with a prybar or wrecking bar. Nails can usually be pulled with a claw hammer or a nail claw, although for large nails, you may need to use a prybar or wrecking bar. If the nail is headless, or is countersunk, drive it through the wood with a nailset. If you're removing a large number of nails from a flat surface, use a sliding-handle nail puller to make the job easier. This tool has jaws that grab the nail head when the handle is slid down; by rocking the handle against the built-in lever, the nail is pulled out of the wood. However, this type of nail puller is fairly expensive, and you may want to rent one.

To remove screws or bolts, you can usually use the same tool you would use to install them: Screws call for a screwdriver—manual or power—or a power screw gun or reversible variable-speed electric drill with a screwdriver bit. If you have many screws to remove, you'll appreciate the convenience of a power tool. Lag screws and carriage bolts will require a wrench or socket wrench of the appropriate size for the head and nut, respectively; you'll need two wrenches for regular machine bolts. For extra gripping strength, use locking pliers. If you encounter a rusted nut, apply penetrating oil to the bolt shaft, the washer, and the nut; let it soak in, then try to loosen the nut.

To remove a screw that has a damaged head, drill a pilot hole in the head, insert a screw extractor into the hole, and turn the extractor with a tap wrench. If this doesn't work, use a prybar to pry the joint far enough apart to work a hacksaw in; cut through the shaft of the screw.

DECK MAINTENANCE

Keeping your deck free of debris is probably the most important aspect of deck maintenance. Dirt on the deck and stairs gets ground in by foot traffic, wearing the finish down. Good drainage is required so that the deck can dry properly after it gets wet; leaves and needles can block drainage channels, impeding proper drying. Sweep the deck regularly to remove leaves and other loose items, and spray it with a garden hose to further remove dirt. Don't overlook the stairs—they're probably the heaviest traffic area of the deck and may need cleaning more frequently than the decking. Refinishing the stairs more frequently than the rest of the deck is a preventive measure that will help keep dirt particles from damaging the wood.

Debris that collects between butt joints in deck boards or between parallel boards should also be removed: Use a hard spray of water from a garden hose to dislodge it, following up with a putty knife to knock out any recalcitrant litter. Boards should be adequately spaced to allow proper drainage. If your deck boards are too close together, cut a wider gap between them as described on the following page.

To give the entire deck a chance to dry, move deck furniture, planters, and other accessories periodically.

Inspect your deck regularly and repair any problems you find. Check the condition of the boards, looking for nail stains, splintering, splits, and cupping *(page 93)*. Look for popped nails (nailheads that have worked loose and are exposed above the surface of the decking), unstable railings or stairs, and rotted wood (either on the surface of the deck or below). Check for rot wherever two pieces of wood meet, on any surfaces where water may collect, and at ground level on wood in contact with the ground. Wood may show no visible signs of rot, or it may appear spongy or discolored. To test for rot, insert an awl or the tip of a sharp knife into the wood. If the awl or blade penetrates easily, or if the wood seems soft and crumbles instead of splintering, it is likely rotten and needs to be replaced.

Insect damage may also be a problem. Remove any loose finish from areas you suspect. Look for tiny holes or tunnels, or powdery or pitted surfaces. If you think your deck has suffered insect damage, consult a pest-control professional.

Dealing with deck nails

TOOLKIT
- Claw hammer
- Nailset
- Screwdriver (optional)

Resetting popped nails

Since it is the nature of wood to tend to swell and contract over time, nails that were once seated firmly can slowly work loose. This means that resetting nails is a regular task for most deck owners.

To reset rising nails, punch them flush with or slightly below the deck's surface with a hammer and nailset.

If you find that some nails pop frequently, you can reinforce them or replace them. To reinforce them, first set them with a nailset then fasten a galvanized deck screw next to the nail so that the head of the screw overlaps the head of the nail. Or, you can pull the nail and replace it with a galvanized deck screw.

QUICK FIX

STRENGTHENING SEPARATING JOINTS

Joints between the various parts of a deck may separate over time; repositioning the offending members and reinforcing the joint will usually solve the problem. Loosening may occur where the stair stringers meet the joists or rim joist, where railing posts meet the rim joist or joists, and where the joists meet the ledger. There are framing connectors available for most situations; turn to page 100 for more details.

If stringers have worked loose, first move the staircase back into position by tapping against the front edge of the top stair tread with a hand-drilling hammer; protect the stair

with a scrap of 2x4. Then, fasten the stringer to the rim joist or joist with a framing anchor or carriage bolt.

To reinforce a loose railing post that's nailed or screwed to a joist or the rim joist, drill through both the post and the joist and fasten them tightly together with carriage bolts. Or, you can secure the post with strap-type connectors.

Reposition a joist that has pulled away from the ledger by hitting it at the other end with a hand-drilling hammer; protect the wood with a scrap of lumber. Once the joist is repositioned, secure it to the ledger board with a joist hanger.

CLEANING OR REFINISHING A DECK

Of all the steps involved in deck restoration, cleaning probably involves the most labor, especially if you haven't done it in a while. But this is an important step; once your deck is clean, you may find that it's in better shape than you thought.

Start by cleaning between the decking. For a healthy deck, maximum air circulation must be maintained around each board; the debris that builds up between deck boards slows drainage, keeping wood moist and encouraging the growth of mildew. First spray with water from a garden hose, then scrape out whatever debris remains with a putty knife.

Dirt tracked over and ground into a deck can eventually turn it dusty gray; in shady areas, mildew can build up and make the wood slippery when it's wet. But the hardest weathering comes from the sun's ultraviolet rays, which break down the wood tissue's lignin—a plastic-like polymer binding the cellulose fibers together. The end product of degraded lignin is cellulose in minute strands, and these give boards a tired-looking gray surface.

In order to rejuvenate your deck, you'll have to determine which of these problems applies to your situation, and choose your cleaning method accordingly.

To determine if your deck is simply dirty, mix a sudsy solution of water and laundry detergent and use a stiff fiber brush to scrub this into a small area of the deck. If the deck is clean when you rinse this solution off, then the problem is dirt, and you can continue to wash the deck this way, rinsing it with a garden hose. To test for mildew, apply undiluted household liquid bleach to a small inconspicuous area of the deck, let it stand for about 30 seconds, and then rinse it off with water. If the deck comes clean, mildew is at least part of the problem. Stains may also be caused by chemicals in the wood being drawn up to the surface through exposure to weather, or by iron from the use of ungalvanized nails or from contact with other metal. To test for these stain problems, use oxalic acid. You can buy oxalic acid crystals at a home

center or hardware store (mix a solution of 4 ounces of the crystals to 1 quart of water), or use an oxalic acid-based cleaning product. Apply either liquid to a small, inconspicuous area. Let it stand 5 minutes, then scrub with a stiff fiber brush. If you have stains caused by weathering or iron, the deck will come clean when you rinse off the oxalic acid.

Once you've discovered the source of your deck's discoloration, look into deck-cleaning or deck-restoring products. Check the ingredients: Oxalic acid will clean stains caused by chemicals in the wood or by iron. It doesn't kill mildew, but it may brighten a mildewed surface. Chlorine bleach-base products will kill mildew, but they may also leave the wood looking washed out, since chlorine bleach has a tendency to break down the lignin that holds the wood fibers together. A deck cleaned with bleach will have a surface layer of loose fibers, which may keep any finish you then apply from adhering properly.

There are also products that are less toxic than acid or bleach; important both for the environment and for the person applying the product. Many of these products are sodium percarbonate-base (similar to what is used in nonchlorine bleach). When this type of product is in use, the sodium percarbonate breaks down into hydrogen peroxide, which bleaches and helps remove the grayed cellulose cells; and sodium carbonate, which cleans the wood. To remove the old cellulose, brush the wood with a stiff fiber brush, then rinse.

Certain deck-restoration products that are also environmentally friendly actually dissolve the weathered cellulose without harming the healthy wood cells. The dissolved wood cells are rinsed off your deck when you rinse off the cleaning solution. The cleaning product itself becomes innocuous when dissolved in water.

Whatever you use, work safely. Wear gloves and goggles when applying the cleaning product—and a respirator if you're using a pressure sprayer—or when scrubbing. Bleach can discolor fabric, so wear old clothes. Never mix different commercial cleaners, or mix them with any household cleaner, unless the manufacturer's directions tell you to. Also follow the manufacturer's instructions for protecting greenery around the deck; even those products that are the least harmful to the environment in their final form may still cause damage to plants when undiluted.

CAUTION: Never mix bleach with any product containing ammonia—a lethal substance is created.

Once you've cleaned your deck, and made any necessary repairs, you'll want to refinish it to help keep it looking its best, and to get the longest life possible from the wood. Choosing and applying a finish is discussed beginning on page 166.

 QUICK FIX

WIDENING THE SPACING
BETWEEN YOUR DECK BOARDS

If your deck's boards are set so close together that a hose can't clean between them, slip an old handsaw into the cracks and work the blade up and down. Some professionals recommend widening the gap between tightly spaced boards by making a pass with a circular saw with the depth of the blade set to match the wood's thickness. Recommended spacing between boards is $^1/_8$ to $^3/_{16}$ inch.

SHOULD I USE A POWER WASHER?

If you have a large deck, consider renting a power washer for the initial cleaning—it will help blast away dirt, as well as the surface layer of grayed cells, and save you a lot of elbow grease. You can also use a power washer to rinse your deck after you've applied a deck-cleaning product. A model that delivers about 1,000 psi of pressure is probably strong enough—more pressure can damage soft wood.

A power washer used incorrectly can also damage the wood. One way to reduce the chance of damage is to choose a nozzle with a 25° or 40° spray arc. Work in line with the wood's grain, holding the spray head at a slight angle about 4 to 6 inches above the deck's surface. Move slowly and evenly, overlapping adjacent sprayed areas. CAUTION: Wear safety goggles whenever you're operating a power washer.

Removing mildew, stains, and old cellulose

TOOLKIT
• Paint roller, mop, or pressure sprayer
• Stiff fiber scrub brush or broom
• Power washer (optional)

Dealing with special problems

Your deck may not simply be dirty; it may be plagued by mildew, iron stains, or discoloration caused by chemicals in the wood, or it may be grayed from unprotected exposure to the elements. There are various products available to deal with some or all of these problems.

Chlorine bleach will remove mildew; make a solution of 1 or 2 cups bleach to each gallon of water, or buy a bleach-base deck-cleaning product. Spray the solution on with a pressure sprayer, or use a roller or mop to spread it evenly over the deck. Let it stand approximately 15 minutes, then spray it off with a garden hose or power washer. Don't scrub unless the product label recommends it; scrubbing can make the deck look worse. Keep in mind that some experts recommend against using bleach, since it will affect the structure of the wood, as described opposite.

Acid-base cleaning products, including those with an oxalic acid base, can be used to clean decks discolored by iron or chemicals in the wood.

You can make your own solution of about 4 ounces oxalic acid crystals to 1 gallon of water, or buy an acid-base deck-cleaning product. Apply the solution with a pressure sprayer, mop, or roller. Wait about 15 minutes, then scrub with a stiff fiber brush or broom and rinse the deck with a hose or power washer.

To deal with dirt, mildew, stains, and grayed cellulose all at once, choose a commercially available deck-cleaning product and follow the manufacturer's directions. Generally, you roll or spray the solution evenly onto the deck. Wait the period of time specified on the label (about 15 minutes), then scrub with a stiff fiber brush or broom, and rinse the deck with a hose or power washer. NOTE: Some of these products may darken the wood, especially redwood and cedar. You may prefer the new color, or you can restore the wood to its original color using an oxalic acid solution or a product supplied by the manufacturer for this purpose.

Preparing to refinish

TOOLKIT
• Paint scraper, wire brush, or putty knife
OR
• Belt sander and sanding block
OR
• Paintbrush, roller, or pressure sprayer
• Stiff fiber scrub brush or broom
• Power washer (optional)

Scraping, sanding, or stripping your deck

To scrape off flaking or lifting finish, use a paint scraper, applying even pressure in the direction of the grain. Be sure to wear goggles or glasses to protect your eyes. In corners or tight places, use a wire brush. Remove debris from cracks with a putty knife, and use a broom or whisk to sweep up any flakes of paint you've loosened.

To remove a finish that's still adhered, with no flaking, sand the surface. Start with a belt sander, moving in the direction of the grain. A sanding block will come in handy for small patches or areas you can't reach with the power sander. Use a coarser grade of sandpaper for rough or heavily coated surfaces and finish up with a finer grade.

You can also use a commercially available stripping product designed to remove finish from exterior wood surfaces. Some of these products will also restore the wood, removing any old cellulose and returning the wood to its original color. Follow the manufacturer's directions for any such product, paying particular attention to the safety recommendations. Generally, you brush, roll, or spray the product on the deck and wait about 15 minutes, or the length of time specified by the manufacturer. Then brush the deck with a stiff fiber brush or broom, and remove the product with water from a hose or power sprayer.

REPAIRING DECKING

You'll eventually need to make some minor repairs to your decking. Boards may become warped or cupped over time, they may not be level with the boards around them, or you may find that some or all of the deck boards are damaged, cracked, or rotted and need to be replaced.

To salvage cupped boards, see the instructions in the tip below. To raise a board so its surface is level with those around it, brace it with shims from underneath the deck as described below. If you need to replace a board, follow the directions also found below.

If the decking surface is too damaged to be repaired by cleaning, but most boards are still sound, consider turning the boards over and reusing them. Do this the same way you would to replace a board; remove a few boards at a time, turn them over, and fasten them.

Raising a deck board

TOOLKIT
• Paintbrush for applying preservative
• Claw hammer

Inserting shims
If the surface of a board is not level with those around it, raise it by inserting shims underneath. Use either pre-cut shims or a cedar shingle broken off to approximately the same width as the deck board. If you're using precut shims, coat them with preservative.

Insert one shim from each side of the joist; tap both of them in between the joist and the bottom of the board, using a hammer, until the board is even with those next to it.

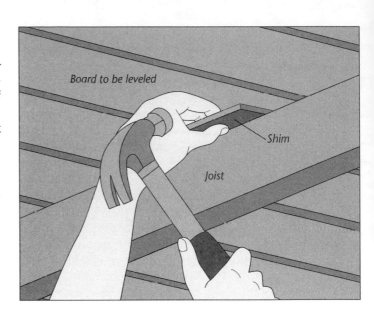

Board to be leveled

Shim

Joist

Replacing a board

TOOLKIT
• Claw hammer or nail claw; or screwdriver, screw gun, or electric drill
• Hand-drilling hammer
• Combination square
• Circular saw

Removing a board
Remove the nails with a claw hammer or nail claw, or nail puller. Or, you can hit the board from underneath with a hand-drilling hammer, if you have easy access to the underside of your deck. If you intend to turn the board over and reuse it, use a block of scrap wood to protect the bottom surface of the board from the blows. To remove screws, use a screwdriver, screw gun, or electric drill with the appropriate bit. Remove the board.

Cut a replacement board to the appropriate length (unless you're turning the original board over) and, using a nail as a spacer *(page 127)*, nail the board in place. If you're reusing a board, nail through the existing nail holes.

 ASK A PRO

HOW CAN I FIX A CUPPED DECK BOARD?
If the board is only slightly cupped, remove the nails and re-fasten it with galvanized deck screws: Fasten the screws tightly enough to flatten the board. If this doesn't work, remove the screws and the board. Set the depth of cut on a circular saw to about one-third the thickness of the board, and make several cuts in the back of the board along the length of the cup. Fasten the board in place with galvanized deck screws. If this doesn't solve the problem, you'll have to replace the board.

REPAIRING RAILINGS

Your deck railings are both functional and aesthetic: To keep them safe and looking good, inspect them periodically and make any necessary repairs. Over time, the railing posts may become loose if they're simply nailed in place. To strengthen them, install bolts or lag screws. Counterbore holes for the screws through the post and the structural member of the deck that it's attached to. Install lag screws with washers.

To replace a baluster or rail, remove the fasteners holding it to the rails or posts. Cut a new baluster or rail exactly like the one you've removed; if possible, use the old one as a model. Install the new baluster or rail, keeping the proper spacing between the new piece and the existing ones. If you're replacing several balusters, the job will be easier if you cut a scrap of wood to size to use as a spacer.

To replace a cap rail, remove the nails or screws holding it in place; to loosen nails, hammer up on the bottom of the rail. Use the old cap rail to mark the appropriate length and any angled cuts on a new piece of lumber of the same dimensions. Cut the new piece, and install it using the same type of fasteners as on the piece you removed. At mitered corners, toenail the adjacent cap rails together.

To replace a railing post that isn't a continuation of a post holding up the deck, first remove any rails attached to it. Then remove any fasteners connecting the post to the structural member of the deck. Using the old post as a template, mark and cut new dimension lumber to the appropriate length and shape. Position the new post, and install it with bolts, lag screws, or framing connectors. To replace a railing post that's an extension of a structural post turn to page 181.

If your posts are sound but your railing seems to lack strength, you can reinforce the posts by installing braces between them, as shown below.

QUICK FIX

REINFORCING A CAP RAIL
Make a brace from lumber of the same dimensions as the cap rail, sawing it to the same width as the post. Position the brace under the cap rail against the post. Drill pilot holes in the brace and nail or screw it to the post. For extra strength, nail or screw the cap rail into the brace from the top.

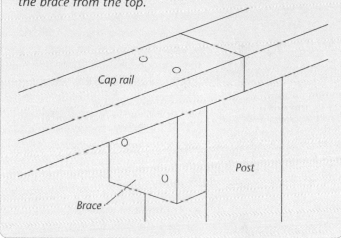

Reinforcing a railing post

TOOLKIT
- Circular saw
- Claw hammer

Adding a brace
To reinforce a railing post, install a brace made of 2-by lumber between it and the next post along the railing. Position the lumber diagonally between the posts, with the top of the brace against the weak post and the bottom against the next post. Mark the brace for length, and indicate the required angle on each end, then cut it to fit using a circular saw.

Choose the appropriate framing connectors for your situation: A selection is shown on pages 100 and 101, and many other varieties are available. Position the brace and nail the framing connector to both the brace and the posts.

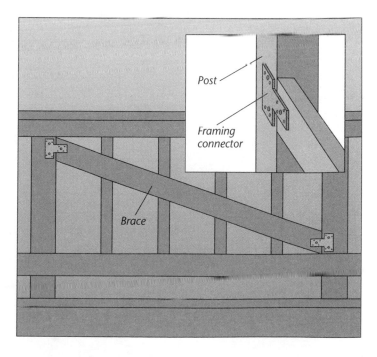

REPAIRING STAIRS

One way to strengthen your deck stairs is to install framing connectors *(page 100)* where the stringers join the deck. If the stairs have pulled away from the deck at the top, the stringers may have moved out of position at the bottom. To raise them up again, drive shims—use cedar shingles—between the bottom of the stringers and the concrete pad they rest on.

Stair treads may be attached in various ways: Placed on top of notched stringers, or supported by cleats or metal stair angles. To replace a damaged stair tread, first remove the fasteners holding it in place. To loosen

nails, hammer up on the bottom of the tread. Cut a new tread, using the old one as a guide if possible, and fasten it in place. If the tread is made up of more than one board, use a nail as a spacer. Usually, the spacing between the boards on the stairs matches the spacing between the deck boards.

If a stringer is weakened by cracking or splitting, reinforce it; if it's badly damaged, replace it. Both of these procedures are shown below. Before you do either, you'll have to remove any treads, railings, posts, or balusters that are in the way.

Reinforcing a stringer

TOOLKIT
- Circular saw
- Hand-drilling hammer
- Tape measure
- Combination square
- Electric drill
- Screwdriver

Installing a support
Cut a length of lumber (2x4 or thicker) at an angle to fit tightly under the damaged area as a brace. Position the brace on a board under the stringer and tap it into place with a hand-drilling hammer.

Using lumber of the same thickness as the stringer, cut a support to extend about 6" past each side of the damaged section; shape it to match the stringer if necessary to cover the damage. Fasten screws in pairs along the length of the support, starting with two at each end. Space the screws 10" to 12" apart (closer for shorter supports). Reinstall any parts of stairs or railing you removed.

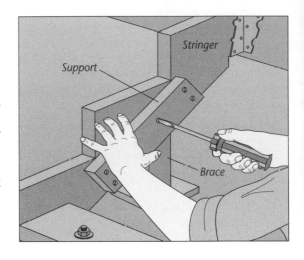

Replacing a stringer

TOOLKIT
- Tape measure
- Adjustable T-bevel (optional)
- Circular saw
- Crosscut saw
- Claw hammer

For a notched stringer:
- C-clamp
- Carpenter's level

Installing the stringer
To mark the new stringer, you can remove the old stringer, place it on top of the new stringer, and trace the outline, including any notches or angles. Or, measure along the bottom edge of the other stringer to determine the length of the new stringer. Use an adjustable T-bevel to determine the required angles at the top and bottom of the new stringer. At the top, find the angle between the lower edge of the stringer and the joist or beam to which it's attached *(inset)*; at the bottom, measure between the lower edge of the stringer and the concrete pad. Cut the new stringer to length and angle the ends.

If you need to notch the new stringer, clamp the new one to the existing stringer, aligning it at both ends, and use a pencil to mark the notches *(left)*. Cut the notches with a circular saw, finishing the corners with a crosscut saw. Then, hold the stringer in place, with the bottom resting against the concrete pad and the top against the beam or joist. Place a tread on one of the notches and position a carpenter's level on it. Adjust the position of the stringer until the tread is level; having a helper makes this task easier.

Finally, fasten the stringer to the deck in the same position as it was originally. Install framing connectors, as shown at left, or carriage bolts if the stringer meets a parallel member of the deck, such as a joist. Reinstall any parts of the stairs or railing that were removed.

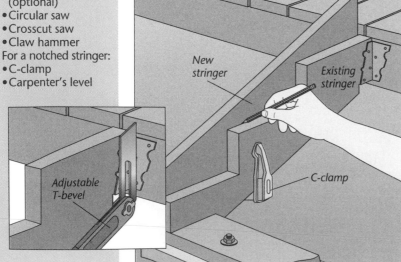

REPAIRING JOISTS

To strengthen the structure of your deck, install framing connectors at joints, such as between joists and the rim joists, between joists and beams, and between joists and the ledger. Choose the appropriate connector for your situation—probably joist hangers *(page 100)* or seismic or universal anchors *(page 101)*—and nail it in place.

Another way to reinforce a joist is to add solid blocking between it and the joists on either side of it. Measure the distance between two joists and cut lumber of the same dimensions as the joist to this length. Install the blocks in the middle of the span, offsetting them from one another; center each block under a deck board. Face-nail through the joist into the blocking.

If a joist is slightly rotten, you can reinforce it with supports as described below. If a joist is cracked, hold it up with a jack and install supports to strengthen it; instructions for this procedure are given on the following page.

Sometimes reinforcing a section of a joist is not enough. In that case, you'll have to install an entire new joist alongside it for support *(page 178)*.

 QUICK FIX

REMOVING ROTTEN JOIST ENDS
If the ends of cantilevered joists have rotted, you can cut them off. Carefully remove any deck boards in the way, and the rim joist, if there is one. Be sure to cut the joists far enough back to remove the rotten section of each one. Apply preservative to the cut ends, then install a new rim joist, if desired.

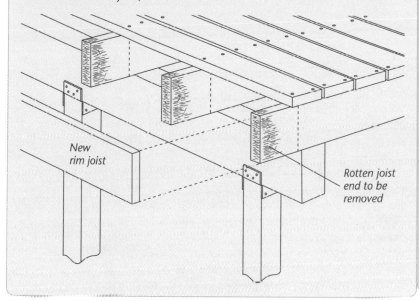

New rim joist

Rotten joist end to be removed

Reinforcing a rotted area

TOOLKIT
• Paintbrush
• Tape measure
• Circular saw
• Combination square
• Screwdriver or claw hammer

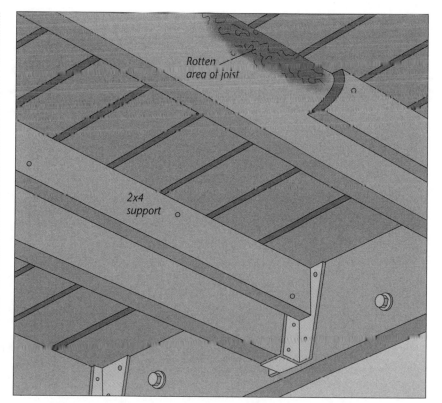

Rotten area of joist

2x4 support

Installing a support
To reinforce rotten joists, first apply preservative to the rotten area. Then cut a 2x4 or 2x6 board to make a support; it should be long enough to extend past the rotten section by about 6" on each end. Screw or nail the support onto the side of the rotten joist, staggering the fasteners every 10" to 12".

Reinforcing a cracked joist

TOOLKIT
- Claw hammer
- Jack
- Tape measure
- Circular saw
- Electric drill
- Wrench

Installing supports

Nail a piece of 2x6 or 2x8 to the bottom edge of the damaged section of the joist, as a temporary pad for a jack to push against. Support the joist with a jack positioned directly under the temporary pad.

For the supports, use lumber of the same dimensions as the joist and cut them about 4' to 6' longer than the damaged section of the joist.

On each side of the joist, use nails to hold the supports in place temporarily while you drill holes for carriage bolts through the joist and both supports. Stagger the holes, placing them about 12" apart.

Tap the bolts through the holes, put on washers, and tighten the nuts with a box or open-end wrench or a socket wrench.

USING JACKS

House jacks are either screw type or hydraulic. Whichever type you use, place a temporary support under the load as a precaution—this is especially necessary with a hydraulic jack, which may tend to slip.

Position the jack directly under the joist or beam. Place a 2x6 or 2x8 as a pad between the jack and the deck. Set the jack on a length of 2x10 or a concrete slab for a footing. Make sure the footing is level before you install the jack—dig out the ground or, on a slope, add a concrete block underneath. Once the jack is set up, push it into plumb; check with a carpenter's level on two adjacent sides.

Extend the reach of a house jack *(near right)* with a length of 4x4; turn the screw adjuster for the final adjustments.

Raise the extension of an adjustable jack post *(far right)* to within a couple of inches of the surface being supported and slip the pin into the hole to lock it. Raise the jack the final few inches by turning the screw adjuster at the top.

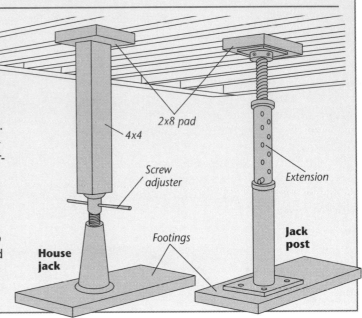

2x8 pad
4x4
Screw adjuster
Extension
Footings
House jack
Jack post

Reinforcing an entire joist

TOOLKIT
- Tape measure
- Combination square
- Circular saw
- Claw hammer
- Hand-drilling hammer (optional)
- Jack (optional)

Installing a new joist

Rather than replacing a badly damaged or rotted joist, install another one a few inches away from it. Fasten the new joist in place using the same method as for the other joists: They'll either be on top of, or butted against, two beams, or a beam and a ledger. Use a framing connector, such as a joist hanger *(page 100)* or a universal anchor *(page 101)* to secure the joist.

Cut a new joist to fit next to the old one. Nail framing connectors to each end of the new joist, then position it about 3" to 4" away from the existing joist; the space will allow air to circulate and help keep rot from spreading to the new joist. With helpers, lift the joist into position. If the joist must sit on top of beams (or a beam and a ledger), pivot it to insert first one end, then the other, between the framing member and the decking. It may help to angle it slightly, then tilt it upright, tapping it into place with a hand-drilling hammer; this is a difficult task, so be patient. To raise the ends of a crowned joist, jack them up slowly until they're properly positioned.

Insert a 4x4 block between the new joist and the damaged one every 2'; face-nail through both joists into the blocks. Leave out the blocks closest to the ends until you've attached the framing connectors, so you'll have room to swing your hammer. Nail the framing connectors in place, and remove the jacks.

REPAIRING BEAMS

Beams, like joists, may be cracked, rotten, or otherwise damaged and need to be reinforced or replaced. Reinforcing a beam, as described below, is essentially the same as reinforcing a cracked joist (*opposite page*). To replace a beam, you'll need to support the joists while you remove it; this procedure is described below.

Reinforcing a beam

TOOLKIT
• Claw hammer
• Jack
• Tape measure
• Circular saw
• Electric drill
• Wrench

Installing supports
Support the damaged part of the beam with a jack; first nail a piece of 2x6 or 2x8 to the bottom of the beam as a temporary support for the jack.

Cut supports about 5' longer than the damaged section of the beam from lumber the same width as the beam but only half its thickness. Position the supports on opposite sides of the beam; drive in a few nails to hold them in place while you drill holes for carriage bolts through the supports and the beam. Stagger the holes about 12" apart along the length of the damaged section. Tap the bolts in and install washers and nuts.

Replacing a beam

TOOLKIT
• Tape measure
• Claw hammer
• Jacks
• Wrench (optional)
• Nail claw (optional)
• Crosscut saw (optional)
• Combination square
• Circular saw
• Hand-drilling hammer (optional)
• Carpenter's level

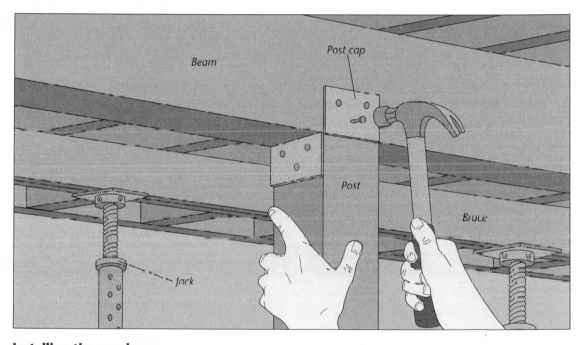

Installing the new beam
Support the joists with braces placed about 3' from the beam, on both sides. Nail two 2x10s together to make each brace and raise them on jacks, parallel to the beam, until they fit tightly against the joists; position one jack every 6' to 8'.

Remove any pieces, such as a stringer or railing post, that are attached to the beam, and remove the fasteners or framing connectors holding the joists to the beam. Remove all the nails in the post cap; have a couple of helpers support the beam while you do so. Tilt the post enough to slide the post cap out. (If you can't do this, disconnect the bottom of the post as well, and reattach it after the beam is replaced. If the post is sunk into the concrete footing, cut it off and reinstall it as shown on page 181.)

Remove the beam, tapping it with a hand-drilling hammer, if necessary, to dislodge it. Or, saw it into smaller sections for easier removal. Cut a new beam from lumber of the same dimensions as the old one. Position the new beam between the posts and the joists; tap it into position with a hand-drilling hammer if necessary. Near each post, slide a post cap onto the beam. Tilt the post out of the way, then reposition it in the post cap. Plumb the post, then nail the post cap in place (*above*). NOTE: You can install T-straps at the joints between the beam and the posts instead.

REPAIRING LEDGERS

If your deck's design incorporates a ledger, it's an integral part of the deck's structure, and therefore it is important to keep it in good repair.

To reinforce a ledger fastened to wood framing, drill pilot holes and install additional lag screws with washers, spacing them about 16 inches apart, and staggered. Tighten the screws with a socket wrench.

To reinforce a ledger fastened to a brick or masonry wall, insert additional expanding anchor bolts, staggering them about 16 inches apart along the ledger.

For even more support, install a ledger support; if the ledger is past repair, replace it. The procedures are illustrated below; choose the appropriate fastener, as described above. See page 108 for ledger installation details.

Installing a ledger support

TOOLKIT
- Tape measure
- Combination square
- Circular saw
- Jacks
- Electric drill
- Wrench

Supporting a ledger

Cut a ledger support about 4' to 6' longer than the damaged section of the existing ledger; use lumber of the same dimensions as the ledger. Support the ledger with jacks, placing them about 7' apart. See page 178 for information on using jacks. Raise the jacks until they hold the support ledger tightly against the existing ledger. Drill staggered holes for the fasteners every 16" along the ledger support, then install the fasteners.

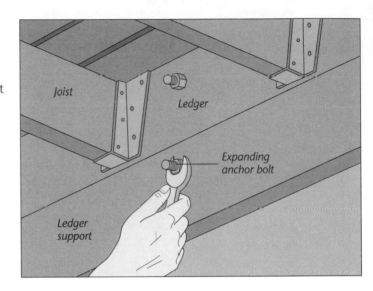

Joist

Ledger

Expanding anchor bolt

Ledger support

Replacing a ledger

TOOLKIT
- Claw hammer
- Tape measure
- Jacks
- Nail claw (optional)
- Wrench
- Combination square
- Circular saw
- Electric drill

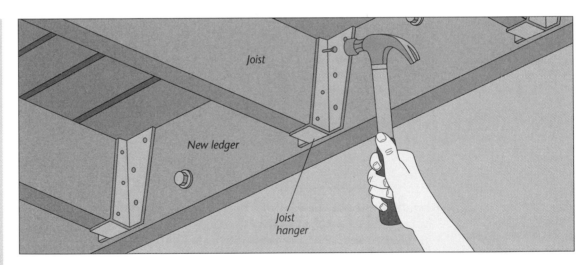

Joist

New ledger

Joist hanger

Installing a new section

Support the joists 3' to 4' from the section of the ledger you're replacing: Nail two 2x10s together to make a brace and raise it on jacks set about 7' apart. Have helpers hold the brace while you raise the jacks. Remove any nails or framing connectors holding the joists to the ledger, and, with your helpers supporting the ledger, remove the fasteners holding it to the wall. Remove the ledger. NOTE: Once you've disconnected the joists from the ledger, the deck is no longer supported at that end. Be careful not to bump into any of the supporting jacks, and don't let anyone walk on the deck while it's unsupported. If you must replace the entire ledger, do one section at a time, so part of the deck is always supported.

Next, cut a new section from lumber of the same dimensions as the existing ledger. Have your helpers hold it in place while you drill holes and insert fasteners, staggered 16" apart. Finally, fasten the joists to the new ledger using joist hangers (above).

REPAIRING POSTS

To reinforce a post, bolt another post of the same dimensions to one side of it; drill holes through both posts to install the bolts. Or, bolt a length of 2x4 to each side of the post.

To reinforce the entire deck structure, you can add bracing between the posts, as discussed on page 120. Hold a 1x6, 2x4, or 2x6 board diagonally at the top of one post and the bottom of the post next to it. Mark the board at the outside edge of each post, and cut it along this line. Drill pilot holes and fasten the braces with at least two nails or screws at each end. Repeat on the back of the posts, angling the brace the opposite way, so that the two braces form an X.

If a post is rotten, you'll need to replace it. Posts may be attached to the concrete footings in various ways: They may be sunk directly into them; they may sit in a post anchor set in the footing; or they may rest on a pier block, either attached to a nailing block or in a post anchor. A post right in concrete is most likely to rot. If it does, cut it off flush with the top of the footing and bolt a post anchor to the remaining wood, or use a side anchor as shown below.

Where the ground below has settled or washed away, you may need to replace an old footing. Break up the footing with a sledgehammer, if necessary, to remove it, then cast a new one *(page 115)*.

Replacing a post

TOOLKIT
- Jack
- Prybar or nail claw
- Claw hammer
- Crosscut saw (optional)
- Hand-drilling hammer (optional)
- Tape measure
- Circular saw
- Carpenter's level
- Electric drill
- Wrench

1 Removing the post
Support the structure above the post with a jack *(page 178)*. If a post anchor was used, pull out the nails holding the post to the post anchor with a prybar or nail claw. To loosen the nails, pry the plate away from the post with a prybar, then hammer it back in place.

If the post is embedded in concrete, saw it off flush with the top of the footing using a crosscut saw. If the post is set on a nailing block, remove the nails holding the post to the block.

Remove the post; if necessary, tap it gently with a hand-drilling hammer to loosen it.

2 Installing a new post
The length of the new post will depend on the method of attachment: If the old post was set in a post anchor, simply measure the post. Otherwise, measure the distance between the beam and the footing (or the nailing block attached to the foot-

ing) and subtract the height that the post anchor will hold the post above the footing or nailing block; cut the new post to this length. If you'll be using a side anchor as shown, cut the new post to the same length as the distance between the footing and the beam.

The next step is to install the new post. If the old one was set in a post anchor, insert the new one into the anchor, check it for plumb with a carpenter's level, and fasten it in place. If the old post was embedded directly in the concrete or set on a nailing block and the wood is in good shape, use the type of post anchor that can be attached to wood. Insert the new post in the anchor, check it for plumb, and fasten it in place.

If the old wood is not strong enough to accept a post anchor, use side anchors. Have a helper hold the post on top of the footing, and drill a hole in the footing (using a masonry bit) to one side of the post, to fasten the side anchor to the footing. Insert an expanding anchor bolt in the hole, and fasten the side anchor in place. Plumb the post and fasten it to the side anchor with lag screws. Repeat to fasten another side anchor to the other side of the post *(left)*.

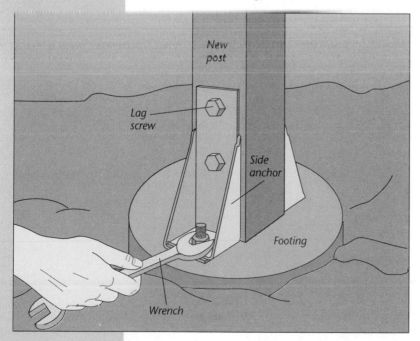

New post

Lag screw

Side anchor

Footing

Wrench

DECK PLANS

U sing one of the professionally designed deck plans in this chapter can simplify the planning stage of your project and result in a more professional looking deck. At the end of this chapter are four plans for overheads to complement your deck; they can be adapted to a variety of deck styles.

The plans shown have been designed for specific sites; differences in plan styles, foundations, materials, and details reflect the individual designers' preferences. You'll probably want to adjust the plan you choose to suit your own needs. Variations may be influenced by locale, style, needs, and cost. Scale your deck in relation to your home, and use landscaping to help the deck blend in with your garden. You may choose to have a plan built by a contractor, but you should be able to build most of the decks shown if you're moderately skilled and have a helper.

Look over the chapter on deck materials *(page 89)* for lumber and fastener choices, and tips on estimating quantities of materials. Sometimes the designer has specified the type of lumber. Change it if you like, but check the spans for the lumber you choose and make any necessary adjustments.

Before you begin, you must check your plan with local building authorities and get any required permits; specifications, such as depth of footings, vary depending on locale. Building is full of surprises, so expect to make minor changes as you go along.

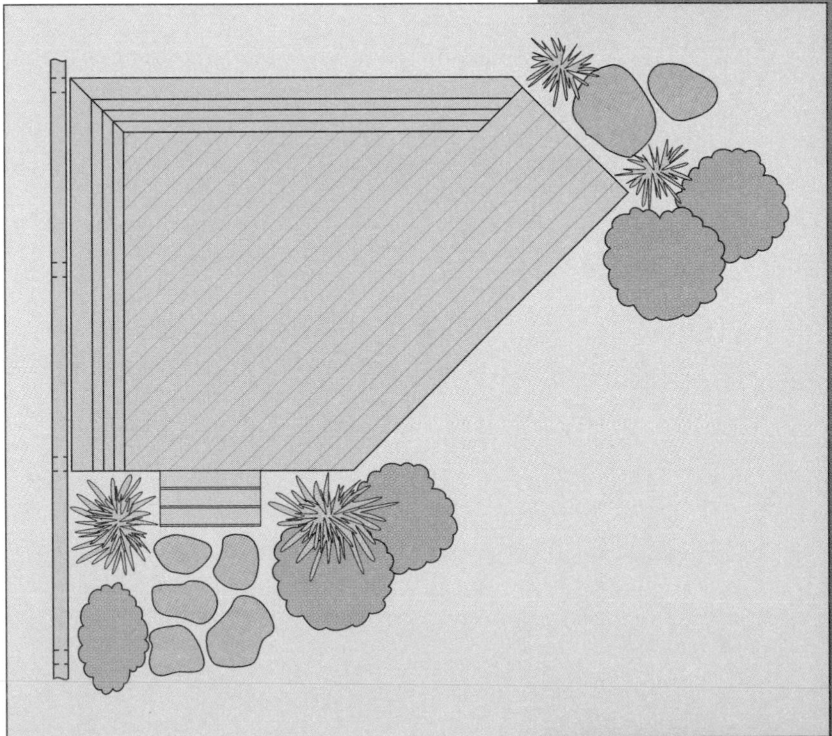

The plan views in this chapter, such as the one shown at right, will give you an idea of what the deck you choose will look like when it's finished.

ADJUSTING PLANS

Chances are that none of the plans in this book will fit your needs exactly. If the dimensions of your property call for a different size of deck, you'll need to make adjustments in the design you choose. You might also want to adjust a plan to make the deck better complement your house and the natural terrain of your lot, or suit your style of outdoor living. You'll find a variety of options for deck components in the chapter starting on page 61; the ones in the plans may not be the most optimal for your situation. It's also important to check building code requirements and apply them to the plan; for instance, most codes allow a maximum distance of 4 inches between railing members, although some allow 6 inches.

To make adjustments, think about a deck from the top down. Draw exactly what you want the decking to look like from above, then make the appropriate changes in the substructure, working from the joists to the beams, then to the posts and the footings. Sometimes you can change the size or configuration of the deck simply by increasing the length of certain deck members, such as beams and joists. However, increasing the length of one member usually means increasing its size or adding extra supports. For example, if you increase the length of a beam to handle additional joists, you may also need to increase its size or add more posts to support it properly. Different species of lumber allow different maximum spans; once you've decided what kind of lumber to use, check the span tables on pages 73 and 74, and adjust the spans in the deck plan you choose, if necessary. For more information on reading and drawing plans, see the section beginning on page 54.

RAISING OR LOWERING A DECK

Raising the height of the deck often means more than simply using taller posts. If a deck is 30 inches or more above the ground, you should also add railings for safety. (Check your local building codes for specific requirements for railings.) If you go higher than 3 feet, you'll need to crossbrace the perimeter posts.

If you lower a deck, it's always a good idea to leave at least 6 inches between the ground and wooden deck members, even if you're using pressure-treated lumber. However, this clearance is only mandatory for untreated wood. Any wood set within 6 inches of the ground

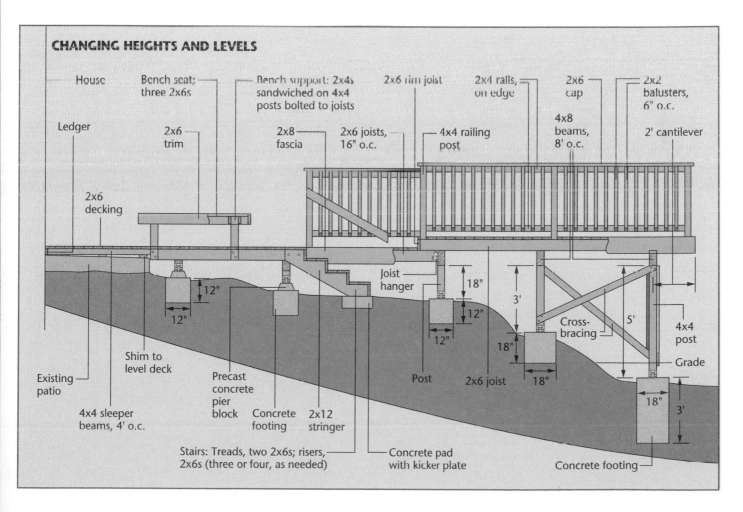

CHANGING HEIGHTS AND LEVELS

House · Bench seat; three 2x6s · Bench support: 2x4s sandwiched on 4x4 posts bolted to joists · 2x6 rim joist · 2x4 rails, on edge · 2x6 cap · 2x2 balusters, 6" o.c.

Ledger · 2x6 trim · 2x8 fascia · 2x6 joists, 16" o.c. · 4x4 railing post · 4x8 beams, 8' o.c. · 2' cantilever

2x6 decking

Joist hanger · 18" · 3' · 12"

Cross-bracing · 5' · 4x4 post

Grade

Shim to level deck · Precast concrete pier block · Concrete footing · 2x12 stringer · Post · 2x6 joist · 18" · 18"

Existing patio

4x4 sleeper beams, 4' o.c.

Stairs: Treads, two 2x6s; risers, 2x6s (three or four, as needed) · Concrete pad with kicker plate · Concrete footing

12" · 12"

18" · 3'

must be pressure treated or naturally decay resistant, such as redwood or cedar heartwood.

MAKING A DECK LARGER

This is usually fairly easy. Depending on the deck's configuration, simply increase the length (you may have to do some splicing if you're making big changes) or number of joists and beams. If necessary, add posts and piers to support the new beams. If you're increasing the size of the deck along a side that is attached to the house, you'll also have to increase the length of the ledger.

You can safely extend joists over a beam to enlarge a deck, but don't exceed one-quarter of the joist span.

MAKING A DECK SMALLER

This is just the opposite of enlarging a deck. Shorten or decrease the number of joists and beams; this means you may be able to shorten a ledger or decrease the distance between ledger and beam (or two beams). Then reposition the posts and footings accordingly.

MAKING AN ATTACHED DECK FREESTANDING

You'll need to replace the ledger with a beam of the same length supported by posts. You can cantilever the joists over the beam, as long as you don't exceed one-quarter of the joist span.

MAKING A FREESTANDING DECK ATTACHED

This is essentially the opposite of making a deck freestanding. Replace the beam and posts with a ledger, of the same length as the beam, fastened to the house. The ledger must be positioned where the beam originally was, not simply at the end of the joists, so if the joists extended past the beam on the original design, you'll have to shorten them.

MAKING A DECK MULTILEVEL

There are a number of ways to change a single-level deck into a multilevel one; for details, turn to page 75. The illustration on the previous page shows a deck with two levels, built on a slope.

CHANGING A DECK'S SHAPE

This is simplest with square or rectangular decks. Basically, you follow the same rules as for enlarging or decreasing a deck's size, adjusting the length and number of appropriate joists and beams, increasing their size as necessary, and designing an adequate substructure.

You can build a larger deck by linking together smaller, simpler modules, as shown below. For example, begin by following one of the plans in the book to build a module or section that attaches to the house. Then attach other sections to this basic module, using common beams. You can also connect decks at an end joist or rim joist so long as you increase the thickness of the joist so it's as strong as a beam.

One way to wrap a deck around your house is to extend one of the ledgers out past the corner so that it acts as a beam for the rest of the deck. In the example below, it's the ledger for the new deck module that extends past the house. You might have to increase the ledger's size or double up the extended portion to enable it to handle the load. Then add new beams and joists according to your decking pattern.

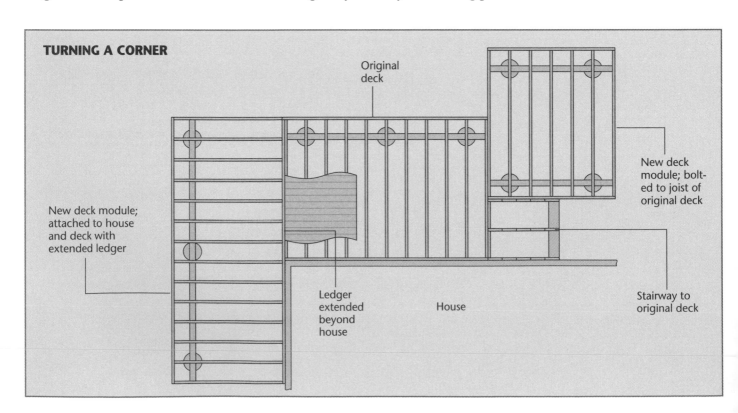

TURNING A CORNER

Original deck

New deck module; bolted to joist of original deck

New deck module; attached to house and deck with extended ledger

Ledger extended beyond house

House

Stairway to original deck

LOW-LEVEL DECK

A low-level deck like this one can transform any unused part of your yard into a comfortable outdoor floor that's ideal for almost any outdoor activity, from sunbathing to picnicking. Because this deck is so small (8 feet by 12 feet), it will fit in a yard of just about any size. Its construction is simple, but includes all the basic components of most freestanding, low-level decks.

BUILDING NOTES

For sloping terrain, as shown here, you'll need posts supporting the deck at the low end; cut the posts to the length required to make the deck level on your slope. At the high end, you can place the beam directly on the piers. Use precast piers with post anchors.

If the terrain is level, you can omit all the posts, placing the beams right in the piers' post anchors.

To fasten the last joist in place flush with the end of the beams, use a universal anchor.

This low deck can be attached to the house or built freestanding, as a garden retreat.

MATERIALS LIST

Use pressure-treated lumber for the structural members, decay-resistant lumber such as cedar or redwood heartwood for the decking, and corrosion-resistant hardware.

Lumber	
Posts	4x4
Beams	4x8
Joists	2x6
Decking	2x6
Fascia	2x10
Masonry	
Pier blocks	Precast concrete
Concrete	12" square footings
Hardware	
Nails	3¼" or 3½" for decking; nails for framing connectors
Connectors	Post caps; joist hangers; universal anchors

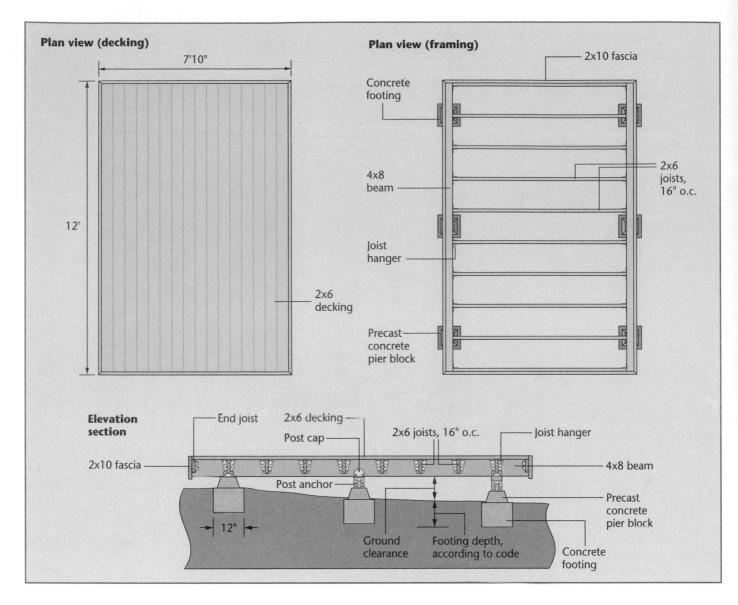

Plan view (decking)

7'10"

12'

2x6 decking

Plan view (framing)

2x10 fascia

Concrete footing

4x8 beam

2x6 joists, 16" o.c.

Joist hanger

Precast concrete pier block

Elevation section

End joist

2x6 decking

Post cap

2x6 joists, 16" o.c.

Joist hanger

2x10 fascia

Post anchor

4x8 beam

Ground clearance

Footing depth, according to code

Precast concrete pier block

Concrete footing

12"

TO ADAPT THIS PLAN

To build a higher deck from this plan, use longer posts between the piers and the beams. To add a step use 6x6 pressure-treated land-scape timbers, a large flat rock, or a concrete slab where you want to access the deck. Check your local building code for the max-imum deck height allowed before you have to add a railing; generally, it's 30 inches.

To attach this deck to your house, replace one of the beams with a ledger attached to the house, as shown in the illustration at right. For information on attaching a ledger to different wall materials, see the section on mounting a ledger *(page 108)*.

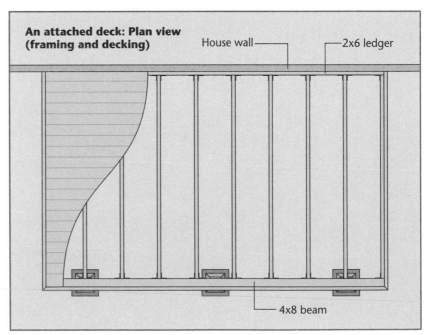

An attached deck: Plan view (framing and decking)

House wall

2x6 ledger

4x8 beam

SINGLE LEVEL DECK WITH STAIRS

This 12-foot square deck, built with framing connectors for extra strength, will provide ample space for outdoor activities.

TO ADAPT THIS PLAN
The deck posts are sandwiched between the beams, so to add a railing or overhead, extend the posts above the deck to the required height, cut the deck boards to fit around the posts, and support their ends with cleats.

BUILDING NOTES
This deck is attached to the house with a ledger, so you could reduce the foundation work required by shortening the beams—consult the span charts.

Attaching the decking with deck clips makes a smooth deck surface, with no exposed nailheads.

PLAN REPRINTED COURTESY OF
THE SIMPSON STRONG-TIE COMPANY

MATERIALS LIST
Use pressure-treated lumber for the substructure, decay-resistant lumber such as cedar or redwood heartwood or pressure-treated wood for the decking, and corrosion-resistant hardware.

Lumber	
Posts	4x4
Beams/ledger	2x6
Joists	2x6
Decking	2x6
Fascia	2x8
Stairs	2x10 stringers; 2x6 risers (optional); 2x12 treads
Masonry	
Pier blocks	Precast concrete
Concrete	Footings and stair pad
Hardware	
Nails	3" for fascia; 3½" for framing; nails for framing connectors
Screws	⅜"x4" lag screws for ledger
Connectors	Post anchors; post-beam connectors; joist hangers; seismic anchors; stair angles; deck clips

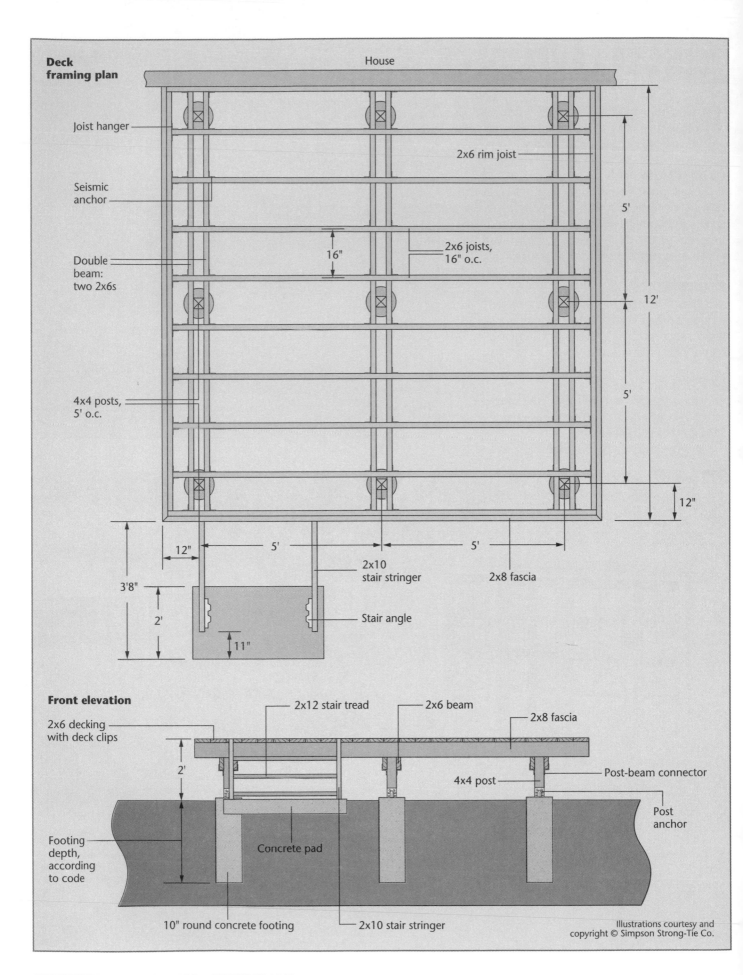

Deck framing plan

House

Joist hanger

Seismic anchor

Double beam: two 2x6s

4x4 posts, 5' o.c.

2x6 rim joist

2x6 joists, 16" o.c.

16"

5'

12'

5'

12"

12"

5'

2x10 stair stringer

2x8 fascia

3'8"

2'

Stair angle

11"

Front elevation

2x6 decking with deck clips

2x12 stair tread

2x6 beam

2x8 fascia

2'

4x4 post

Post-beam connector

Post anchor

Footing depth, according to code

Concrete pad

10" round concrete footing

2x10 stair stringer

Illustrations courtesy and copyright © Simpson Strong-Tie Co.

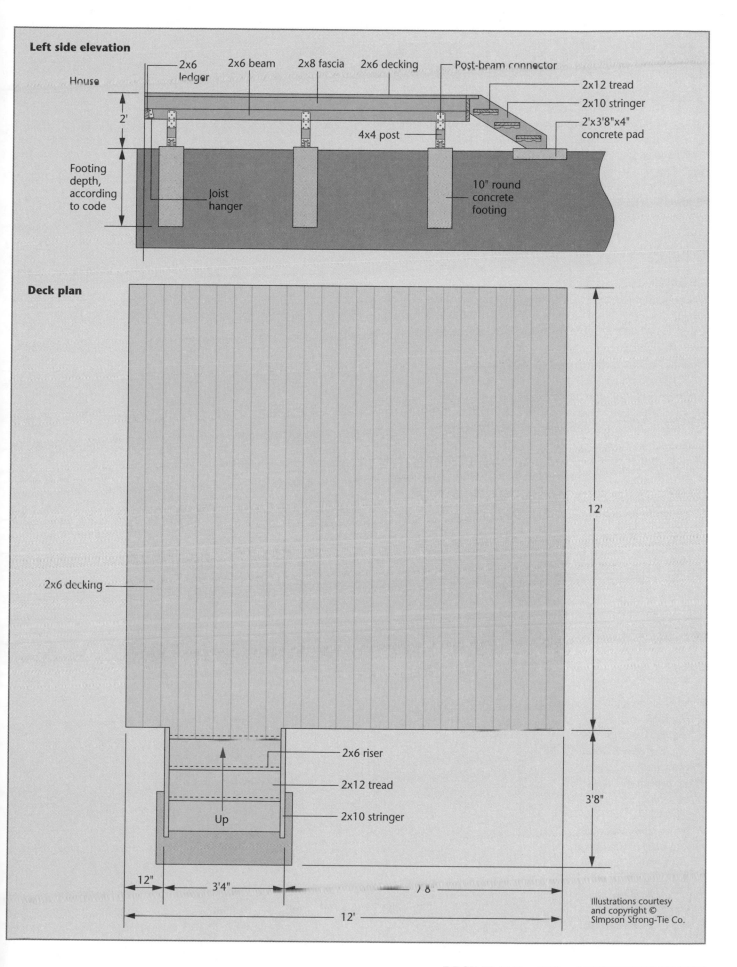

Left side elevation

House

2x6 ledger

2x6 beam

2x8 fascia

2x6 decking

Post-beam connector

2x12 tread

2x10 stringer

2'x3'8"x4" concrete pad

2'

4x4 post

Footing depth, according to code

Joist hanger

10" round concrete footing

Deck plan

2x6 decking

12'

2x6 riser

2x12 tread

Up

2x10 stringer

3'8"

12"

3'4"

? 8

12'

Illustrations courtesy and copyright © Simpson Strong-Tie Co.

COMPACT DECK WITH STEPS

A number of stylish accents add interest to this rectangular deck: The radius-edge decking gives the deck surface a decorative touch, and the chamfer on the rail and the 45° angled cuts on the balusters complete the finished look.

TO ADAPT THIS PLAN

You can build this deck to accommodate a slope by adjusting the height of the posts as required. You may also need to lengthen or shorten the stairway.

BUILDING NOTES

Be sure to cut the posts long enough to extend the required height above the surface of the decking for the railing. Notch the decking to fit around the posts, and add cleats to the sides of the posts, to support the decking. Use scrap pieces of 2x8 lumber for the cleats.

A 2x10 fascia is fastened to the outside of the stair stringers, so that the notches are not visible. Face-nail the fascia to the stringers after the treads are in place but before you attach the railing balusters. You'll also need to notch the bottom tread to fit around the post—support the notched board with a 2x4 cleat nailed to the post—and add a spacer to fill the gap between the rail and the post at the bottom of the steps.

MATERIALS LIST

Designed for pressure-treated lumber; choose lumber rated for ground contact for members in or close to the ground, and lumber rated for aboveground use for the rest of the deck.

Lumber	
Posts/beams	4x4 posts; 2x8 beams
Joists/ledger	2x8 joists; 2x10 ledger
Decking	5/4 (actual size 1") x6 (radius edge)
Fascia	2x10
Stairs	2x6 ledger, rail; 2x12 stringers; 5/4x6 treads (radius edge); 2x10 fascia; 2x2 balusters
Railings	2x6 top rail; 2x2 balusters
Masonry	
Concrete	10" square footings
Hardware	
Nails	3 1/4" for framing; 3" for fascia, bridging, cleats, balusters; 2 1/2" for decking; nails for framing connectors
Screws	1/2"x6" lag screws for ledger; 1/4"x4" lag screws for rails
Bolts	1/2"x6" for deck beams to posts; 1/2"x8" for stair platform beams to posts
Connectors	Joist hangers
Finishes	Water-repellent sealer

This deck has certain design features that make it stand apart from other basic decks: The platform at the top of the stairs means that the stairs take no space away from the main surface area of the deck, and the posts supporting the deck also serve as railing posts.

PLAN REPRINTED COURTESY OF THE SOUTHERN PINE COUNCIL

Plan

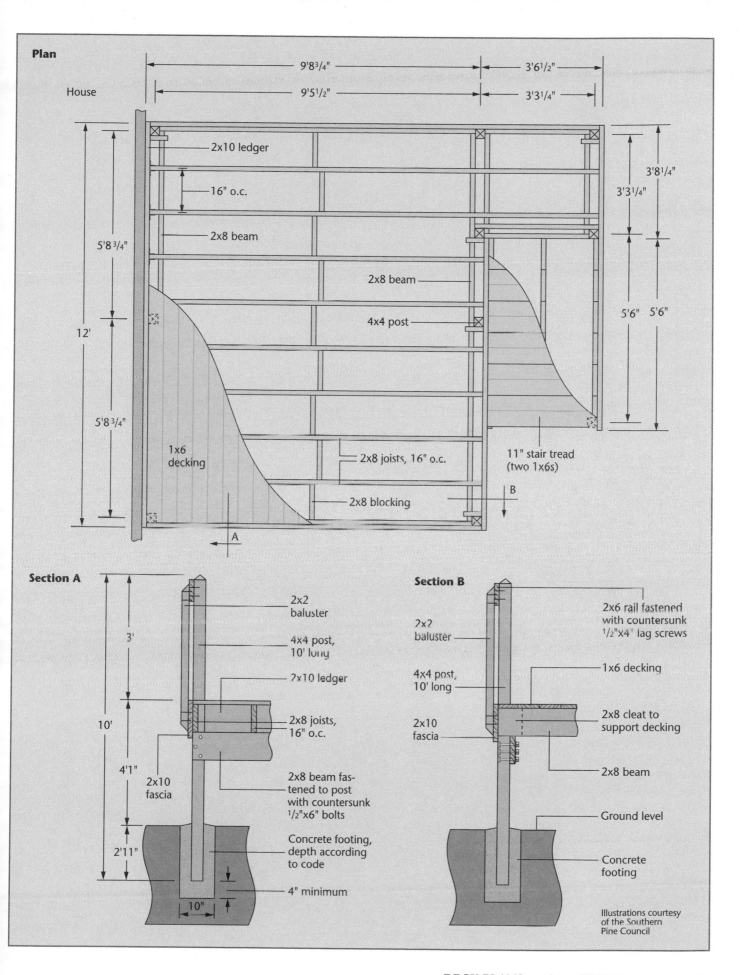

House

9'8³/4"

3'6¹/2"

9'5¹/2"

3'3¹/4"

2x10 ledger

16" o.c.

2x8 beam

2x8 beam

4x4 post

3'8¹/4"

3'3¹/4"

5'8³/4"

12'

5'6"   5'6"

5'8³/4"

1x6 decking

2x8 joists, 16" o.c.

11" stair tread (two 1x6s)

2x8 blocking

A

B

Section A

3'

10'

4'1"

2'11"

2x2 baluster

4x4 post, 10' long

2x10 ledger

2x8 joists, 16" o.c.

2x10 fascia

2x8 beam fastened to post with countersunk ¹/2"x6" bolts

Concrete footing, depth according to code

4" minimum

10"

Section B

2x2 baluster

4x4 post, 10' long

2x10 fascia

2x6 rail fastened with countersunk ¹/2"x4" lag screws

1x6 decking

2x8 cleat to support decking

2x8 beam

Ground level

Concrete footing

Illustrations courtesy of the Southern Pine Council

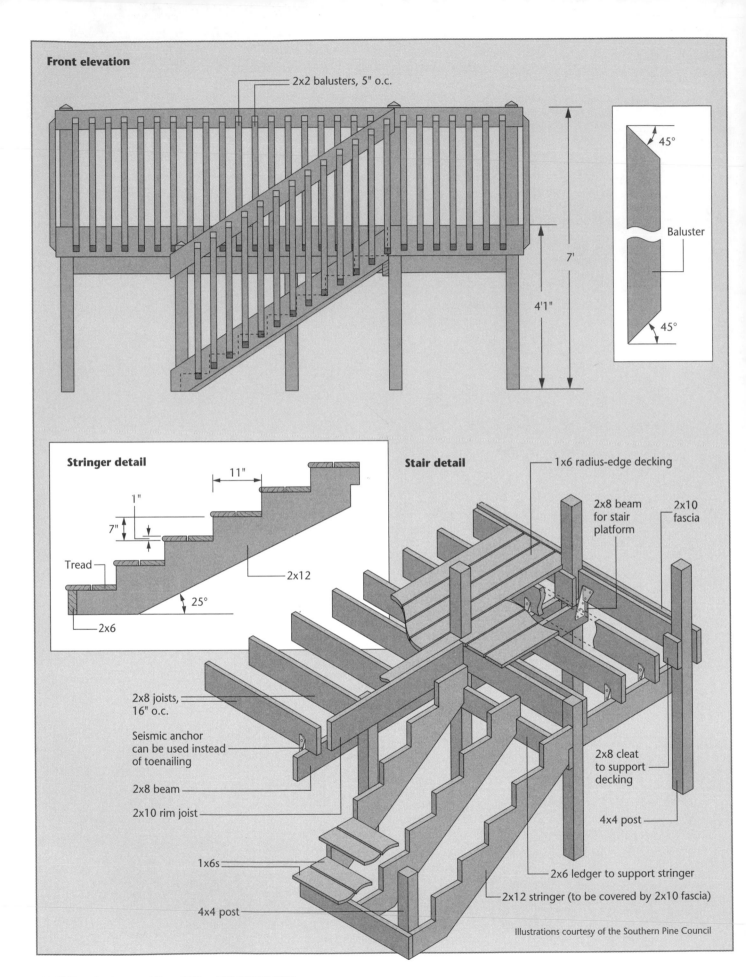

Front elevation

2x2 balusters, 5" o.c.

7'

4'1"

45°

Baluster

45°

Stringer detail

11"

1"

7"

Tread

2x6

25°

2x12

Stair detail

1x6 radius-edge decking

2x8 beam for stair platform

2x10 fascia

2x8 joists, 16" o.c.

Seismic anchor can be used instead of toenailing

2x8 beam

2x10 rim joist

1x6s

4x4 post

2x8 cleat to support decking

4x4 post

2x6 ledger to support stringer

2x12 stringer (to be covered by 2x10 fascia)

Illustrations courtesy of the Southern Pine Council

FREE-FLOATING DECK

This deck adds versatile outdoor space to a small city yard. The angled sides and diagonally laid decking add interest to the essentially rectangular design. The corner bench provides a place for sunning or reading, or, with the addition of a small table, a pleasant spot for backyard dining.

TO ADAPT THIS PLAN

This plan is readily adaptable, and because the deck is small, compact, and freestanding, it can be located almost anywhere.

Consult the span tables on pages 73 and 74 if you want to enlarge the overall size. If you decide to run the decking parallel to either of the benches, the foundation as shown in the plan will still work. By using a ledger, the deck can be attached to your house or other structure; by lengthening the posts and adding a skirt below the fascia, it can accommodate a small slope.

BUILDING NOTES

A simple rectangle cut short at 45° on two sides, this deck is easy to build. The entire substructure is a series of 2x8 joists and rim joists, nailed to posts on precast piers and connected to one another at either 90° or 45°. The bench support posts are nailed to 2x8 bracing between joists.

One concrete footing is cast as a support pad beneath the step; the step's supporting frame is hung from the deck fascia on joist hangers.

Lay decking on the diagonal and be sure to bring the boards flush against the bench posts. To simplify this step, cut the deck boards to fit before putting the bench seat on (but after the bench posts are in place). Drop the deck boards down over the bench posts. Alternatively, cut the deck boards so that there is a joint at the bench posts. Just add the bench seat and access step, and the deck is finished.

MATERIALS LIST

Designed for pressure-treated lumber (structural members), Clear Green redwood (visible members), and galvanized hardware.

Lumber

Posts	4x4
Joists/blocking	2x8
Decking	2x8
Step	2x4 kicker plate, framing 2x6 riser, tread 2x8 tread
Bench	2x4 posts, framing, seat boards, fascia, blocking beneath seat; 2x8 seat boards, blocking beneath decking

Masonry

Pier blocks	Precast concrete
Concrete	Footings; 3'x12"x6" deep stair pad

Hardware

Nails	3½" for decking, seat boards; 3½" casing for mitered fascia; nails for framing connectors
Bolts	⅜" anchor bolts for kicker plate
Connectors	Joist hangers for 90° and 45° connections
Finishes	Clear water sealer

DESIGN: JEFFREY MILLER, LANDSCAPE ARCHITECT
"I designed this simple perennial-bordered platform to be a remote gathering place floating in a larger garden plan. Access to this urban getaway is via a flagstone path past herb and vegetable gardens."

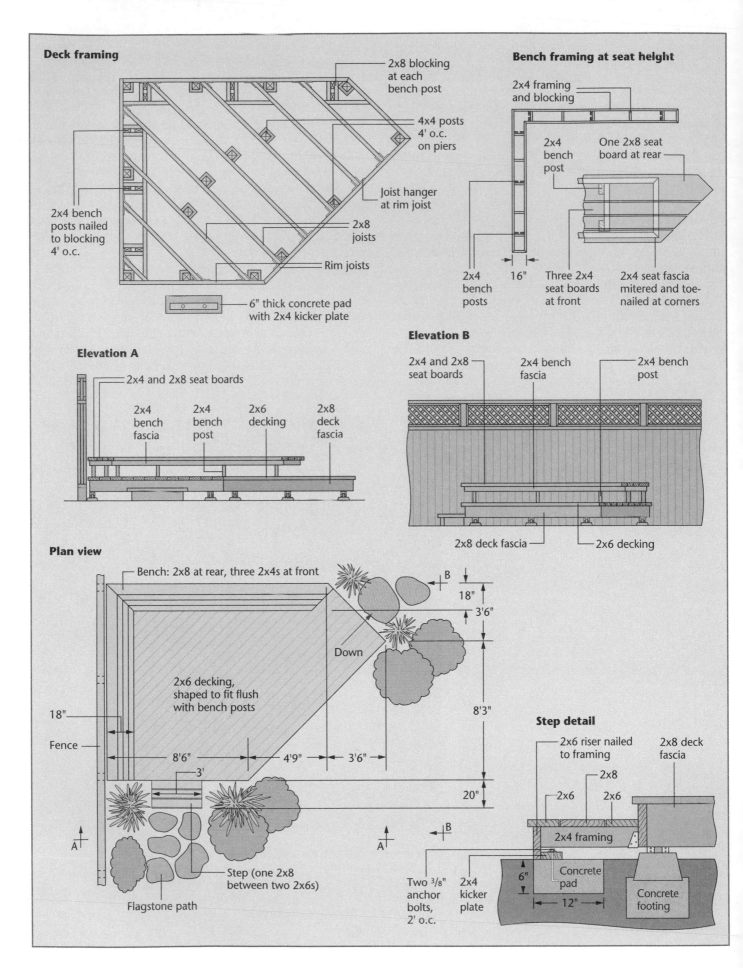

Deck framing

2x8 blocking at each bench post

4x4 posts 4' o.c. on piers

2x4 bench posts nailed to blocking 4' o.c.

Joist hanger at rim joist

2x8 joists

Rim joists

6" thick concrete pad with 2x4 kicker plate

Bench framing at seat height

2x4 framing and blocking

2x4 bench post

One 2x8 seat board at rear

2x4 bench posts

16"

Three 2x4 seat boards at front

2x4 seat fascia mitered and toe-nailed at corners

Elevation A

2x4 and 2x8 seat boards

2x4 bench fascia

2x4 bench post

2x6 decking

2x8 deck fascia

Elevation B

2x4 and 2x8 seat boards

2x4 bench fascia

2x4 bench post

2x8 deck fascia

2x6 decking

Plan view

Bench: 2x8 at rear, three 2x4s at front

B

18"

3'6"

Down

2x6 decking, shaped to fit flush with bench posts

18"

Fence

8'6"

4'9"

3'6"

8'3"

20"

3'

Step (one 2x8 between two 2x6s)

Flagstone path

A

A

B

Two 3/8" anchor bolts, 2' o.c.

2x4 kicker plate

Step detail

2x6 riser nailed to framing

2x8 deck fascia

2x8

2x6

2x6

2x4 framing

Concrete pad

6"

12"

Concrete footing

STREETFRONT DECK

In just over 350 square feet, this plan provides both a distinctive entry area (defined by a fence and a change in direction of the decking boards) and an area for entertaining or relaxing, bordered by planters.

For a fully integrated design, match the siding and finish on the fence to the style of your house.

TO ADAPT THIS PLAN

This easy-to-build deck works best on a flat or gently sloped site. You could build the deck off any side of the house, wrapping it around a corner to allow access from different rooms.

Use the divider fence to separate adjacent spaces outside different rooms—for instance to distinguish the area off a family room from that off a bedroom.

If privacy is a problem, you can fence around the entire deck (here, stone planters serving as low walls form a sufficient barrier from the street). If your house is masonry, you can build a matching wall instead of a wooden fence; frame the deck to go around its footings.

BUILDING NOTES

The on-edge decking allows greater spans, so joists can be placed further apart than for standard decking. When laying out the joists, keep two things in mind: the perpendicular change in decking direction at the fence, and the position of the fence. If you choose to lay all decking in the same direction, you must change the direction of the joists from that shown in the plan.

To install the decking, lay the 2x4 decking boards alternately with 2x3½x½x¼-inch spacers, both on edge, over each joist. Nail each spacer into the previous 2x4 with one 3½-inch nail, then toenail the 2x4 to the top of the joist with one 2½-inch nail.

MATERIALS LIST

Designed for pressure-treated lumber (structural members), surfaced redwood (visible members), and galvanized hardware.

Lumber	
Posts	4x4
Beams/joists	4x6
Ledgers	2x6
Decking	2x4, on edge
Fascia	2x10
Other	¼" exterior-rated plywood shims
Masonry	
Pier blocks	14" precast concrete
Hardware	
Nails	3½"; 2½" for decking; nails for framing connectors
Bolts	⅜" lag screws for house ledgers; anchor bolts for stone planter ledgers
Connectors	Joist hangers, post anchors, post caps

DESIGN: NICK WILLIAMS & ASSOCIATES
"This low-maintenance design spares the homeowners deck repair. Decking is laid on edge to eliminate bowing, cupping, and the sight of nails."

Plan view of framing

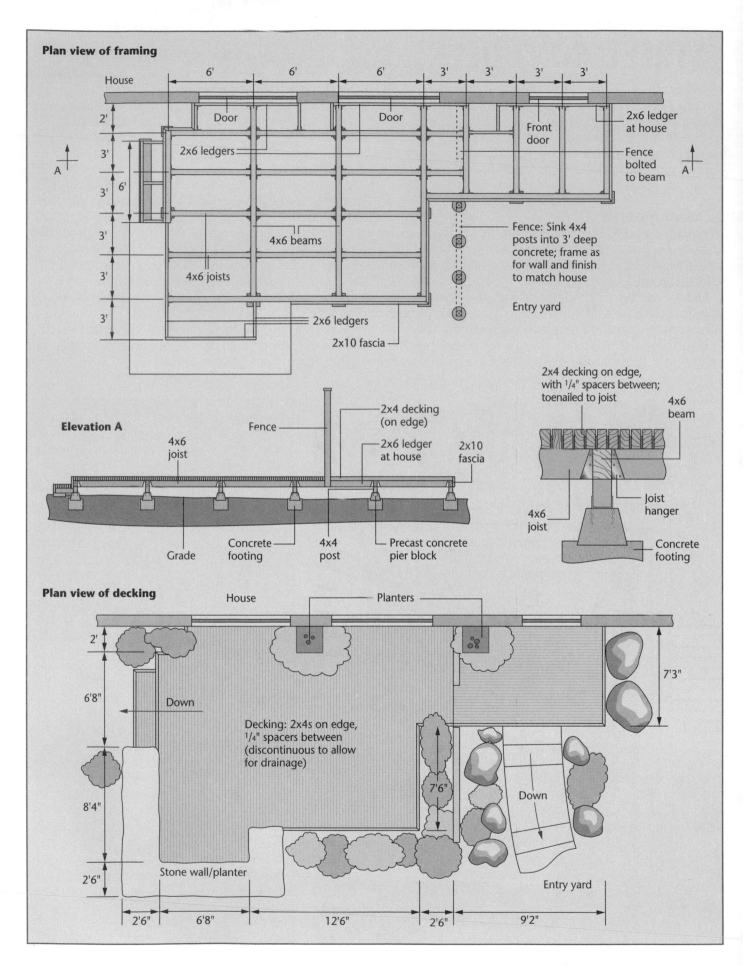

House

6' 6' 6' 3' 3' 3' 3'

Door   Door

Front door

2x6 ledger at house

2x6 ledgers

Fence bolted to beam

2'

3'

3'

6'

3'

3'

3'

A

A

4x6 beams

4x6 joists

Fence: Sink 4x4 posts into 3' deep concrete; frame as for wall and finish to match house

Entry yard

2x6 ledgers

2x10 fascia

Elevation A

2x4 decking on edge, with ¼" spacers between; toenailed to joist

4x6 beam

4x6 joist

Fence

2x4 decking (on edge)

2x6 ledger at house

2x10 fascia

Joist hanger

4x6 joist

Concrete footing

Grade   Concrete footing   4x4 post   Precast concrete pier block

Plan view of decking

House   Planters

2'

7'3"

6'8"

Down

Decking: 2x4s on edge, ¼" spacers between (discontinuous to allow for drainage)

7'6"

Down

8'4"

Stone wall/planter

2'6"

Entry yard

2'6"   6'8"   12'6"   2'6"   9'2"

RECYCLED PATIO

This deck, which covers an old slab patio, serves as a shady outdoor extension of the living room. The low bench/planter units bring flowers closer to eye level without obstructing the view of the garden.

TO ADAPT THIS PLAN

To build this deck on any level lot, use piers on footings spaced 8 feet on center. If the floor level of your house is well above grade, raise the deck to that height with posts on piers. Continue the siding to the ground to disguise the substructure. If your patio already has an overhead, attach beams alongside its support posts with ½-inch machine bolts.

For less shade, reduce the number of 2x3s in the trellis—or eliminate them completely. For the feel of an old-fashioned enclosed porch, fasten screen panels between the perimeter support posts.

The height and depth of benches may be adjusted for comfort. The seat continues under the backrest to become the planter bottom. Planter depth may be adjusted to accommodate container plants. For permanent plantings, line the planters with galvanized sheet metal or copper inserts; some other waterproofing ideas

are described on page 164. Provide drainage holes all the way down through the decking to prevent rotting of the boards underneath.

If you waterproof the area beneath the bench, it can be used to store toys, gardening gear, or seat cushions. Construct a lift-up door from a portion of the seat; attach a frame to its underside and hinge it to the 2x6 planter wall. Be sure its ends rest securely on two 2x3 box frames below.

BUILDING NOTES

Piers are required only beyond the edges of the concrete patio slab. On the slab, anchor the beams to the concrete with metal angles or straps.

The steps are actually one small pad atop another. To build them, frame and block the lower step with 2x4s, then repeat the shape for the upper step, using smaller dimensions.

For the overhead, you can use a band saw to make the notches and decorative cuts in the rafters and header.

Be sure the trellis is square to the side of the house. Select attractive looking 2x3s, since they will be visible from below. Set the 2x3 end trim so that its bottom is

DESIGN: RICHARD ROCHA, PILOT CONSTRUCTION COMPANY
"We wanted to extend the living room into the rear garden. The need for shelter overhead influenced me to design a room-like deck enclosed by planters, a place where small children can safely play."

flush with the bottom of the other 2x3s. Plumb the posts and level the header, then measure back to the ledger to establish the length of the rafters, extending them 2 feet beyond the notch.

If any decking boards have bad ends, conceal them beneath the bench. Save the best 2x6s for the bench seats and the center of the deck.

The two sections of each gate have an uneven number of pickets, so that when they're closed, the curves will peak at the centers. To build them, fasten the pickets to the rails with screws, attach the latch to the center to hold the two sections shut, screw the hinges to the ends, and then secure them to planters.

MATERIALS LIST

Designed for pressure-treated lumber (structural members), surfaced redwood (visible members; rough lumber may be used for the overhead trellis), and galvanized hardware.

Lumber	
Beams	4x8
Joists	2x8
Ledgers	2x8
Decking	2x6
Trim/ Fascia	$\frac{1}{4}$"x1$\frac{1}{2}$" lath at top, bottom, and corners of planter sides, and bottom of bench side; 1x4 at front of bench seat; 2x3 around trellis top; 2x6 sandwich at posts
Stairs	2x6 treads; 2x4 framing, blocking, risers; 1x4 trim
Trellis	4x4 posts; 4x8 header; 2x6 ledger, rafters; 2x3 trellis
Bench/ Planters	2x6 seat deck, back; 2x4 caps; 2x3 framing; 1x6 tongue-and-groove siding
Gates	2x3 rails; 1x4 pickets
Masonry	
Pier blocks	12" precast concrete
Concrete	18" footings under piers; base for bricks
Hardware	
Nails	3$\frac{1}{2}$"; nails for framing connectors
Screws and bolts	$\frac{3}{8}$"x5" lag screws for attaching ledger; brass wood screws for gate; bolts for steel straps
Connectors	Joist hangers for rafters; post anchors; post caps; steel straps or angles for attaching beams to slab
Other	Hinges, latches, barrel bolts for gates
Finishes	Paint to match house trim

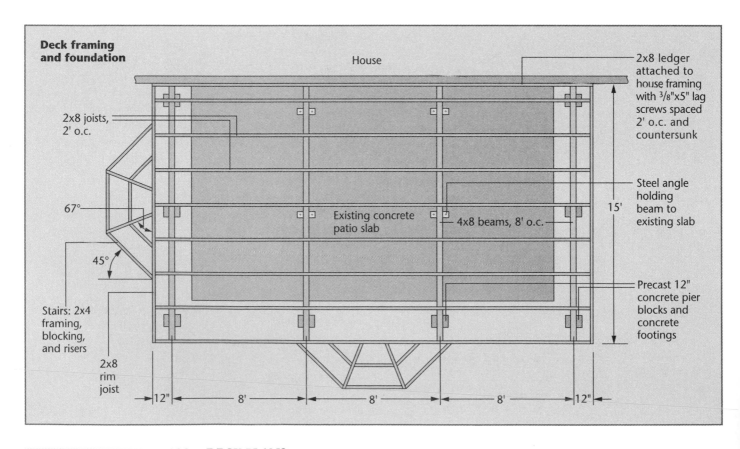

Deck framing and foundation

House

2x8 ledger attached to house framing with $\frac{3}{8}$"x5" lag screws spaced 2' o.c. and countersunk

2x8 joists, 2' o.c.

67°

45°

Stairs: 2x4 framing, blocking, and risers

2x8 rim joist

Existing concrete patio slab

4x8 beams, 8' o.c.

Steel angle holding beam to existing slab

15'

Precast 12" concrete pier blocks and concrete footings

12" 8' 8' 8' 12"

Elevation section A

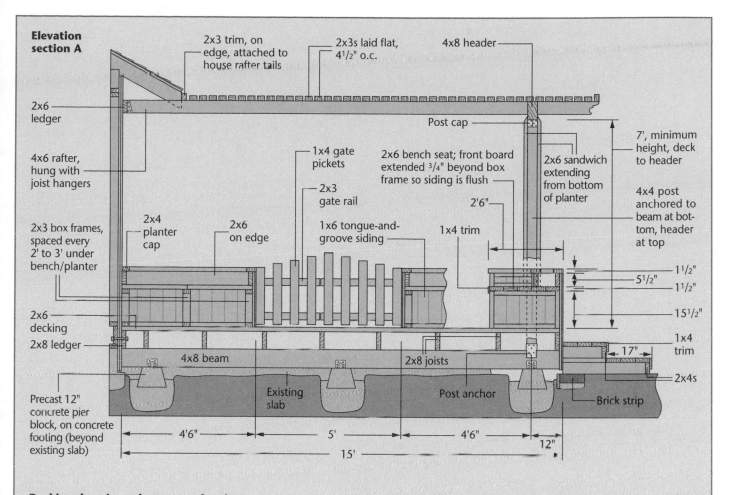

2x3 trim, on edge, attached to house rafter tails

2x3s laid flat, 4 1/2" o.c.

4x8 header

2x6 ledger

Post cap

7', minimum height, deck to header

4x6 rafter, hung with joist hangers

1x4 gate pickets

2x6 bench seat; front board extended 3/4" beyond box frame so siding is flush

2x6 sandwich extending from bottom of planter

4x4 post anchored to beam at bottom, header at top

2x3 gate rail

2'6"

2x3 box frames, spaced every 2' to 3' under bench/planter

2x4 planter cap

2x6 on edge

1x6 tongue-and-groove siding

1x4 trim

1 1/2"

5 1/2"

1 1/2"

15 1/2"

2x6 decking

2x8 ledger

4x8 beam

2x8 joists

Post anchor

1x4 trim

17"

2x4s

Precast 12" concrete pier block, on concrete footing (beyond existing slab)

Existing slab

Brick strip

4'6"   5'   4'6"   12"

15'

Decking, benches, planters, and stairs

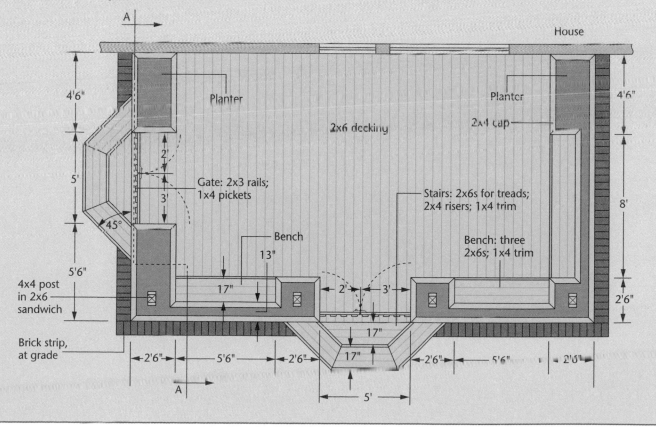

A

House

4'6"

Planter

Planter

2x4 cap

4'6"

5'

2'

Gate: 2x3 rails; 1x4 pickets

2x6 decking

3'

Stairs: 2x6s for treads; 2x4 risers; 1x4 trim

8'

45°

Bench

13"

5'6"

17"

Bench: three 2x6s; 1x4 trim

4x4 post in 2x6 sandwich

17"

2'   3'

2'6"

Brick strip, at grade

A

2'6"   5'6"   2'6"   2'   3'   2'6"   5'6"   2'0"

17"

17"

5'

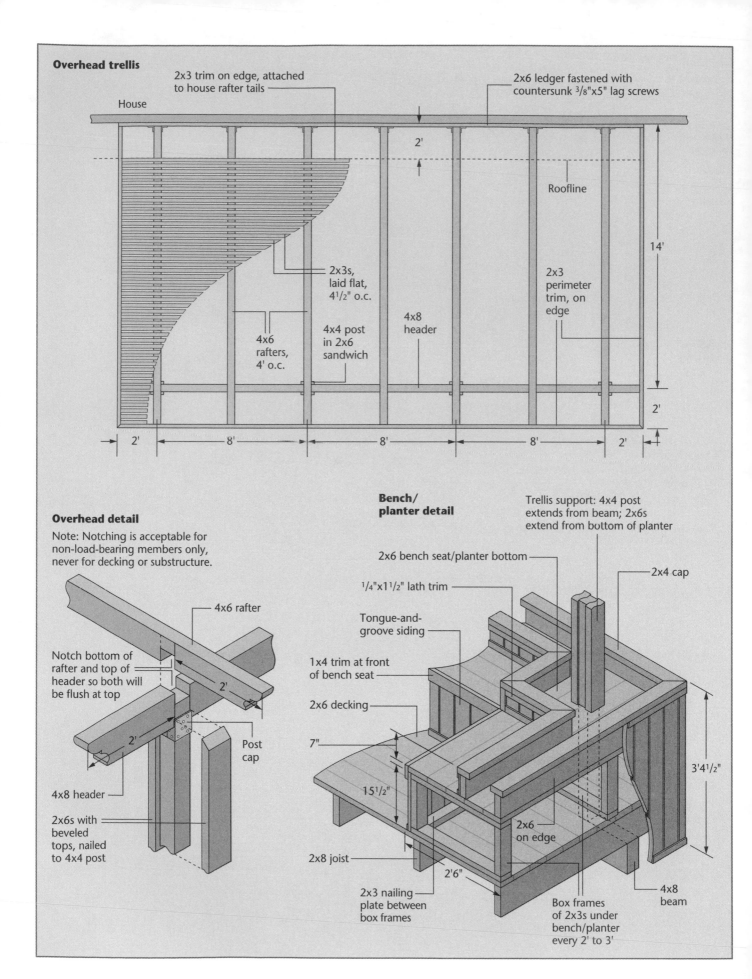

Overhead trellis

2x3 trim on edge, attached to house rafter tails

House

2x6 ledger fastened with countersunk 3/8"x5" lag screws

2'

Roofline

14'

2x3s, laid flat, 4 1/2" o.c.

2x3 perimeter trim, on edge

4x8 header

4x6 rafters, 4' o.c.

4x4 post in 2x6 sandwich

2'

2'

8'

8'

8'

2'

Overhead detail

Note: Notching is acceptable for non-load-bearing members only, never for decking or substructure.

4x6 rafter

2'

2'

Notch bottom of rafter and top of header so both will be flush at top

Post cap

4x8 header

2x6s with beveled tops, nailed to 4x4 post

Bench/ planter detail

Trellis support: 4x4 post extends from beam; 2x6s extend from bottom of planter

2x6 bench seat/planter bottom

2x4 cap

1/4"x1 1/2" lath trim

Tongue-and-groove siding

1x4 trim at front of bench seat

2x6 decking

7"

15 1/2"

3'4 1/2"

2x6 on edge

2x8 joist

2'6"

2x3 nailing plate between box frames

Box frames of 2x3s under bench/planter every 2' to 3'

4x8 beam

SPA DECK

This spa is sheltered from both wind and neighbors by a protective screen. Low planters (extending barely 8 inches above the deck) and a continuous bench complete the design. Simple lines and symmetry create its clean look. Located across the lawn from the house, the deck draws the eye to the spa as the garden's focal point.

TO ADAPT THIS PLAN

This plan is designed for a corner of a flat yard. You could also use it on a gentle slope by adjusting the height of the posts. Since the tall screen has a wraparound effect, it is most successful when positioned facing the house. The plan could work along a side of a rear garden if the area itself were separated by a tall hedge, for example. Otherwise, the exposed side would reveal the back of the screen.

Size and shape of the deck may vary according to the spa you purchase. You can use a different-sized spa within the dimensions shown, or you can increase or decrease the entire deck to accommodate a larger or smaller spa. Remember to verify all dimensions and check electrical and plumbing access against the spa manufacturer's instructions. If you change any dimensions, refer to the lumber span charts on pages 73 and 74.

BUILDING NOTES

Verify the dimensions of your new spa and map the deck and footing locations before beginning any excavation. Remember that no members of the deck are actually attached permanently to any part of the spa. Be sure to inset the front row of footings 12 inches to avoid conflict with the stair stringers. You must also provide adequate drainage away from the deck and spa.

Prepare a base for the spa—either a concrete slab or compacted rock. Make provisions for the electrical requirements of the spa: You'll probably want to call in an electrician for this. Be sure that you have enough power and that all work complies with local codes.

DESIGN: W. JEFFREY HEID, ASLA, LANDSCAPE ARCHITECT

"To establish a major focal point in a fairly small garden and to provide privacy from adjacent neighbors, I angled this deck around the spa and shielded it with a screen that supports climbing vines."

The size and location of your equipment access hatch will be determined by the design of your spa. Frame this removable portion of decking so that it rests upon surrounding beams and install the handle flush in order to protect bare feet.

After the main portion of the deck is built, protect the insides of the 2x12 bottomless planter frame by nailing a waterproof liner under the 2x6 cap. Caulk the nail holes.

When bolting the exterior posts on each side of the deck into their bases, the bolts should be long enough to later accommodate the 1x6 vertical siding that will be applied below the decking. Remove the bolts, apply the fascia board, and reinsert the bolts. Attach the top of the siding to the side of the 4x6 beam with nails.

MATERIALS LIST

Designed for pressure-treated lumber (structural members), Construction Heart surfaced redwood (visible members), and galvanized hardware.

Lumber	
Posts	4x4 (redwood for screen; pressure-treated for deck)
Beams	4x6; 2x6 headers
Decking	2x6; 2x2 trim
Siding	1x6
Stairs	2x12 stringers; 2x6 treads, risers; 2x4 kicker plates
Screen	2x6 caps; 2x4 rails; 2x2 uprights
Planters	4x4 frame bases; 2x12 frames; 2x6 caps
Benches	4x4 posts; 2x8 trim; 4x4 braces, seat, trim; 1/4" spacers
Masonry	
Pier blocks	Precast concrete
Concrete	18"x18" interior footings; 12"x12" exterior footings; 12"x12" (or shallower 18"x18") screen footings; 6" deep stair pads
Hardware	
Nails	3 1/2" for decking; 2 1/2" for 2x2s and trim
Bolts	1/2"x8" machine bolts for siding; 3/8"x6" machine bolts for stair stringers; washers, nuts
Connectors	Post anchors; steel straps (interior footings); joist hangers; universal anchors
Other	Flush-mount chest pull for hatch; reinforcing bar
Finishes	Two coats redwood sealer
Other	Waterproof membranes for planters

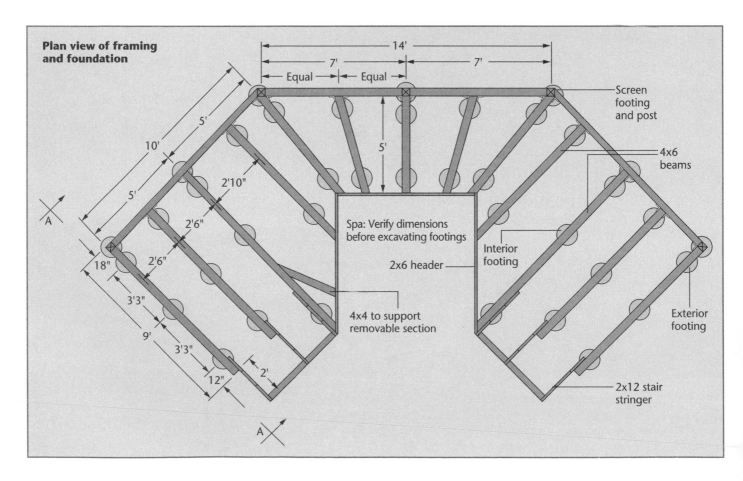

Plan view of framing and foundation

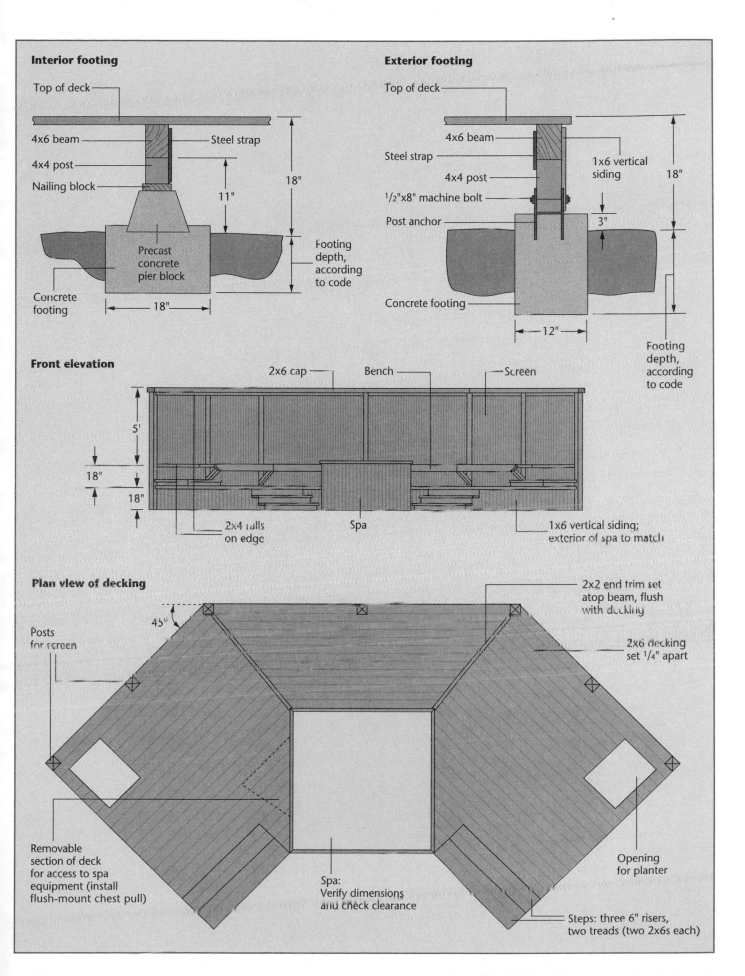

Interior footing

Top of deck

4x6 beam

Steel strap

4x4 post

Nailing block

Precast concrete pier block

Concrete footing

11"

18"

18"

Footing depth, according to code

Exterior footing

Top of deck

4x6 beam

Steel strap

4x4 post

1/2"x8" machine bolt

Post anchor

Concrete footing

1x6 vertical siding

18"

3"

12"

Footing depth, according to code

Front elevation

2x6 cap

Bench

Screen

5'

18"

18"

2x4 rails on edge

Spa

1x6 vertical siding; exterior of spa to match

Plan view of decking

2x2 end trim set atop beam, flush with decking

Posts for screen

45°

2x6 decking set 1/4" apart

Removable section of deck for access to spa equipment (install flush-mount chest pull)

Spa: Verify dimensions and check clearance

Opening for planter

Steps: three 6" risers, two treads (two 2x6s each)

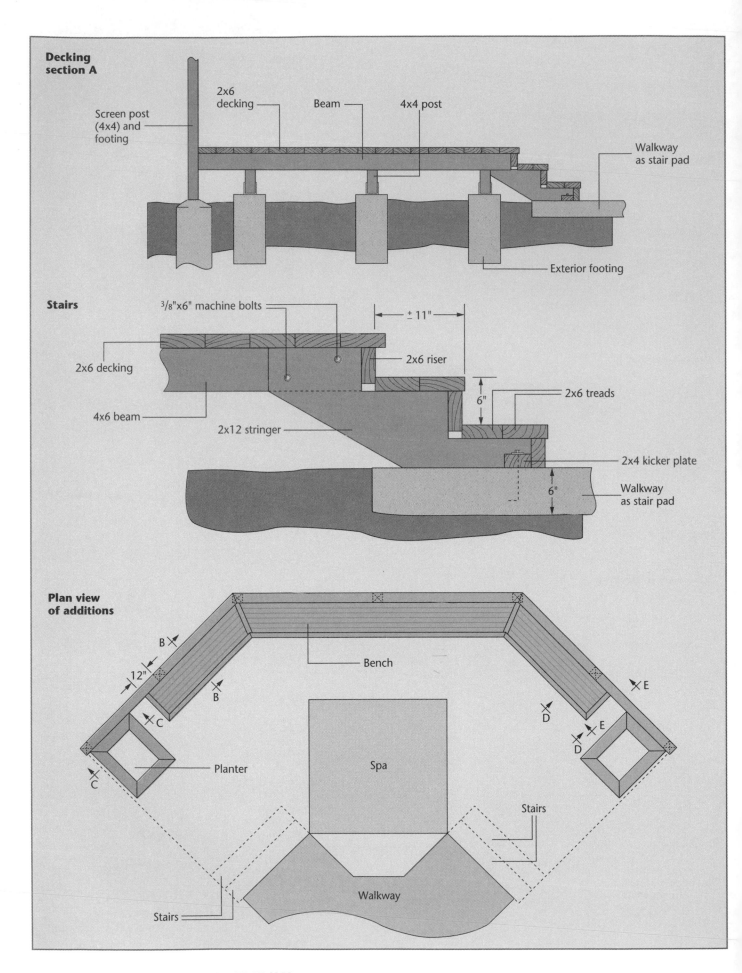

Decking section A

Screen post (4x4) and footing

2x6 decking

Beam

4x4 post

Walkway as stair pad

Exterior footing

Stairs

3/8"x6" machine bolts

±11"

2x6 decking

4x6 beam

2x12 stringer

2x6 riser

6"

2x6 treads

2x4 kicker plate

6"

Walkway as stair pad

Plan view of additions

B

12"

B

C

C

Bench

Planter

Spa

Stairs

Walkway

Stairs

E

D

E

D

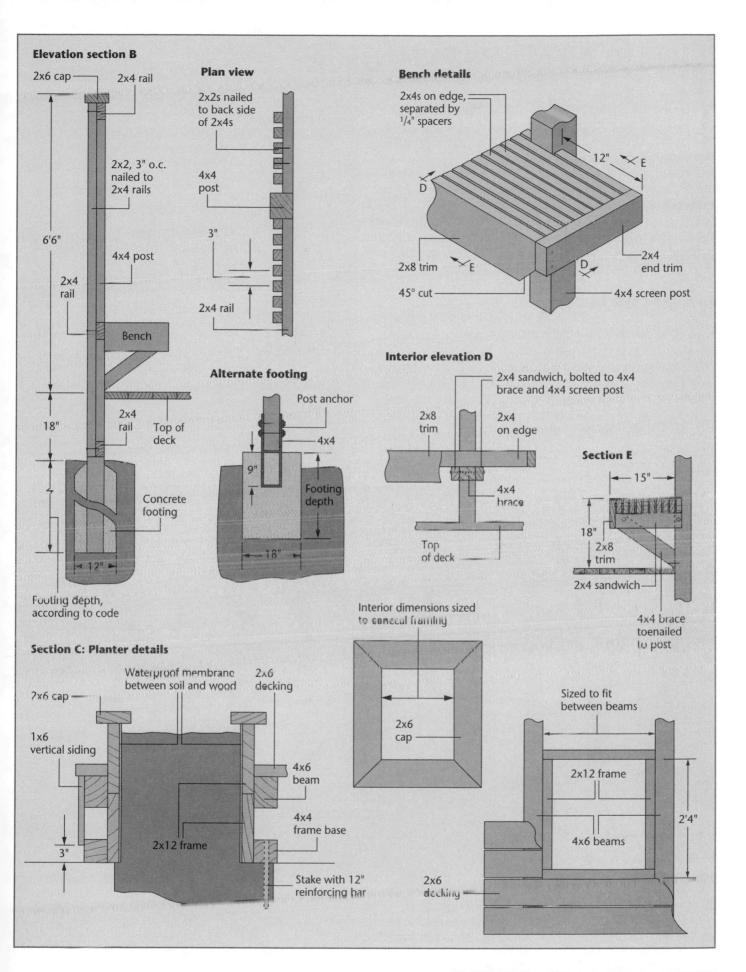

Elevation section B

2x6 cap
2x4 rail
2x2, 3" o.c. nailed to 2x4 rails
6'6"
4x4 post
2x4 rail
Bench
Top of deck
2x4 rail
18"
Concrete footing
12"
Footing depth, according to code

Plan view

2x2s nailed to back side of 2x4s
4x4 post
3"
2x4 rail

Bench details

2x4s on edge, separated by ¹⁄₄" spacers
12"
E
D
2x8 trim
E
45° cut
D
2x4 end trim
4x4 screen post

Alternate footing

Post anchor
4x4
9"
Footing depth
18"

Interior elevation D

2x4 sandwich, bolted to 4x4 brace and 4x4 screen post
2x8 trim
2x4 on edge
4x4 brace
Top of deck

Section E

15"
18"
2x8 trim
2x4 sandwich
4x4 brace toenailed to post

Section C: Planter details

2x6 cap
Waterproof membrane between soil and wood
2x6 decking
1x6 vertical siding
4x6 beam
4x4 frame base
2x12 frame
3"
Stake with 12" reinforcing bar

Interior dimensions sized to conceal framing
2x6 cap

Sized to fit between beams
2x12 frame
4x6 beams
2'4"
2x6 decking

ANGULAR LOW-LEVEL DECK

The angular projection on this clean-lined deck intrudes very little into the garden, yet increases the deck's square footage by about a third. A built-in planter/bench echoes its form.

To enhance the sleekness of the design, all wood surfaces were sanded to a smooth finish, then stained to match the doors of the house.

This deck is ideal for a house with simple lines on a flat lot. Its low level and tidy fascia float it neatly over a lawn. And, because the decking is laid on the diagonal, it creates an illusion of spaciousness.

TO ADAPT THIS PLAN

Although tucked into an L-shaped area here, the design would have the same sleek effect across the straight back of a house, in a side yard, or at an entry.

To maintain the lean, seamless look, do not enlarge the plan beyond the length of available lumber for decking. To conserve lumber and reduce the amount of mitering, joists may be run perpendicular to the ledger, though the pattern made by the fasteners in the diagonal decking will no longer be at a 90° angle.

MATERIALS LIST

Designed for pressure-treated lumber (structural members), surfaced Clear All Heart redwood or cedar (visible members), and galvanized hardware.

Lumber	
Joists/ledgers	2x6
Decking	2x6
Trim	2x2 nosing over joists/rim joists
Benches	2x4, 2x8 legs; 2x6 trim, blocking, seat; 2x2 siding; 2x4 bracing, caps
Planters	2x2 siding; 2x4 bracing, caps
Masonry	
Pier blocks	Precast concrete
Concrete	Footings
Hardware	
Nails	3¹/₂" for structure; nails for framing connectors
Screws	3" for decking; ¹/₄" lag screws for ledger
Connectors	Joist hangers
Finishes	Protective pigmented coating
Other	6-mil plastic for planter liners

DESIGN: DAVID KIRK, CR, CGR; THE KIRK COMPANY
"To avoid a 'boat dock' effect, this plan employs a modified octagon in its seating area. A seamless diagonal surface makes it seem larger than it is."

BUILDING NOTES

Use galvanized hardware; deck screws are suggested for easier maintenance.

A 2x2 nosing caps all the decking edges, for decoration and durability. Line planters with 6-mil plastic, slit the bottom for drainage, and fasten the liner to the top edge of the planter before installing the 2x4 cap. To permit easy transplanting and prolong the life of the wood, use seasonal plants in pots, rather than planting directly in the planters. Cut a 2x6 to sit atop bricks or blocks inside the chamber; conceal any voids with dried sphagnum moss, available at nurseries or garden centers.

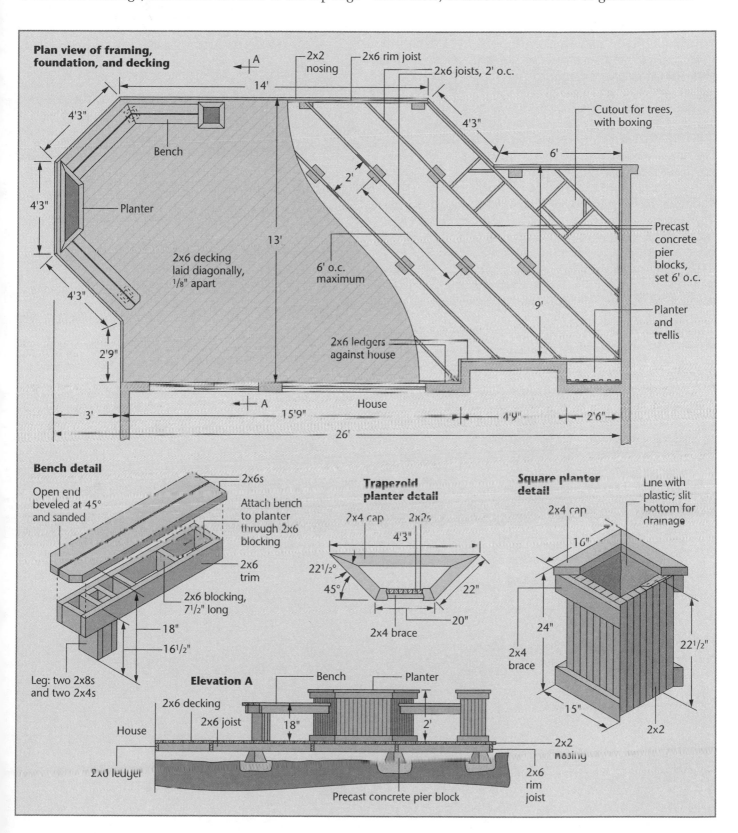

Plan view of framing, foundation, and decking

A

14'

2x2 nosing
2x6 rim joist
2x6 joists, 2' o.c.
4'3"

4'3"

Bench

Cutout for trees, with boxing

6'

4'3"

Planter

4'3"

13'

2'

2x6 decking laid diagonally, 1/8" apart

6' o.c. maximum

Precast concrete pier blocks, set 6' o.c.

9'

Planter and trellis

2'9"

2x6 ledgers against house

A

15'9"

House

4'9"

2'6"

3'

26'

Bench detail

2x6s

Open end beveled at 45° and sanded

Attach bench to planter through 2x6 blocking

2x6 trim

2x6 blocking, 7 1/2" long

18"

16 1/2"

Leg: two 2x8s and two 2x4s

Trapezoid planter detail

2x4 cap   2x2s

4'3"

22 1/2°

45°

22"

2x4 brace

20"

Square planter detail

2x4 cap

Line with plastic; slit bottom for drainage

16"

24"

2x4 brace

22 1/2"

15"

2x2

Elevation A

Bench   Planter

2x6 decking

2x6 joist

House

18"

2'

2x2 nosing

2x6 ledger

Precast concrete pier block

2x6 rim joist

SPLIT-LEVEL DECK

A deck on two levels, such as this one, allows you to use different areas for different outdoor activities.

TO ADAPT THIS PLAN

You could build the railings with horizontal rails rather than vertical balusters and cleats. In either case, make sure that the space between the rails or balusters does not exceed that allowed by your local code—usually 4 inches, although it may be 6 inches in some areas.

BUILDING NOTES

If you use wood that's not decay resistant for the posts, you'll need to raise them at least 6 inches off the ground. You can use precast concrete pier blocks, or cast the concrete above ground level in a form. Either of these options will raise the finished height of your deck, so make any necessary adjustments—for one thing, you'll need to add another tread to the stairs.

The 2x6 nailer shown in section C *(page 211)* is face-nailed to the rim joist between the stringers. The stringers are face-nailed into the ends of the nailer and fastened to it with universal anchors and 3½-inch nails.

Deck clips hold the deck boards securely with no visible fasteners on the surface.

MATERIALS LIST

Use pressure-treated lumber for structural members, pressure-treated lumber or redwood or cedar heartwood for the decking, and galvanized hardware.

Lumber	
Posts	4x4
Beams	2x6
Joists	2x6
Decking	2x6
Fascia	2x8
Stairs	2x10 stringers; 2x6 risers; 2x12 treads
Railing	4x4 posts; 2x6 cap rails; 2x4 bottom rails; 2x2 balusters; 2x2 cleats
Hardware	
Nails	3"; 3½ "; nails for framing connectors
Screws	3/8"x4" lag screws for ledger, 1/4"x1½" lag screws for stair hardware
Connectors	Post anchors; post-beam connectors; joist hangers; seismic or universal anchors; deck clips; stair angles; railing ties
Masonry	
Concrete	10" round footings; stair pad

Dual-level decks don't have to be difficult to construct; the use of a wide variety of framing connectors in this deck makes the job go quickly.
PLAN REPRINTED COURTESY OF SIMPSON STRONG-TIE COMPANY

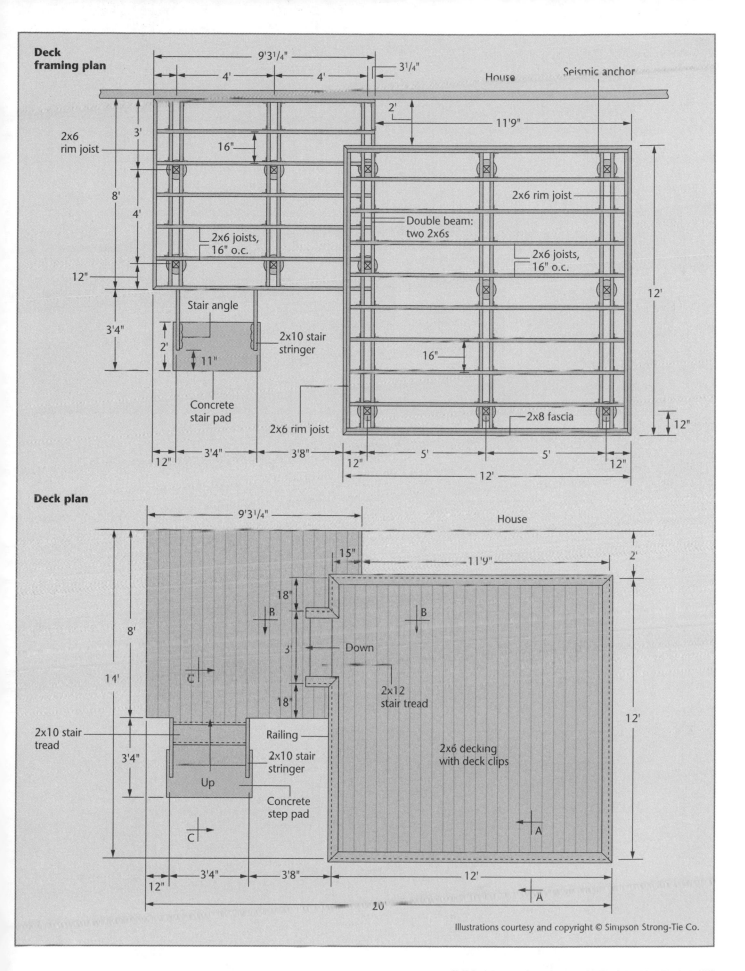

Deck framing plan

9'3¼"

4' 4' 3¼"

House   Seismic anchor

2' 11'9"

2x6 rim joist

3'

16"

8' 4'

12"

2x6 joists, 16" o.c.

Stair angle

3'4" 2' 11"

2x10 stair stringer

Concrete stair pad

2x6 rim joist

12" 3'4" 3'8" 12" 5' 5' 12"

12'

2x6 rim joist

Double beam: two 2x6s

2x6 joists, 16" o.c.

12'

16"

2x8 fascia

12"

Deck plan

9'3¼" House

15" 11'9" 2'

18" B B

8' 3' Down

C 2x12 stair tread

18"

14' 2x6 decking with deck clips

12'

2x10 stair tread

3'4" Railing

2x10 stair stringer

Up Concrete step pad

C A

12" 3'4" 3'8" 12' A

20'

Illustrations courtesy and copyright © Simpson Strong-Tie Co.

Front elevation

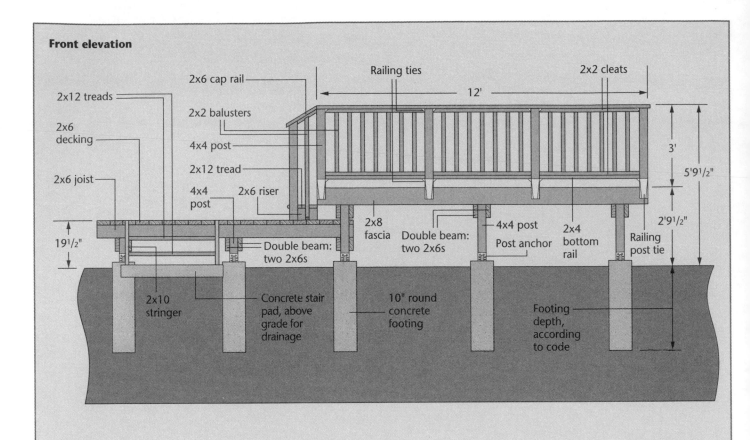

- 2x6 cap rail
- Railing ties
- 2x2 cleats
- 12'
- 2x12 treads
- 2x2 balusters
- 2x6 decking
- 4x4 post
- 2x12 tread
- 2x6 joist
- 4x4 post
- 2x6 riser
- 3'
- 5'9¹/₂"
- 2'9¹/₂"
- 19¹/₂"
- 2x8 fascia
- Double beam: two 2x6s
- 4x4 post
- Post anchor
- 2x4 bottom rail
- Railing post tie
- Double beam: two 2x6s
- 2x10 stringer
- Concrete stair pad, above grade for drainage
- 10" round concrete footing
- Footing depth, according to code

Left side elevation

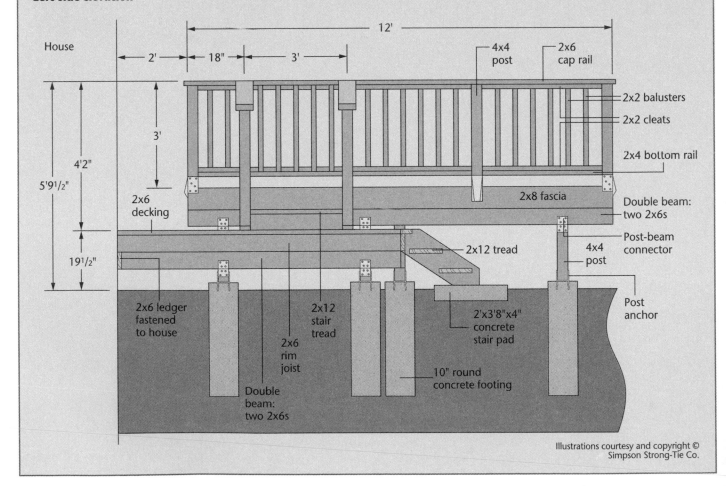

- House
- 12'
- 2'
- 18"
- 3'
- 4x4 post
- 2x6 cap rail
- 3'
- 4'2"
- 5'9¹/₂"
- 19¹/₂"
- 2x6 decking
- 2x2 balusters
- 2x2 cleats
- 2x4 bottom rail
- 2x8 fascia
- 2x12 tread
- Double beam: two 2x6s
- Post-beam connector
- 4x4 post
- 2x6 ledger fastened to house
- 2x6 rim joist
- 2x12 stair tread
- 2'x3'8"x4" concrete stair pad
- Post anchor
- Double beam: two 2x6s
- 10" round concrete footing

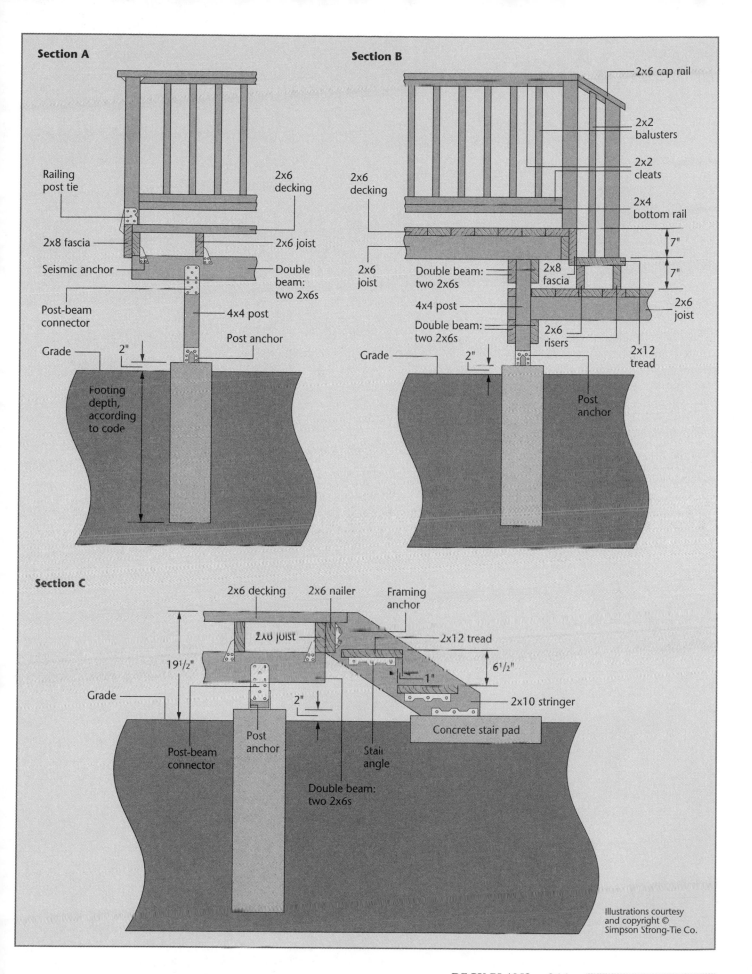

Section A

Railing post tie

2x6 decking

2x8 fascia

Seismic anchor

2x6 joist

Post-beam connector

Double beam: two 2x6s

4x4 post

Post anchor

Grade

2"

Footing depth, according to code

Section B

2x6 cap rail

2x2 balusters

2x2 cleats

2x4 bottom rail

2x6 decking

7"

7"

2x6 joist

Double beam: two 2x6s

2x8 fascia

4x4 post

2x6 joist

Double beam: two 2x6s

2x6 risers

2x12 tread

Grade

2"

Post anchor

Section C

2x6 decking

2x6 nailer

Framing anchor

2x8 joist

2x12 tread

19 1/2"

6 1/2"

Grade

2"

1"

2x10 stringer

Post-beam connector

Post anchor

Stair angle

Concrete stair pad

Double beam: two 2x6s

SPACE-SAVING ANGLE

The diagonal orientation of this plan leaves space to plant on three sides, resulting in a deck surrounded with greenery. It also provides the largest deck possible with the least intrusion into garden space.

TO ADAPT THIS PLAN

Although it overlooks a small garden here, this design would be equally comfortable in the woods, or as an entry. Build it on any side of the house, at a corner, or nestled into an L. You could use this deck as an area for adult entertaining, with the stairs leading down to a children's play space.

To change the length or width of the deck, add or subtract joists and adjust their length (see the lumber span tables on pages 73 and 74). Height is easily adjusted by changing the size of the posts and the number of steps or size of the risers. Without the posts, this deck can be built just a step above garden level.

Adjust the railing, if necessary, to conform to your local building code; you may have to add another rail.

BUILDING NOTES

Using metal framing connectors to build this deck gives it added strength.

Extend the bench fascia around the exposed ends and miter the corners. Before ripping the 2x4 block behind the backrest, check the angle to be sure it's comfortable.

You might want to round the inside corners of the cap rail for comfort, and rout out the back side of the stair handrail to create a finger grip.

MATERIALS LIST

Designed for pressure-treated lumber (structural members), surfaced redwood (visible members), and galvanized hardware.

Lumber	
Posts	4x4
Beams	4x8
Joists	2x6
Blocking	2x6 atop beams and ledgers, and at bench and rail posts
Ledgers	4x8 for deck; 2x4 for benches
Decking	2x6
Fascia	2x8
Stairs	2x12 stringers; 2x6 treads; 2x4 risers
Railings	4x4 posts; 2x6 cap, rails, stair handrail; 2x4 stretchers; 1½" dowel
Bench	4x4 posts; 2x6 seat, trim; 2x4 supports, blocks (ripped); 2x2 trim
Masonry	
Pier blocks	12" precast concrete
Concrete	18"x18" post footings; 18"x6' stair pad
Hardware	
Nails and screws	3½" nails or deck screws; nails for framing connectors; ⅜"x6" lag screws for handrail
Bolts	⅝" bolts for ledgers and sandwiched blocking; ½" bolts at all other vertical connections to posts
Connectors	Post anchors; post caps; angled joist hangers at beam to ledger; sloped joist hangers at top of stringers; 8"x8"x2" angle irons at foot of stringer; 3"x3"x5" angle irons at joists to posts, blocking

DESIGN: ANN CHRISTOPH, ASLA, LANDSCAPE ARCHITECT

"The diagonal deck takes advantage of the largest dimension of the yard and provides a privacy/planting area in front of the master bedroom, ensuring leafy seclusion on both sides."

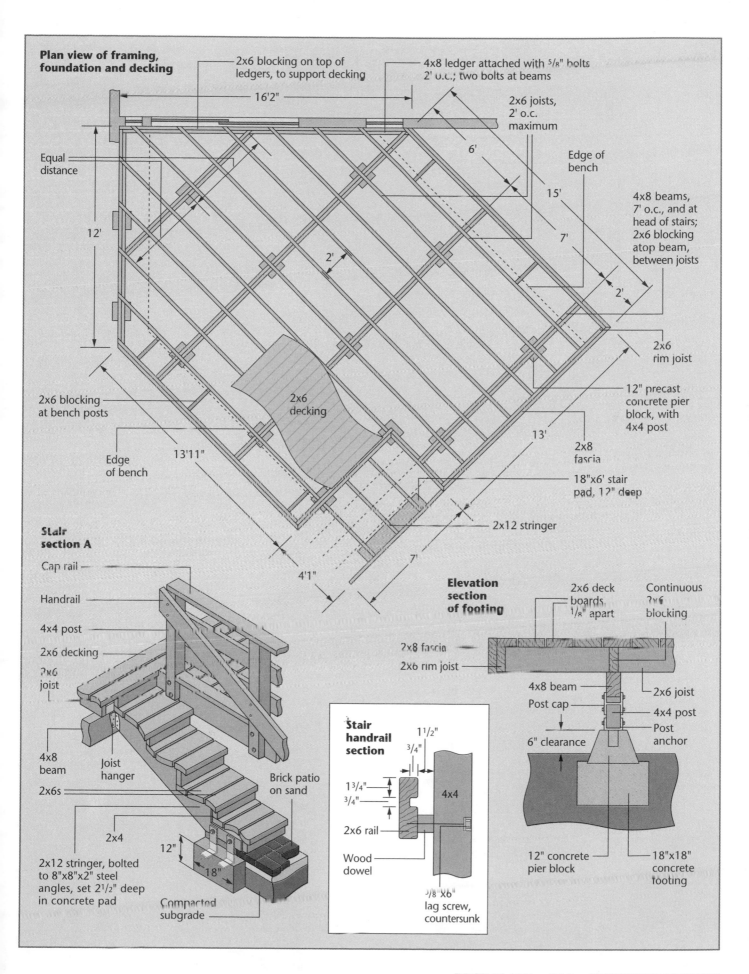

Plan view of framing, foundation and decking

2x6 blocking on top of ledgers, to support decking

4x8 ledger attached with $^5/_8$" bolts 2' o.c.; two bolts at beams

16'2"

2x6 joists, 2' o.c. maximum

6'

Edge of bench

Equal distance

15'

12'

7'

4x8 beams, 7' o.c., and at head of stairs; 2x6 blocking atop beam, between joists

2'

2'

2'

2x6 rim joist

12" precast concrete pier block, with 4x4 post

2x6 blocking at bench posts

2x6 decking

Edge of bench

13'11"

13'

2x8 fascia

18"x6' stair pad, 12" deep

2x12 stringer

4'1"

7'

Stair section A

Cap rail

Handrail

4x4 post

2x6 decking

2x6 joist

4x8 beam

Joist hanger

2x6s

2x4

Brick patio on sand

12"

18"

2x12 stringer, bolted to 8"x8"x2" steel angles, set 2$^1/_2$" deep in concrete pad

Compacted subgrade

Stair handrail section

1$^1/_2$"

$^3/_4$"

1$^3/_4$"

$^3/_4$"

4x4

2x6 rail

Wood dowel

$^3/_8$"x6" lag screw, countersunk

Elevation section of footing

2x6 deck boards, $^1/_8$" apart

Continuous 2x6 blocking

2x8 fascia

2x6 rim joist

4x8 beam

Post cap

6" clearance

2x6 joist

4x4 post

Post anchor

12" concrete pier block

18"x18" concrete footing

Plan view of bench and rail framing

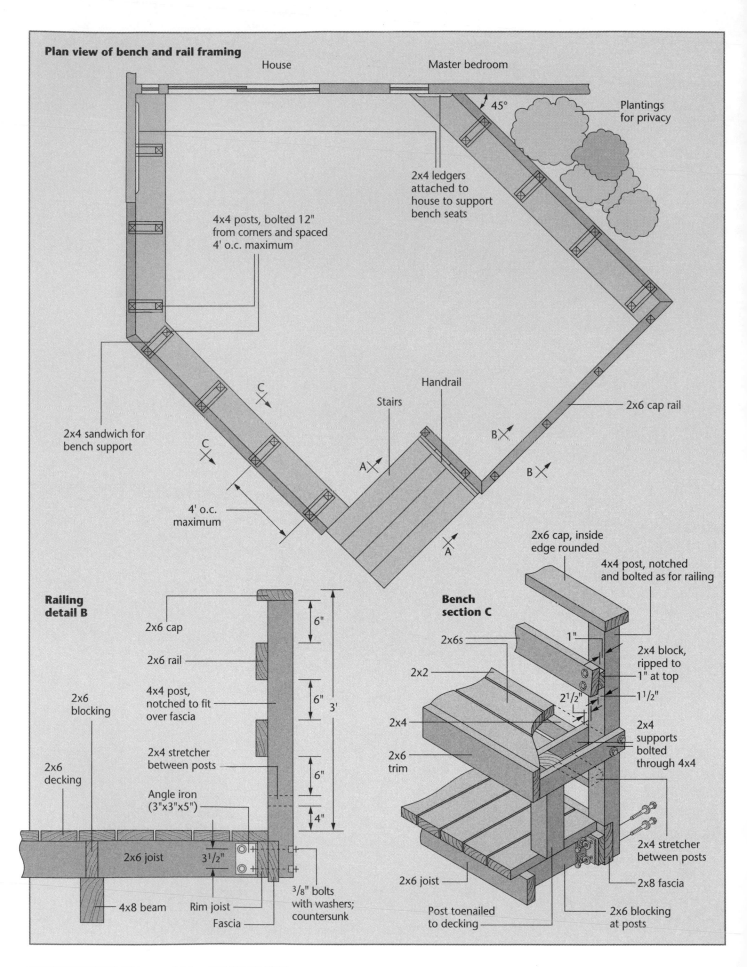

House

Master bedroom

45°

Plantings for privacy

2x4 ledgers attached to house to support bench seats

4x4 posts, bolted 12" from corners and spaced 4' o.c. maximum

2x6 cap rail

2x4 sandwich for bench support

Handrail

Stairs

C

C

A

B

B

4' o.c. maximum

A

Railing detail B

2x6 cap

2x6 rail

4x4 post, notched to fit over fascia

2x4 stretcher between posts

Angle iron (3"x3"x5")

2x6 blocking

2x6 decking

2x6 joist

4x8 beam

Rim joist

Fascia

3/8" bolts with washers; countersunk

3 1/2"

6"

6"

3'

6"

4"

Bench section C

2x6 cap, inside edge rounded

4x4 post, notched and bolted as for railing

2x6s

2x2

1"

2x4 block, ripped to 1" at top

2 1/2"

1 1/2"

2x4

2x6 trim

2x4 supports bolted through 4x4

2x6 joist

Post toenailed to decking

2x4 stretcher between posts

2x8 fascia

2x6 blocking at posts

CAPTURING LOST SPACE

An overhead arbor and a privacy screen seclude the partially shaded deck and spa area on which this plan focuses. A shower is ingeniously tucked between two studs in the exterior wall of the house, with plumbing hidden inside the house; over the shower's drain, a wooden grate is fitted into the patio surface of concrete pavers. You can increase privacy at the spa by planting vines to cling to the arbors.

Past this calm outdoor soaking area, the side yard terraces downhill in a series of interrelated planters, retainers, and paved patios that lead to a play yard and garden at the rear of the house.

Square corners appear throughout the design, rhythmically repeated in the spa, privacy screen, arbors, and wooden retaining walls. Detailing is in a tranquil Northwest/Japanese style.

Outdoor lighting at the steps and under the trees makes the spa suitable for nighttime use.

TO ADAPT THIS PLAN

This plan is a wonderful solution for a narrow side yard. Although it was built on a slope here, it would also work well on a level lot.

Some obvious changes will be required, depending on the particular spa you choose: Decking height, the size of the spa opening, and location of and access to spa equipment will all be determined by the model of spa you select. But you should locate the spa in a quiet spot with easy access back into the house, and be sure that both your house and your neighbor's are

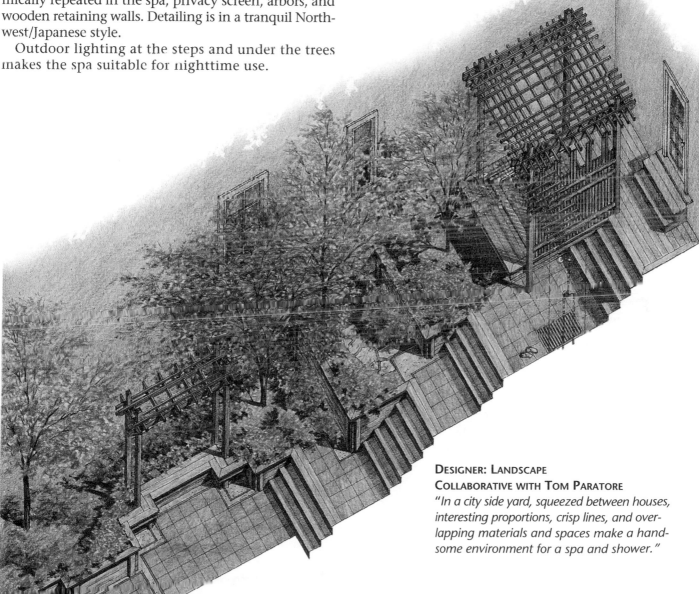

DESIGNER: LANDSCAPE COLLABORATIVE WITH TOM PARATORE
"In a city side yard, squeezed between houses, interesting proportions, crisp lines, and overlapping materials and spaces make a handsome environment for a spa and shower."

MATERIALS LIST

Designed for pressure-treated lumber (structural members), Clear Green redwood (visible members; Construction Heart rough redwood where specified), and galvanized hardware.

Lumber	
Posts	4x4 rough
Beam/joists	2x6
Ledgers	2x8
Decking	2x6
Rim joists	2x6; 2x10
Fascia	1x6 over 2x10 rim joist at stair no. 4
Stairs	2x12 stringers; 2x6 treads; 2x4 risers, kicker plate
Retainers	2x8 caps; 2x6 rough sides
Arbors/screen	4x4 rough posts; 2x4 beams; 2x3 rails; 2x2 lattice, screen, shower arbor ledger; marine plywood shower backboard in 2x2 frame
Spa skirt	2x6
Masonry	
Pier blocks	12" precast concrete
Concrete	Footings for retainer posts; pad for stairs
Gravel	Footings; shower grate drainage
Hardware	
Nails	3½", 3½" casing for arbor 2x4s; 3¼" casing for arbor 2x3s; 3" casing for arbor 2x2s; nails for framing connectors
Screws	³⁄₈"x6" lag screws with washers for ledgers
Connectors	Deck clips at spa surround; joist hangers
Other hardware	Metal drain pan; pipe to sewer; shower head; handles; pipes
Finishes	Marine enamel
Other	Caulking for house siding near shower

high enough above grade at the site of the spa to ensure privacy for bathers.

The width of your side yard will determine the width of decks, patio areas, planting areas, and steps.

BUILDING NOTES

Use Construction Heart rough redwood for all vertical elements, including stairs, retaining walls, posts, and some arbor uprights. All wood that won't be visible is pressure-treated Douglas-fir. Arbor fasteners are galvanized casing nails, which are less conspicuous than common nails and do not detract from the beauty of the wood.

You'll have to follow the manufacturer's specifications for the spa's foundation and installation, but ideally, the top of the spa will be flush with your deck. Remember that the spa must be supported independently of the deck. Be sure to determine where you'll require access to the spa equipment and adjust joist locations, if necessary, before you build. Install extra joists and blocking for fastening purposes if you intend to miter the corners of the spa deck. Deck clips are specified around the spa to help provide a smooth walking surface for bathers, and Clear Green redwood is used for the same reason.

The shower head is set in a backboard of marine plywood that is framed with 2x2s and enameled an aquamarine color to match the spa. Instead of marine plywood, you could use pressure-treated plywood rated for exterior use. Be sure to caulk all holes in the shower area and in the side of the house where the ledgers are attached. When you're attaching the ledgers to the house, shim them out from the wall with washers to prevent rot.

The privacy screen shown in Elevation section B *(page 218)* is supported by 4x4 posts. Three 2x3s are set on edge between them and serve as rails for the tightly spaced upright 2x2s. Note the pattern created by mixing two different lengths. The moon arbor over the spa shares two of the same posts as the privacy screen; they should be cut after deck level is established and arbor and detail levels have been determined. Arbor beams sandwich the posts and are topped by two layers of 2x2s at intervals that open up toward the center. The shower arbor extends from one of these 2x4 beam sandwiches, continues across to the house, and rests on a 2x2 ledger. Additional 2x2s, laid crosswise, complete the job.

Plan view of framing

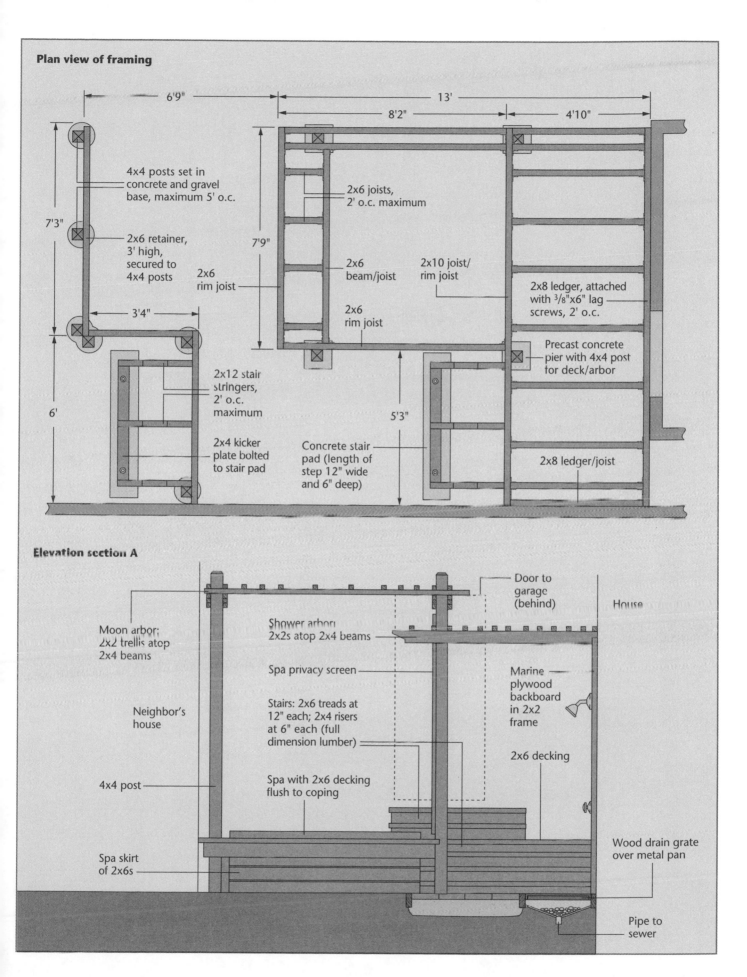

6'9"

13'

8'2"

4'10"

7'3"

7'9"

3'4"

6'

5'3"

4x4 posts set in concrete and gravel base, maximum 5' o.c.

2x6 retainer, 3' high, secured to 4x4 posts

2x6 rim joist

2x6 joists, 2' o.c. maximum

2x6 beam/joist

2x6 rim joist

2x10 joist/ rim joist

2x8 ledger, attached with ³/₈"x6" lag screws, 2' o.c.

Precast concrete pier with 4x4 post for deck/arbor

2x8 ledger/joist

2x12 stair stringers, 2' o.c. maximum

2x4 kicker plate bolted to stair pad

Concrete stair pad (length of step 12" wide and 6" deep)

Elevation section A

Door to garage (behind)

House

Moon arbor; 2x2 trellis atop 2x4 beams

Shower arbor: 2x2s atop 2x4 beams

Spa privacy screen

Neighbor's house

Stairs: 2x6 treads at 12" each; 2x4 risers at 6" each (full dimension lumber)

Marine plywood backboard in 2x2 frame

2x6 decking

4x4 post

Spa with 2x6 decking flush to coping

Spa skirt of 2x6s

Wood drain grate over metal pan

Pipe to sewer

Elevation section B

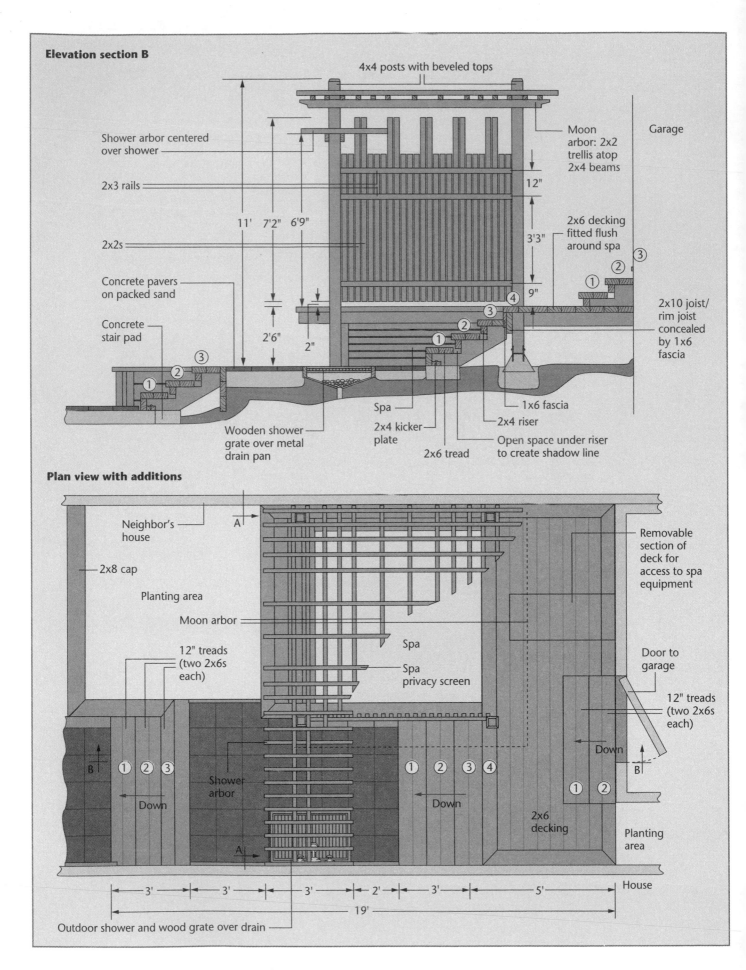

4x4 posts with beveled tops

Shower arbor centered over shower

2x3 rails

2x2s

Concrete pavers on packed sand

Concrete stair pad

Moon arbor: 2x2 trellis atop 2x4 beams

Garage

12"

2x6 decking fitted flush around spa

3'3"

9"

11' 7'2" 6'9"

2'6"

2"

2x10 joist/ rim joist concealed by 1x6 fascia

Wooden shower grate over metal drain pan

Spa

2x4 kicker plate

2x6 tread

1x6 fascia

2x4 riser

Open space under riser to create shadow line

Plan view with additions

Neighbor's house

2x8 cap

Planting area

Moon arbor

12" treads (two 2x6s each)

Shower arbor

Down

Down

Spa

Spa privacy screen

Removable section of deck for access to spa equipment

Door to garage

12" treads (two 2x6s each)

Down

2x6 decking

Planting area

House

3'   3'   3'   2'   3'   5'

19'

Outdoor shower and wood grate over drain

MEANDERING DECK

These rectangular decks tie pre-existing areas together, making the gazebo and distant patio part of a more functional whole. Decking is all on a single level, but the change in surface board size and direction adds interest to the serene design. Simple geometric shapes contribute to the ordered feeling. (Photo on page 9.)

TO ADAPT THIS PLAN

A small, level yard containing separate, presently unconnected elements is perfect for this deck. If you have an unused area, perhaps behind your garage or in a large side yard, this plan yields a secluded retreat. It would also impart organization to a large, flat yard.

Think of each deck as a separate unit; this plan has four, but you could drop or add components. You can also change the length or width of any unit to link existing elements in your garden.

BUILDING NOTES

The 4x4 beams are nailed to the nailing blocks on the precast pier blocks. However, a low-level deck plan like this one could be fastened directly to an existing concrete slab *(page 131)*.

To prevent weeds and simplify future garden maintenance, begin by using a pre-emergent weed killer, then lay 4- to 6-mil polyethylene sheeting covered with gravel where the decks will be built.

DESIGN: JOLEE HORNE, LANDSCAPE DESIGNER
"I retained the existing gazebo and added a lawn, patio, and decking to complement it. Together, they surround the new fish pond, create a focal interest, and suggest oriental balance and style."

MATERIALS LIST

Designed for pressure-treated lumber (structural members), surfaced redwood (visible members), and galvanized hardware.

Lumber (decks)	
Beams	4x4
Decking	Clear All Heart; 2x4 for small decks, 2x6 for large decks,
Fascia	2x4, 2x6 Select
Masonry (decks)	
Pier blocks	Precast concrete
Concrete	12" square footings
Hardware (decks)	
Nails	3½" or 3¼" (or wood screws)
Lumber (benches)	
Posts	4x4 Construction Heart
Bracing	2x6 Clear All Heart
Seating/trim	2x6 Clear seating; 2x4 Clear trim
Masonry (benches)	
Concrete	12" square footings
Gravel	Drain rock, 4" to 6" deep
Hardware (benches)	
Nails	3½" or 3¼"
Bolts	½"x8" carriage bolts

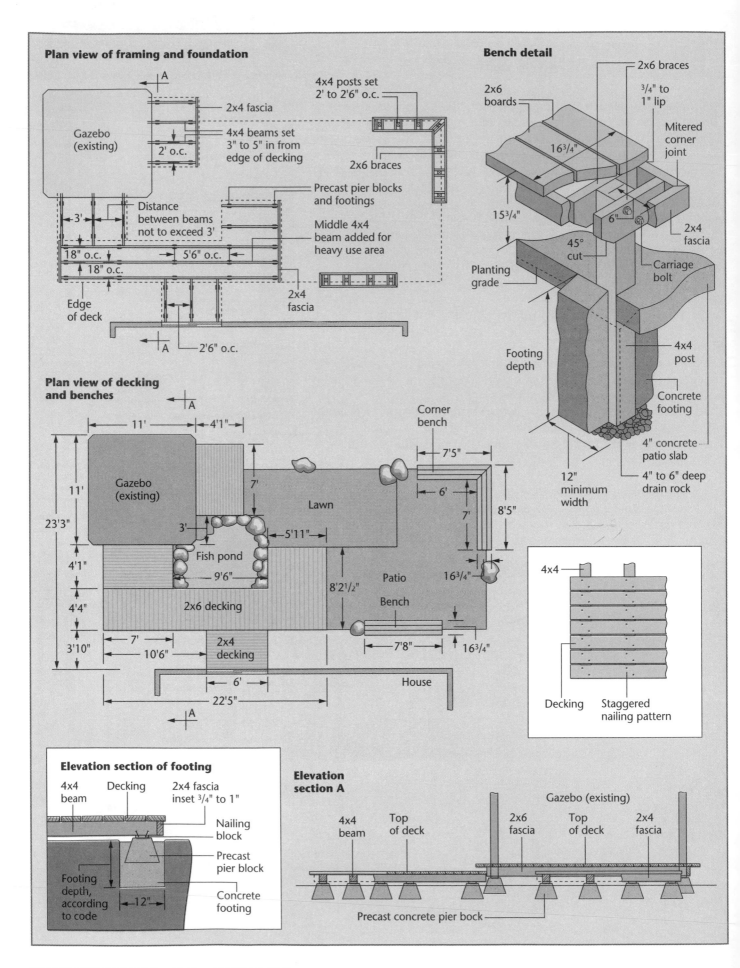

Plan view of framing and foundation

Gazebo (existing)

2x4 fascia

4x4 beams set 3" to 5" in from edge of decking

2' o.c.

4x4 posts set 2' to 2'6" o.c.

2x6 braces

Precast pier blocks and footings

Middle 4x4 beam added for heavy use area

2x4 fascia

3'

Distance between beams not to exceed 3'

18" o.c.

5'6" o.c.

18" o.c.

Edge of deck

2'6" o.c.

A

Bench detail

2x6 braces

2x6 boards

¾" to 1" lip

Mitered corner joint

16¾"

15¾"

6"

2x4 fascia

45° cut

Carriage bolt

Planting grade

4x4 post

Footing depth

Concrete footing

4" concrete patio slab

12" minimum width

4" to 6" deep drain rock

Plan view of decking and benches

A

11'

4'1"

Gazebo (existing)

7'

11'

23'3"

3'

Fish pond

5'11"

9'6"

2x6 decking

4'1"

4'4"

7'

2x4 decking

3'10"

10'6"

6'

22'5"

A

Lawn

Corner bench

7'5"

6'

7'

8'5"

16¾"

Patio Bench

8'2½"

7'8"

16¾"

House

4x4

Decking

Staggered nailing pattern

Elevation section of footing

4x4 beam

Decking

2x4 fascia inset ¾" to 1"

Nailing block

Precast pier block

Concrete footing

Footing depth, according to code

12"

Elevation section A

4x4 beam

Top of deck

Gazebo (existing)

2x6 fascia

Top of deck

2x4 fascia

Precast concrete pier bock

PATIO PLATFORM

This multilevel deck and stair system is an integration of elements that fit together like a carefully thought-out puzzle. A closer look reveals that decks become steps, steps become benches, benches become planters, and the entire structure frames and overlooks the charming brick patio.

Weather was a major factor in this particular design. Though the arbor-shaded upper deck off the kitchen makes an attractive transition to the lower garden, this area is often too windy for comfort. But the conversation nook at patio level, with its matching arbor and lower position, is very sheltered and cozy.

The perimeter fence not only defines the property but also serves as a backrest to the benches. A coordinating outdoor dining table was built to complete this cohesive design; details for the table are found on page 161.

TO ADAPT THIS PLAN

Though designed for a flat yard behind a house with an elevated first floor, this deck can be adapted to a variety of sites, for example, a lot with a gentle downslope.

You can use this plan to enclose any small space, providing privacy outdoors even in an urban neighbor-hood. Or align this deck to overlook a larger garden from its long side.

Some tailoring of dimensions is likely to be required. If your house is closer to ground level, eliminate a step or two as needed (the reverse, of course, is also true). You can easily shorten or extend the length or width of either the upper or lower deck, and turn the corner where it is most appropriate for your lot.

You can also adjust the size of the conversation nook by changing the lengths of the benches around its three sides. But keep in mind the relationship between the levels: The benches are three risers above the main deck, and the tops of the planters are three risers above them.

Another possibility is to replace the brick of the original design with a third, lower level of decking. For continuity of design, run the boards in the same direction as the two existing decks.

DESIGN: DAVID AND ROBERT TRACHTENBERG WITH SALO RAWET
*"Our goal was to link the kitchen and the garden
with a series of interconnected spaces. The upper
deck leads to a lower deck, which sits just one foot
above the patio and its arbor-covered nook."*

BUILDING NOTES

All lumber used in the deck's substructure is pressure treated. The designers of this plan feel that more scarce and costly woods should be conserved and used only where their beauty can be fully appreciated.

Locate a structural member such as framing or the band joist when attaching the ledger to the house *(page 108)*. Pack the holes in the house with clear silicone for water protection. For each lag screw, use one washer on the front of the ledger and two or three washers between the ledger and the house. Floating the ledger in this way will protect the house from moisture and any future deterioration.

Here there are no concrete footings under the pier blocks, but in many areas, footings are required. Follow your local building code regulations.

The level changes are accentuated by the use of 2x6 stair treads, which run in the opposite direction to the 2x4 decking for much of the deck's length.

If you're building the fence and the deck at the same time, additional seat support can be cantilevered off the 4x4 fence posts by lining them up with the 4x4 bench posts. Sandwich both posts between common blocking beneath seat level.

MATERIALS LIST

Designed for pressure-treated lumber (structural members); surfaced Clear redwood (decking, planter caps, bench seats, and railing); rough redwood (all other visible members); and galvanized hardware.

Lumber	
Posts/beams	4x4 posts; 4x6 beams
Joists/ blocking	2x6, lowest landing only; 2x8; 2x12 rim joist for upper deck; 2x4 blocking
Ledgers	2x6 for lower deck and as header between brick and wraparound step; 2x12 at house
Decking	2x4
Fascia	2x12 upper deck; 2x4 lower deck
Stairs	2x12 stringers; 2x4 risers; 2x6 treads
Railings	2x6 caps; 2x4 rails; 2x2 balusters; 4x4 posts
Arbors	2x10 beams; 2x6 rafters, notched at beams; 2x4 rafter atop beam, kitchen arbor only; 2x2s as top layer, patio arbor only; 4x4 posts; 2x6 ledger
Benches	2x4 trim, blocking; 2x6 seating; 4x4 posts
Planters	2x6 sides, retainers; 2x4 nailers at posts; 4x4 posts
Masonry	
Piers	Precast concrete blocks (at corners, except at kitchen)
Concrete	Footings
Gravel	Beneath footings and planters, 4" to 6" deep
Hardware	
Nails	3" for joists, decking; 3½" at pier blocks, headers; 3½" casing for visible vertical members, set in; nails for framing connectors
Bolts and screws	⅜"x6" lag screws at ledgers; ¼" bolts for post connections
Connectors	Joist hangers for 2x6, 2x8
Other	Caulk at ledger holes; roofing felt to line planters

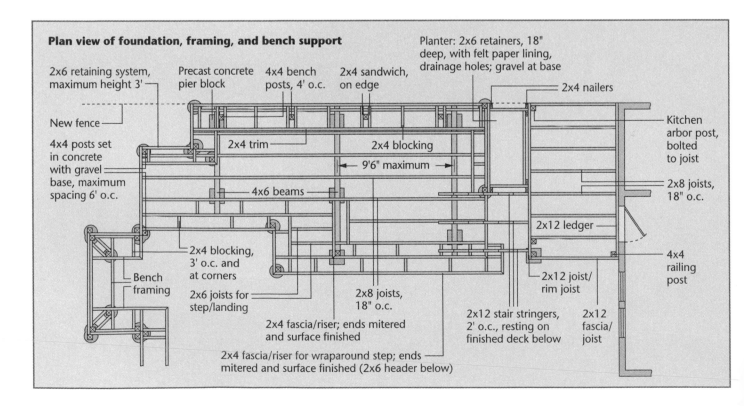

Plan view of foundation, framing, and bench support

2x6 retaining system, maximum height 3'

New fence

4x4 posts set in concrete with gravel base, maximum spacing 6' o.c.

Bench framing

Precast concrete pier block

2x4 trim

4x6 beams

2x4 blocking, 3' o.c. and at corners

2x6 joists for step/landing

4x4 bench posts, 4' o.c.

2x4 sandwich, on edge

2x4 blocking

9'6" maximum

2x4 fascia/riser; ends mitered and surface finished

2x4 fascia/riser for wraparound step; ends mitered and surface finished (2x6 header below)

2x8 joists, 18" o.c.

Planter: 2x6 retainers, 18" deep, with felt paper lining, drainage holes; gravel at base

2x4 nailers

2x4 blocking

2x12 ledger

2x12 joist/ rim joist

2x12 stair stringers, 2' o.c., resting on finished deck below

2x12 fascia/ joist

Kitchen arbor post, bolted to joist

2x8 joists, 18" o.c.

4x4 railing post

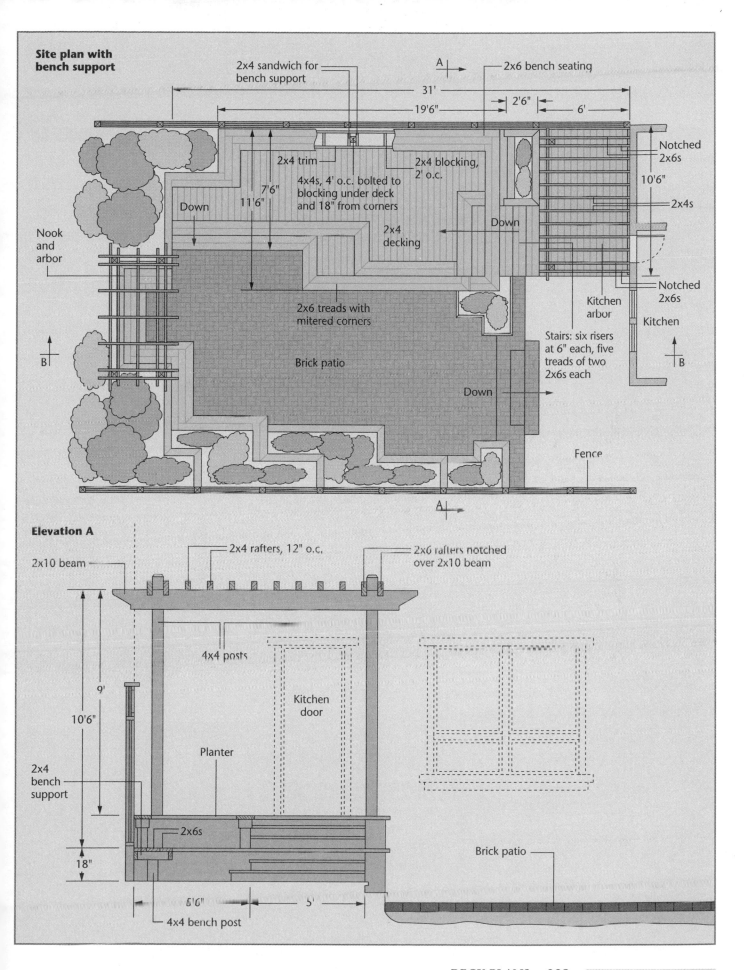

Site plan with bench support

2x4 sandwich for bench support

A

2x6 bench seating

31'

19'6"

2'6"

6'

Notched 2x6s

2x4 trim

2x4 blocking, 2' o.c.

10'6"

2x4s

7'6"

11'6"

4x4s, 4' o.c. bolted to blocking under deck and 18" from corners

Down

Down

2x4 decking

Nook and arbor

Notched 2x6s

Kitchen arbor

Kitchen

2x6 treads with mitered corners

B

Stairs: six risers at 6" each, five treads of two 2x6s each

B

Brick patio

Down

Fence

A

Elevation A

2x4 rafters, 12" o.c.

2x6 rafters notched over 2x10 beam

2x10 beam

4x4 posts

Kitchen door

9'

10'6"

Planter

2x4 bench support

2x6s

18"

Brick patio

5'6"

5'

4x4 bench post

Elevation B

Nook and arbor

Kitchen arbor

Planters

Stairs

Planters

Upper deck

Main deck

Bench

Two steps

Brick patio on sand

Partial elevation section B

2x4 sandwich on post supporting bench seat of three 2x6s

2x6 header; 2x4 fascia on top

2x4 fascia

Gravel

Brick patio

2x6 blocking

2x4 decking

Bench trim: 2x4s, front and rear

Planter

2x10 beam

2x6 end rafter

2x6 cap

2x6 ledger

Kitchen

2x2 baluster

2x4 rail

2x4 decking

2x8 joist

2x6 ledger

4x6 beam

4x4 post

2x12 stringer

4x4s, 4' o.c. and 18" from corners, bolted to blocking under deck

4x4 post supports deck, handrail, and arbor

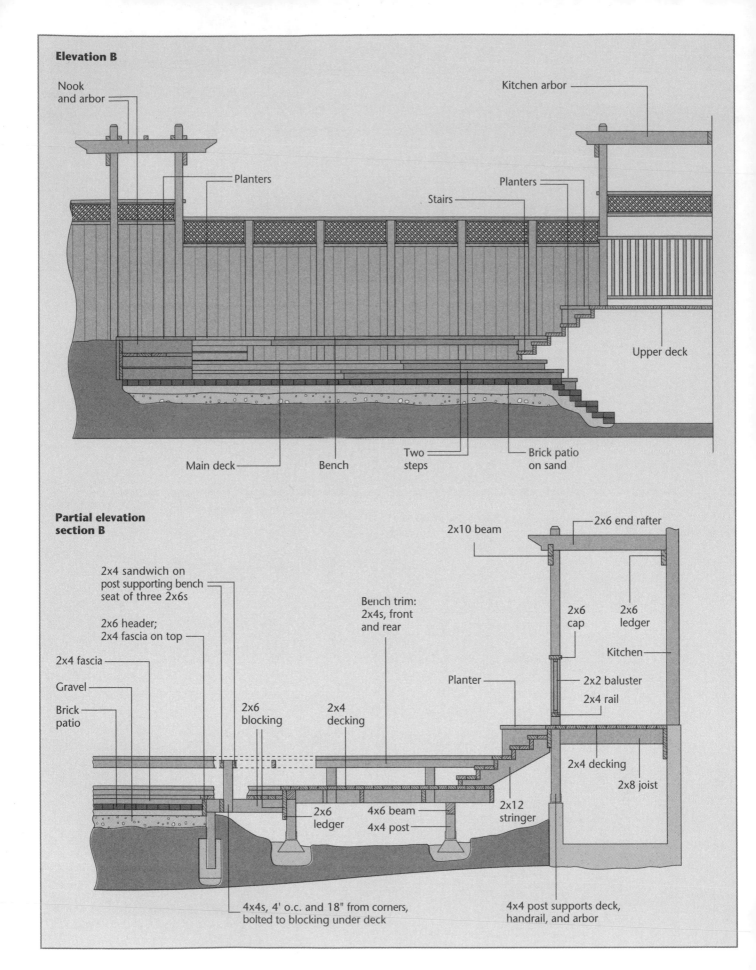

DOUBLE-DECKER

This multilevel deck unifies a number of distinct areas. Because many posts would interfere with the use of the lower deck, large posts, which allow longer spans and thus fewer posts, support the upper deck. Stairs were positioned at a corner to save space. Storage was built under the stairs and under the side of the upper balcony.

TO ADAPT THIS PLAN

In many areas, you can use standard precast pier blocks on footings; follow your local building code regulations.

Although designed for a flat lot behind a two-story house, this deck could be built in a side yard instead. Modify the size of the deck according to the length of the back of your house and the depth of your lot.

BUILDING NOTES

For the benches, space pairs of 4x4 legs a maximum of 45 inches apart between the bench corners. Top each pair with a 2x4 brace. Then, position the first 2x4 seat board on edge and, using a 3-inch nail, fasten a 3/8-inch spacer to it at every brace and again midway between the legs. Continue with the other 2x4s and spacers. Trim the bench with mitered 2x6s on edge. To prevent tipping, connect all the benches or toenail their legs to the decking.

Build the sides of each planter first, attaching 2x6s to 1x4 braces; then fasten 2x6s across both ends to form a box. Toenail the mitered 2x4 cap on from the inside. Line with water-resistant material and provide for drainage.

Frame walls for the storage area and cover them with siding. For an access door, attach siding to a Z-shaped frame of 1x4s. For the roof, trim about 2 inches off the tops of the joists, enough to fit a layer of 1/2-inch exterior-rated pressure-treated plywood and 2x2 sleepers. Nail the plywood to the joists, cover it with bitumen roofing membrane, and lay the sleepers on top of it. Toenail the sleepers into the 2x12 frame, but not through the roofing membrane. Finally, lay the decking in place and nail it to the sleepers—use 2 1/2-inch nails.

DESIGN: MILI CHARNO & ASSOCIATES

"To replace a cramped upper deck and inadequate concrete patio, I created a two-story deck—with 1,350 square feet of outdoor living space—plus a planting bed and two generous storage areas."

MATERIALS LIST

Designed for pressure-treated southern pine, .40 retention (structural members), Construction Heart redwood (visible members), cedar (storage siding), and galvanized hardware.

Lumber for upper deck	Posts/beams	6x6 posts; 2x12 beams
	Joists/ledgers	2x10 joists; 2x12 ledgers
	Decking	2x6
	Fascia	2x12
Lumber for lower deck	Posts/beams	4x4 posts; 4x6 beams
	Joists/ledgers	2x6
	Decking	2x6
	Fascia	2x12
Other lumber	Stairs	2x12 stringers; 2x6 treads, risers; 4x4 posts for landing
	Railings	2x6 caps; 2x4 rails, posts; 2x2 balusters
	Storage	1x8 siding; 1x4 frame for door; 2x2 sleepers; ½" exterior-rated pressure-treated plywood
	Benches	⅜" spacers; 2x4 seating, braces; 2x6 trim; 4x4 legs
	Planters	1x4 braces; 2x6 siding; 2x4 caps
Masonry	Concrete	Footings in 4' postholes
	Gravel	Planter drainage
Hardware	Nails	2½" casing for trim, balusters; 3" for framing, decking, seat boards; nails for framing connectors
	Bolts	Expanding anchor bolts at ledgers for masonry; ⅜" lag screws for wood framing
	Connectors	2x6, 2x10, 2x12 joist hangers
	Other hardware	Hinges, latches for storage areas
Other		Bitumen roofing membrane for storage areas; waterproof lining for planters

Plan view of foundation and framing (lower deck)

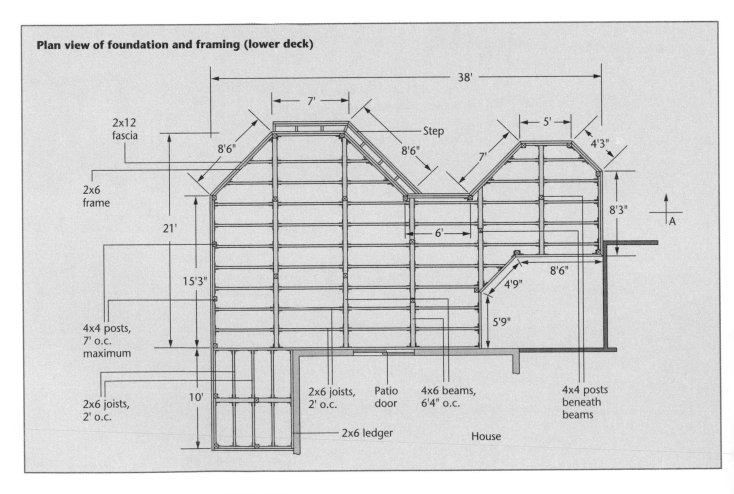

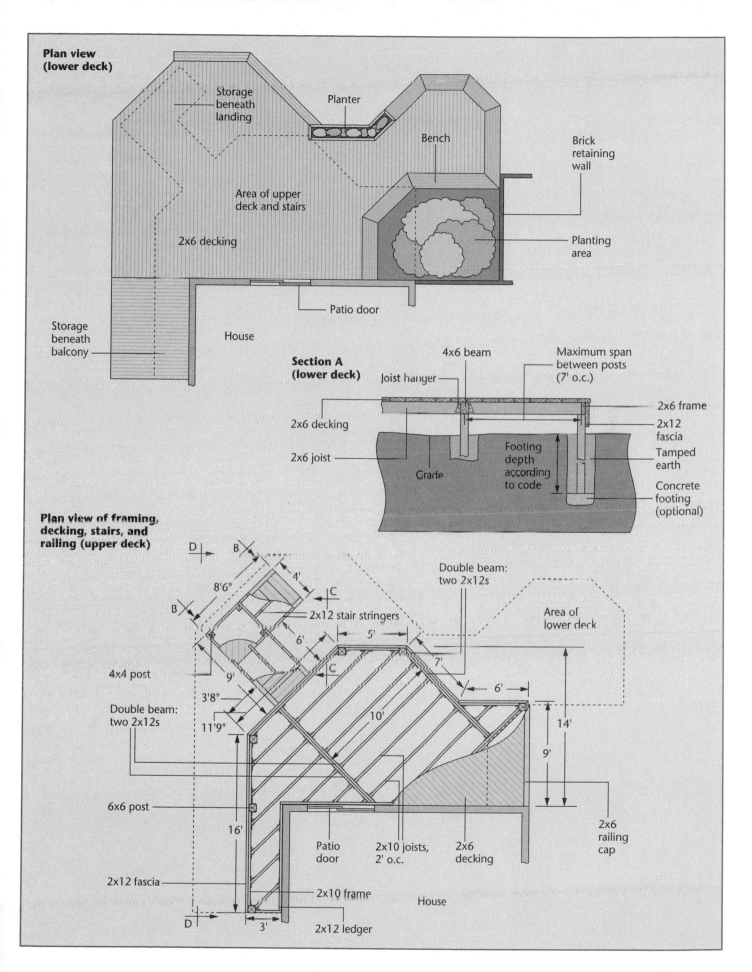

Plan view (lower deck)

Storage beneath landing

Planter

Bench

Brick retaining wall

Area of upper deck and stairs

2x6 decking

Planting area

Patio door

Storage beneath balcony

House

Section A (lower deck)

4x6 beam

Maximum span between posts (7' o.c.)

Joist hanger

2x6 frame

2x6 decking

2x12 fascia

2x6 joist

Grade

Footing depth according to code

Tamped earth

Concrete footing (optional)

Plan view of framing, decking, stairs, and railing (upper deck)

D

B

8'6"

4'

C

B

2x12 stair stringers

Double beam: two 2x12s

Area of lower deck

6'

5'

7'

C

4x4 post

9'

6'

3'8"

14'

Double beam: two 2x12s

11'9"

10'

9'

6x6 post

16'

Patio Door

2x10 joists, 2' o.c.

2x6 decking

2x6 railing cap

2x12 fascia

2x10 frame

House

3'

2x12 ledger

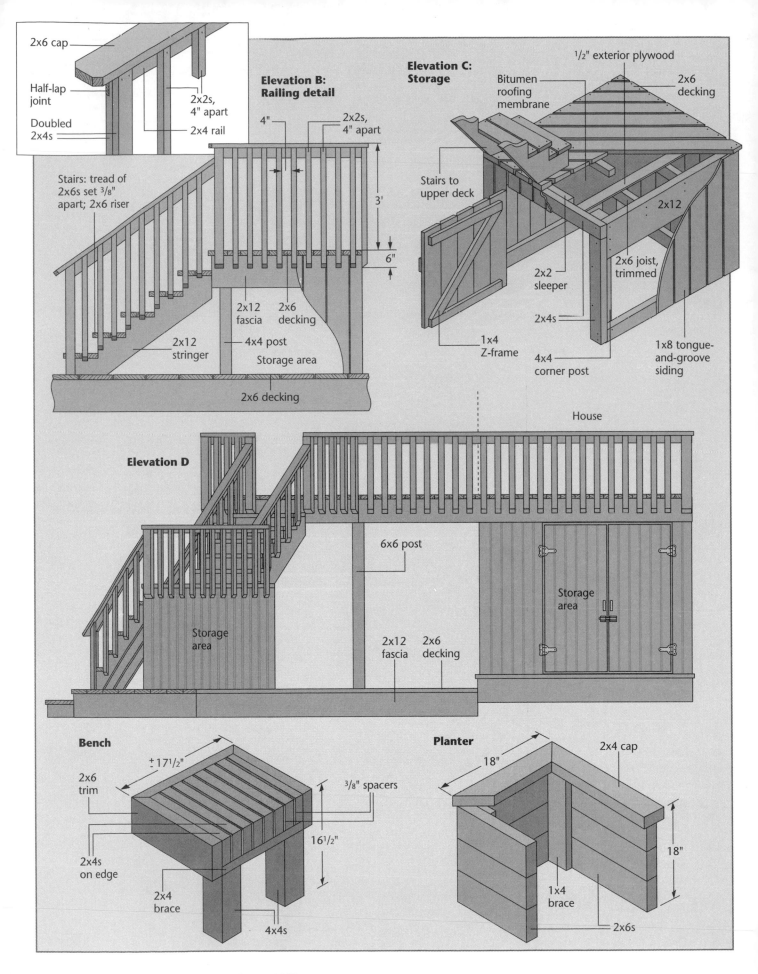

2x6 cap

Half-lap joint

Doubled 2x4s

2x2s, 4" apart

2x4 rail

Elevation B: Railing detail

4"

2x2s, 4" apart

3'

6"

Stairs: tread of 2x6s set ³/₈" apart; 2x6 riser

2x12 fascia

2x6 decking

2x12 stringer

4x4 post

Storage area

2x6 decking

Elevation C: Storage

¹/₂" exterior plywood

Bitumen roofing membrane

2x6 decking

Stairs to upper deck

2x12

2x6 joist, trimmed

2x2 sleeper

2x4s

1x4 Z-frame

4x4 corner post

1x8 tongue-and-groove siding

Elevation D

House

6x6 post

Storage area

2x12 fascia

2x6 decking

Storage area

Bench

± 17¹/₂"

2x6 trim

³/₈" spacers

2x4s on edge

16¹/₂"

2x4 brace

4x4s

Planter

18"

2x4 cap

18"

1x4 brace

2x6s

DECK FOR A STEEP SLOPE

Situated just below the crest of a sloping backyard, this multilevel deck takes advantage of the scenery without obstructing the view from the house. And its projections cantilevered out over the slope create a seating area from previously unusable space.

An important consideration here was to locate the new wood decking adjacent to the concrete pool decking just below, yet far enough from the water so it would not be subject to the spotty bleaching and hastened deterioration bathers' splashes can cause.

TO ADAPT THIS PLAN

The interesting angles and curves of this design would be attractive almost anywhere—even if built as one level on a flat lot. This plan can be built on any slope, provided the footings meet local building codes. In a situation where the deck will be only a few inches above grade, you can set all the footings as shown in the foundation detail for flat areas *(page 230)* and remove the railings.

For a large, flat deck, eliminate level changes and rely on changes in the decking pattern for visual interest.

The entire deck may be enlarged or made smaller, but for best results, maintain the original proportions.

BUILDING NOTES

Begin by laying out the perimeter of the deck to make sure that your hillside can accommodate the plan. If not, adjust placement or size of the component decks.

Choose the longest straight beam line in each section and use it to determine the footing locations.

Two tasks may require professional help. On steep slopes, hire someone to drill footing holes with an auger attached to a truck or tractor drilling rig. (Size and construction of footings are a function of deck size

MATERIALS LIST

Designed for pressure-treated lumber (structural members), All Heart redwood (exposed members), and galvanized hardware.

Lumber	
Posts/beams	4x4 posts; 4x6 beams
Joists/blocking	2x6
Decking	2x6
Fascia	2x6 at steps; 2x12 at straight sides; on curve, two 1x12s each milled to ¹/₂" and laminated
Railings	Curved: three 4" benderboards, each ³/₈" thick, laminated; Straight: 2x6 caps; 2x4 rails; Both: 2x2 balusters
Benches	4x4 posts; 2x6 seat boards, braces, trim; 2x4 seat boards
Masonry	
Concrete	12" square footings, various depths
Hardware	
Nails	3¹/₂"; 2¹/₂" for decking; nails for framing connectors
Bolts	³/₈" for bench posts and balusters
Connectors	Post anchors; post caps
Other	No. 3 reinforcing bars

DESIGN: PETER KOENIG, LANDSCAPE DESIGNER
"My challenge, on a steep lot with an existing pool, was to increase the limited outdoor entertaining space and provide a comfortable place from which to enjoy an unusually scenic view."

and soil conditions; consult your local building code.) And on any site, laminating the curved railing and fascia can be tricky for inexperienced do-it-yourselfers.

The table shown in the illustration on the previous page was not part of the original design. To build this table, use the drawing of the bench section (*opposite*) as

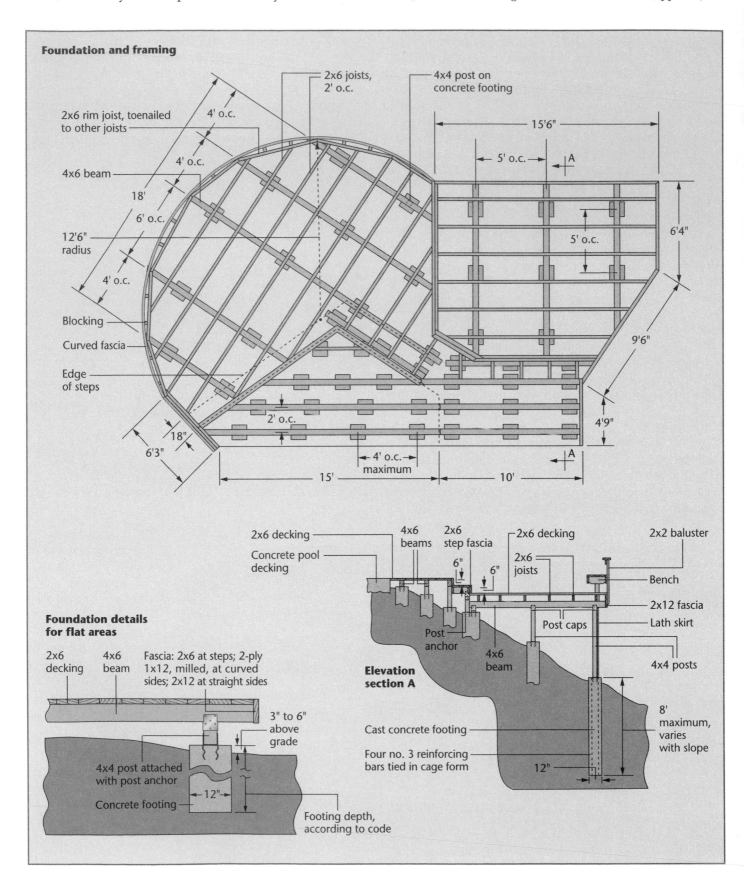

Foundation and framing

2x6 joists, 2' o.c.

4x4 post on concrete footing

2x6 rim joist, toenailed to other joists

4' o.c.

4x6 beam

18'

4' o.c.

6' o.c.

12'6" radius

4' o.c.

Blocking

Curved fascia

Edge of steps

18"

6'3"

2' o.c.

4' o.c. maximum

15'

10'

15'6"

5' o.c.

A

5' o.c.

6'4"

9'6"

4'9"

A

Foundation details for flat areas

2x6 decking

4x6 beam

Fascia: 2x6 at steps; 2-ply 1x12, milled, at curved sides; 2x12 at straight sides

3" to 6" above grade

4x4 post attached with post anchor

Concrete footing

12"

Footing depth, according to code

2x6 decking

Concrete pool decking

4x6 beams

2x6 step fascia

2x6 decking

2x2 baluster

6"

6"

2x6 joists

Bench

2x12 fascia

Post caps

Lath skirt

Post anchor

4x6 beam

Elevation section A

4x4 posts

Cast concrete footing

Four no. 3 reinforcing bars tied in cage form

12"

8' maximum, varies with slope

a guide. The table's surface matches the 2x6 decking. The side trim matches the step fascia; miter the trim at the corners. The legs match the bench posts, but they're not bolted to the substructure. The outline of the tabletop follows the angles created by the benches. Adjust the dimensions of the table to suit your needs.

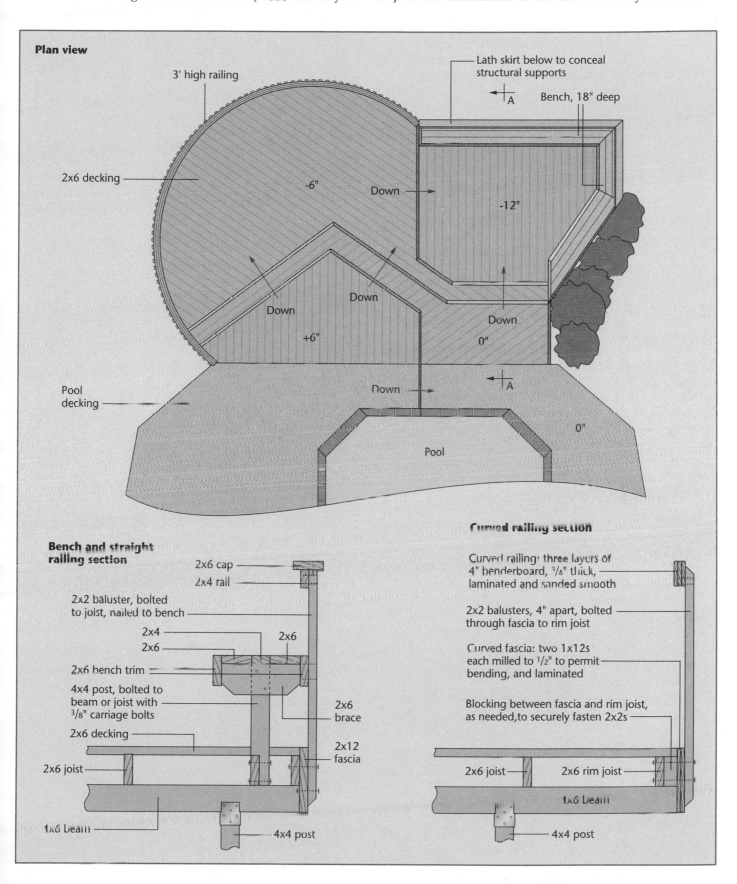

Plan view

3' high railing

2x6 decking

Pool decking

Lath skirt below to conceal structural supports

Bench, 18" deep

-6"

Down

-12"

Down

Down

Down

+6"

0"

Down

Pool

0"

Bench and straight railing section

2x6 cap

2x4 rail

2x2 baluster, bolted to joist, nailed to bench

2x4

2x6

2x6 bench trim

4x4 post, bolted to beam or joist with ³⁄₈" carriage bolts

2x6 decking

2x6 joist

1x6 beam

2x6 brace

2x12 fascia

4x4 post

Curved railing section

Curved railing: three layers of 4" benderboard, ³⁄₈" thick, laminated and sanded smooth

2x2 balusters, 4" apart, bolted through fascia to rim joist

Curved fascia: two 1x12s each milled to ¹⁄₂" to permit bending, and laminated

Blocking between fascia and rim joist, as needed, to securely fasten 2x2s

2x6 joist

2x6 rim joist

1x6 beam

4x4 post

EXTENDED DECK

This long deck, cantilevered over a slope, integrates natural features of the site. Cantilevering over a slope extends the view and usable space, and running the diagonal decking parallel to the long side of the plan emphasizes the new expansiveness of the outdoor area. (Photo on page 10.)

TO ADAPT THIS PLAN

You can modify the height of the deck (depending on your slope) and the design of the fence/railing behind the bench (here, it matches the board-and-batten house siding). The shape of the deck will be influenced by the shape of the side of your house and by the locations of any natural features you wish to incorporate.

Although designed as a cantilevered platform, this deck would be suitable on a gentle slope or even in a flat yard where, with its closed fence and generous bench (with storage potential), it could serve as a children's play area.

BUILDING NOTES

Before building a deck over a steep slope, check with an architect or structural engineer for the foundation needed for your site. Also, see the span tables on pages 73 and 74.

To connect the two beams that meet at the 135° angle, miter their ends so they butt together, centered over the post. At both inner and outer sides of the joint, bend a 12-inch by 12-inch T-strap to fit across both beam-to-beam and beam-to-post seams; then attach it. Leave room above it to attach an additional $2^{1}/_{16}$-inch by $23^{5}/_{16}$-inch strap tie. Be certain this meets your local code; you may have to use other standard connectors, or have two steel

MATERIALS LIST

Designed for pressure-treated Douglas-fir (structural members), surfaced redwood (visible members), and galvanized hardware.

Lumber	
Posts	4x4
Beams	4x12; 4x10 on 16" footings
Joists/blocking	2x10
Ledgers/bracing	2x10 ledgers; 2x6 bracing
Decking	2x6
Fascia	2x8; 1x4
Open railings	4x4 posts; 2x6 caps; 2x4 rails; 2x2 balusters
Fence/railing	2x8 caps; 2x4 framing; 1x12 siding; 1x4 battens
Bench	2x6 back, seat, front plate; 2x4 support, back plate
Other	2x8 plate on concrete grade beam
Masonry	
Concrete	8" wide and 24" deep (continuous) grade beam; 24" and 16" round footings
Hardware	
Nails	$3^{1}/_{2}$"; nails for framing connectors
Bolts	Machine bolts ($^{5}/_{16}$"x5" for railing balusters to rim joist, and $^{1}/_{2}$"x7" for railing posts to rim joist); $^{1}/_{2}$"x10" anchor bolts (plate to grade beam)
Connectors	Joist hangers at ledger; T-straps for post-to-beam; strap ties for beam-to-beam; post anchors; post caps
Other	No. 5 reinforcing bars; low-voltage light fixture

DESIGN:
GARY MCCOOK,
LANDSCAPE
CONTRACTOR
"Cantilevered over a slope and around an olive tree and a boulder, this deck works with a brick patio to provide pleasantly varied outdoor living space."

connectors custom-fabricated. Attach the railing's 4x4 posts and 2x2 balusters with machine bolts that extend through the post or baluster, the fascia, and the rim joist behind.

Consider using the space beneath the bench seats for storage. You could provide access doors at the ends or build a portion of the seat on a hinged frame to be lifted for access. Waterproof the insides.

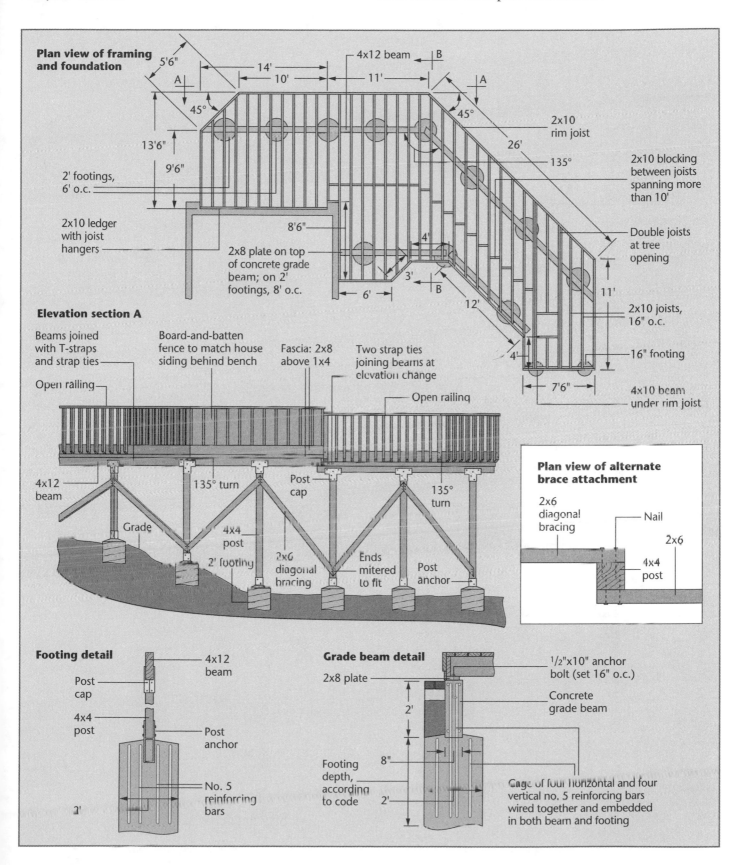

Plan view of framing and foundation

5'6"
14'
10'
11'
4x12 beam
B
A
A
45°
45°
2x10 rim joist
13'6"
26'
135°
2x10 blocking between joists spanning more than 10'
9'6"
2' footings, 6' o.c.
2x10 ledger with joist hangers
8'6"
Double joists at tree opening
2x8 plate on top of concrete grade beam; on 2' footings, 8' o.c.
4'
3'
6'
B
12'
11'
4'
2x10 joists, 16" o.c.
16" footing
7'6"
4x10 beam under rim joist

Elevation section A

Beams joined with T-straps and strap ties

Board-and-batten fence to match house siding behind bench

Fascia: 2x8 above 1x4

Two strap ties joining beams at elevation change

Open railing

Open railing

4x12 beam

135° turn

Post cap

135° turn

Grade

4x4 post

2'6 diagonal bracing

Ends mitered to fit

Post anchor

2' footing

Plan view of alternate brace attachment

2x6 diagonal bracing

Nail

2x6

4x4 post

Footing detail

4x12 beam

Post cap

4x4 post

Post anchor

No. 5 reinforcing bars

2'

Grade beam detail

2x8 plate

Footing depth, according to code

8"

2'

2'

1/2"x10" anchor bolt (set 16" o.c.)

Concrete grade beam

Cage of four horizontal and four vertical no. 5 reinforcing bars wired together and embedded in both beam and footing

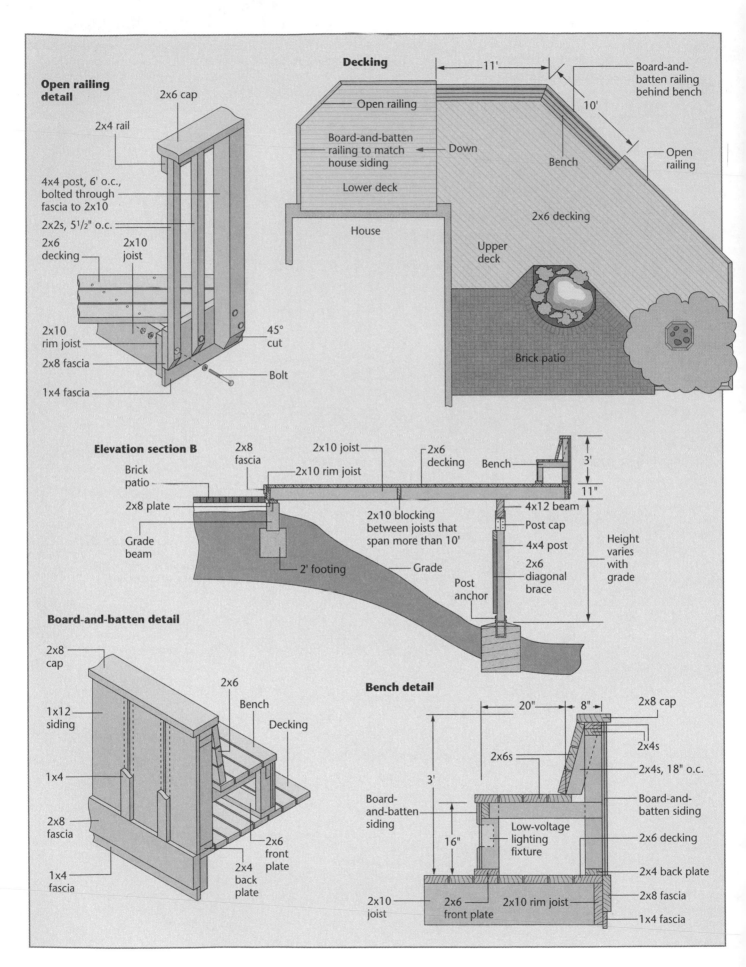

Open railing detail

2x6 cap

2x4 rail

4x4 post, 6' o.c., bolted through fascia to 2x10

2x2s, 5½" o.c.

2x6 decking

2x10 joist

2x10 rim joist

2x8 fascia

1x4 fascia

45° cut

Bolt

Decking

11'

10'

Board-and-batten railing behind bench

Open railing

Board-and-batten railing to match house siding

Down

Bench

Open railing

Lower deck

House

2x6 decking

Upper deck

Brick patio

Elevation section B

Brick patio

2x8 plate

Grade beam

2x8 fascia

2x10 rim joist

2x10 joist

2x6 decking

Bench

2x10 blocking between joists that span more than 10'

2' footing

Grade

Post anchor

4x12 beam

Post cap

4x4 post

2x6 diagonal brace

3'

11"

Height varies with grade

Board-and-batten detail

2x8 cap

1x12 siding

1x4

2x8 fascia

1x4 fascia

2x6

Bench

Decking

2x4 back plate

2x6 front plate

Bench detail

20"

8"

2x8 cap

2x4s

2x4s, 18" o.c.

2x6s

Board-and-batten siding

Board-and-batten siding

2x6 decking

2x4 back plate

2x8 fascia

1x4 fascia

Low-voltage lighting fixture

3'

16"

2x10 joist

2x6 front plate

2x10 rim joist

GARDEN PENINSULA

This plan features three levels of decking: a railed upper balcony; a lower balcony that functions as an L-shaped covered walkway; and, three steps down, a circular platform with built-in seating.

TO ADAPT THIS PLAN

To build an attractive single level deck, eliminate the upper balcony; cut the posts to end beneath the bench of the wraparound deck.

If you increase the depth of the balconies (the distance from ledger to rail) or the cantilevering, consult an architect or engineer about the need for additional support. The circular peninsula can be built larger, but keep it in proportion to the balconies. For clean lines, keep the circular deck's diameter plus the width of the garden steps less than the length of the decking boards.

BUILDING NOTES

Locate your ledgers at the level of the first floor of the house. Then calculate how many steps you'll need to reach the circular peninsula (and how many between the peninsula and the garden). Locate the second-story ledger and calculate the height of your support posts from the top of the footing to the top of this upper ledger.

Before building the staircase and landing to the upper balcony, extend the decking surface of the walkway level around the corner of the house and all the way back under the first flight of stairs, creating a small, low deck that could also be used as a storage area.

MATERIALS LIST	
Designed for pressure-treated lumber (structural members), Clear Green redwood (visible members), and galvanized hardware.	
Lumber (circular deck)	
Posts/joists	4x4 posts; 2x6 joists
Blocking	2x6
Decking	2x4
Fascia	6" benderboard, 3/8" thick
Benches	4" benderboard, 3/8" thick for fascia; 1x1 seat back ledger; 1x10 backs; 1x12 seat wedges; 2x4 posts, blocking; 2x6 caps
Lumber (first story)	
Posts/joists	4x4 posts; 2x8 joists
Ledgers	2x8
Decking	2x4
Rail/bench	2x2 seat joists, seat slats, back slats; 2x4 back supports, seat trim (front and back); 2x6 back slats, rail caps
Lumber (second story)	
Posts/beams	4x4 posts; 2x12 beams
Joists/ledgers	2x10
Decking	2x4
Railings	4x4 posts; 2x2 balusters; 2x4 top rails, end balusters; 2x6 caps
Lumber (all stairs)	2x12 stringers; 2x4 treads, kicker plate
Masonry	
Pier blocks	Precast concrete
Concrete	12" round post footings; footings under pier blocks; stair pad
Hardware	
Nails	2 1/2" casing for 1x1s; 3" casing for 2x2s; 3 1/2" for 2x4s; 3 1/2" casing for 2x6 caps; 4" for framing; nails for framing connectors
Bolts	Carriage: 3/8"x6" (bench supports to posts); 1/2"x8" (for second-story beam-post sandwich)
Screws	1/2"x5" lag screws at ledgers
Connectors	Joist hangers; post anchors
Finishes	Clear water sealer

DESIGN: JEFFREY MILLER, LANDSCAPE ARCHITECT

"In this small city garden, a pair of narrow balconies reach out from the house for daylight and views. A circular bench-lined peninsula extends into the yard as an outdoor gathering spot."

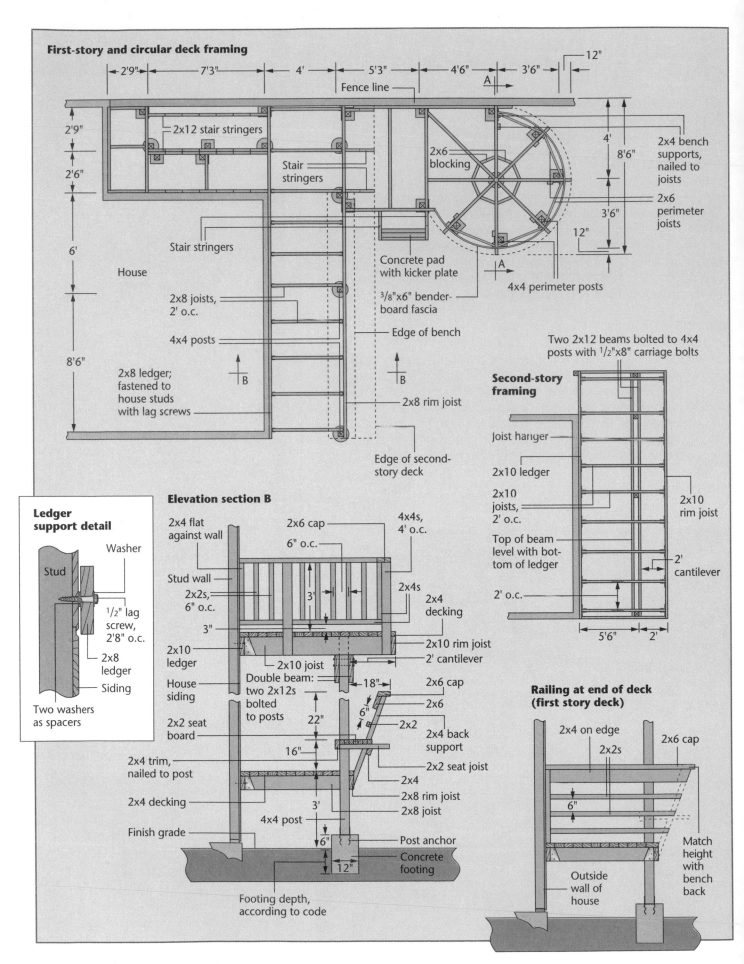

First-story and circular deck framing

2'9" · 7'3" · 4' · 5'3" · 4'6" · 3'6" · 12"

Fence line

A

2'9"

2x12 stair stringers

2'6"

Stair stringers

6'

House

8'6"

Stair stringers

2x8 joists, 2' o.c.

4x4 posts

2x8 ledger; fastened to house studs with lag screws

B

2x6 blocking

Concrete pad with kicker plate

³⁄₈"x6" bender-board fascia

Edge of bench

2x8 rim joist

B

Edge of second-story deck

A

4'
8'6"
3'6"
12"

2x4 bench supports, nailed to joists

2x6 perimeter joists

4x4 perimeter posts

Ledger support detail

Washer

Stud

¹⁄₂" lag screw, 2'8" o.c.

2x8 ledger

Siding

Two washers as spacers

Elevation section B

2x4 flat against wall

Stud wall

2x2s, 6" o.c.

3"

2x10 ledger

House siding

2x2 seat board

2x4 trim, nailed to post

2x4 decking

Finish grade

2x6 cap

6" o.c.

3'

2x10 joist

Double beam: two 2x12s bolted to posts

22"

16"

3'

4x4 post

6"

12"

Footing depth, according to code

4x4s, 4' o.c.

2x4s

2x4 decking

2x10 rim joist

2' cantilever

18"

6"

2x6 cap

2x6

2x2

2x4 back support

2x2 seat joist

2x4

2x8 rim joist

2x8 joist

Post anchor

Concrete footing

Two 2x12 beams bolted to 4x4 posts with ¹⁄₂"x8" carriage bolts

Second-story framing

Joist hanger

2x10 ledger

2x10 joists, 2' o.c.

Top of beam level with bottom of ledger

2' o.c.

2x10 rim joist

2' cantilever

5'6" · 2'

Railing at end of deck (first story deck)

2x4 on edge

2x2s

2x6 cap

6"

Outside wall of house

Match height with bench back

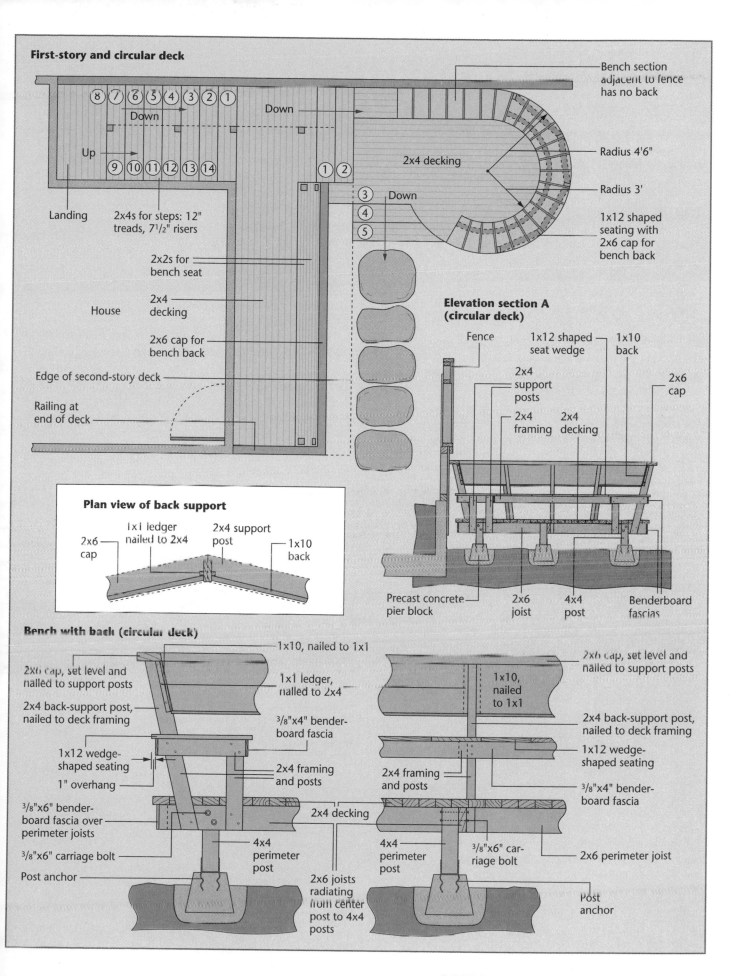

First-story and circular deck

Bench section adjacent to fence has no back

Down

Down

⑧ ⑦ ⑥ ⑤ ④ ③ ② ①

Down

Up

⑨ ⑩ ⑪ ⑫ ⑬ ⑭

① ②

2x4 decking

Radius 4'6"

Radius 3'

③ Down
④
⑤

1x12 shaped seating with 2x6 cap for bench back

Landing

2x4s for steps: 12" treads, 7½" risers

2x2s for bench seat

House

2x4 decking

2x6 cap for bench back

Edge of second-story deck

Railing at end of deck

Elevation section A (circular deck)

Fence

1x12 shaped seat wedge

1x10 back

2x4 support posts

2x6 cap

2x4 framing

2x4 decking

Plan view of back support

2x6 cap

1x1 ledger nailed to 2x4

2x4 support post

1x10 back

Precast concrete pier block

2x6 joist

4x4 post

Benderboard fascias

Bench with back (circular deck)

1x10, nailed to 1x1

2x6 cap, set level and nailed to support posts

2x6 cap, set level and nailed to support posts

1x1 ledger, nailed to 2x4

2x4 back-support post, nailed to deck framing

⅜"x4" benderboard fascia

2x4 framing and posts

1x12 wedge-shaped seating

1" overhang

⅜"x6" benderboard fascia over perimeter joists

⅜"x6" carriage bolt

Post anchor

4x4 perimeter post

2x6 joists radiating from center post to 4x4 posts

2x4 decking

4x4 perimeter post

⅜"x6" carriage bolt

1x10, nailed to 1x1

2x4 back-support post, nailed to deck framing

1x12 wedge-shaped seating

⅜"x4" benderboard fascia

2x4 framing and posts

2x6 perimeter joist

Post anchor

MULTILEVEL DECK

Extending across the full width of the backyard, this deck gracefully accommodates a gentle slope. Wide steps zigzag uphill to handle the transition. Diagonal decking creates an illusion of greater space, and built-in planters soften the design's angular contours.

TO ADAPT THIS PLAN
This plan can easily be adapted for a downslope by reversing the direction of the steps so they lead down to the next level—which might overlook a dramatic view. Where the outlook is uninspiring, build the upper (rear) level higher, and it will itself supply a view.

Built on a single level, this plan would still gain visual interest from the directional changes of the decking and repeated use of angles.

Placing a privacy screen across the narrowest area could divide this large deck into two distinct smaller ones serving separate rooms.

BUILDING NOTES
Depth of footings will vary with climate and soil conditions; check with your local building department.

To save wood, you can space the joists farther apart, but first check the span tables on pages 73 and 74.

The arbor is optional. You might want to use it outside a large glass window or door to frame your view. If you want to use the 3-by lumber called for in the original plan, you'll have to have it custom-milled, or you can substitute standard 2-by lumber, place the posts 6 feet on center and adjust the spacing of the smaller battens between.

When finishing the bench seat, add trim to all sides and miter the corners. Leave about 1/4 inch between individual seat boards and between seat boards and trim. Use brass wood screws, rather than nails, to minimize clothing snags.

To build the planter, sink the posts into footings, nail exterior-rated plywood sides to the inside face of the posts, apply building paper (overlap it by several inches at each seam), then cold-mop with waterproof material such as bitumen roofing compound. Apply diagonally cut 2x6 boards to the outside, between posts. For a very finished look, miter the 2x6 boards at the corners and the 2x8 cap as well.

DESIGN: ROBERT MOWAT ASSOCIATES
"This multilevel deck has three activity areas. The lower level lets entertaining and dining spread outward from the house. The upper level captures the small yard's only summer sun."

MATERIALS LIST

Designed for pressure-treated lumber (structural members), surfaced Construction Heart redwood, rough where specified (visible members), and galvanized hardware.

Lumber

Beams	4x6
Joists	2x6
Decking	2x6
Stairs	2x10 rough stringers; 2x6 treads, risers
Arbor	6x6 rough posts; 3x8 rough beams; 3x3 rough battens
Planters	4x4 rough posts; 2x8 caps; 2x6 siding; 2x4 under caps; exterior plywood
Benches	4x4 rough posts; 2x12 rough retainers; 2x8 trim; 2x6 rough blocking; 2x4 seats

Masonry

Concrete	18" round footings, for planters, arbor; 12" round footings for deck (depth may vary); 12"x3'x6" deep pad for side stairs
Gravel	3/8" drain rock, 3" deep, beneath footings and inside planter

Hardware

Nails	3 1/2" ; nails for framing connectors
Screws	Brass wood screws for bench seat, trim
Bolts	5/8" for arbor beams; 1/2" for seat posts
Connectors	Joist hangers; post anchors
Other	Building paper, cold-mop waterproofing

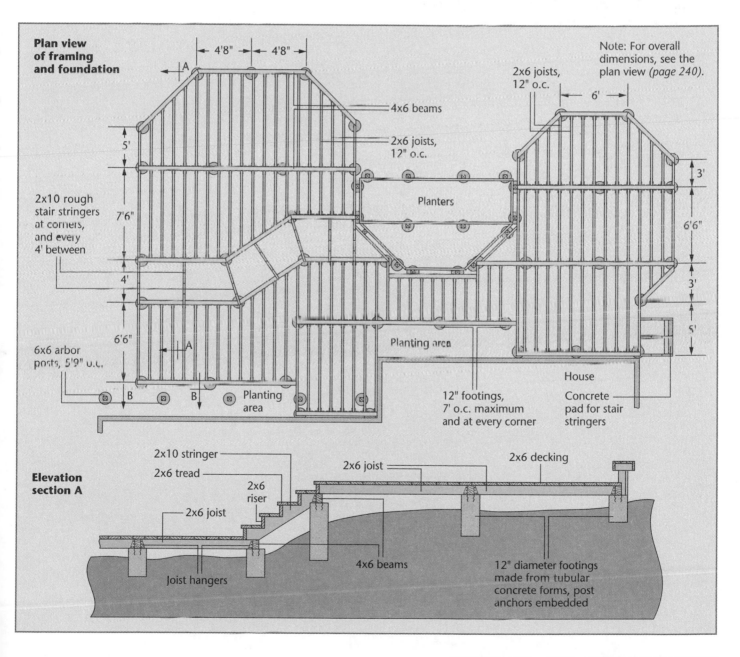

Plan view of framing and foundation

4'8" 4'8"

Note: For overall dimensions, see the plan view (page 240).

2x6 joists, 12" o.c.

4x6 beams

2x6 joists, 12" o.c.

6'

5'

3'

2x10 rough stair stringers at corners, and every 4' between

7'6"

Planters

6'6"

4'

Planting area

3'

6'6"

House

5'

6x6 arbor posts, 5'9" o.c.

Planting area

12" footings, 7' o.c. maximum and at every corner

Concrete pad for stair stringers

Elevation section A

2x10 stringer
2x6 tread
2x6 riser
2x6 joist

2x6 joist

2x6 decking

Joist hangers

4x6 beams

12" diameter footings made from tubular concrete forms, post anchors embedded

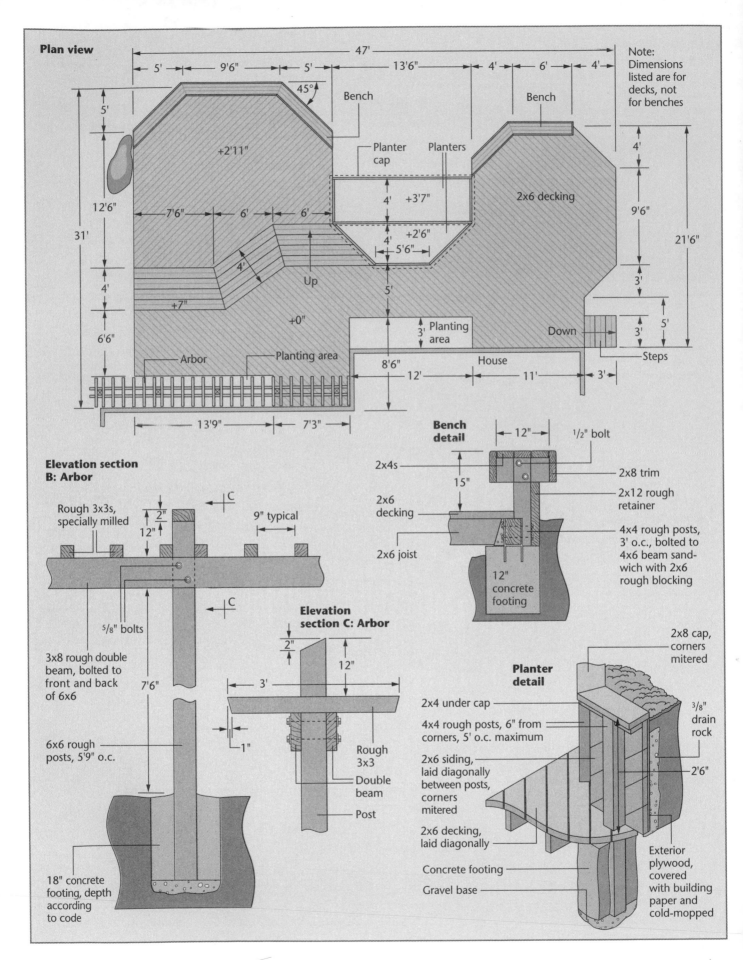

Plan view

Note: Dimensions listed are for decks, not for benches

47'

5' · 9'6" · 5' · 13'6" · 4' · 6' · 4'

45°

Bench

Planter cap

Planters

Bench

+2'11"

5'

12'6"

31'

7'6" · 6' · 6'

4' +3'7"

2x6 decking

4'

9'6"

21'6"

4'

4' +2'6"

5'6"

3'

5'

4'

6'6"

+7"

Up

+0"

5'

3' Planting area

Down

3'

5'

Steps

Arbor

Planting area

8'6"

12'

House

11'

3'

13'9" · 7'3"

Elevation section B: Arbor

Rough 3x3s, specially milled

2"

12"

9" typical

C

C

⁵/₈" bolts

3x8 rough double beam, bolted to front and back of 6x6

7'6"

6x6 rough posts, 5'9" o.c.

18" concrete footing, depth according to code

Elevation section C: Arbor

2"

12"

3'

1"

Rough 3x3

Double beam

Post

Bench detail

12"

½" bolt

2x4s

15"

2x6 decking

2x6 joist

12" concrete footing

2x8 trim

2x12 rough retainer

4x4 rough posts, 3' o.c., bolted to 4x6 beam sandwich with 2x6 rough blocking

Planter detail

2x8 cap, corners mitered

2x4 under cap

4x4 rough posts, 6" from corners, 5' o.c. maximum

2x6 siding, laid diagonally between posts, corners mitered

2x6 decking, laid diagonally

Concrete footing

Gravel base

³/₈" drain rock

2'6"

Exterior plywood, covered with building paper and cold-mopped

240 DECK PLANS

DECK WITH A VIEW

This plan fashions a large entertaining area from a strip of land at the crest of a steep hill. An upper deck becomes a sofa seat for a lower deck; planters support the sofa's backrest; and armrest/end tables are a finishing touch. The table echoes the shape of the deck's front end. From the house, the diagonal decking directs the eye toward the planters and the view beyond. (Photo on page 27.)

TO ADAPT THIS PLAN

The foundation for this deck is unusually hefty because the site is in earthquake country, and the owners entertain very large groups. The continuous footings and decorative stone wall shown here require extensive concrete and masonry work. To determine the degree of support required at your site (and simplify foundation design if your circumstances permit it), consult an architect or engineer.

Sofa height is determined by the relationship between deck levels. But you can alter the length or width of the decked area and contour it to suit the shape of your house. You could also buy ready-made cushions and tailor the dimensions of the seat to fit

DESIGN: ROBERT ENGMAN, AIA, ARCHITECT

"Designed as a substantial outdoor living space, this deck takes advantage of a sunny exposure and fine outlook. The seating area steps down with the slope, preserving the view from the house."

MATERIALS LIST

Designed for pressure-treated lumber (structural members), surfaced Western red cedar (visible members), Clear Heart redwood (siding), and galvanized hardware.

Lumber

Posts	4x4
Beams	4x8
Joists	2x6 upper deck; 2x8 lower deck
Blocking	2x6 atop interior footings
Ledgers	2x8
Bracing	2x6 at stone wall
Decking	2x6
Interior stairs	2x12 stringers; 2x6 treads; 2x4 risers
Exterior step	4x12
Railings	4x4 posts; 2x8 caps; 2x3 rails; 3/4"x2 1/4" trim; 1x8 fascia
Planter/sofa	2x8 armrest/end table frame; 2x6 backrest; 2x4 frame, caps, armrest trim; 2x2 under caps; 1x8 siding; 1x6 trim; 3/4" marine plywood planter bottom, armrest top; 3/8" plywood planter interior sides
Table	2x12 legs and feet; 3/4" finish plywood top

Masonry

Concrete	Footings (all continuous): perimeter and interior, 9" wide with 2x4 mudsill; for stone wall, 2'4" wide; for step, 6" wide and 15" deep; 8" precast blocks (grout-filled)
Gravel	Drain rock at perforated pipe

Hardware

Nails	3 1/2"
Bolts and screws	5/8" at steps, post-to-rail; 1/2" anchors in interior footing, stone wall; 1/2" lag screws for table
Connectors	Post caps; joist hangers
Other hardware	1/2" copper pipe balusters; 4" perforated drainpipe at stone wall; 3/4" drainpipe for planter/sofa; 1/2" threaded rod brace for table masonry anchors in stone wall
Other	No. 4 and no. 3 reinforcing bars; no. 3 stirrups. For planter/sofa: galvanized sheet-metal liner, 12" tiles, bitumen protective coating, all-weather cushions; for table: waterproof membrane, granite top

them. The granite table tops could be replaced by tile, and in place of the custom-milled siding, you could substitute standard tongue-and-groove or plain siding.

BUILDING NOTES

The planter/bench unit is not as complicated as it looks. After you complete the two decks, measure 3½ feet back from the outer edge of the upper one; this is the edge of the planter. Build the planters (or install purchased ones). Then construct 2x4 frames and attach them to the front side, where the sofa backrest will be. Rip braces for the backrest, and bases for them, at 12° (or any comfortable angle) from 2x6s; rip 2x4 top rails at the same angle. Nail the braces, bases, and top rails together, and nail them to the 2x4 frames. Cover the backrest with three horizontal 2x6s. Frame and secure the armrest/end tables at the ends of the backrest. Top the end tables with ¾-inch marine plywood (or exterior-rated pressure-treated plywood) and granite or tile.

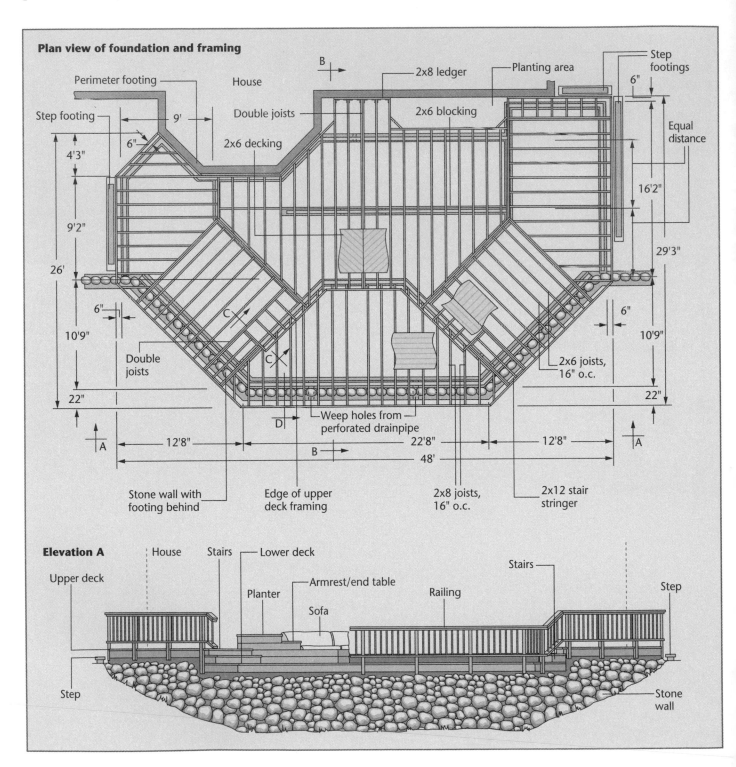

Plan view of foundation and framing

Elevation A

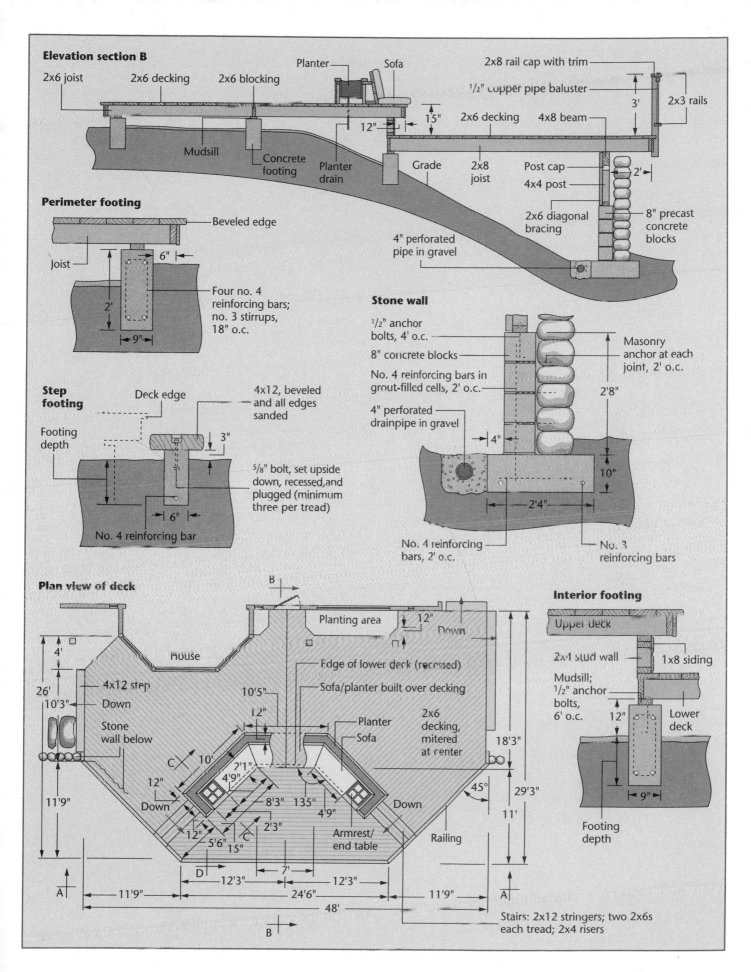

Elevation section B

2x6 joist · 2x6 decking · 2x6 blocking · Planter · Sofa · 2x8 rail cap with trim · 1/2" copper pipe baluster · 2x3 rails · 3' · Mudsill · Concrete footing · Planter drain · 15" · 12" · 2x6 decking · 4x8 beam · Grade · 2x8 joist · Post cap · 4x4 post · 2x6 diagonal bracing · 8" precast concrete blocks · 2' · 4" perforated pipe in gravel

Perimeter footing

Beveled edge · Joist · 6" · 2' · 9" · Four no. 4 reinforcing bars; no. 3 stirrups, 18" o.c.

Step footing

Deck edge · 4x12, beveled and all edges sanded · Footing depth · 3" · 5/8" bolt, set upside down, recessed, and plugged (minimum three per tread) · 6" · No. 4 reinforcing bar

Stone wall

1/2" anchor bolts, 4' o.c. · 8" concrete blocks · No. 4 reinforcing bars in grout-filled cells, 2' o.c. · 4" perforated drainpipe in gravel · Masonry anchor at each joint, 2' o.c. · 2'8" · 4" · 10" · 2'4" · No. 4 reinforcing bars, 2' o.c. · No. 3 reinforcing bars

Interior footing

Upper deck · 2x4 stud wall · 1x8 siding · Mudsill; 1/2" anchor bolts, 6' o.c. · 12" · Lower deck · Footing depth · 9"

Plan view of deck

B · Planting area · 12" · Down · House · 4' · 26' · Edge of lower deck (recessed) · Sofa/planter built over decking · 2x6 decking, mitered at center · 18'3" · 4x12 step · Down · 10'3" · Stone wall below · 10'5" · 12" · Planter · Sofa · 10' · C · 2'1" · 4'9" · 135° · 4'9" · Down · 45° · 29'3" · 12" · Down · 8'3" · Armrest/end table · 11' · 11'9" · 12" · C · 2'3" · 5'6" · 15" · 7' · Railing · D · 12'3" · 12'3" · A · 11'9" · 24'6" · 11'9" · A · 48' · B · Stairs: 2x12 stringers; two 2x6s each tread; 2x4 risers

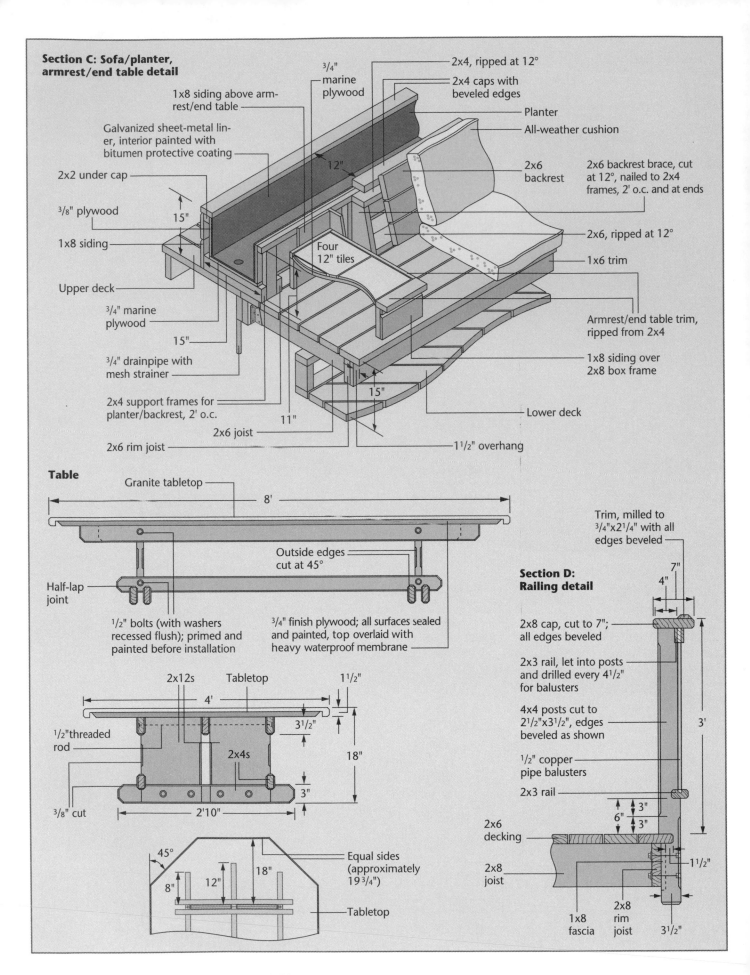

OVERHEAD: SPACE FRAME

This large space frame shows that not much is required to define an outdoor area; it frames the outdoor space yet still allows light into an adjacent house.

The posts are sandwiched between pairs of 2x6 beams. The two layers of beams, also fastened to short connector posts, create interesting patterns of shade on this fairly large deck. On a smaller deck, a simple structure of posts joined by beams at the perimeter of the deck may be enough to create a sense of enclosure.

You can plan a space frame as part of the deck, extending the deck posts for the overhead as well, or fasten the overhead posts to the deck's substructure. For information on building overheads, turn to the chapter beginning on page 135.

On a higher deck, a railing could be added, running between the posts. Use 2x6s for rails, and 2x2s for balusters. For intermediate posts, use 4x4s; bevel their tops and notch them to match the overhead posts.

LANDSCAPE ARCHITECT: MICHAEL WHITMORE AND ASSOCIATES FOR THE AMERICAN WOOD COUNCIL
Little more than posts connected at the tops to pairs of 2x6s, this airy structure creates a sense of enclosure, whether over an expansive deck or a more intimate small one.

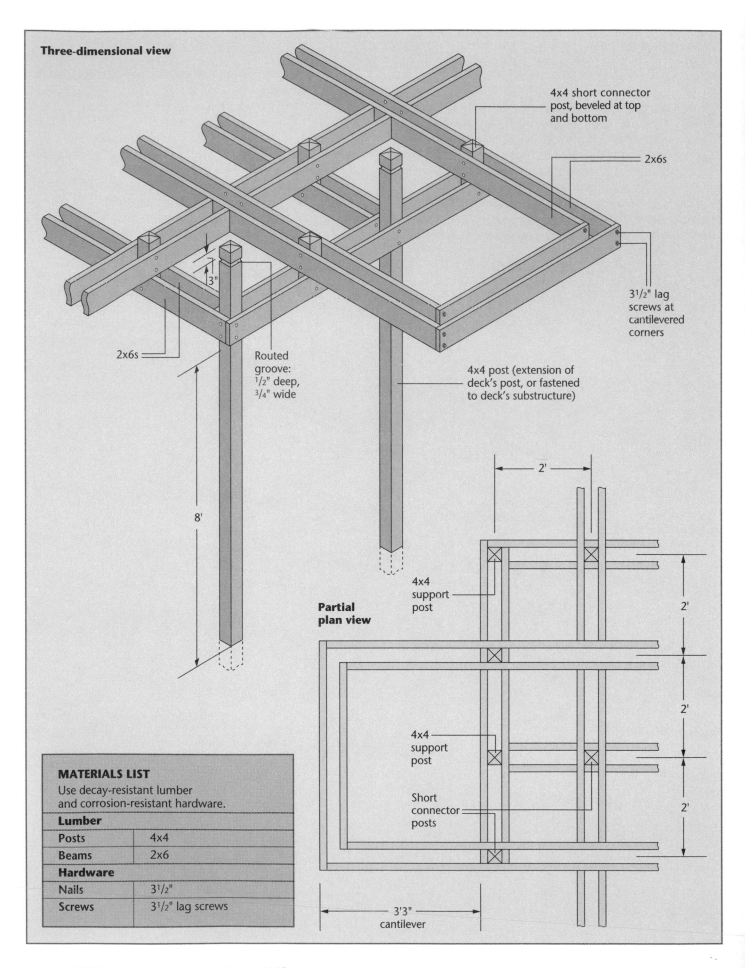

Three-dimensional view

4x4 short connector post, beveled at top and bottom

2x6s

$3\frac{1}{2}$" lag screws at cantilevered corners

3"

4x4 post (extension of deck's post, or fastened to deck's substructure)

2x6s

Routed groove: $\frac{1}{2}$" deep, $\frac{3}{4}$" wide

8'

2'

4x4 support post

Partial plan view

2'

2'

4x4 support post

2'

Short connector posts

3'3" cantilever

MATERIALS LIST	
Use decay-resistant lumber and corrosion-resistant hardware.	
Lumber	
Posts	4x4
Beams	2x6
Hardware	
Nails	$3\frac{1}{2}$"
Screws	$3\frac{1}{2}$" lag screws

OVERHEAD: CORNER SHELTER

Built-in benches, bamboo shades for privacy, potted plants, and some outdoor furniture all help to create a comfortable outdoor environment. This overhead is integrated with a free-standing deck, but could be added to an existing deck instead.

The entire overhead structure is built from redwood. The posts, made from 6x6s, support both the deck and the cover. They should be set in concrete footings that are sized according to your local building code regulations and climate. For general information on building overheads, see page 135.

The overhead beams are 2x10s sandwiched to the posts and bolted in place. The cover is composed of pieces milled to 2½ inches by 2½ inches actual size. The first piece is toenailed to the beam from both sides, but the others are toenailed only from one side. A spare piece is used as a spacer. You'll have to special order the lumber, or substitute a standard size and adjust the spacing.

The ends of the benches are also supported by the main posts. In the middle, they rest on 2x6 cleats nailed to each side of short 4x4 bench posts.

MATERIALS LIST	
Designed for redwood heartwood, and corrosion-resistant hardware.	
Lumber	
Posts	4x4
Beams	2x10
Covering	2½"x2½" actual size
Benches	4x4 posts; 2x6 cleats, seat boards
Hardware	
Nails	3½", 2½" for cover
Bolts	⁵⁄₁₆"x8" machine bolts

LANDSCAPE ARCHITECT: RUDY YADAO ASSOCIATES

This shade-casting overhead can turn any deck—or a segment of a larger deck—into a perfect spot for informal entertaining.

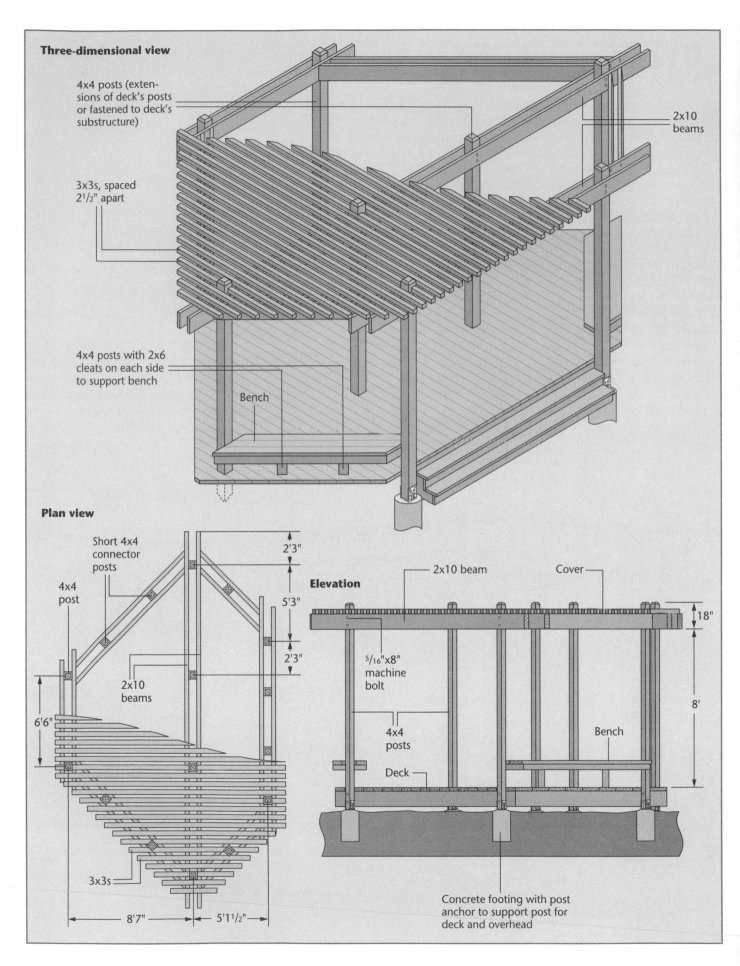

Three-dimensional view

4x4 posts (extensions of deck's posts or fastened to deck's substructure)

3x3s, spaced 2¹/₂" apart

4x4 posts with 2x6 cleats on each side to support bench

Bench

2x10 beams

Plan view

Short 4x4 connector posts

4x4 post

2x10 beams

3x3s

2'3"

5'3"

2'3"

6'6"

8'7"

5'1¹/₂"

Elevation

2x10 beam

Cover

18"

⁵/₁₆"x8" machine bolt

4x4 posts

Bench

8'

Deck

Concrete footing with post anchor to support post for deck and overhead

248   DECK PLANS

OVERHEAD: BACKYARD PAVILION

Cozy enough for just one or two, but with plenty of room for a small crowd, this 12-foot-square pavilion offers benches and a lath-style roof for shade over your deck.

Posts for an overhead must be firmly attached to the deck's substructure, or you can continue the deck's posts upward to support the overhead's roof. In this case, four posts at each corner rise from the foundation to support the deck, benches, and roof framing. At each corner, 2x8 beams sandwich the tops of the posts; an upper layer of 2x8s running in the opposite direction repeats this. The look of paired 2x8s on the upper layer is continued by attaching three equally spaced pairs of 2x8s on top of the lower layer. These may be short, as shown in the plan view and three-dimensional view on the following page, or they may extend across the space, as shown below.

Four rafters run from one post at each corner to a 4x4 hub at the center. The upper edges of the rafters are beveled to support the 1x2 roofing.

MATERIALS LIST

Use decay-resistant lumber, and corrosion-resistant hardware.

Lumber

Posts/beams	4x4 posts; 2x8 beams
Rafters/hub	4x6 rafters; 4x4 hub
Trim	4x6
Roofing	1x2
Benches	2x6 supports; 2x6 seat boards; 2x4 trim

Hardware

Nails	2" nails for roofing; 3$\frac{1}{2}$" nails for framing
Bolts	$\frac{1}{2}$"x5$\frac{1}{2}$" machine bolts; $\frac{1}{2}$"x7" machine bolts

ARCHITECT: THOMAS HIGLEY

Quadrupled corner posts tie this gazebolike structure together from the foundation to the roof.

Three-dimensional view

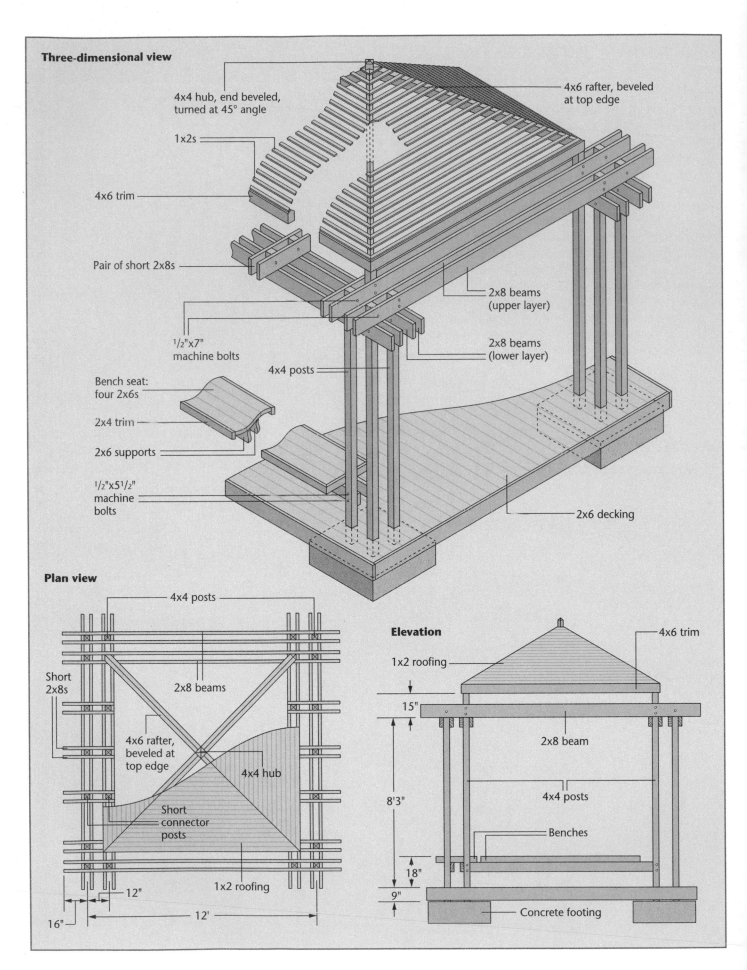

4x4 hub, end beveled, turned at 45° angle

1x2s

4x6 trim

Pair of short 2x8s

1/2"x7" machine bolts

Bench seat: four 2x6s

2x4 trim

2x6 supports

1/2"x5 1/2" machine bolts

4x6 rafter, beveled at top edge

2x8 beams (upper layer)

2x8 beams (lower layer)

4x4 posts

2x6 decking

Plan view

4x4 posts

Short 2x8s

2x8 beams

4x6 rafter, beveled at top edge

4x4 hub

Short connector posts

1x2 roofing

12"

16"

12'

Elevation

4x6 trim

1x2 roofing

15"

2x8 beam

4x4 posts

Benches

8'3"

18"

9"

Concrete footing

OVERHEAD: OPEN GAZEBO

A grove of lanky cedar trees provides a dignified setting for a gazebo tailored to entertaining. Groups of four cedar posts support the open rafters and the two built-in benches. (Photo on page 35.)

Posts for a gazebo can be fastened to the deck's substructure, or the deck's posts can be made longer. For this gazebo, the posts continue down beneath the gazebo's decking, where they're anchored in footings. At each corner, built-in planters between the posts add seasonal color. A series of 1x2s wrap around the post tops, creating texture and visual interest. Trim is fitted to the bottom of the posts at deck level.

The 2x6 rafters cross at the ridge; 1x4s nailed to each side of the rafters enhance the design. Both the rafters and the trim are fitted together with angled half-lap joints. For more information on building an overhead, such as a gazebo, turn to the chapter beginning on page 135.

MATERIALS LIST
Designed for cedar heartwood, corrosion-resistant hardware.

Lumber	
Posts	4x4
Beams	2x8
Rafters	2x6
Ridge boards	2x6
Trim	1x4 for rafters; 1x2 for tops of posts; 2x3 for bottoms of posts
Benches/planters	2x4 seat boards; 1x6 trim
Hardware	
Nails	1½" for 1-by trim; 3" for 2-by trim; 3½" for rafters to beams
Bolts	½"x7" machine bolts
Other	Galvanized steel liner for planter

ARCHITECT: ROBERT G. SLENES AND MORTON SAFFORD JAMES III FOR BENNETT, JOHNSON, SLENES & SMITH
This airy gazebo's sophisticated design, uncluttered lines, and natural finish perfectly complement its serene setting.

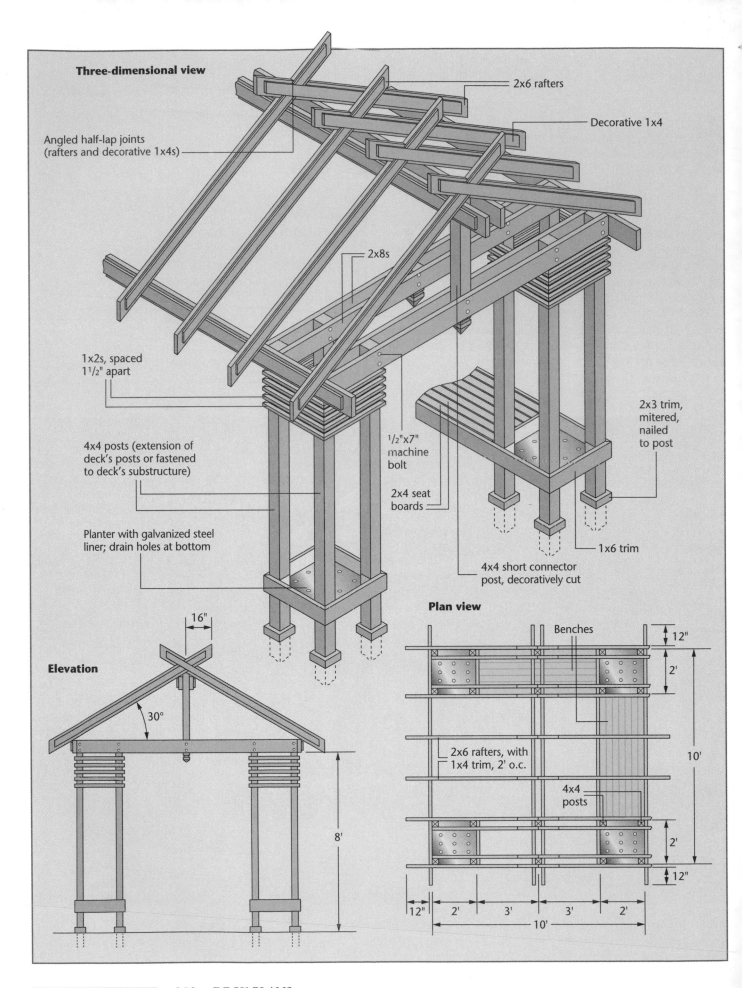

Three-dimensional view

2x6 rafters

Decorative 1x4

Angled half-lap joints (rafters and decorative 1x4s)

2x8s

1x2s, spaced 1¹⁄₂" apart

2x3 trim, mitered, nailed to post

4x4 posts (extension of deck's posts or fastened to deck's substructure)

¹⁄₂"x7" machine bolt

2x4 seat boards

1x6 trim

Planter with galvanized steel liner; drain holes at bottom

4x4 short connector post, decoratively cut

Elevation

16"

30°

8'

Plan view

Benches

12"

2'

2x6 rafters, with 1x4 trim, 2' o.c.

4x4 posts

10'

2'

12"

12" 2' 3' 3' 2'

10'

PROJECT PLANS

The preceding chapter gives you a variety of deck plans that can be adjusted to the size of your house and yard. In the appendix that follows you will find yet more well designed decks and gazebos for which you can order plan packages. There is also a small selection of outdoor-furniture projects and deck enhancements such as planter boxes and benches. With these plans in hand, you can tackle a building project yourself or hire a professional carpenter or builder to do the work. Pages 254 and 255 provide information on how to order plans, including suggestions on the number of copies you will need, pricing, and an order form. Simply choose the plan that's right for you from the descriptions beginning on page 256, and then place your order.

Before You Order

Plan packages for the projects on the following pages include all of the information you'll need to successfully build the projects. When you order a plan set, you will receive complete, large-scale drawings, details, and specifications. The plans call-out part sizes, and most present detailed step-by-step instructions for assembly. Several offer plans for alternate sizes, enabling you to adapt the project to suit your outdoor living space. Before filling out the order form on the following page, note the information that follows.

HOW MANY PLAN SETS WILL YOU NEED?

Each plan package contains two complete sets of plans. Though a single set should suffice for a simple project such as a picnic table, the spare set may come in handy if you like to make modifications or scribble notes on your plans. For more complex designs, you may need several sets, particularly if you intend to obtain bids from two or three builders or carpenters.

If your building department requires a permit for a structure such as an attached deck or gazebo, figure you'll need one set each for yourself, the building department, and any builders or subcontractors involved in the project.

SERVICE AND PLAN DELIVERY

Company service representatives are available to answer questions and assist you in placing your order. Every possible effort is made to process and ship orders within 48 hours.

RETURNS AND EXCHANGES

Each set of project plans is specially printed and shipped to you in response to your specific order; consequently, requests for refunds cannot be honored. However, if the prints you order cannot be used, you may exchange them for another plan. For an exchange, you must return all sets of plans within 30 days. A nonrefundable service charge will be assessed for all exchanges; for more information, call our toll-free number (1-800-721-7027).

COMPLIANCE WITH LOCAL CODES AND REGULATIONS

Because of climatic, geographic, and political variations, building codes and regulations vary to some extent from one area to another. These plans are authorized for your use expressly conditioned on your obligation and agreement to comply strictly with all local building codes, ordinances, regulations, and requirements, including permits and inspections at the time of construction.

ARCHITECTURAL AND ENGINEER SEALS

With increased concerns about energy costs and safety, many cities and states now require that an architect or engineer review and "seal" a plan for a large structure, such as a house-attached multi-level deck, prior to construction. To find out whether this is a regulation in your area, contact your local building department.

LICENSE AGREEMENT, COPY RESTRICTIONS AND COPYRIGHT

When you purchase your plans, you are granted the right to use the documents to construct a single unit only.

All the plans in this publication are protected under the Federal Copyright Act, Title XVII of the United States Code and Chapter 37 of the Code of Federal Regulations. Each designer retains title and ownership of the original documents. The plans licensed to you cannot be used by or resold to any other person, copied, or reproduced by any means. If you require additional plans, you must order additional packets (again, each packet contains two complete sets of plans).

Complete the order form on the following page in three easy steps. Then mail in your order, or, for faster service, call our toll-free number (1-800-721-7027).

Ordering Plans

1. PLANS AND ACCESSORIES

Price Code	Description	Price
A	Small decks and projects	$12.95
B	Raised and combination decks	$15.95
C	Multi-level decks	$19.95
D	Gazebos and deck/gazebo combinations	$24.95

Prices subject to change
Each plan package contains two sets of plans

2. SHIPPING AND HANDLING

Determine shipping and handling charges from the chart below.

Shipping and Handling Charges

Type of Service*	Plan Package	2 Plan Packages	3 Plan Packages
U.S. Regular	$4.95	$7.95	$9.95
U.S. Express	$12.50	$15.50	$18.50
Canada Regular	$7.45	$9.95	$12.45
Canada Express	$18.00	$20.50	$23.00

* U.S. Regular (5-7 working days) U.S. Express (2-3 working days)
Canada Regular (2-3 weeks) Canada Express (7-10 working days)

3. CUSTOMER INFORMATION

Choose the method of payment you prefer. Include a check, money order, or credit card information, complete the name and address portion, and mail the order form to:

Sunset/HomeStyles Plan Service
P.O. Box 75488
St. Paul, MN 55175-0488

**For faster service, call
1-800-721-7027**

PLAN CHECKLIST

Plan number(s) _____ Price code(s) _____

Number of packages _____ $ _____
(see chart at left)

Subtotal	$ _____
Sales tax (Minnesota residents only, add 6.5%)	$ _____
Shipping and handling	$ _____
GRAND TOTAL	$ _____

☐ Check/money order enclosed (in U.S. funds)
☐ VISA ☐ MasterCard ☐ AmEx ☐ Discover

Credit card # _____

Exp. Date _____

Signature _____

Name _____

Address _____

City _____ State/Province _____

Country _____

Zip/Postal code _____

Daytime phone (___)_____

Please check if you are a contractor ☐

Mail form to: Sunset/HomeStyles Plan Service
P.O. Box 75488
St. Paul, MN 55175-0488

Or fax to: 651-602-5002

**FOR FASTER SERVICE,
CALL 1-800-721-7027
INTERNATIONAL CALL
651-602-5002**

Source code: SSPP03

OCTAGON SUN DECK

SOM-2040
PRICE CODE A
- Plans for three different sizes:
  9', 12', and 16'
- Includes options to personalize
  the deck to suit your needs
- Step-by-step instructions

EASY FREESTANDING DECK

UC-2062-B
PRICE CODE A
- Three sizes: 8' X 12', 12' X 12',
  and 16' X 12'
- Easy-to-follow professional
  blueprints
- Dimensional drawings and details

PATIO DECK

AB-1366
PRICE CODE A

- Includes plans for four different
  sizes: 12' X 10', 12' X 14',
  14' X 10', and 14' X 14'
- Details on benches, railing,
  and stairs
- Complete materials list

CASUAL CURVED DECK

SOM-2010
PRICE CODE A

- Four different deck sizes: 8' X 16',
  10' X 16', 12' X 16', and 12' X 20'
- Planter and bench plans included
- Step-by-step instructions

TWO LEVEL DECK

UC-13008
PRICE CODE B
- Overall size 14' X 15'
- Upper deck 12' X 9'
- Lower deck 8' X 8'
- Unique, contemporary design

OUTSIDE CORNER DECK

HPM-1107
PRICE CODE B
- 10' X 12'
- Wrap-around deck with two stairways
- Detailed instructions

INSIDE CORNER EXTENSION DECK

HPM-1109
PRICE CODE B
• 18' X 18'
• Plenty of room for deck furniture and entertaining
• Two stairways for easy access

ENTRY PORCHES

UC-13013
PRICE CODE A
• Both porches 8' X 5'9"
• Contemporary and colonial styles
• Can be free standing or attached to any type of home

OPEN GARDEN DECK

HPM-1101
PRICE CODE B
• 16' X 16'
• A versatile, open deck leading to your backyard
• Built-in benches wrap around the edge of the deck

INSIDE CORNER DECK

HPM-1103
PRICE CODE B
• 16' X 16'
• Maximize your living space with this deck tucked into the corner of your home

SPLIT LEVEL DECK

SOM-2080-7
PRICE CODE B
• Plans for three deck sizes:
12' X 14', 16' X 14', 20' X 14'
• Can be easily adapted for
any height

OCTAGON DECK WITH STEPS

HPM-1105
PRICE CODE B
• 16' X 16'
• A unique deck suitable for any
home
• Step-by-step instructions

BI-LEVEL DECK

AB-1375
PRICE CODE B
- Upper deck sizes: 12' X 12', 10' X 12', and 8' X 12'
- Lower deck sizes: 16' X 16', 10' X 12', and 8' X 10'
- Great for sloping lots

MID-LEVEL DECK

SOM-2070-9
PRICE CODE B
- Three different sizes included: 14' X 10', 16' X 12', and 20' X 12'
- Step-by-step instructions
- Includes options to personalize the deck

TRELLIS DECK

AB-1378
PRICE CODE B
• Four different sizes included:
  16' X 20', 16' X 16', 14' X 20',
  and 14' X 16'
• Overhead structure for shade
• Complete materials list

CUSTOM SPLIT-LEVEL DECK

SOM-2090
PRICE CODE B
• Plans include 12' X 8' upper level
  deck, stair storage platform, and
  22' X 16', 24' X 16', or 26' X 16'
  lower-deck options
• Bench and planter plans included
• Step-by-step instructions

TWO-LEVEL SPA DECK

UC-13020
PRICE CODE C
- Overall size 20' X 14'
- Upper deck 10'9" X 11'3"
- Lower deck 14' X 14'
- Designed for self-contained portable spas

HIGH-LOW DECK

UC-13011
PRICE CODE C
- Upper deck 10' X 8'
- Lower Deck 15'6" X 13'
- Features an optional fire pit and two movable benches

SHADED DECK

UC-13009
PRICE CODE C
• 16' X 10' X 9'6" high
• Simple, free-standing, shaded deck
• Ideal for entertaining on hot summer days

MULTI-LEVEL DECK WITH SPA

SOM-2100-3
PRICE CODE C
• Includes plans for 18' X 10' upper level deck, 5' stair storage platform, and 27' X 20' lower level deck
• Elaborate plan with three decks leading to your backyard spa

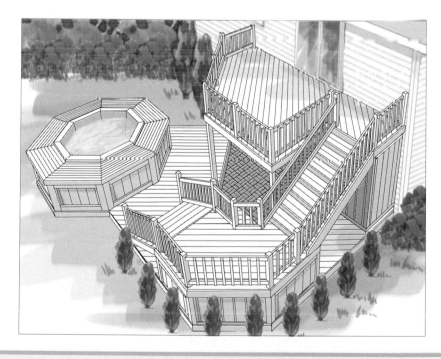

NOSTALGIC GAZEBO

SOM-8020
PRICE CODE D
- Plans for three different sizes: 9', 12', and 16'
- Elegant design for use throughout the seasons
- Step-by-step instructions

DECK WITH GAZEBO

UC-13002
PRICE CODE D
- 24' X 15'6"
- Height floor to peak: 12'2"
- Enjoy your deck year-round with a shaded gazebo for outdoor eating and special events

TIERED DECK WITH GAZEBO

UC-13031
PRICE CODE D
• Deck: 28'6" X 15'6"
• Gazebo: 8' across with roof and side railings
• Sprawling outdoor entertaining area with three decks, a walkway, and a cozy gazebo

CLASSIC GAZEBO

HPM-1601
PRICE CODE D
• 16' across the floor
• Detailed materials list
• Construction guidelines

ADIRONDACK CHAIR

UC-2070-B
PRICE CODE A

- Easy-to-follow professional blueprints
- DImensional drawings and details

DECK RAILINGS

UC-13023
PRICE CODE A

- Includes plans for five styles: contemporary (double and single bevel), colonial, and traditional 2' X 2' and 2' X 4'
- Easily adaptable to any outside structure

PICNIC TABLES

UC-2051-RB
PRICE CODE A

- Rectangular design 72" X 60" X 30"
- Octagonal design 56" X 56" X 30"

DECK ENHANCEMENTS

UC-13014
PRICE CODE B

- Includes plans for a 2' X 2' planter box, 7' X 5'6" decorative screen, 6' X 1'8" bench, and 2'6" X 1'5" end table

DECKS GLOSSARY

Actual size
The size of lumber after it has been surfaced, as opposed to nominal size.

Anchor bolt
Used to fasten wood to concrete; the bolt, usually J-shaped, is set into freshly cast concrete with the threaded end projecting above the surface.

Balusters
Thin, vertical members of a railing that divide up the space between posts.

Band joist
In a house, the framing member fastened across the ends of the floor joists.

Batterboard
A horizontal board held in the ground with a stake at each end; used to stretch string lines for laying out the deck foundation.

Blocking
Pieces of wood installed between joists to give rigidity to the structure.

Cantilever
To extend past the edge of the supporting member, such as when a joist extends past the last beam. "Cantilevered" is also used to describe a deck that juts out over a slope.

Cap rail
Part of a railing; the horizontal member laid flat across the tops of the posts.

Chamfer
A decorative angled cut along the edge of a piece of wood, to remove the corner where two adjacent surfaces meet.

Cleat
A small piece of wood attached to one member in order to support the end of another. Cleats are often attached to stringers to support stair treads, or to posts to support decking.

Crown
The higher edge of a warped piece of lumber; also known as "crook."

Dado
A channel with square sides and bottom cut across a piece of lumber.

Dead load
The weight of the deck materials themselves that the structure must be able to support.

Decay resistant
Wood that is resistant to decay caused by fungi. Redwood and cedar heartwood are naturally decay resistant. Other woods can be pressure treated against decay.

Dimension lumber
Lumber graded for strength and intended for structural framing. From 2" to 4" thick and at least 2" wide.

Elevation
A side view of a structure, showing vertical dimensions and relationships. An elevation section shows a vertical slice of the structure.

Expanding anchor bolt
A combined anchor and bolt used to fasten wood to masonry. The anchor bolt is tapped into a hole drilled in the masonry and a nut is tightened on the outside of the wood.

Face nail
To drive a nail through one piece into another with the nail at right angles to the surface.

Fascia
Decorative trim installed around the edge of the deck to cover the rim joist, end joists, and ends of deck boards. Nonstructural.

Fasteners
Any kind of hardware used to fasten one item to another; typically, nails, screws, and bolts.

Flashing
Sheet metal used to protect a joint from water, such as between a ledger and the house. Can be bought already formed in a Z-shape.

Footing
The underground part of a concrete foundation. Distributes the weight of the deck.

Framing connectors
A wide variety of metal connectors used to join wood to wood, or wood to concrete. Form stronger joints than nailing.

Frost line
The maximum depth at which freezing can occur in a particular locale.

Galvanized
Fasteners that are covered with a hard coating of zinc that resists corrosion. Galvanized fasteners should be used for all outdoor applications. Hot-dipped galvanized are the best quality.

Grade
Ground level. Also, the slope of a lot, usually away from the house.

Ground-fault circuit interrupter
A device that cuts a circuit in the event of a current leakage; required outdoors and in other damp areas. It is either built into the circuit or installed in an individual receptacle. Abbreviated GFCI.

Heartwood
The inactive wood nearest the center of the tree, as opposed to sapwood. Redwood and cedar heartwood is resistant to decay.

Kicker plate
A board laid flat on a concrete pad to support the bottom end of stair stringers. Attached to anchor bolts embedded in the pad.

Knee bracing
Short diagonal bracing fastened between a beam and the top of a post to add lateral stability.

Lattice
A gridwork of wood strips; used for screens, skirts and overheads. Can be bought preassembled or constructed out of lath.

Ledger
A structural member attached to a house or other structure; supports the ends of joists.

Live load
The load on the surface of a deck or overhead due to people, furniture, snow, etc.

Miter
A cut at any angle other than 90°. Also, to make such a cut.

Nominal size
The size of a piece of lumber when it is first cut from the log, before being surfaced. Lumber is sold by these sizes.

On center
A measurement of the spacing between a series of objects as measured from the center of one to the center of the next. Abbreviated "o.c.". Spacings given in plans are generally measured on center.

Overhead
A structure such as a trellis built over the deck to give shade or to support climbing plants.

Pier
A block of concrete set on top of a footing to keep posts raised above grade. Can be purchased precast or cast in place.

Plan view
A view of a structure shown from above. A plan view of a deck shows the framing or the decking.

Plumb
Perfectly vertical. Also, to make vertical.

Pressure treated
Lumber that has been commercially treated with chemicals to protect it from decay and termites. More effective than a brush-on treatment.

Radius-edge decking
Lumber specifically intended for decking. Milled with slightly rounded edges. Available in thicknesses of 1" or 1⁵/₃₂".

Rim joist
A type of joist fastened across the ends of the other joists, and intended to keep the structure rigid.

Rip
To cut a board parallel to the wood grain.

Rise
The vertical distance covered by a stairway.

Riser
The vertical part of a step.

Run
The horizontal distance covered by a stairway.

Site plan
Map of a lot showing the house, landscaping, and microclimatic features.

Skirt
A screen installed below the deck to hide the deck substructure or to protect items stored underneath the deck.

Sleeper
A length of pressure-treated lumber laid down and fastened to a concrete or brick patio to provide a nailing surface for decking.

Span
The distance a member covers from the center of one supporting member to the center of the next.

Stringer
The diagonal part of a stairway supporting the risers and treads. Can be notched or cleated to support the stair treads.

Substructure
The framework of posts, beams, and joists supporting the decking.

Toenail
To drive a nail at an angle through one piece and into another.

Tread
The part of a step that is horizontal.

INDEX

A-B-C-D

Adhesives, 98
Architects, 59
Barbecues, 45
Beams, 67, 68, 117
  built-up, 119
  cantilevered, 73
  installation,
    117, 119-120
  overheads, 141, 144
  repair, 179
  replacement, 179
  sizes and spans,
    74, 141
  splicing, 120
  steel, 91
Benches, 49, 157
  attached, 14, 16,
    36-39,158-159
  bench and railing
    combinations, 157
  freestanding, 157, 158
  with built-in over-
    heads, 36, 37, 160
  with planters, 43
Bolts, 99
  removal, 170
Bridges, 47
Building codes, 53
  bracing, 70
  bridging/blocking, 70
  foundations, 69
  load calculations, 72
  railings, 81
Building contracts, 60
Building materials, 90
  see also Lumber
Cantilever, 72-73
Carpeting, 90
Cellulose removal,
  172, 173
Cleaning, 171, 172-173
Climate, 50-52
Compact decks, 14-15
  plans, 190-192
Concrete, 91, 113-116
  decking, 90
  formula, 113
  stair pads, 123
Contractors, 59-60
Decay
  cut ends of pressure-
    treated wood, 117
  decay-resistant
    wood, 95
  finishes, 166-167
  protecting post ends,
    69
  reinforcing rotted
    joists, 177
  removing rotted
    joist ends, 177
  shifting accessories
    to allow drying, 165

Deck clips, 98
Decking, 63, 90, 125
  bowed boards, 127
  carpeting, 90
  concrete, 90
  cupped boards, 174
  direction of boards,
    49
  elastomeric surface
    coatings, 91
  fiberglass, 91
  installation, 125-128
  installation over
    patios, 131-132
  joint patterns, 63
  lumber sizes, 65
  nonslip surfaces, 90
  nonwood, 25, 90
  patterns, 63, 64-65
  repairs, 174
  sizes and spans, 73
  space between
    boards, 63, 172
  splitting when
    nailing, 126
  surrounding natural
    obstacles, 66
  tiles and pavers, 90
Decking modules, 66
Design elements,
  45, 48-49
  deck shapes, 46-47
Designers, 59
Design software, 54
Detached decks, 6, 14,
  16, 17, 21, 46
  plans for detached
    deck, 193-194
  plans for low-level
    deck, 185-186
Diagonal orientation
  plans, 212-214
Dining areas, 45
Doors
  enlarging or
    moving, 49
Drainage, 106, 107
  waterproof decks,
    134

E-F-G

Easements, 53
Elastomeric surface
  coatings, 91
Enclosed decks, 24
  plans, 197-200
Entry decks, 8, 14, 47
  plans for streetfront
    deck, 195-196
Fasteners, 97-99
  avoiding splitting
    boards, 126

for framing connectors,
  101
  location, 125
  removal, 170
Fiberglass, 25, 90, 91
Finishes, 166-167
Footings, 69, 111,
  115-116
Foundations
  building code, 69
  concrete, 113-115
  footings, 69, 111,
    115-116
  layout, 111-112
  piers, 69, 111,
    115-116
  stairs, 123
Framing connectors,
  100-101
  fasteners, 101
Freestanding decks.
  see Detached decks
Gardens, 45, 49
Gates, 85
Gazebos, 34, 35
  plans, 251-252
Grading, 106

H-I-J-K-L

Hardware
  deck clips, 98
  framing connectors,
    100-101
  see also Fasteners
Hillside decks, 10-11,
  27, 58
  plans for extended
    deck, 232-234
  plans for large deck
    with a view,
    27, 241-244
  plans for steep
    slope, 229-331
Hot tubs. see Spas
Jacks, 178
Joists, 67, 68
  bridging/blocking,
    70, 71
  cantilevered, 72-73
  installation, 121-122
  reinforcing rotted
    joists, 177
  removing rotten
    joist ends, 177
  repair, 177-178
  spacing and spans, 73
  splicing, 122
Ladders, 144
Lag screws, 99
Lattice panels, 149
Ledgers, 68, 108
  installation, 108-110
  overheads, 142
  repair, 180
  replacement, 180

Legal restrictions, 53
Liens, 60
Lighting, 154-155
Load calculations, 72-74
Low-level decks, 8-9,
  14-17
  plans, 185-188
  plans for angular deck,
    206-207
  plans for deck with
    stairs, 187-189
  plans for meandering
    deck, 219-220
Lumber
  bowed, 127
  brush-on preservative,
    117
  characteristics, 92-93
  decay-resistance, 95
  defects, 93, 127
  estimating, 96
  finishing, 166-167
  grades, 94-95
  grain, 93
  moisture content,
    92-93
  overheads, 148
  plywood, 96
  pressure-treated,
    95, 117
  pricing, 95
  sizing, 94
  sizes for decking, 65
  sizes related to spans,
    73-74
  strength groupings,
    73
  substructures, 91
  woven woods,
    148-149

M-N-O

Maintenance, 171
  cellulose removal,
    172, 173
  cleaning, 171,
    172, 173
  shifting accessories to
    allow drying, 165
  stain removal,
    172, 173
  strengthening joints,
    171
  see also Finishes,
    Repairs
Mechanic's liens, 60
Multilevel decks,
  10-13, 19, 46
  changing levels, 75
  plans for deck with
    patio platform,
    221-224
  plans for garden
    peninsula, 235-237

plans for large deck
  for a gentle slope,
    238-240
plans for multilevel
  spa deck, 215-218
plans for split-level
  deck, 208-211
plans for two-level
  deck, 225-228
stairs, 29
Nails, 97, 98, 101
  avoiding splitting
    boards, 126
  popped, 171
  removal, 170
Obstacles, 10, 66, 128
Outdoor rooms, 24
Overheads, 20, 23, 34-
  35, 36, 49, 135
  beams, 141, 144
  bracing, 144
  cantilevered, 141
  combined with
    benches, 36,
    37, 160
  combined with
    screens, 88
  covers, 148
  design, 136
  finishes, 152
  ledgers, 142
  louvered slats,
    151-152
  lumber, 148
  open-style covers,
    148-149, 150-152
  plans for backyard
    pavilion, 249-250
  plans for bench com-
    bined with over-
    head, 36, 160
  plans for corner
    shelter, 247-248
  plans for large space
    frame, 245-246
  plans for open
    gazebo, 35,
    251-252
  posts, 142-143, 144
  rafters 141,145-147
  shade, 136, 150, 151
  solid roofs, 34, 149
  span tables, 141
  structure, 140
  styles, 137-139
  wood decay, 148

P-Q

Paints, 167
Patios
  plans for multilevel
    deck with patio plat-
    form, 221-224
  plans for recycled
    patio, 197-200

ACKNOWLEDGMENTS

Thanks to the following:
Akzo Nobel Coatings, Inc., Troy, MI
APA—The Engineered Wood Association, Tacoma, WA
Jon Arno, Troy, MI
Association of Professional Landscape Designers, Chicago, IL
Benjamin Moore & Co., Ltd., Montreal, Que.
Biddle Co., St. Louis, MO
Bio-Wash Canada, Whistler, B.C.
Building Officials and Code Administrators International,
    Country Club Hills, IL
CaddCon Designs, Baltimore, MD
California Redwood Association, Novato, CA
Cepco Tool Co., Spencer, NY
Chapel Valley Landscaping Co., Woodbine, MD
Chemical Specialties, Inc., Charlotte, NC
City of Stockton Permit Center, Stockton, CA
Mary Daniels Desktop Publishing and
    Graphic Design, Eugene, OR
Davison Design, Vancouver, B.C.
Deckmaster Inc., Sebastopol, CA
Dekbrands, Alvadore, OR
E-Z Deck, Nisku, Alberta
Feeney Wire Rope, Oakland, CA
The Flood Company, Hudson, OH
Garden Concepts, Glenview, IL
Georgia-Pacific Corporation, Atlanta, GA
Gilbert Whitney & Johns, Whippany, NJ
Tom Gorman, University of Idaho, College of Forestry,
    Wildlife, and Range Sciences (Forest Products
    Department), Moscow, ID
Hart Tool Co., Inc., Huntington Beach, CA
Hickson Corp., Smyrna, GA
International Conference of Building Officials, Seattle, WA
Macon Bureau of Inspection and Fees, Macon, GA
Martin Industries, Florence, AL
Giles Miller-Mead, Brome, Que.
Mobil Chemical Co. (Trex Composite Lumber), Winchester, VA
National Roofing Contractors Association, Rosemont, IL
Northwestern Steel and Wire, Sterling, IL
Powder Actuated Tool Manufacturers' Institute, Inc.,
    St. Charles, MO
PPG Architectural Finishes, Pittsburgh, PA
The Private Garden, Lake Forest, IL
PVC Lumber Corporation, Montreal, Que.
Simpson Strong-Tie Co., Pleasanton, CA
Southern Forest Products Association
    (Southern Pine Council), Kenner, LA
UGL Zar Products, Scranton, PA
Urban Associates, Hamilton, Ont.
Western Red Cedar Lumber Association, Vancouver, B.C.
Western Wood Products Association, Portland, OR
Wolman Wood Care Products, Pittsburgh, PA
Wm. Zinsser & Co., Inc., Somerset, NJ

*For their valuable contribution to this book,
we would also like to thank each of the designers
whose plans and ideas are included.*

Picture Credits
p. 3 Philip Harvey
p. 6 courtesy Western Red Cedar Lumber Association
p. 7 Philip Harvey
p. 8 Philip Harvey
p. 9 *(upper)* Tom Wyatt
p. 9 *(lower)* courtesy UGL Zar Products
p. 10 *(upper)* courtesy Western Red Cedar Lumber Association
p. 10 *(lower)* Russ Widstrand
p. 11 *(both)* courtesy Western Red Cedar Lumber Association
p. 12 courtesy The Flood Company
p. 13 *(upper)* courtesy Western Wood Products Association
p. 13 *(lower)* courtesy CaddCon Designs
p. 14 *(upper)* courtesy Western Wood Products Association
p. 14 *(lower)* courtesy Western Red Cedar Lumber Association
p. 15 *(upper)* courtesy Southern Pine Council
p. 15 *(lower)* Tom Wyatt
p. 16 *(upper)* courtesy Western Red Cedar Lumber Association
p. 16 *(lower)* courtesy Southern Pine Council
p. 17 *(upper)* Philip Harvey
p. 17 *(lower)* courtesy Georgia-Pacific Corporation
p. 18 courtesy California Redwood Association
p. 19 *(upper)* courtesy California Redwood Association
p. 19 *(lower)* courtesy Wolman Wood Care Products
p. 20 courtesy California Redwood Association
p. 21 *(upper)* courtesy Georgia-Pacific Corporation
p. 21 *(lower)* Tom Wyatt
p. 22 courtesy Western Wood Products Association
p. 23 *(upper)* Jack McDowell
p. 23 *(lower)* Philip Harvey
p. 24 *(upper)* Stephen Marley
p. 24 *(lower)* Tom Wyatt
p. 25 *(upper)* courtesy E-Z Deck
p. 25 *(lower)* courtesy Mobil Chemical Co.
p. 26 courtesy CaddCon Designs
p. 27 Philip Harvey
p. 28 *(both)* courtesy Western Red Cedar Lumber Association
p. 29 *(upper)* courtesy Western Wood Products Association
p. 29 *(lower left)* courtesy Western Wood Products Association
p. 29 *(lower right)* courtesy Southern Pine Council
p. 30 *(upper)* Richard Nicol
p. 30 *(middle)* courtesy Southern Pine Council
p. 30 *(lower)* courtesy Western Red Cedar Lumber Association
p. 31 *(upper)* courtesy CaddCon Designs
p. 31 *(lower)* courtesy Western Red Cedar Lumber Association
p. 32 *(upper)* courtesy Feeney Wire Rope
p. 32 *(lower)* Philip Harvey
p. 33 *(upper)* Jack McDowell
p. 33 *(middle)* Tom Wyatt
p. 33 *(lower)* Ells Marugg
p. 34 *(upper)* courtesy California Redwood Association
p. 34 *(lower)* courtesy Western Red Cedar Lumber Association
p. 35 *(upper)* Stephen Marley
p. 35 *(lower)* Philip Harvey
p. 36 *(upper)* courtesy California Redwood Association
p. 36 *(lower)* Tom Wyatt
p. 37 *(upper)* courtesy Western Wood Products Association
p. 37 *(lower)* courtesy Akzo Nobel Coatings, Inc.
p. 38 *(upper)* courtesy Akzo Nobel Coatings, Inc.
p. 38 *(lower)* courtesy Western Red Cedar Lumber Association
p. 39 *(upper)* Richard Nicol
p. 39 *(lower)* courtesy Pro Shop
p. 40 *(upper)* Stephen Cridland
p. 40 *(lower)* Patrick Barta
p. 41 *(upper)* courtesy Western Red Cedar Lumber Association
p. 41 *(lower)* Richard Nicol
p. 42 *(upper)* Robert Mowat
p. 42 *(lower)* Norman A. Plate
p. 43 *(upper)* courtesy Western Red Cedar Lumber Association
p. 43 *(lower)* courtesy Western Wood Products Association